Reliable Linux
Assuring High Availability

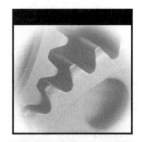

Reliable Linux
Assuring High Availability

Iain Campbell

Gearhead Press™

Wiley Computer Publishing

John Wiley & Sons, Inc.

NEW YORK · CHICHESTER · WEINHEIM · BRISBANE · SINGAPORE · TORONTO

Publisher: Robert Ipsen
Editor: Theresa Hudson
Consulting Editor: Donis Marshall
Developmental Editor: Kathryn A. Malm
Managing Editor: Angela Smith
Text Design & Composition: MacAllister Publishing Services, LLC

Designations used by companies to distinguish their products are often claimed as trademarks. In all instances where John Wiley & Sons, Inc., is aware of a claim, the product names appear in initial capital or ALL CAPITAL LETTERS. Readers, however, should contact the appropriate companies for more complete information regarding trademarks and registration.

This book is printed on acid-free paper. ♾

Published by John Wiley & Sons, Inc., New York

Published simultaneously in Canada.

This publication is designed to provide accurate and authoritative information in regard to the subject matter covered. It is sold with the understanding that the publisher is not engaged in professional services. If professional advice or other expert assistance is required, the services of a competent professional person should be sought.

The Gearhead Press trademark is the exclusive property of Gearhead Group Corporation.

Library of Congress Cataloging-in-Publication Data:

Campbell, Iain.
   Reliable Linux : assuring high availability / Iain Cambell.
     p. cm.
   ISBN 0-471-07040-8
  1. Linux. 2. Operating systems (Computers) I. Title.
   QA76.76.063 C357 2001
   005.4'32--dc21   2001006155

Printed in the United States of America.

10 9 8 7 6 5 4 3 2 1

A Note from Gearhead Press

Gearhead Press is dedicated to publishing technical books for experienced Information Technology professionals—network engineers, developers, system administrators, and others—who need to update their skills, learn how to use technology more effectively, or simply want a quality reference to the latest technology.

Gearhead Press emerged from my experience with professional trainers of engineers and developers: people who truly understand first-hand the needs of working professionals. Gearhead Press authors are the crème de la crème of industry trainers, working at the companies that define the technology revolution. For this reason, Gearhead Press authors are regularly in the trenches with the developers and engineers that have changed the world through innovative products. Drawing from this experience in IT training, our books deliver superior technical content with a unique perspective that is based on real-world experience.

Now, as an imprint of John Wiley & Sons, Inc., Gearhead Press will continue to bring you, the reader, the level of quality that Wiley has delivered consistently for nearly 200 years.

Thank you,
Donis Marshall
Founder, Gearhead Press
Consulting Editor, Wiley Computer Publishing

Gearhead Press Books in Print

To my parents, Colin and Gladys Campbell, who chose to invest so much of what they had in their children and keep so little for themselves. Here is a small token in return.

Acknowledgments

While my name appears on the cover of this book, many others have contributed in various ways to this effort, and I want to take a moment to acknowledge them here.

First, I need to acknowledge the vision and years of effort put into Linux by its creator, Linus Torvalds. Wherever the future of Linux may lie, the computing world has been irrevocably changed by his dedication to the concept of open source software. Linus, however, represents the tip of the programming iceberg, and I need to acknowledge too the assistance of a number of Linux developers, maintainers and administrators who write the code this book is about and who supplied information and in some cases reviewed portions of the text. Among these are Ted Tso, Neil Brown, Hans Reiser, Phil Edelbrock, Mark Lord, Doug Gilbert, Alan Kennington, Russell Kroll, Nigel Metheringham, Stephen Tweedie, Steve Lord, Lorien Golaski, Peter Breuer, Tim Burke, Peter Braam, Philipp Reisner, and Corin Hartland-Swann. In addition are many others whose voluntary contributions to support mailing lists were invaluable sources of information.

To an author, editors sometimes seem like necessary evils. The honest author, however, recognizes his shortcomings and gratefully acknowledges the assistance of his editors. Among the staff at Gearhead Press, I want to thank Trudy Neuhaus not only for her editorial input, but for the risky decision to take me on as an author in the first place (and for being a delightful dinner guest). Thanks also go to Donis Marshall, who took the greater risk by agreeing to foot the bill for Trudy's decision and who also devoted his editorial efforts on my behalf. Many thanks go to the tireless J.W. (Jerry) Olsen, whose patience and dedication added so much to the finished product, and to Linda and Al McKinnon, who cast a technical editorial eye over my shoulder. At Wiley Computer Publishing, credit is due to Ben Ryan and Kathryn Malm for managing the project through its many phases to a successful conclusion.

On the home front, thanks are due Jeff Page of Qenesis Technologies and Doug Barwell of OSI Computers, who supplied hardware for my guinea pig servers. Thanks too to Brian Whelpton of Whelpton Associates, who released me to take on this project and who will be as happy as I am now that it is done and I can get back to my "real" job.

Finally, I must credit my wonderful family for their unconditional love and support. Many times one of you prayed at the dinner table for "Jesus to help Daddy finish his book." Well, your prayers have been answered and I can finally come out of my office and return to the privilege and joy of being husband of the loveliest wife and father to the best children in the world.

About the Author

Iain Campbell is a mechanical engineer by profession, graduating in 1986 from Ryerson Polytechnic Institute in Toronto. After a year in the manufacturing industry, Iain returned to Ryerson as an engineer on the staff of the Institute's Centre for Advanced Technology Education (CATE), where he spent nine years working in manufacturing automation, computer aided design, and industrial robotics. Much of the engineering and analysis software he used ran on Sun or IBM UNIX platforms; and as few others knew much about it, he began to see the value of learning it himself. The seductive UNIX spell began to draw him deeper, and by the end of his time at CATE he was coding in C, building kernels, and teaching UNIX systems administration for Sun Microsystems and IBM. He left the University in 1996 to form his own company and now teaches and consults for IBM and other corporate clients.

Iain started using UNIX-based systems and cruising the Internet in the late 1980, and can remember being without email for several days when a infamous worm made the rounds. When he tried to tell people about it, they were puzzled and needed the term email explained. He had his first exposure to Linux several years later and can recall wheeling a PC down to the Electrical Engineering department network and installing a Slackware distribution using kernel version 0.99. The most fun he ever had with UNIX was building a manufacturing cell that was remotely programmed and operated from a distance of several miles. The whole cell was controlled by an original IBM PC fitted with a multiport serial card and running QNX, a real-time UNIX-like operating system.

Iain is married with four children and lives in a small town just the right distance from Toronto, Ontario—far enough to avoid the traffic, but close enough to hear the traffic reports on the radio and appreciate what he is missing.

Contents

Introduction

Selling insurance must be one of the more difficult challenges in marketing. After all, you are asking your customer to lay out money with no immediate return. In fact, if there is never a claim, the customer loses every penny of every premium paid with no apparent benefit. But if the unthinkable happens, nobody wants to be without a good insurance policy. I hope and trust that none of you will have to face floods, fire earthquakes, or the like; but I can almost guarantee that if you manage a computer system for more than a year or two, you will have to deal with a power failure, or a disk failure, or an operating system failure. Do you have adequate insurance?

With the support of such industry giants as IBM, Oracle, SAP, Dell, and Compaq, Linux has clearly become a major platform for deploying open systems servers of all kinds. Much has been written about choosing, configuring and running server software of all kinds on the Linux platform. But what about the underlying hardware and operating system software? Can you rely on it? The most stable and efficient web server is useless when a disk crashes, or the operating system fails. It is essential that a reliable server platform take into consideration the certainty that something someday *will* fail! This book addresses the risks of hardware and operating system failures and presents strategies to create your own insurance policy against data loss and unnecessary downtime.

Audience

This book should be useful to a technical manager, Linux system administrator, network administrator, or applications developer. The issues, tools, and techniques presented are applicable to Linux platforms of all sizes, from a small single processor server through a midsize multiprocessor box, up to a multiserver cluster.

The examples detailed in this book focus primarily on reliability of the entire environment in which these servers exist. This book assumes the reader has a working knowledge of the Linux environment. If you can install Linux and have a basic working knowledge of creating user accounts, creating and mounting file systems, and configuring basic network functions, you should be able to follow the examples.

Installing Linux itself is not discussed in this book, but many excellent references are available to help you in that area. To prepare yourself to get the most value from this book, I recommend *Installing and Administering Linux*, and *Customizing and Upgrading Linux*, both by Al and Linda McKinnon, companion books to this one and published by Wiley.

Structure

The book is divided into three sections. The first, "Planning for Reliability," discusses the importance of planning strategies to protect your business operations when servers fail. This involves technical issues, but must go beyond the technical to include the entire business operation. When a server goes down, it takes a business process with it. The connection between the technical failure and the business process it affects must be understood, and a plan needs to be in place to recover both the server, and the process. Before you can start implementing protections, you must also know specifically what it is that can go wrong, and how severe the effect of any failure would be on the your business. If you know that, you know where you need to spend your money most effectively.

The second section, "Building a Reliable Server," starts with a chapter on the state of the art in reliable hardware, covering topics such as hot-swap hardware, temperature monitoring, and reliable power supplies. Chapter 4 discusses how you can install and configure Linux with reliability as a priority. Chapter 5 is devoted entirely to reliable disk storage, with complete coverage of the software RAID available in the current, v2.4 Linux kernel. Closing out this section are chapters on monitoring production servers, and backup/recovery strategies.

The third section, "Linux Reliability Enhancements," looks at several reliability enhancements new to the Linux world. Chapter 8 covers logical volume management, a powerful new way to manage disk storage now incorporated into the current production Linux kernel. Chapter 9 reviews recent file system developments, including the new journalling file systems of ReiserFS, XFS, JFS, and ext3 as well as two network file systems, enbd and drbd, and the cluster file systems of GFS and InterMezzo. The section closes with a chapter on server clustering, which examines a number of current Linux based approaches for building highly available server clusters.

Examples

I have included relevant examples when possible. Working with Linux poses a challenge: Linux is not a static entity. It changes on a weekly-even daily-basis, so the version of the kernel or a supplementary utility that I based my examples on at the time I wrote them will almost certainly have changed to some extent by the time this book finds it way into your hands. As some of the functionality I cover is new, I am sure it will have changed before you see it, as I have in some cases been working from beta test releases in developing my examples. You will need to double check the appropriate references for the version of the code you use and adjust them as necessary to ensure that they will work for you.

Linux and Other UNIX Versions

This book is focussed primarily on Linux, that flavor of the UNIX operating system created and still maintained by Linus Torvalds. I have chosen the Red Hat Linux distribution (*www.redhat.com*) for my examples, as it is currently the most popular North American Linux distribution The principles presented, however, are equally applicable to any Linux distribution, although some utilities will behave differently or exist in different forms in other distributions. You will need to consult the references applicable to your distribution and version in these cases.

All of the theory I present and much of the practice is also equally applicable to other open source UNIX variants such as FreeBSD, OpenBSD or NetBSD. Note that anything referred to as kernel functionality will be specific to the Linux kernel and may not be found in other UNIX variants.

Typographical Conventions

This book uses the following typographical conventions.

`Fixed width`

is used in examples to indicate command line input and output, shell script fragments, or the contents of configuration files. The fixed width font is also used within normal text to indicate a command line, a flag, or command option.

`Fixed width bold`

is used in examples to indicate text a user inputs.

Italic

is used for directory paths, filenames, and command names as well as identifiers such as user IDs or host names. It also is used on occasion for emphasis.

<pointy brackets>

are used in examples where you must substitute your own specific information for what the brackets contain.

\#

indicates a root privilege user's command line prompt.

$

indicates a low privilege user's command line prompt.

Acronyms and Abbreviations

Acronyms used without definitions are frustration. I avoid doing so when possible. Also, the book includes a glossary containing acronyms as well as any other technical terms that might need definition.

I have used the standard abbreviations M for mega (1,000,000) and K for kilo (1,000) as well as b for bit and B for byte. Hence, 100 KB stands for 100 kilobytes, and 2 Mb represents 2 megabits.

Planning for Reliability

Business Recovery Planning

"Be prepared."

—The Boy Scout Motto

My challenge in this section is to convince you that you need a Business Recovery (BR) plan and show you how to develop one suited to your business. This sounds about as interesting as watching grass grow. If you are a system administrator or an application developer, you will be tempted to skip to the technical implementation details in Parts Two and Three. Don't! If you are responsible in any capacity for keeping servers going, then anything you can do to keep them going every hour of every day is useful. You know that high reliability requires foresight, planning, and a bit more money invested than just putting a system together out of the box, plugging it in, and crossing your fingers. Whether you are a system administrator or developer, manager or business owner, you have a part to play in identifying and justifying the resources needed to build a solid and reliable server platform. This section helps you to do that.

If you are a system administrator or developer, you are mostly interested in the hands-on implementation details. I plan to give you lots of that in Parts Two and Three. But you also need to function as part of a larger team. The servers and applications you create and run are key to the success of the business as a whole. For this reason, you need to work with end users and managers to integrate your technical functions into the larger business function.

If you are a manager, you need a tool to assess the risk factors in your servers and the downtime cost so that you know how much money to allocate and where to allocate it. You also need to understand the advice you get from your technical staff, so you can weigh the risks and solutions. When a server goes down, it affects the whole business operation, and a disaster plan that considers only a server itself in isolation and not the broader functions the server supports will not keep you from trouble. You need to understand the challenges your technical experts face and work together with end users to develop a plan that does not involve unreasonable technical demands. It must protect your business operation, and achieve that goal at an acceptable cost. This section gives you a methodology to develop such a plan.

If you are a small business owner, then you are both the manager and the technical staff (and the receptionist, accountant, and janitor) and you'll take all the help you can get. I know. I'm a small business owner myself. If you manage a large environment, then you are expected to spend a significant portion of your time designing proactive BR strategies for every aspect of the business for which you are responsible. Large companies also have access to fully qualified architects, system analysts, and IT department managers. In the case of both large and small businesses, documents need to be prepared and BR drills need to be orchestrated and constructed to prove the plan before the inevitable strikes.

If you already know what a BR plan is and you have one in place, congratulations. Appendix A supplies a sample BR plan. You can compare yours with mine, and then use the hands-on information in the rest of the book to integrate your new Linux servers into your existing reliable infrastructure.

What Is Business Recovery Anyway?

Just what is in a BR plan and what good is it to you? Many businesses make backups of their critical data on a regular basis and consider that adequate insurance. While a good backup plan is essential, it is only part of the whole picture.

Consider the case of a hard disk crash. The first hint of trouble may be a call for help from an end user when a client application doesn't seem to be responding. It may take several minutes to eliminate the possibility that the problem lies at the client end and begin to suspect that something is wrong with the server. If the server has only one disk and it has crashed, then the server will be staring at you, dead and mute. You can see it's dead, but what killed it? It could be the disk, but it could also be a power supply failure, a motherboard failure, or maybe the operating system crashed. You will have to investigate further.

You try to reboot. If you can get as far as the Basic Input-Output System (BIOS), that rules out the power supply; and by using the BIOS diagnostics, you would have a good chance of determining if the motherboard was indeed deceased or if there may be some other hardware problem. Let's say the disk checks out okay in the hardware diagnostics, so you try to boot from it, but the boot fails. Obviously something is wrong with the disk, but what? The next thing you need to try is booting from a boot diskette. If that works for you, then you at least have a running operating system and you can attempt to read whatever may or may not be on the damaged disk. Do you have a valid boot diskette for each sever? Do you have a problem determination procedure? Who do you have on site to carry it through? These are all elements of a comprehensive BR plan that prepares you for emergencies.

If you determine that the disk is in fact kaput, you need to lay your hands on a replacement. Do you have a spare? Is it good? Is it compatible? If you answer no to these questions, where are you going to get a compatible replacement? What model or type do you need? You need it ASAP; is this liable to cost you a premium price?

So far you are still down and have been staring sadly at your backup tapes for an hour. Once you have the replacement drive installed, you have to start the restore procedure. Do you have a restore procedure? Restoring from a backup is rarely as simple as putting the tape in and closing the door. If the operating system is lost, you may have to start by reinstalling it, then adding your application software, and finally adding your application data. Now you're back in business, right? Well, yes, but you have only the data up to the last time you backed up the system. All of the data entered since your last backup is lost and will have to be regained somehow. Do you have a plan? And how long will that take? Is it possible that some information simply gets lost in the shuffle and never gets found? Of course, you find that out next week—when your best customers don't get their orders and you have to explain why.

Ouch. This does not sound like fun. A good BR plan does the following:

- Outlines possible points of failure
- Rates the likelihood of failure of each point
- Describes procedures for monitoring points of failure
- Outlines the physical and human resources needed to remedy the problem

- Includes guidelines for having those resources available
- Documents procedures for detecting and recovering from failure

In short, it makes failure detection and recovery as painless as possible. A good BR plan goes beyond dealing with failures when they occur. It should be proactive by monitoring servers while they are working well and searching for warning signs of impending doom, and then alerting you to brewing problems before they cause an actual collapse. Should the worst happen, a good BR plan is prepared. Where reasonable, spare parts should be kept in stock and clear, up-to-date procedures for restoration of lost machines should be close at hand. Finally, restoring the machine itself does not necessarily get your business back on its feet. You may need contingency plans for your business processes that kick in during an outage so that you do not lose valuable current data and can add that data back into the system when it comes back up.

To make all of this work, managers, technical teams, and client users need to have input into the development of the BR plan. A good BR plan is not solely a technical challenge. Certainly the technologies that I examine later in this book play a critical part, but it is not just the computer that needs to work; the whole business process built on top of the computer must be reliable. That's why you need to read this section!

What Is the Cost of Failure?

Are you convinced yet? If not, let's look at the bottom line: money. Let's determine how much money server downtime will cost you. It will help you to see the importance of the BR plan and give you some idea how much money you should be spending on your plan.

Consider Table 1.1, which lists annual server downtime both as a percentage and as a number of hours for a 24-hour, 7-day-a-week operation.

Table 1.1 Annual Downtime

DOWNTIME PERCENTAGE	DOWNTIME IN HOURS PER YEAR
0.01%	0.88
0.10%	8.76
0.27%	24.0
1.00%	87.6

Notice that 0.01 percent downtime is only 53 minutes per year! That's pretty impressive (and undoubtedly pretty expensive to achieve). How about 0.1 percent? That represents about nine hours of downtime per year. This seems more reasonable. Surely most businesses can survive an outage of less than one day in a year. Maybe, but consider that you cannot choose when that outage will occur. It could happen in the middle of the night on New Year's Day, when your entire operation is closed for the holidays. In that case, it may cost you little or nothing in lost business.

Unfortunately, it is more likely to happen on the busiest business day of the year. Why? If you leave your car idling in the driveway on a cool winter day, could the engine overheat and fail? Yes. Is it likely? Realistically, no. It is, however, much more likely that the engine will overheat and fail when you are loaded up for a vacation and passing a string of trucks on the freeway on the hottest day in the summer. The same is true of computer hardware and software. Failure is more likely to occur when the machine is being pushed to its limits, which is generally when you can least afford it. If the servers running a major stock exchange were to fail in the last minutes before the bell tolls to end the day's trading, it could cost millions. In that case, even 5 minutes of downtime—never mind 53—would be a major disaster.

Let me put it another way. I've been talking in terms of downtime, and observed that at 0.1 percent downtime we only lose a day or so a year. But, that means that all of our servers have to be up 99.9 percent of the time all year. That is a pretty reliable machine! How many of your servers have been up 99.9 percent of the last three or four years? Let's look at 1 percent downtime, then. At that rate, your server is out of commission for *87 hours per year*. That's close to four solid 24-hour days out of service. And that is with servers running perfectly 99 percent of the time, day in and day out, year after year. Remember, too, that when a server goes down, all of its clients go down, too. In an enterprise network, servers commonly rely on other servers, so an outage of one server can have a significant domino effect.

How much might all that downtime cost you? It can be difficult to arrive at the exact cost of an outage since there are a number of variables and some hidden costs. If your server is a direct revenue generator, such as an online Web store, you could arrive at a figure for the average revenue generated by the site on a per-hour basis and use that figure to arrive at a downtime cost. I'll call this the *Basic Hourly Loss*. Of course the revenue flow will vary between your peak times and slow times. You would be prudent to consider something closer to the worst case than the best, of course. For example, on one Web site that I help to administer, almost half of the Web traffic occurs in six hours—only one quarter of the day. In a business-to-business setting in North America, most if not all of the day's transactions may occur during a business day of 12 hours or so (taking time zones into account). If the business is international, your server may be busy close to 24 hours a day. To be safe, you should multiply the basic hourly loss by a factor that assumes the outage happens at a bad time for your business. I'll call it the *Time of Day factor*.

In business it is often said that timing is everything, and that applies equally to good timing and bad. If you are beginning to do business on the Web and your site goes down three times in a week, but for only 20 minutes per outage, you have accumulated only an hour of downtime in a week, or an uptime of 99.4 percent. That's pretty good reliability. On the other hand, if those three outages occurred at busy times, your Web site may acquire a reputation for unreliability, which could cost you future business. It is never news when a Web site stays up, but it sure can be when they go down. You need another factor to account for this. I'll call it the *Bad Publicity factor*.

While the server is down, your business may have to fall back on manual processes to keep functioning. If those processes are paper-based, they may be time consuming and eventually someone will have to sit down and re-enter the information into the system when it comes back up. I'll call this the *Extra Paperwork factor*. Also, what if an outage results in employees unable to do their work? I once consulted in an auto assembly plant where anything that stops the line means a direct revenue loss on the order of *$25,000/minute*, plus the cost of hundreds of idle workers. That is why those lines rarely stop! In addition, consider other operational overhead besides direct labor. I'll add another factor, then, called the *Wasted Labor and Overhead factor*.

To get a downed server back up, you will have to stop what you are doing and move to solve the problem. In the case of smaller firms, there may not be sufficient in-house expertise. An outside consultant may have to be called in, costing money and time. Whether you tap in-house or outside expertise, you need to account for it. I'll add an *Expert Help factor*.

What if the outage results in data loss? If you are not using any of the data replication techniques I'll be talking about in Chapter 4, "Installing and Configuring for Reliability," it is virtually impossible to come through a disk crash with no loss of data at all. Without a reliable backup strategy, the data loss could be devastating. Let's be positive, though, and say you do have a good backup (you *do* have good backups, don't you?). Then you have minimized your data loss. That's good, but how long will it take you to restore from your backup and recover the data lost since the backup was made? Add the *Data Recovery Time factor*.

In the case of a hardware failure, it may be necessary to source new hardware. If you keep spares, then that becomes part of the cost of your insurance. If you don't, however, replacing your hardware may take time. Should a server fail tomorrow, how long would it take you to provide a replacement hardware specification to a supplier? How long would it take the parts to arrive? Add in the *Source New Hardware factor*. How do you know that you will be able to get exact replacements for your hardware? These days, anything that was current on the market a year ago can be hard to find today. You may have to replace the failed parts with newer, possibly different technology. It may take extra time to get that new technology working properly. Add in the *New Technology factor*.

Do you see what I mean? You must consider many factors to determine the true bottom line cost of a server failure. I've talked about those that occur to me. This is not meant to be a comprehensive list and there will be factors unique to your business that you will have to deal with as you build your own BR plan. When all the factors are added up, it will cost some multiple of the base-per-hour lost revenue. In the following sidebar, I have worked out a downtime cost example for a small business that has done

---

HOW MUCH IS THIS GOING TO COST ME?

Here is an example of downtime cost calculations. This is for a small business with annual gross revenue of $200,000. On a 24-hour-per-day, 365-day-per-year basis, that would represent an income of about $23 per hour. I'll take that as my Basic Hourly Loss, should the servers on which that revenue flow depends fail. The factors I described in the text add up like this:

- **Time of Day.** If the majority of the business is transacted during the business day, then it is reasonable to at least double the basic rate, so add $23 per hour of downtime.

- **Bad Publicity.** As this is a small company, I'll assume the number of customers is small enough and close enough to the company that there will not be a serious problem, I'll add only $2 per hour, but be careful. This one is unpredictable. It could get much worse.

- **Extra Paperwork.** It is reasonable to assume that one or possibly more employees need to work manually while the server is down to do the work the server normally does. If one employee can keep up with what the computer normally does, then I probably shouldn't have the computer, so let's say it takes three people to manually duplicate the computer's function, and their average burdened cost is $20 per hour—each. Add $60 per hour.

(continued)

- **Wasted Labor and Overhead.** The down server idles three unskilled workers. Add $30, plus $15 in overhead, for a total of $45 per hour.

- **Expert Help.** My small company has to bring in an outside expert to help with this one. The expert has a minimum four-hour billing policy for an on-site call. At an hourly rate of $75 per hour, add $300.

- **Data Recovery.** It takes the expert one hour to respond to my page and arrive at my door. When she arrives, it takes her only 15 minutes to diagnose the problem, but it takes 2 hours and 45 minutes to fully resolve it and get back into production. Unfortunately the fix involves restoring from last night's backup, which takes 45 minutes. Now I have to reenter all of the day's transactions. If the breakdown occurred half way through the day, add 4 hours of labor for two data entry clerks at $20 per hour, for a total of $160.

- **Source New Hardware.** The outside expert really knows her stuff, but even she can't breath life into a dead power supply. It takes her an extra hour to source a replacement power supply. Add $75.

- **New Technology.** The new power supply doesn't fit my old case. Back to the supplier for a second unit. Cost: one more hour. Add another $75.

Now, let's add up the damage for the four hours of total downtime:

Basic Hourly Loss	$23 × 4 = $	92
Time of Day	$23 × 4 = $	92
Bad Publicity	$ 2 × 4 = $	8
Extra Paperwork	$60 × 4 = $	240
Wasted Labor and Overhead	$45 × 4 = $	180
Expert Help	$	300
Data Recovery	$	160
Source New Hardware	$	75
New Technology	$	75
Total Cost for Four Hours of Downtime		$1,222

($305.50 per hour of downtime)

Now, if I set my goal to keep my server running 99 percent of the time, I will still have 88 hours of downtime each year, making my annual downtime cost 88 × $305.50, or $26,884. If my server is up only 95 percent of the time, I would have 438 hours of downtime to deal with, costing me 438 × $305.50, or $133,809. That is more than half of my entire gross revenue!

This example uses a small company. As the size of the operation grows, so do the losses. One industry survey of large corporate IT departments recorded annual downtime costs of $700,000, and that was for servers with uptimes of 99.9 percent.

little beyond having a simple on-site backup as their loss insurance policy. Too many companies have proceeded no further than this. If you have insurance, congratulations! Readers who have gotten this far and are thinking they have some work to do, fear not and read on. Help is on the way. The values for the factors I have used are estimates; they almost always will be. Work it out yourself with numbers suited to your business, and remember, although the base loss rate is in terms of gross revenue, the actual amount lost comes straight off your bottom line.

How Much Should I Spend on Insurance?

If I have convinced you that downtime will cause you significant loss, then you should do something to protect yourself. This will undoubtedly cost money. To help determine how much you should spend, consider the two graphs in Figure 1.1. The sample downtime calculation in my previous example assumed the cost of downtime to be constant, irrespective of the length of the downtime period. In fact, due to the domino effect on the overall business process, the hourly cost tends to escalate as the length of the downtime period increases. For example, your staff may be able to manually accumulate incoming orders to be processed when the system comes back up, but they will only be able to do that for a limited period of time before it affects their regular duties. Should the outage last more than a few hours, it may become necessary to bring in extra staff to cope, and thus the costs escalate.

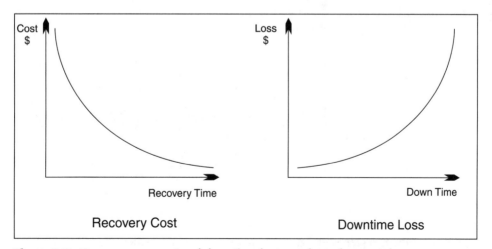

Figure 1.1   Here, recovery cost and downtime loss are charted separately.

If you are dealing with material flows, downtime may hamper your ability to order raw materials. For a short interruption, you may have enough raw material on hand to keep going until the system comes back on line, at which time a double order can be placed to replenish stocks. If the outage lasts long enough that you begin to run out of critical items, however, the costs again escalate.

Finally, there are cases in which your customer may have imposed a performance requirement on you. If you are unable to meet shipment times, for example, there may be a penalty cost to you over and above the revenue lost for the late or missed shipment. A short interruption in your system may not push you into that penalty zone; a longer outage may render you helpless to avoid the penalty. On the recovery side, the speed of recovery greatly affects the cost of the reliability solution. By duplicating all components of the server and making extensive use of specialized hardware and software components, it is possible to build machines that can operate in the 99.99 percent availability range, but it is costly. A more reasonably priced solution can be created, but you will have to accept a longer time to recover.

Following the standard practice in a cost benefit analysis, the optimum BR plan budget is obtained by placing the two graphs atop one another, as shown in Figure 1.2. The curves cross at the cost benefit target point, where the cost of insurance just equals the cost of loss. Any solution that places you to the left of the target shortens the recovery time further than its cost

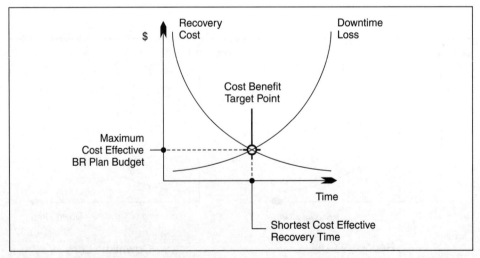

Figure 1.2   The two graphs in Figure 1.1 are more meaningful when charted together, as shown here.

warrants, while any solution to the right saves you money on your BR plan, but will cost you too much in downtime.

Building Your BR Plan

I've tried my best to convince you to develop a BR plan. Let's say I've succeeded. (I'm an optimist.) How do you go about doing it? In the spirit of the Linux HOWTOs, I've written a BR plan HOWTO.

LINUX HOWTOS

One of the commonly voiced objections to the commercial use of open source software has always been the issue of documentation. It has been argued that although the code itself may be well enough written, the documentation is poor and often out of date. The authors of the code, while they may be brilliant programmers, are not necessarily best suited to writing documentation, and as there is no revenue associated with open source, who is going to write and maintain good documentation? The open source community responded to these concerns by founding the Linux Documentation Project (LDP). The LDP manifesto describes the project as "a loose team of volunteers with minimal central organization." However, a visit to the LDP Web site (www.linuxdoc.org) reveals a well-organized body of several hundred up-to-date documents distributed from a worldwide group of 250 mirror sites.

One of the most popular document categories maintained by the LDP are the HOWTOs. These are short, subject-specific papers giving practical hands-on implementation instructions for a particular task, usually with numerous examples. Subjects range from the fundamental to the specific, such as

Cable_Modem HOWTO. Answers basic questions on how to connect your Linux box to a cable modem or cable Internet provider.

Hardware HOWTO. Lists most of the hardware supported by Linux and helps you locate any necessary drivers.

Hebrew HOWTO. Describes how to configure your Linux machine to use Hebrew characters on X-Windows and Virtual Consoles.

In addition to the HOWTOs, the LDP maintains the man (online manual) pages and is now beginning to produce longer documents, called Guides. These are full-length books, some of which are available in print as well as online. The LDP also produces a monthly ezine, *The Linux Gazette*, containing tips, tricks, and Linux news of all sorts. It can be found at www.linuxdoc.org/LDP/LG. LDP documents are professionally written and can be enormously helpful. Don't run Linux without them!

I've written this HOWTO in the form of a seven-point checklist. When you can check off all seven steps, you're done.

1. **Make a list of computer-dependent business functions, prioritized by downtime impact.** A business function might be something like billing, new order entry, online sales, or customer followup. You prioritize by determining how long you can be without this function before it starts costing you money. For example, online sales or new order entry would be a high priority. Any downtime at all could cost you a sale. Billing, while obviously important, could probably be deferred until tomorrow with little cost, as long as you have a good contingency system to make sure you don't miss sending out bills altogether. Customer followup may not be time critical either, unless you are primarily a service-based business that depends on fast customer service response.

   One quick way to build a list of computer-dependent functions is to ask each of your employees to write on a sticky note the top three functions that take up his or her time in an average working day. Add to each note your assessment of the time and revenue priority of each of these functions. If you can, try to assign an amount of time you can survive without the function being performed before it costs you money. Now stick all of these notes on a wall and compile an ordered list of all of the functions putting the ones that have the highest time assessments at the top of the list.

   It is also interesting to try to estimate for each function the amount of money it would cost you should the function be unavailable. Time can play tricks on you here. It may be that a short disruption, say an hour or so, may have negligible effect. Remember, though, how costs escalate as the period of downtime lengthens.

2. **Identify the data you need to keep those critical business functions going.** By data I mean the applications' own binary code as well as production data. You should be able to list actual data directory names and names of application configuration files on each server you manage. List them in the same priority sequence as you listed the functions they support in step 1. If you are managing well-structured applications that were installed properly, most if not all of the code for each application will be in a single directory. Likewise, well-structured data is contained in as few directories as possible, ideally only one per application. Take care not to overlook small configuration files that may be in a system generic directory such as /etc.

As you list each data object, carry over the time factor from your list in step 1. The idea is to come up with a list of critical data objects and the amount of time you can survive without those objects being available.

3. **List what could go wrong.** The goal here is to consider all the things that could break and the likelihood of each type of failure. This is commonly called *Risk Analysis*. Consider hardware failures such as crashed disks, cooling fans, or failed peripheral cards. Also take into consideration site risks such as power outages, fire, flood, or other natural disasters, especially if you are located in a high-risk area. You should also consider the possibility of operating system or application errors that may result in business function downtime. You must also consider the unpleasant possibilities of hacker intrusion or virus infection. It makes sense to consider a security violation as a form of failure, since recovering from a security breach will require you to take an application out of production to resecure it.

   The extent to which you are actually at risk is difficult to assess and involves some speculation. Some things are certainly more likely than others (disk crashes are inevitable, I'm afraid). Large-scale calamities such as fire or flood, while perhaps less likely, would be so damaging that you would be foolish to ignore them. I'll go into this subject in more detail in Chapter 2, "Risk Analysis," giving you lists of specific risks to consider. The one thing I have learned here is never say never.

4. **Identify and list in priority order your high-risk data.** In step 2 you identified data that needs protection, and in step 3 you determined what kind of failures threaten that data. Now, you put the results of steps 2 and 3 together. You look at the highest failure possibilities and what data entities those failures would affect. If one or more of the most critical data objects turn out also to be at significant risk, those data objects make the top of the list in this step. The BR plan should allot the most time and money to protecting these high-risk, mission-critical data objects.

5. **Defend yourself!** Now you know what you should fear the most, and you can start putting together a defense. Bring together the users of your business application and your technical staff, and work out plans of action to cover each of the failure modes you have isolated. The higher up a data object is in your step 4 list, the more money and time you should devote to protecting it. As you work down the list, you may decide at some point to accept the risk and

implement no defense if the defense cost appears to exceed the potential loss.

Make sure that no one group dominates this step; each party has important input. The end user of the application may point out a critical function that the technical implementer has entirely over-looked. At the same time, the techie may point out a critical compo-nent that no one but the technical staff really appreciates the importance of. If you are a manager, listen; you may learn all sorts of things you didn't know!

6. **Do it!** You now have the information necessary to support a budget proposal to build your BR plan. If you are in production now, then you are at risk now, so start the process.

7. **Keep doing it!** This one might not be so obvious. Like most business mechanisms, a BR plan needs to be maintained. Nothing is so con-stant as change, especially where computers are involved. Your most critical server will probably be replaced in the next year or so, and old recovery procedures will need to be updated. Applications will come, be upgraded, and possibly go. Production data will continue to grow. Today's backup solution will be inadequate for the data volumes you will manage two years from now. Consequently, the money budgeted to build the BR plan needs to be extended to an ongoing annual budgetary commitment to properly maintain the BR plan. Also, part of the value of developing a BR plan is that you start to *think* BR. Thus for every new project you undertake, you should (in its planning stage) consider the possibilities of failures and spec-ify defenses to integrate with your existing overall BR plan.

One of the most involved parts of this process is step 3, analyzing what poses a risk to your data. To help you through that task, the next chapter leads you through this risk analysis process in detail. I have also provided a sample BR plan in Appendix A, which should provide a good starting point for the development of your own plan.

What You Can Do Now

1. Consider your most important server and go through the exercise of calculating a downtime cost, should that machine go out of service for 1 percent of a production year. At the same time determine what the uptime record has been for that machine. The idea is to get an idea of your current downtime costs.

2. Use this current downtime cost figure to put together a budget proposal for the development of a BR plan. This should focus the attention of IT management on the importance and the cost benefit of a good BR plan so that there is strong commitment from management for the project.

3. Put together a team to produce a BR plan. The team should include players from each area of your corporate organization that either supplies or relies upon a data processing function.

4. Use the sample BR plan in Appendix A to build your own plan.

Risk Analysis

Know thine enemy.

Risk analysis involves identifying all the possible things that could go wrong, and the relative likelihood of each in fact going wrong. This is a complicated task, as there are usually a number of things that could go wrong, and the likelihood of any particular failure can only be estimated. Risk analysis is thus more art than science. You can improve the reliability of a risk analysis by your knowledge of risks particular to your situation and by keeping records of failures as they happen in order to build a history. The more you know of the past, the better you are able to predict the future.

This chapter steps through a risk analysis of a Linux server. Risks are divided into four areas, starting with server hardware, followed by server software, human factors, and finally natural disaster. Failure modes are listed in a tabular format, with an assessment of the impact of each failure on your operations, the likelihood of the failure, and the defenses available to you against the failure. The severity and likelihood of each failure is listed as low, medium, or high; these are my own ratings and are based on my own observation and experience. Your particular situation may not be subject to some of the risks detailed; on the other hand, you may be at higher risk than the norm. If computer failures were completely predictable, I wouldn't be writing this book and you wouldn't be reading it.

My intent is for you to use this chapter as a framework to assess your own situation. All of the defenses listed are introduced briefly in this chapter; the technical details you will need to implement them are the subject of the last two sections of this book. The Chapter Reference column in each table shows you in which chapter the implementation details for each defense are detailed. I've chosen to list the failures in order of greatest likelihood first. This was purely arbitrary; it may make more sense to order your list in terms of severity.

Server Hardware Failure

Clearly the reliability of your server's hardware is a key issue, and forms the foundation upon which everything else rests, so I have chosen to consider this first. Table 2.1 lists my server hardware failure risk table.

You will notice that the highest risk items in the table involve mechanical components, as opposed to purely solid-state components such as peripheral cards or memory. The fact is, mechanical components wear out. Solid-state components may fail if abused, but rarely do they wear out as such. If you can keep the in-case temperature under control, and the machine is not physically disturbed, then the purely electrical components should normally be the least of your worries. As disk drives are one of the most mechanically complex components of any computer, and are in constant use, they stand at the top of the list for probable failure.

Dealing with Hard Disk Failure

The first listed defense against disk failure is operational monitoring. Often when building a Business Recovery (BR) plan you can become fixed on after-the-fact recovery and overlook the opportunity to be proactive, attempting to see failure coming as well as dealing with it when it arrives. In the case of disk failures, it is possible for a drive to begin logging I/O errors before it fails completely. In most cases, unfortunately, especially in the case of a head crash, the drive deteriorates rapidly after the first sign of trouble. As a result, monitoring must be done on an ongoing basis with a rapid response time. To do this effectively requires an automated system.

Losing a hard disk is listed as high severity because the data on a failed disk should be considered irrevocably lost. In desperate cases, it may be possible to physically dismantle the failed drive and recover some of the

Table 2.1 Server Hardware Risks and Defenses

FAILURE	LIKELIHOOD	SEVERITY	DEFENSE	CHAPTER
Hard Disk	High	High	Operational Monitoring	6
			Redundant Disk Hardware (RAID)	5
			Hot Swap Disk Hardware	3
			Reliable Backups	7
			Server Clusters	10
Cooling Fan(s)	High	High	Operational Temperature Monitoring	3,6
			Operational Fan Failure Monitoring	3
			Multiple Redundant Fans	3
			Server Clustering	10
External Power Supply	High	High	Uninterruptible Power Supply (UPS)	3
			Backup Site Power	3
Network Failure	High	High	Redundant Network Hardware	3
			Multiple External Service Connections	3
Tape Drive	High	Low	Operational Monitoring	6
			Hot Swap Spare	3
Internal Power Supply	Medium	High	Redundant Power Supply	3
Internal Peripheral Card	Low	Low	Operational Monitoring	6
			Redundant Card	3
			Spare Hardware on Hand	3
Ram or Motherboard	Low	High	Operational Monitoring	6
			Spares on Hand	3

data. There are disaster recovery companies that specialize in this type of work; however, it is expensive and time consuming, and the amount of recoverable data varies widely. This should be considered only as a last resort—never a viable first line of defense.

Redundant Disk Solutions

If that is not acceptable, you may want to consider using a redundant array of inexpensive disks, or RAID. This involves using several separate disks to store your data so that there is a complete duplicate copy of the data held within the array. Any one of the disks could now fail, without losing any data. If the disk hardware can be replaced without bringing the server down, the failed disk can be replaced and the data it held recovered from the remaining good disks with no downtime at all. This is obviously an ideal solution. Until recently, however, RAID was not a commonly used solution, especially in smaller servers, due to the relatively high cost of the extra disk storage required. The steady drop in the cost of hard disks and improvements in the software implementations in the latest Linux kernel have made RAID a much more affordable option. There are a variety of different types of RAID solutions, implemented in hardware, software, or a combination of both. All of the variations are possible in a Linux environment. I devote all of Chapter 5, "Building Reliable Disk Storage," to the topic of redundant disk storage.

UNUSUAL DISK FAILURES

At times disks can fail for what seem unlikely reasons. A colleague with a number of years experience in large server environments shared this interesting observation: "Most of the disk failures that I have experienced have happened as a result of shutting down a large stable system that has been running for many months for routine maintenance. During the maintenance period of less than 30 minutes the disks stopped spinning and cooled. The disk alignments were affected by the change of temperature and they could not spin again to reboot. Your systems are at risk even when prescheduled extended periods of downtime occur. This would be the one time that a disk would fail without an error warning of any kind being logged."

I had a similar experience with some of my first UNIX workstations. This group of machines had the same make and model of operating system disk. None of these disks failed in 24/7 operations over several years. However, if the server were shut down for any reason, usually to move it to a different location in our case, there was a high probability that when powered on, the disk would not spin up. Using highly unscientific means (picking the machine up and shaking it) we could sometimes free the stuck platter and get the machine going. We only fully solved the problem by replacing the problematic drives with new ones.

The Importance of Backups

Even if you implement multiple redundant hot swap disks, it is still critical that you include a comprehensive backup policy. Disk crashes are not the only source of data loss. Problems in the operating system or applications can damage or destroy data. Operational errors can all too easily cause data loss also. It may be necessary to maintain historical snapshots of data for accounting, legal, or tax purposes. Finally, an off-site backup is essential for your protection in case of a large-scale site loss.

Server Clusters

A broader approach to protecting against disk failure is server clustering. This involves grouping several servers together with a connecting management infrastructure, the objective of the cluster being either high-speed parallel computing or redundancy for high availability. A simple cluster would be a pair of servers, typically one production machine and a warm standby. Software runs on both machines to detect the failure of any functionality, whereupon a recovery procedure is started. Disk storage is usually shared in some way between the machines so that, should the primary production server fail, the warm standby would be able to take over the disk from the failed production machine and bring the data back into production ASAP.

This is a complex technology with the greatest challenge to its success being the ability of the application to inherit data from a failed machine and be able to successfully use it. There are a number of competing server cluster implementations available for a Linux server farm. I'll be examining them in Chapter 10, "Server Clustering."

Keeping Your Cool

Next to disk failure, overheating due to cooling failure is probably the next major hardware concern. Most servers have at least two, often more, cooling fans that run 24 hours a day, seven days a week. They can and do fail, leading to potentially damaging in-case temperatures.

Good Maintenance Is Cheap Insurance

One of the most obvious things you can do that I often see overlooked is to enforce good maintenance practices. Not all fans are inlet fans, some are designed to exhaust and don't usually have filters. Cooling fans that work by drawing air into the case are normally fitted with filter screens to catch dust. These screens must be cleaned at regular intervals or they will clog up and reduce the effectiveness of the fan. This is such a simple thing to do; yet it is often overlooked. Fans that operate by exhausting air from the case are often fitted with a coarser screen, which is less likely to clog. In this case, however, there is commonly no provision for filtering the air drawn into the case, so dirt and dust build up inside the case. I am less happy about cleaning inside cases than I am cleaning an externally accessible filter screen. Any thing that has the potential to disturb the hardware in the case is trouble in the making. I know of several large-scale computing board and case designs that have known weaknesses in terms of being sensitive to disturbance. If they are running fine and you don't touch them, you have no problems.

Building a Server Room

If you find a lot of dust building up in cases or plugging fans, maybe you need to examine the server room environment. You do have a server room, don't you? Even in a small server installation, it is worthwhile to locate the server in its own space. The air supply can be properly filtered and regulated, and it is generally easier to control temperature and humidity in a smaller room than a larger one. Should the building air conditioning fail and the temperature in the server room climb to 120 degrees, you may still have a temperature problem, even if none of the server cooling fans fails. A small, self-contained, reasonably inexpensive air conditioning unit may be all it takes to keep those servers cool and running, even if you have to sweat it out in the main office.

Water is another consideration in terms of where to put a server. Any location that is below grade should be avoided, if possible. Water has a funny habit of finding holes in the ground, and if you put your server in a hole in the ground, there's a good chance some water might find it one day. I'm not necessarily thinking about a large-scale flood, either. All it takes is for a toilet to overflow two floors up on the weekend for enough water to find its way downstairs to cause grief. The top floor of a building is also not ideal, especially if the building has a flat roof. A good friend of mine once gave me the same advice when I was looking for an apartment. He had once worked for a property management company that operated a number of high-rise apartment towers. He observed that many top floor penthouses were strongly prone to leaky ceilings, as flat roofs are notoriously difficult to seal perfectly.

If you are working in a larger-scale server installation, you may consider a raised floor, machine room style environment. The Uptime Institute (www.upsite.com) has developed a four-tier system for classifying machine room environments. A tier one environment is associated with uptimes of 99.8 percent, and is estimated to cost $400 per square foot of floor area. At the top of the scale, a tier four installation is expected to support 99.991 percent uptime, at an estimated cost of $1,000 per square foot. This is overkill for most small to mid-sized PC server installations today. It would only be justifiable for large, multiple server installations or in situations where an existing machine room designed for a previous generation of computing technology is still in service, and you can take advantage of the excellent environment it will provide. I do want to make the point, however, that the server critical to your corporate mission deserves a decent home and will benefit from it in reliability.

Fan and Temperature Monitoring

Many motherboards now support built-in on-board sensors to monitor CPU temperature, fan speed, or case intrusion. Many of these devices use a standard two-wire bus known as the i2c bus. There is good Linux support for this bus in the 2.4 kernel, and there are applications available to enable you to read these sensors and monitor them. Systems administrators can write scripts that trigger alarms, initiate shutdown, or start fail over processes in the event a fan fails or temperatures rise beyond dangerous levels. This kind of functionality was previously associated with expensive large-scale servers. Today these sensors are available on low-cost, mass-market motherboards, and are well worth the small effort it takes to specify them and use them.

Of course it never hurts to have two of everything, and fans are no exception. Unless noise is a factor, I usually like to see as many fans in a server as can be fitted. Most cases are supplied with mounting for extra fans. Since fans are cheap, I take the opportunity to fill every fan hole with a fan unit.

Keeping the Power Flowing

A stable and reliable supply of electrical power to your site is clearly a necessity for a reliable server. Unfortunately, you may have less control over that than you might like. Should you have the luxury of deciding on the geographical location of your servers, reliable power is going to be one of your top considerations. There are of course many other factors that come into play, and in reality you may find yourself in a location that regularly experiences power shortages or outright outages. I live in a northern location in which several outages during the winter months are a certainty and must be planned for. An uninterruptible power supply (UPS) is a must in these cases, and there is good Linux support for a number of the most popular external UPS units.

In a larger site, you may also put in place backup power from your own generator. Installing such a generator is beyond the scope of this book, but realize that in the case of a fail over from line to generator, there is almost always a power dip that needs to be smoothed over. Generator power may also not be as stable as line power, so even though you have your own power should you need it, a UPS is still a requirement.

Dealing with Network Failures

A network failure may be either internal or external to the server. From a hardware point of view, the Network Interface Card (NIC) could fail, as could the physical cable connection. As the NIC is a solid-state device, the likelihood of failure is small, but you may not wish to overlook it. It is possible to install a duplicate warm standby NIC in the server, although there are problems with this approach. The Linux clusters I'll be presenting in Chapter 10 implement monitor code designed to isolate things like a NIC failure and initiate a recovery process. In practice, however, it is more likely that a server is isolated from the network as a result of a problem originating on the network rather than a problem local to the server itself.

Label Those Cables

I cannot suggest strongly enough that you are positively religious about labeling cables. If you suspect a cabling problem and you have no labels, the likelihood of unplugging the wrong cable and making things worse is just far too high. Commercial adhesive wire label books are available at any industrial electric supply, and are well worth the investment. I have stood by too many sites watching people plugging and unplugging cables trying to isolate a fault by trial and error. The few minutes and dollars it takes to put some labels on when you install the cabling can pay off enormously six months from now. The other critical element of a well-managed physical network is a complete and up-to-date topology diagram. When I teach networking classes, I ask the question, "How many machines does it take to make a network?" The answer I'm looking for is two. If you have

NOW WHERE DOES THIS ONE GO?

I once read a wonderful article written by a network analyst newly hired by a company that had created a dedicated network management position for the first time. As no one had been in charge to that time, their networks were a mess. Specifically, there was no overall diagram that could be used to trace network connections. It took this analyst three months to go back over the entire network and document it, labeling and correcting loops and redundant cabling as he went. At the end, he was left with one cable disappearing into a wiring duct. He had no idea at all where the other end went. All he could do was to cut the cable and wait for the phone to ring. It never did! This is not the situation you want to find yourself in; it does not help your server reliability.

two machines, you have a network; if you have a network, you need a network topology diagram. Developing a topology diagram for only two machines seems silly. But the point is this: if you don't start the diagram when you have two machines, you still won't have it when you have 20. It is when you have more machines to deal with that the troubles escalate, confusion sets in, and you could really use that diagram. Start it now, not later. I've provided a topology diagram in the sample BR plan in Appendix A, so you can get an idea of the sort of information needed.

Another invaluable tool is a cable tester. You need one that allows you to place the tester at one end of the cable and a wrap plug at the other so that long cables and cables fished through walls can be tested without having to remove them. Again, I have seen far too much time wasted trying to fix what at first seems to be an operating system driver, or network routing problem that turns out to be nothing more than a bad cable. I have learned in troubleshooting network issues to check the hardware first, not last, and a simple cable tester is often all you need.

External Network Redundancy

If your server relies on external connectivity, it may be a good idea to have a secondary external connection. This may be of limited use, however. If the external failure is within your service providers network, an alternate provider may be able to offer backup connectivity. If the reason that your main provider failed is due to some natural disaster, or a large-scale disruption in the general communications infrastructure in your area, there is a good chance that any backup provider will be affected also. In this case you may want to consider a backup site located at some distance from your primary site. This requires that you have a plan of action in terms of either moving your servers to the alternate site, or having backup servers already in place at the alternate site. In the latter case, you will need a way to move your current data from the primary to the backup site in case of a fail over. If there is normally good network connectivity between the two sites, Linux supplies some interesting network file systems that may help you distribute that data in production. Then in case of fail over, your production data will already be at the backup site. This also offers alternatives to off-site tape backups that can be time consuming to recover. I'll be talking about these options in Chapter 9, "Alternative File Systems."

Tape Backup Failures

Although CD-R and CD-RW are well supported under Linux, magnetic tape is still the most popular backup media by far. Tapes have capacities in the gigabytes, while the CD formats, as well as other removable media devices such as zip drives are typically limited to hundreds of megabytes. Whichever format you choose, it is critical to test your backups on an ongoing basis. Just because the backup appeared to finish doesn't mean it is good. Tape drives are mechanical devices, and need maintenance. Heads and capstan rollers should be cleaned on a regular basis, the same way that there should be a maintenance schedule for keeping fan screens clean. Your backup procedures should always test existing backups. I call it Campbell's Law of Backups. Your backup procedure should read back at least some of every backup at the time it is written to ensure that the tape is good. Also, for every backup tape you create, you should be drawing one from storage and testing to make sure it is *still* good. I have heard too many stories of people who need to pull a backup in a crisis and discover that it is no good.

Some sites reuse tapes; others will use a tape only once. If you choose not to reuse a tape, either physically destroy it or use a bulk eraser to ensure that none of your data is left on the tape when it leaves your site. Store tapes in a secure location. Make sure that as well as being cool and dry, your tape storage location is free from strong magnetic fields. Storing tapes on top of or beside a CRT monitor, for example, is *not* a good idea.

If you begin to have trouble with a tape drive, it is tempting to peg repair at a low priority, after all it doesn't affect production, right? Not until something crashes and you need it. Do you ever check the air in your spare tire? Speaking of spares, a spare tape drive is not a bad idea, although you may consider it overkill. Replacing the tape drive could mean bringing the server down, if it is not a hot swap unit. If you want to avoid this, you could attach the tape drive to a second, non-mission-critical internal server. Then you could bring the tape server down if necessary without affecting production.

Alternatives to Magnetic Tape

If you don't like the idea of magnetic tape, you may want to consider using disk as a backup media. The almost continuous drop in hard disk prices has brought disk storage to the point of being cheaper than tape on a per-megabyte-stored basis. There are removable media drives in the 20-40 GB range that can be had for a reasonable cost. I will be going into more detail on options in this area in Chapter 7, "Backup and Recovery Strategies."

Internal Power Supply Problems

The power supply internal to the server is primarily solid state, with the exception of a cooling fan. If you have secondary cooling fans inside the case and you are monitoring the in-case temperature, then you should be reasonably well prepared for a power supply fan failure. As the rest of the power supply is solid state, there should be little cause for concern, right? Well, yes, but should that power supply fail, the server is going to crash. And it doesn't matter how many levels of disk redundancy you have, and how many extra fans, your data is not going to survive unscathed. So, although the likelihood of internal power supply failure may not be high, the severity is. The only real way to protect yourself is to source a server case with power supply redundancy. These cases typically have several power supply modules whose total capacity exceeds the maximum possible draw of a fully populated case. Thus, one module may fail without crashing the server. Needless to say, you would expect these modules to be hot swappable.

It is also possible to have a power supply that does not actually fail, but slips outside of the acceptable range of output voltage. This can be a difficult problem to isolate, as the only symptom may be random CPU errors that are practically untraceable. Most motherboards that offer hardware monitoring capabilities will monitor power supply output voltage. This is definitely one to add to your monitoring scripts.

On a side note, one way to protect your dynamic data from a sudden and total failure such as an internal power supply, is to use file systems that support journalling. I'll talk about these in Chapter 9.

Motherboard, Memory, or Peripheral Card Failure

Once a machine is built and is in service, the chances that a memory module or a motherboard will fail in service are small. If it is necessary to open the case and move, add, or replace anything inside, the disturbance is a potential cause of problems. The card-edge style of connector found on most mass market PCs does not give the most positive and reliable connection in the industry. Machines designed for industrial or military application make use of much more robust and durable components at every level. Of course, such cases are much more expensive, too. If a motherboard is abused during handling such that it cracks, this can result in a broken trace. This may not be immediately obvious if the crack is only a hairline. As the temperature of the board rises, however, the action of thermal expansion can pull the crack and the trace open, causing a fault. Although this kind of problem can be hard to pinpoint, it usually happens pretty soon after the machine is put into service, hopefully during preproduction testing.

Servers tend to have a narrow range of peripheral cards. They may have a video card, although as servers are almost always on a network, it is common to administer them over the network and leave the servers themselves headless (that is, without a video card or monitor). It is easy to set up a login prompt on a serial port for emergencies when, for any reason, the machine falls off the network. A serial terminal or laptop can be plugged in via a simple serial cable and the machine can be run from there. The network card itself can be duplicated, as I described earlier.

A disk controller failure would, on the face of it, be a showstopper. In the case of IDE disks, however, the controller is usually on the motherboard, hence a controller failure is synonymous with a motherboard failure. In the case of SCSI disk, the controller is more often a peripheral card, although there are some motherboards offering on-board SCSI controllers. You could protect against loss of the SCSI controller by using disk mirrors such that a complete redundant data copy is made on separate drives attached to separate SCSI controllers.

Server Software Failure

Table 2.2 lists my server software failure risk table.

To assess all the software vulnerabilities of any server would fill many books. I will only try to deal here with broad areas of risk. Each piece of

Table 2.2 Server Software Risks and Defenses

FAILURE	LIKELIHOOD	SEVERITY	DEFENSE	CHAPTER
Dynamic data overruns	High	Medium	Monitoring quotas	6 6
Daemon crash or race	High	High	Monitoring	6
Bugs and upgrades	High	High	Maintenance	6
Security breach	High	High	Security policy maintenance	6
Viruses and worms	Medium	High	Security policy maintenance	6
Boot failure	Low	High	Proper configuration	5

application software has its own idiosyncrasies, which you will become well familiar with and will have to deal with. This presentation considers issues that are of general application to most, if not all, Linux server installations.

Managing Dynamic Data

Although some applications deal with static data, most work with data sets that are dynamic. Commercial servers commonly accumulate data on transactions of one sort or another. They may be financial in the case of sales, they may be accounting for the movement of goods in a manufacturing or warehouse distribution operation, or accumulating data on employees in a personnel management system. Such dynamic data generally grows; rarely does it shrink. Consequently, you must allow for the ever-increasing disk space demanded by this data. While the standard Linux file system is dynamically extensible, the underlying disk management system is not. It is based on fixed-size disk partitions. Should these partitions become full, the application will no longer be able to record further data and, in the worst case, may even crash or corrupt the existing data. So, it is important to do two things: Store each application's data in a separate partition, thus problems in one data partition would not affect another. Monitor these partitions on an ongoing basis, track usage and predict in advance when the partition will fill. Downtime can then be scheduled to add or restructure disks to provide more space as required

One new approach that greatly helps in this area is Logical Volume Management (LVM), one of the features of the 2.4 kernel. LVM allows disk storage to be restructured dynamically. LVM replaces the old concept of fixed-size disk partitions with much smaller allocations of disk space termed physical extents (PEs). These extents can be concatenated to form storage spaces termed logical volumes (LVs) for file systems or raw data. The useful thing is that this concatenation can span disks, allowing two or three disks to appear to the application as one contiguous storage space. Thus, should your data approach filling a disk, a second disk can be added to expand the storage. What is even better is that these changes can be done online, with little or in some cases no operational downtime. In fact both

THE DANGER OF LOG JAMS

One specific concern in terms of disk usage is log files. The nature of any log file is that it is a continuously growing file and so must be managed. Logs can be divided into two categories, those maintained by the operating system, and those associated with applications. In a simple world, I could monitor these logs, determine the growth rate, and budget disk space accordingly. Most of the time, this approach works well, and Linux provides a mechanism for automatically rolling log files over, allowing a new log to be started and the old one renamed. The old log can then be pulled off disk and stored offline, freeing online disk storage space.

Problems can arise, however, should something go wrong that causes the log files to grow at an accelerated pace. It may be that the problem being logged is not in itself serious, but if a side effect is to balloon the log file to the point that it fills a disk partition, then the small problem has become a bigger problem. Unfortunately, it is not possible to predict when such a problem might arise. The best protection is to ensure that the log files are kept in a partition that, if it fills, will not bring the application or the server down.

Another good idea is to be careful with the verbosity of your logging. Many applications and operating system logging functions support the ability of logging terse messages, or much more verbose output. For debugging purposes, logs can be told to record things associated with the normal function of the code, as well as actual errors. Too often these debugging or verbose messaging flags are overlooked when the machine is moved into production, and a log jam results.

LVs and file systems can be dynamically increased or decreased in size. As this code matures and improves in stability, it should become a standard element of any Linux server installation. I've devoted Chapter 8, "Logical Volume Management," to the discussion of LVM.

Another data management tool is disk quotas. In the case where the ownership of data in a partition is divided among several users, it is possible for one user to use all of the remaining free space in the partition. Should that happen, none of the other users or applications will be able to store any more data. Disk quotas can be used in this case to dynamically monitor and control the amount of storage used within a partition on a per-user basis. Quotas can be set per user, or per user group. There is a grace period allowed a user who is over quota to correct the problem before an absolute limit is placed on his or her disk usage.

Tracking Those Devilish Daemons

All of the UNIX flavors have used the term daemon to denote a process that runs all the time and performs a fundamental operating system or application task. Thus, much of the real work that happens on a Linux server is done by one daemon or another. Should something go wrong, usually a bug in the daemon's code, daemons will occasionally either race or crash. A buggy daemon that enters a race condition will use all of the CPU cycles it can get from the operating system to run around in circles and do nothing useful. This usually stops the other applications cold, and can also severely impair the operating system from getting anything much else done. To defend against this condition, you will want to monitor the process table and watch the CPU usage of the major processes. You will need to know the normal bounds of CPU usage, and you can then watch for out-of-bound conditions. Thus, monitoring for and detecting racing daemons is straightforward. Unfortunately, once you have discovered the problem, there is rarely a nice fix. Usually, it is necessary to kill the racing daemon process, often with adverse affects on data or connections to the functionality that the daemon implemented.

A buggy daemon may race, but it may also simply crash. In this case, you will monitor the process table for the simple existence of the daemon. Should the daemon die, you can restart it. Unfortunately, however, the data the daemon was acting on may now be damaged as a result of the crash, and the daemon may quickly crash again. Your monitor may then restart it, and continue a vicious cycle that could be as damaging as a race condition. Writing monitors is discussed in Chapter 6, "Monitoring Linux in Production."

As both races and crashes are often caused by faults in code, the importance of testing new application code in an offline, non-mission-critical environment cannot be over stressed. Any new application, or upgrade to an existing application should be thoroughly tested before placing it into production. A modest investment in some test hardware and test time may prevent costly production hassles. As the old saying goes, an ounce of prevention is worth a pound of cure.

Linking Downtime and Security

Server security and downtime are closely connected. While this is not a book on security, it is important to see that a breach in security can cause downtime, and that scheduled downtime may be necessary to implement or maintain your security systems. A security breach that results in wholesale destruction of data or the server operating system will obviously bring the server down. The procedure to recover from such a breach, however, is really the same as it would be for a major disk crash, CPU crash, or site loss. You should have procedures in place for these possibilities. No one likes to think of having to use those procedures to recover from a malicious action, but the situation is clear and the procedures will be there.

A much more dangerous security breach is one in which you discover unauthorized access at a high level of privilege, yet nothing appears to be missing or malfunctioning. It is tempting to simply overlook the breach and hope that nothing damaging was really done. You change all the passwords and breath a sigh of relief that you got over the situation without any downtime or data loss. The problem is that you still do not know what might have been done. Have any of the binaries on the server been tampered with? Is it possible that these tampered binaries are now steadily leaking data to an unsecure destination or corrupting existing data? Is there a logic bomb planted somewhere in the server that will go off and destroy everything next New Year's Day? If the breach occurs at a high enough level of privilege, you cannot rule any of these possibilities out. Consequently, the only sure response is to bring the server out of production and completely re-install it from a secure backup. Clearly this is not the solution you want to implement, but you really have no choice.

Is there something you could do to ward off this kind of trouble? You may wish to consider including as a part of your monitoring policy a security scanner such as *tripwire*. Originally written at Purdue University, tripwire is now available as open source under the GPL (www.tripwire.org). It compares the sizes and parameters of critical files, including a checksum value, against a reference database of file parameters created from the system when in a known secure state. Any discrepancies between the current state of the system and the reference database indicate a security anomaly, which can be investigated.

An even more robust solution can be found in the Linux Intrusion Detection System, or LIDS (www.lids.org). This is a new kernel patch that allows a security administrator to protect key files and the kernel itself from tampering, even by someone with root privilege. This system has promise in providing significant protection from root security breaches. That kind of strong protection is good for security, and what is good for security is often good for uptime as well.

Resolving Boot Problems

Booting an operating system is a complex process. Once the base kernel is located by the boot loader and copied into memory, the kernel must find and configure drivers for any hardware it is to support. Then basic parameters such as network addresses and names must be set, local and remote file system mounts must be done, and user interfaces started. Finally, the application servers must be started up. There is a substantial body of data stored in numerous configuration files that must be present and correct for all of this to work properly.

It is essential to ensure that any operating system or application configuration you do will survive a reboot. It is easy to say that the machine should only be rebooted by the administrator, and should there be a problem, the administrator will be there to fix it at the time. There are two problems with this idea: One is that you cannot control entirely when a server will get rebooted. The other is that you may have a surprising amount of difficulty remembering the details of all of the configuration the machine needs to do its job. When I do any configuration changes or upgrades to a server, I always do a test reboot when I'm done. If production needs make it impossible to reboot at the time of the changes, I schedule a test reboot at the earliest possible opportunity.

Human Errors

A complete discussion of risk cannot be finished without considering plain old-fashioned mistakes, accidental or deliberate. A good friend of mine has a T-shirt that says on the back, pobody's nerfect. Well, it's true. It is certain that the highly skilled staff who build and operate your servers will make mistakes. Plan for it. The following sections describe some of the things you should be prepared for.

Managing Hardware Servicing Risks

I once had a discussion in a class of system administrators. We were talking about common causes of downtime and one of my students commented that, at their site, normal maintenance or upgrade servicing was a real problem if the hardware service technician failed to properly communicate with other staff onsite. Here is the sort of scenario he was talking about: You have a scheduled downtime window on one of your servers to upgrade the memory. Your hardware is maintained by an outside contractor who arrives at your site to do the upgrade. Because he knows you have a short window to do the upgrade, he goes straight to the machine, powers it off and installs the new memory, then powers it on again. He did a great job in record time and he is pleased with himself. Problem is, he upgraded the wrong server. There are three identical machines all next to each other, but none are clearly identified. He was *sure* it was the one in the middle. What he didn't know was that the function of the machines had changed since his last visit and it was really the one on the left he should have upgraded. The middle machine was the production database server. There is now a big mess to clear up.

How can this kind of mistake be avoided? Every piece of mission critical hardware in your server room should be clearly identified. A name which has meaning to your own staff is good, as well as a short description of what the machine does, in case someone from outside your site needs to be brought in, possibly in an emergency. Also, machines should never be powered off unless the person responsible for the software application running on that machine is present or has specifically authorized and clearly identified the machine to be touched. The idea is to ensure that the software is in the proper state to allow the hardware to be shut down. Finally, access to the server room should be restricted to those who should know what they are doing. In the memory upgrade case, the contractor did not check with the site staff before going ahead with the upgrade. On the other hand, he shouldn't have been able to get into the server room unless the local staff let him in.

Minimizing Scheduled Downtime

Scheduled downtime is an unavoidable necessity. Hardware upgrades or reconfigurations demand it, as does software maintenance and upgrading. Downtime is downtime, however, whether planned or not, and all downtime is bad. Therefore, it is important to make sure that you make optimal use of scheduled downtime, and use no more of it than is absolutely necessary. While you can certainly allow yourself extra time in the downtime window for contingency, you really should do all you can to make the window as small as is necessary, and that requires good planning.

When you are working in a fixed downtime window to add or replace hardware components, assume that things will go wrong. Assume, for example, that a connector will get jammed, or a pin bent or broken. Where reasonable, have extra parts on hand. Make sure that any new hardware you get is going to fit before you get into the shutdown and discover that it doesn't. Always allow yourself an option to roll back to the previous working configuration. Do a dummy run through the upgrade to make sure you have all the necessary tools and components. I have been held up on a job for lack of the smallest darn part enough times to have learned that lesson. If some new components can be installed alongside your production hardware before the shutdown, so much the better. Test each new component as you go. Don't install everything, and then just turn it on. If you have installed several new components and it doesn't turn on, which one is the problem? Do your testing incrementally so that one new thing at a time gets tested in an environment that is known to be good. Invest in the proper tools. Tools are generally a lot cheaper than downtime.

Haste Makes Waste

In the rush to get a new product into production, you decide to go with a new piece of hardware (or software, for that matter) that you have not yet had the opportunity to test. In these days of just-in-time production and design build, time to market has become a passion. In today's competitive world, there is no doubt that time to market is a critical element of business success. But the advantage of being first in the market can evaporate quickly if, once you get there, your operation is plagued with problems and your customers jump ship to your competitor's more reliable servers. Don't allow market pressures to push you into what your technical expertise tells you is dangerous territory.

If you use contracted services, ensure that the contract includes a liability clause to cover business loss due to the contractor's error. If the contractor resists such a clause, maybe you should look for a different contractor.

Managing Software Change

Make sure software change management is properly managed. Invest in an offline server to use as a test machine. Use it to test all software patches, upgrades, or configuration changes before they go into production. Your customers are customers, not guinea pigs. Don't do your software experiments on them. If possible, review with the application developer what you plan to do before you do it. There may be known problems that they can alert you to. These could be issues with a specific make or hardware model, or issues of a particular version of the application under a certain version of the operating system. If there are known issues, they often have a known solution. Research that before you find yourself with a buggy server and no time left in your scheduled downtime window.

In the case of Linux, make use of Internet mailing lists and discussion groups, and USENET newsgroups. They can yield valuable information from people who work in the same trenches as you. If you find a bug in a piece of proprietary software, you can certainly report it to the software vendor. You then sit back and wait. In the open-source world, it is not at all unusual to simply e-mail the developer directly. While it is true that these developers are largely volunteers and are not obliged to respond to your problem, most of the developers wouldn't have taken on the project if they didn't want to in the first place. In my experience, they are generally very responsive to reported problems.

Natural Disasters

None of us want to consider this one, but it has to be done. Should your site experience a major flood, fire, earthquake, or similar large-scale disaster, what are you going to do to recover your business? If your site is going to be out of action for days or weeks, you must have an alternate site. There are several ways of approaching this, dependent largely on the size of your business and the amount of money you can justify for the task.

Maintaining Your Own Backup Site

If your business already has a site at a reasonable distance from your primary site, this is obviously the first choice. Keep in mind that the backup site needs to be far enough away so that it is unlikely to be affected by the same disaster as could take the primary site out. A few miles is probably not far enough.

The first consideration at the backup site is hardware. You must assume that the hardware at the primary site is either destroyed or inaccessible, so you need to make provisions for replacement hardware at the backup site. This can clearly be expensive if you have no use for servers at the backup site. You can choose to specify a cheaper server platform for the backup machine, but make sure it will work properly with the operating system and application installation that will come from your backups. If there is no budget at all for a spare server, keep a detailed inventory of all the hardware from the primary location, and information regarding local suppliers who could get you the hardware quickly, should the need arise. The inventory and supplier information needs to be written in a format that requires no extra explanation. You will be busy enough digging yourself out of the mess at the primary site while the new hardware is being sourced at the backup site. If the information you supply is incomplete or unclear, there may not necessarily be competent technical staff at the backup site to interpret it and ensure that the hardware you get is workable.

Once you have the hardware, you need to start restoring the operating system, then the applications, and finally the application data. Obviously, this site is the logical place to store your offsite backups, so those tapes or removable drives should already be there. Again, if there are no technical staff at the backup site, either develop instructions to allow those folks to get the process started, or count on waiting until you or one of your technical staff get there for the restore process to begin. You may want to consider contracting some local expertise to help out in such a case.

If your servers need external network connectivity, which is almost a certainty, you need to ensure that the backup site has enough of the proper kind of external connections to get the job done. The physical network infrastructure may also be different at the backup site. You may need equipment at the backup site that was not necessary at your site. That is a little point that could be frustrating if it holds up the whole show at a time of crisis. In the case of Internet connectivity, you may also have to arrange with the network service provider at the backup site for the proper addressing you need. It may be necessary to change IP address and DNS name resolution information if you do not own your own IP addresses.

Finally, remember that there is indeed a silver lining to every cloud. When the dust settles, you will need to rebuild your primary site. Now is your chance to improve on all of the things you were never able to change in the old setup, due to production or historical restrictions. The chance to start with a clean sheet may not come often, so take advantage of it when it does. Learn from your experience and you can build a better setup the next time.

The Viability of Using a Mirror Site

The idea of a mirror site is to have two geographically distant sites, each of which is a fully functional mirror of the other. Live data flows between the two sites so that the mirror site server is as up-to-date as if it were a warm standby machine sitting in a rack next to the primary server. Linux now supports file systems such as *enbd* and *drbd* that allow data mirroring over a network connection. I'll be talking about both of these file systems in Chapter 9. The main restriction today is network bandwidth. In order to support disk mirroring with acceptable performance, bandwidth in the order of several megabytes per second is required. That is expensive today, but if Moore's Law applies equally to networking technologies as it does to CPU speed, this will become commonplace in the next few years.

Using Disaster Recovery Service Providers

If the cost of maintaining your own backup or mirror site is prohibitive, you can choose to use a disaster recovery service provider. These companies will assess your server requirements and contract with you to provide a site and equivalent server hardware to your own, in case of disaster. What is important to note is what the service provider will not do. Generally, they do not guarantee to duplicate your hardware exactly, but to functionally duplicate it. This means that the exact operating system configuration that will come off your backup tape may not work out of the box on the replacement hardware. The service provider may or may not have local Linux expertise to assist you. Consider this as you choose your provider. For security reasons, you may not want to store your backups at the service provider's site. In this case, you will have to establish a storage site for the backups that is far enough away from your primary site to serve the purpose. You then need to establish a procedure for getting the tapes from the storage site to the service provider.

Should you choose this option, make sure to do a test failover. Take your own backups and get them up and running on the hardware that the service provider will be supplying you with. If you have separated the operating system as much as possible from your applications, as I describe in Chapter 4, "Installing and Configuring for Reliability," then you may be able to create an operating system backup specific to the service provider's hardware, which can be stored at the service provider's site for you to use. In that case, you only have to install your application and its data. The service provider may actually be willing and able to do the operating system installation as part of the service. It would be nice in cases like these if there were a standard Linux installation, rather than a number of different distributions. Projects such as the Linux Scalability Project (LSP) and the Filesystem Hierarchy Standard (FHS) are helping with this issue, and I fervently hope that the day may come when there is a generic standard Linux installation. Unfortunately, we're not there yet.

What You Can Do Now

1. Using Table 2.1 as a basis, examine your current server hardware and generate a list of your top hardware exposures. Consider which defenses you feel are appropriate to your case and incorporate them into your BR plan.

2. If you have a network, but no network topology diagram, now is a good time to make one. You can use the diagram included in the BR plan in Appendix A as a model.

3. Examine the software you have currently running in light of the risks laid out in Table 2.2. Incorporate defenses into your BR plan as well as into your day-to-day operations.

4. If you don't have a site recovery plan, create it now.

By now, you have all the tools to complete your BR plan. Once it is done, ensure that it is maintained, and use it as a planning tool to ensure that new servers and software conform to the requirements of the plan at the time they are implemented so that you can maintain a consistent, reliable server infrastructure.

PART

Two

Building a
Reliable Server

Choosing the Right Hardware

"Therefore everyone who hears these words of mine and puts them into practice is like a wise man who built his house on the rock. The rain came down, the streams rose, and the winds blew and beat against that house, yet it did not fall, because it had its foundation on the rock."

—Jesus Christ

It is generally agreed that the first and most important part of any structure is its foundation, and the hardware platform of a server is its foundation. What will happen to your server when the rain of component failure falls on it, the streams of ever increasing workload swirl around it, and the winds of constant technology change blow over it? If you do not want your server to fall, a solid hardware foundation is essential, and choosing the right hardware is worth time and effort.

Chapter 2, "Risk Analysis," presented a risk analysis that considered, among other things, a number of possible hardware failures. Table 3.1 is a listing of risks and hardware-based defenses. This table will be the framework for this chapter.

Reliable Disk Hardware

What disk hardware choices are available in the Linux world? Whether you are running Linux on an Intel architecture machine, or one of the many other processor architectures supported by Linux, the majority of the servers you see will use either an ATA (AT, as in PC-AT, Attachment) or a

Table 3.1   Hardware Risks and Defenses

FAILURE	DEFENSE
Hard Disk Crash	Hot Swap Disk Hardware
Cooling Fan(s)	Operational Temperature Monitoring Operational Fan Failure Monitoring Multiple Redundant Fans
External Power	Uninterruptible Power Supply Backup Site Power
Network	Redundant Network Hardware Redundant Network Connections
Tape Backup	Hot Swap Spare Tape Drive
Internal Power	Redundant Internal Power Supply
Internal Peripheral Card	Redundant Card
Motherboard	Spare Motherboard
Memory	Spare RAM

Small Computer Systems Interface (SCSI) device. Larger-scale servers may use Fibre Channel (FC) drives, particularly if they are implementing a Storage Area Network (SAN). I'll outline the advantages and disadvantages of these technologies in the following sections and then you can decide which one is right for you.

AT Attachment (ATA) Drives

These drives are generally, and incorrectly, called IDE drives. The acronym IDE stands for Integrated Drive Electronics, which is simply a way of building a drive rather than an actual technical specification. For example, all SCSI drives integrate a controller into the drive, so you might just as well call a SCSI drive an IDE drive. The proper term, ATA, is derived from the history of the technology. The first PC hard drives used a controller built on a peripheral card sitting in a motherboard bus expansion slot. In the early days of the IBM PC, Quantum had the idea of attaching the drive to the expansion card and sticking the whole thing in the expansion slot. These drives were called hard cards, and their convenience made them very popular. The natural progression was then to attach the controller directly to the drive, and move the unit into a drive bay, freeing an expansion slot, and allowing for a much more substantial and reliable mechanical mounting for the drive unit. Because these drives integrated what used to be a controller card into the drive, they were called Integrated Drive Electronics, or IDE drives. Because they were introduced at the time the PC/AT defined the standard for a small computer bus, they talked to the 16-bit AT bus, so the technical specification for the interface was termed AT Attachment, or ATA. The ATA standard is maintained by technical committee 13 of the National Committee on Information Technology Standards (NCITS), which oversees a Web site for ATA issues at www.t13.org.

The ATA standard has been through several generations of improvement since the days of the PC/AT. The most current versions allow for data transfer rates of up to 100 MB/s, and drives of 40 GB and larger are widely available. Clearly these numbers yield drives well able to handle substantial amounts of data at impressive speed, and the relatively low cost of these drives make them doubly attractive. What are the issues in terms of reliability, though?

ATA Reliability and Redundancy

I have heard it argued that due to the mass market nature of the ATA device, the product quality is lower, and so ATA drives are less reliable than other drive technologies. Is there any truth to this? To test the theory, I visited a major disk manufacturer's Web site and examined the technical specifications for several comparable ATA and SCSI drives. I found that, indeed, the Mean Time Between Failure (MTBF) numbers listed for the SCSI drives were often higher than for comparable ATA drives. On the other hand, the estimated product lifetime and warranty period were in most cases identical for the ATA and the SCSI drives. Which numbers should I believe? My own experience tells me that any drive five years old or more is getting long in the tooth, and I begin to get nervous about it. In specifying their warranty period, the drive manufacturer seems to agree with me, and further they see no difference in this regard between an ATA and a SCSI drive. When reliability is a priority, I like the way that Jakob Ostergaard sums it up in his Software RAID HOWTO: "All disks fail, sooner or later, and one should be prepared for that."

A major consideration in choosing a reliable disk drive technology is the ease with which you can implement redundant disk storage using multiple physical disks and maintaining duplicate data copies on each to protect against data loss in the event one disk crashes. While it is possible to do this with ATA drives, there are clear limitations. The early ATA drives still required a simple expansion card to provide the drive to bus connection.

UNDERSTANDING MTBF FIGURES

If you examine the specifications for a typical hard drive, there will be a Mean Time Between Failures (MTBF) number often quoted. For most drives, ATA or SCSI, these range from 300,000 to over 1,000,000 hours. Translated into years, that would imply a drive lifetime of 34 to 114 *years*! This seems rather fantastic. What you need to realize is that this is intended to be applied to a group of drives, not an individual drive. Further, each drive in the group still has a rated service life that is not to be exceeded.

Let me give you some examples. Consider a drive with a rated MTBF of 525,000 hours (about 60 years) and a rated service life of five years. A group of 12 of these drives running for five years would therefore accumulate an aggregate total of 525,000 hours of use, and based on that aggregate number you should expect one of them to fail somewhere in the five years. If you had a group of 60 drives, you might reasonably expect at least one failure somewhere in the group after only one year of operation, considerably less than the service lifetime. On the other hand, if you had only six drives, they would accumulate only one half the MTBF figure at the end of the service life of the drives. At that time the manufacturer would expect you to replace the drives, as they have reached the end of their service life, and go on another five years with six new drives. Somewhere in the ten total years of service you would expect to see at least one failure.

So, in cases where you have a small number of drives, the MTBF figure is really not terribly significant, the service life is what you should be most concerned with. On the other hand, for a large numbers of drives the MTBF would be useful for predicting the number of failures you would expect to see on an annual basis.

Motherboard manufacturers soon added dedicated ATA controllers directly on their boards, however, allowing the drive to access the bus without using up an expansion slot. It is a fundamental limitation of the ATA standard, however, that each of these controllers supports only two devices. That becomes a limiting factor in a reliable server because the standard motherboard commonly has only two ATA controllers. Let me show you an example.

If you want to implement a single level of disk redundancy, you could choose to install two identical drives and mirror them using the software RAID capability of the Linux kernel (I'll be showing you the details of how to do this in Chapter 5, "Building Reliable Disk Storage"). You will also want a CD-ROM drive for software installation and maintenance purposes, and possibly a CD-R, CD-RW, or tape drive for backups. That comes to four devices in total, and as a typical motherboard has two controllers supporting two devices per controller, according to the ATA standard, this should be fine. As it turns out, there are two problems. Should one of the drives fail, the RAID will try to serve data from the good drive, as it should, and Linux will be happy. Unfortunately, ATA controllers do not take well to the loss of one of their devices. A failure of one will usually cause problems for the other. If you were to put each of the two drives on different controllers, that would be better, until you need to use the tape or the CD. You may be able to survive this, if the CD or tape is not mission-critical in terms of keeping the server going. It means, though, that in order to get your backups working again, you need to service that dead drive ASAP. In a small server, this may be acceptable, but it is a risk you need to be aware of. The second problem is one of performance. The ATA bus does not do well at accessing both disks on the same controller well, and in a disk mirror situation, that is what will be happening on a constant basis. For acceptable RAID performance, it is necessary to place a data disk on a different controller than its mirror, which again requires one drive per controller.

A solution to this problem is to look for a motherboard having more than two controllers. Such boards do exist, and they are not overly expensive. You do have to go looking for them, however. Some may offer two controllers supporting the ATA/33 standard and two supporting the ATA/66 or ATA/100 standard. The 66 and 100 refer to a data transfer rate of 66 MB/s and 100 MB/s respectively. Be aware that in order to get these speeds, you will need compatible drives. These rates are defined in the ATA-4 standard and are significant in that they need an 80-conductor cable for the drive to the controller, unlike the normal 40-conductor ATA cable. In an emergency, it is possible to successfully mix and match older or newer drives and cables, but there is a forest of pitfalls if you get the wrong combination of drive, controller, and cable. Make sure you read your drive, motherboard, and ATA references so that you know what you can or cannot do with your hardware before you have a problem!

Finally, if you have a four-controller motherboard, and everything is working fine, what happens when (you will notice I didn't say *if*) you need more disk space? As I write, 40-GB ATA drives are the largest available; by the time you read this, larger capacities will undoubtedly be on the market. Nevertheless, what if your requirements still exceed the largest drive available? Consider this example. You need storage for 120 GB of data and decide to use a RAID1 array, which allows you to keep a mirror copy of your data on a second disk. If you could source a 120-GB disk, this would be fine, as you would need only two disks. Unfortunately, however, the largest disk you can source is 80 GB, so you will need four disks in total, two pairs of 80 GB each That gives you a data storage capacity of 160 GB, room enough for your data with some expansion room. This means, however, that with a one drive per controller limitation, you will need all four of the motherboard controllers for this RAID array. That leaves you with no controllers left for your operating system disk, CD-ROM, or any other ATA devices. You will need to install at least a fifth and possibly a sixth ATA controller to support all of your ATA devices! This could cause problems if you run out of expansion slots or reach a motherboard limitation on the upper number of ATA controllers. Also, there is a length limitation on ATA cables, and an issue with crosstalk (erroneous signals created in one cable conductor arising from the magnetic field created by the signals flowing in another). If you try to stuff too many ATA drives and controllers in one case, it gets mighty crowded, and the likelihood of data errors arising from cabling congestion rises. In short, ATA does not scale well to large numbers of drives.

Hot Swapping ATA Drives

In my examples so far I have suggested using mirrored RAID arrays to achieve disk redundancy so that if one of the drives fails, the server should keep going until you can replace the bad drive. With standard ATA drives, however, you will need to bring the server down in order to safely replace the failed unit. The ATA standard does not support the ability to hot swap (replacing drives while the machine is running) in any fashion. If you need the speed and downtime reduction hot swapping gives, you can buy a hardware ATA RAID unit. These typically are a pair of standard ATA drives installed into either an external enclosure or special internal bay that allows the drives to be safely hot plugged. As the reason this is being done is to use the drives as a RAID1 array, these units usually supply a modified ATA controller that takes care of the RAID mirroring in hardware. To the operating system, the pair of drives looks like a single ATA drive, and using the Linux software RAID is unnecessary. These units have the advantage of simplicity, although the extra cost of the hot plug enclosure and RAID controller hardware may outweigh the benefits of the cheaper ATA drives.

Serial ATA (SATA)

SATA is the next generation of the ATA bus, currently in the draft specification stages. It offers significant improvements over the current standard, and should be a welcome advance. SATA supports very low voltage signaling (250 millivolt) necessary to support current chip technologies. It is a serial rather than parallel bus, eliminating the bulky, length-limited 80 conductor cable and addresses the contention problem in the current standard wherein the master and slave device on a bus must contend for the available bus bandwidth. This helps performance, with the draft specification starting at an impressive 150 MB/s and projecting the possibility of as much as 600 MB/s in future generations. From a reliability standpoint, the significant feature of the new specification is that it will be hot pluggable by definition at the hardware and also the software level, as SATA drivers are required to be able to handle device reconfiguration due to hot plugging as a base functionality. Perhaps the best thing about SATA is that it is entirely backward compatible with the existing specification, so that current ATA drivers should need little or no modification. SATA could conceivably be a future challenger in larger servers to the current big iron monarch, SCSI. Stay tuned.

Small Computer Systems Interface (SCSI) Drives

SCSI is the drive technology commonly associated with larger server environments. SCSI is a more functional environment than ATA. While ATA really only defines a communications interface, SCSI defines a bus architecture, each SCSI device having its own intelligent controller, talking to other devices to manage the flow of data on the bus. One would compare SCSI with something like the ISA or PCI bus architectures, in which multiple devices can be connected to and share a fast communications channel. SCSI is much more sophisticated in its management of shared resources than is ATA. In a busy multi-disk server, for example, multiple requests will be issued to multiple disks. An ATA controller would service the requests in order, while the SCSI bus is capable of sorting the requests by device, so that once a disk is active and supplying data to the bus, several requests outstanding for that disk will also be serviced. This makes much more efficient use of the bus, speeding data flows and reducing the amount of work a disk may need to do to serve data. Although this is really more a performance issue than a reliability one, it is not entirely unrelated, since anything that causes bottlenecks can result in serious enough problems in applications to blur the line between performance problems and reliability problems. Because SCSI works better in larger environments, it is the disk technology of choice for most middle to large servers.

SCSI Scalability and Reliability

Possibly the most significant benefit of SCSI is its scalability. Because it was designed from the start to be a multiple device bus, a single SCSI controller can support either 7 or 15 disk devices, dependent on the SCSI version you choose. Performance issues generally restrict going to the maximum allowable number of devices per controller, as typically each device is generally fast enough that the bus will become congested before the maximum number of devices is reached. However, as this leads to the use of multiple controllers, there is a benefit in increased reliability. If you want to implement disk redundancy by mirroring, putting each copy on a different controller protects you from controller loss as well as disk loss. Of course, the performance cost of mirroring data can be as bad as the cost of a congested bus! You will find that it is one of those unfortunate principles of life that whatever you do to improve reliability usually carries a performance penalty.

Due to the scalability of the SCSI bus, disk manufacturers associate it with larger commercial usage, and place a stronger emphasis on quality and reliability in their SCSI products. This can be inferred from the higher MTBF figures for SCSI drives. The earlier discussion of ATA drives leaned to the service life and warranty period as a more important measure of reliability than MTBF numbers, where the total number of drives was small. Based on the scalability of SCSI and a larger number of drives, the MTBF figures could become important. This is clear when the number of drives is high enough for the aggregate drive up times to exceed the MTBF figure, in which case I expect failures in advance of the service lifetime, as I explain in the sidebar, "Understanding MTBF Figures." On the other hand, I have seen MTBF figures for SCSI drives of 1,200,000 hours, in which case I would need to have at least 27 drives before I would expect failures in less than a five-year service life.

SCSI Redundancy

As SCSI scales well, it has always been associated with larger, more expensive, and often mission critical servers. Consequently it is much easier to find hardware redundancy solutions for SCSI disks than for ATA drives, and hot plug SCSI hardware is common. Numerous vendors sell a variety of hot plug SCSI products, ranging from external disk enclosures, to server cabinets incorporating hot plug bays and controllers. As SCSI cabling can be a cause of trouble, I prefer hot plug drive bays that allow for cableless operation. In these units the drive itself is mounted in a skeleton frame carrier that can be plugged into any open bay. The address of the drive will be determined by the bay it is plugged into, eliminating the possibility of duplicate addresses and fiddling with drive jumpers or software setup code. These drives make use of a specialized connector that adds extra pins to the normal SCSI connector for power and SCSI address. So-called long pins are used since some connections need to be made before others during a hot plug insertion or removal. These are known as Single Connector Attach (SCA) drives. Although these tend to be more expensive, they are the cleanest way to replace disk hardware quickly, safely, and reliably that I have yet seen.

At the moment, however, there is a restriction to hot plugging at the Linux end. The current SCSI driver does not respond as gracefully to a hot plug event as might be desired. The 2.4 kernel does have a provision for dynamically inserting a new SCSI device without a reboot. The problem is that if the new device has a different SCSI bus ID than the one it replaced, or if it is new device, it may affect the identifier given by the kernel to existing devices. This has the potential to cause confusion to a variety of other things that rely on the device identifier and could cause serious problems. The problem is solvable, but as it affects a number of different operating system levels, it will take some time for the necessary changes to filter through everywhere they are needed. There is an additional problem in the mechanism used to detect that a hot plug has occurred. There is code in development to do this, but it is in the early development stages at the time of this writing. There are current proprietary Linux solutions to this issue, specifically in the cluster products discussed in Chapter 10, "Server Clustering." If you want to implement hot plug SCSI devices in the future, make sure your kernel version will support it. Information on the state of the hot plug project for Linux can be found at linux-hotplug.sourceforge.net.

SCSI Bus Termination

There is at least one thing common to any type of SCSI device, and that is termination. SCSI is a bus architecture, each device attached in a daisy chain cable to the next, with the controller attached somewhere in the chain, too. Data signals can originate from any device and will travel up and down the bus to reach the controller. The daisy chain ends somewhere, however, and this creates an electrical problem. When a signal reaches the end of the cable, it doesn't just fall out the end onto the floor (honest, it doesn't). Instead it reflects and travels back down the cable in the direction it came. Passing through each device on the bus it reaches the opposite end of the cable and reflects again. The signal weakens with every trip, and eventually fades to black, but if this were allowed to happen with every signal, the reflections would become hopelessly muddled up with the true signal, and reliable communication on the bus would be impossible. It's rather like interference on a radio. There is music playing in there somewhere, but you can't hear it for the static.

The problem is solved by a terminator. This is an electrical device attached at each of the two ends of the bus. It's job is to absorb data signals when they reach the end of the cable, preventing any reflections. In the early SCSI buses, these terminators were visible devices plugged in to the last connector at each end of the cable. In modern SCSI based servers, the terminators can be a bit more elusive. SCSI devices, for example, often include an internal terminator. Should the device be the last one on the cable, this internal terminator needs to be activated. This is often done with a jumper setting on the drive itself. If the controller is the last device on the chain, it needs to provide termination. Again, a jumper or a software setting may do this. If a device is added to or removed from a SCSI bus, it is critical that you do not overlook this issue. The removed device may have provided the termination using a terminator internal to the drive. In that case, the replacement drive must supply the termination. If the replacement is new or came from the middle of another SCSI bus, its terminator may not be activated. If the bus is not properly terminated at *both* ends, it will not work. If you accidentally place a terminator part of the way along a bus, all devices between the misplaced terminator and the end of the bus will be cut off, and will not work. These terminator woes are a common cause of SCSI problems when reconfiguring or repairing servers, but they can be avoided with proper planning and foresight.

Single Ended versus Differential SCSI

The original SCSI standard was termed a single ended (SE) bus. This referred to the way in which electrical data signals on the bus were interpreted. In an SE system, a positive voltage is considered to represent a binary one, while zero voltage represents, of course, binary zero. This is simple and cheap—two lasting advantages that made it a popular choice. Problems arise with SE signaling, however, as cable lengths grow, and become crossed or damaged. These problems can lead to signals that are weakened or corrupted. What starts out as a binary one at a device on the bus may be close enough to zero by the end of the bus to be interpreted as such. The original standard used two conductors to carry each signal, one for the signal and one for a reference ground voltage. The solution proposed was to use a system of voltage differences to carry the signal and so was called differential SCSI. A binary one signal would be carried by sending a positive voltage on one conductor and the opposite negative voltage on the other. A zero would result in zero voltage on both conductors. At the receiving end, the difference on the voltages would be compared. The difference between the positive and negative voltage was a relatively large value, where the difference between the two zeroes would be negligible. It was really a simple form of amplifying the signals. The purpose of this was to increase the reliability of the bus by reducing its susceptibility to signal fluctuations and also increase the maximum allowable cable length. The signal reliability was critical to support the higher bus speeds the new standard allowed, and the larger number of devices on the bus meant separate disk enclosures that may need to be several feet away from their servers.

In its first form, differential SCSI used a higher signal voltage than the current design and is now termed High Voltage Differential (HVD) SCSI. It was electronically expensive to implement and not widely used. The current standard defines a low voltage modification called Low Voltage Differential (LVD) SCSI. It is important never to mix an older HVD device with a new LVD device because the LVD device can be damaged physically. Also, the terminators used for HVD SCSI are not the same as those for LVD, and SE SCSI devices use a different kind of terminator again! If you use the wrong terminator, the best you can hope for are devices or controllers that the kernel will not be able to see; the worst is physical damage to devices or controllers. Don't experiment on your production machine. *Make sure you have the proper hardware before you turn anything on.*

Understanding the Rainbow of SCSI Flavors

SCSI technology is more than 20 years old and has spawned a number of variations in its history. It started out in 1979 as a creation of Alan Shugart of Shugart Associates. The original Shugart standard was adopted as an American National Standards Institute (ANSI) standard and was first published as such in 1986. Today the SCSI standard is maintained by technical committee 10 of the NCITS, a sibling to committee 13 of ATA fame. Information about committee 10 and SCSI standards can be found on the Web at www.t10.org. If you are considering a SCSI-based storage solution for your server, you will need a program to understand the different versions; otherwise, it can get very confusing. There are also some pitfalls that can cause serious problems when you start mixing and matching different devices. I'll point those out, too.

SCSI Standards

Technically, there are three different SCSI standards: SCSI1, SCSI2, and SCSI3. SCSI1 is now old enough that you can safely ignore it, unless you inherit a very old server indeed. The SCSI2 standard dates from 1994, and was a substantial advance over the original standard. It is not possible to get SCSI2 drives today, although current drives will in some cases work in backward compatible modes with an older SCSI2 device. In any case, if you have any SCSI2 drives they are likely close to or beyond their service life, and would not be good candidates to run an important server on. The SCSI2 standard did however introduce some important innovations that have carried forward in to SCSI3, the current standard. The challenge in understanding SCSI3 is that it really is a group of standards for several different variations on the SCSI theme, and that is where it gets complicated.

Wide SCSI2 and Fast SCSI2

The original SCSI standard defined a bus eight bits wide. In other words, there were eight data signals carried in the SCSI cable, so a single byte could be transferred on the bus at any one time. The SCSI2 standard allowed an increased width of 16 bits, which became commonly known as wide SCSI. Given the same signaling rate, the wide bus could transfer twice the data than could the narrow bus. SCSI2 also doubled the signal rate on the bus to 10 MHz, twice that of the original standard. Putting these two advances together produced what was known as Fast Wide SCSI2, giving a data transfer rate of 20 MB/s. At the same time, the SCSI2 standard also increased the maximum number of devices on a bus from 8 (which is really 7 devices, as the total number of devices on the bus always includes the controller) to 16, but this only applied if the wide bus option was used.

Ultra SCSI and Ultra2 SCSI

The next generation of standards was the SCSI3 standards, which arrived in 1996. Unlike the earlier SCSI and SCSI2 standard, SCSI3 was really a family of standards governing a number of different aspects of the evolving nature of the bus and included definitions for several distinct flavors of SCSI device. This family of standards is still undergoing revision today. Because there are so many variants all falling under the SCSI3 family, the term SCSI3 is not commonly used; rather, terms more descriptive of the transfer speed of the particular flavor are favored.

The first of the SCSI3 standards is Ultra SCSI. It doubled the signal rate again over SCSI2 to 20 MHz, allowing a 20 MB/s transfer rate on a narrow bus. If the cable length exceeded 1.5 meters, HVD signaling was mandatory. Wide Ultra SCSI is also possible and gives transfer rates of 40 MB/s.

Now things get messy. The SCSI3 family of standards also includes Ultra2 SCSI. (Do not confuse Ultra2 SCSI with the older SCSI2 standard.) Ultra2 SCSI uses a 40 MHz signal rate and comes in narrow and wide flavors, and uses LVD signaling. Narrow Ultra2 has a transfer rate of 40 MB/s, while the transfer rate for Wide Ultra2 is 80 MB/s. Ultra2 controllers and drives are still available and are quite satisfactory for many midrange server applications. Be careful to note that at the signaling speeds used by Ultra2 or faster versions, the conventional ribbon-type cable that serves well for previous, slower versions of the bus is no longer sufficient to reliably carry the data. It is important for reliability that you use cabling specifically designed for these higher transfer speeds. Look for labeling on external cables that specifies either the SCSI version, or that they support LVD signaling. Internal cables will look similar to the older flat ribbon-type of cable, but each pair of conductors in the new ribbon will be separated and twisted together between connectors on the cable. The actual connectors on the cable should be labeled according to the version of SCSI supported.

For a solid and stable bus, cable length is also important. Keep your cables as short as possible. Connectors should be evenly spaced along the cable, and extra connectors should be avoided, if possible. If you do have extras, put the terminator on the last connector, so there are no connectors beyond the terminator. Leftover connectors between the terminator and the physical end of the cable can create problematic signal echoes. On the faster versions of the bus it is also a good idea to place devices as near the ends of the cable as possible. The idea here is to avoid a length of cable between the last device and the terminator as that can also lead to echoes.

Ultra160 SCSI and Ultra160+ SCSI

The SCSI3 standard pushed the performance envelope further with the Ultra160 standard (also known as Ultra160/m). This standard uses the same signal rate and bus width as Wide Ultra2, but doubles the transfer rate to 160 MB/s by sending data on both the rise and the fall of the bus clock pulse, a technique known as *dual edge clocking*. There is no narrow version of Ultra160, hence there is no Ultra160 and Wide Ultra160. Ultra160 uses a wide bus by definition. Ultra160 uses only LVD signaling; there is no SE option.

As Ultra160 pushed the performance envelope further, new reliability features were required. Cyclic Redundancy Checking (CRC) was introduced to protect against the possibility of data corruption, the likelihood of which becomes higher with increased signal rates. Also, the concept of Domain Validation was introduced. Prior to Ultra160, the SCSI controller on a bus would query each device at the time the bus was started to determine the speed at which that device could operate. The entire bus would then operate at the speed of the slowest device. The problem with this method was that the controller believed what it was told. If, for example, all of the devices on a bus told the controller they were Ultra2 devices, the controller would attempt to run the bus at a signal rate of 40 MHz. If there were a problem with a poor cable, or terminator, however, this would create ongoing data corruption problems. Like older controllers, an Ultra160 controller also queries all devices to determine their respective speeds, but once it determines the speed the bus should be able to operate at, it then performs an active data transfer test to verify that the device can actually support the speed it claims. If errors are detected, the controller will reduce speed until the error rates are acceptable, and run the bus at that speed. This ensures that devices slower than Ultra160 can co-exist on an Ultra160 bus (although the slow devices slow the entire bus down), as well as adjusting to possible cable or terminator problems.

There is also an Ultra160+ standard that adds two further performance enhancements, Quick Arbitration and Selection (QAS) and Packetization. Neither of these, however, has a significant effect on reliability.

Ultra320 SCSI

Ultra320 SCSI represents the state of the art. Using LVD signaling and an 80-MHz dual edge clocking bus it achieves a transfer rate of 320 MB/s. While this sounds impressive, it is interesting to note that the specification on one Ultra320 drive I read about gives an internal transfer rate (the rate at which the drive can write to the platter internally) of only 70 MB/s, considerably less than the theoretical bus transfer rate. From a performance point of view, then, this would suggest that any more than four drives per controller could saturate the bus itself. A large server supporting data banks scaling into terabytes would need many disks, and if there is to be a four disk per controller performance limitation, then it will also have multiple controllers. Here for once performance and reliability aid one another, as each controller is in this arrangement a point of failure for only four drives, rather than the 15 it could possibly support.

Mixing and Matching SCSI Versions

It is possible to mix different versions of SCSI device on the same bus. As a general rule, the controller will adjust the bus speed to match the slowest device on the bus. Clearly this can be a significant performance issue. I should point out that there are some combinations that will not work. Some LVD devices can operate in single ended mode, but not all. Those that do are often termed multi-mode devices. Multi-mode terminators are also available, some of which give a visible indication of the mode the bus is operating in. This can be handy for debugging purposes. HVD devices do not play well with any others of any type. Mixing HVD devices with SE or LVD will not only break the bus, it could very well damage devices and/or controllers physically. Be careful!

SE, HVD, and LVD buses all require a different style of terminator. Be sure you have the right one, and don't forget that devices may have internal terminators (though internal terminators are not common in differential devices). Terminators can also be built into the cable itself, a handy option as it means one less thing to keep track of, and possibly lose. SCSI controllers usually have the ability to terminate the bus also, as long as they are the last device and you activate the termination. Whenever you change devices on a SCSI bus, always make sure you get the termination right. The classic symptom of a missing terminator is that none of the devices on the unterminated bus appear at boot. If a bus is terminated before a device, the rest of the bus will be quite happy, but the isolated device(s) will be invisible to the controller.

It is possible to mix wide and narrow devices on the same bus. Again, proper termination is a key in making this work. You will need a special adapter to attach a narrow device to a wide bus. The adapter will need to terminate the extra eight unused data channels on the wide bus as it enters the narrow device; otherwise, those eight channels would be unterminated. It is theoretically possible to attach a wide device to a narrow bus, but as this would halve the transfer rate of the wide device, it makes little sense to do it. There are also dual channel controllers that can support more than one physical cable segment. In this case you might have a narrow segment for your narrow devices and a wide one for your wide devices, each having separate terminated bus cables. Remember, too, that a narrow device can only count to seven. If you put a wide device on a narrow bus, don't configure it to be higher than device ID 7 or it cannot be seen. In the same way, a narrow device on a wide bus cannot talk to wide devices having device IDs greater than seven. This would be a problem if

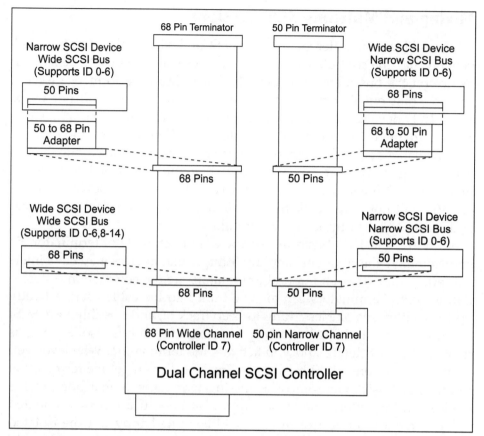

Figure 3.1   SCSI device types can be mixed on the same bus.

the wide controller happened to be numbered device ID 15, for example. Mixed SCSI devices are illustrated in Figure 3.1, shown using a dual channel SCSI controller card. Note that addressing the controller as ID 7 on the wide channel is unusual. Normally the controller is set to the highest possible address (ID 15 in the case of a wide SCSI bus), as the higher addresses have higher priority on the bus.

What about Fibre Channel?

When I said earlier that in a Linux environment you are limited largely to either ATA or SCSI, some readers might ask, "What about Fibre Channel?" FC is a transport layer network protocol that attempts to marry the low-overhead, high-bandwidth characteristics of a local bus protocol like PCI or SCSI with the high-overhead, low-bandwidth performance of a distributed network protocol such as an IP routed Internet. The IP Internet has flexibility, allowing a large number of senders to transmit frames of data to any receiver on the network, with the network handling the delivery. This allows for large number of hosts, distributed over large distances, and great flexibility in changing configuration. A local bus like SCSI, on the other hand, supports a limited number of devices that must be closely situated, and cannot be flexibly reconfigured, but gives far higher bandwidth than the distributed network.

The FC standard offers an interconnect structured like a LAN, using hubs and switches, but offering local bus speeds. FC can be implemented over short distances on copper wiring, but it is really designed to use fiber optic cabling, allowing device-to-device distances of up to 10 kilometers at bandwidths up to a gigabit per second. It is used primarily to implement large-scale, high-speed disk storage infrastructures, commonly called Storage Area Networks (SANs). In this context, people refer to FC drives. FC alone, however, does not support the functionality needed to implement a disk drive in a Linux environment. A Linux FC drive is in fact a SCSI drive that uses FC as its network transport. A Linux host supporting FC drives would have an FC Host Bus Adapter (HBA) with appropriate support drivers. The drives attached to this HBA would have a physical fiber optic connection and use FC to pass data. In fact, the drives also contain a SCSI controller, so the format of the data passed on the FC conforms to the time-honored SCSI standard. Thus the FC drives will appear to the Linux kernel as SCSI devices.

FC drives have excellent high-availability features, allowing for hot addition and removal of drives and hosts into and out of an FC network. The major limitation of FC for many is cost. Most fiber-optics-based technologies tend to combine high performance with high cost (it would seem that you get what you pay for) and FC is no exception. For those contemplating large Linux data environments, however, FC will scale happily to multi-terabyte arrays with excellent performance.

If you want to know more, the University of Minnesota maintains a good FC resource at www.borg.umn.edu/fc. Linux-specific FC information can be found from Sistina Software at www.sistina.com/Pages/fibre_channel.html.

How SMART Is Your Drive?

Years ago IBM developed a technology for their mainframe computer drives they called Predictive Failure Analysis (PFA). PFA relied on error detection and reporting code built into the drive hardware to supply information to the drive's device driver concerning read or write errors, as well as operational information, such as drive case temperature or drive motor current. From that information the firmware attempted to predict if the drive was approaching an unrecoverable failure condition before the crash actually happened. This concept has been reinvented for the PC drive world under the Self Monitoring Analysis and Reporting Technology (SMART).

A SMART drive contains internal instruments capable of recording drive operational characteristics and parameters, which are then reported to the drive controller. Many SCSI drives are SMART compliant, and increasingly ATA drives are also supporting the standard. In fact, SMART will be included in the ATA-4 specification. It is necessary for the operating system device driver to be able to read the values provided by SMART from the drive interface. Linux can be made to read these values fine. The problem is knowing what they mean. This is clearly critical because without it, all you have is a bunch of numbers. Unfortunately, drive manufacturers have not shown a great interest in openly documenting this information. I am hopeful that as Linux gains stature as a serious server platform, these manufacturers will see the value in providing this information. For now, unfortunately, there is little opportunity to make use of this technology in a Linux server.

Disk Drive Operating Conditions

Like any other mechanical device, a disk drive is designed to operate under certain conditions. Service life and MTBF figures all come tied to maximum and minimum figures for operating and nonoperating temperature, humidity, and shock. Drive reliability can be substantially affected by these factors. When a drive is not running, the platter is still and the drive heads are in a safe parked position, consequently the drive is less susceptible to damage. As a result, the shock a nonoperating drive can survive can be as much as ten times greater than what it could survive while running. As the mechanism inside the drive is so sensitive, however, that still means that manufacturers use engineered packaging methods to transport drives, as even the nonoperating shock thresholds can be exceeded if you drop the thing on the floor. When you get a new drive, look at the packaging. If you ever need to ship that drive, you need the same sort of packaging if you want the best chance of the drive surviving.

Once the drive is installed and running, it becomes much more sensitive to shock and vibration, although as most servers are located in office environments, this is rarely a problem. It does emphasize the fact, however, that you should never move or disturb a running server. Also, in a small server situation, don't place the server in a location that will expose it to being bumped or otherwise knocked about. One small office server I saw was placed on the floor directly below a desk. When the cleaner came in and ran the vacuum cleaner over the carpet, he banged the vacuum head hard into the server case three or four times each night. I had the machine moved up off the floor the next day.

In office environments, the building ventilation system is relied upon to keep temperature and humidity within acceptable limits. Why is it, then, that purpose-built computer machine rooms have special climate control to maintain the environment even more carefully than in the surrounding office? In fact, temperature and humidity in a regular office environment can vary more than you might want, especially if the central system malfunctions. If your investment in servers and your reliance on them is sufficient, consider building a machine room if you don't already have one. If yours is a small- to medium-sized operation, choose a closed room in the middle of the building, away from windows and restrooms (which have running water supplies that will one day leak) and equip it with its own ventilation and air conditioning system. That way you are not reliant on the building's central system when it fails. A closed room also has the advantage of allowing you to filter the air entering the room to keep down dust and dirt levels. Dust is a nuisance in that it can clog up cooling fan screens and lead to overheating problems. Keeping your servers in a separate room also places them out of the way of the normal traffic and disturbance of a working office.

When you read the specification for drive operating temperature, remember that this is the temperature of the drive itself—not the server case temperature and certainly not the room temperature. Several busy drives located one atop the other inside the case can build up a local hot spot, driving disk temperatures into the danger zone. If your server will have three or more drives, you need to ensure that there is plenty of air moving across the drive bays. Some drives will even include in their specifications a figure for minimum airflow over the drive. Drives supporting SMART often include a temperature sensor mounted on or in the drive itself that can be used to monitor temperature levels—if only they would tell us how to interpret the values. I'll be showing you a way to mount your own temperature sensors inside a case in the next section, if your drive can't do this itself.

Disk Drive Warranties and Warranty Replacement

ATA drives commonly carry a three- to five-year warranty and SCSI Drives usually carry a five-year warranty. If you have a large number of drives relative to the MTBF ratings for the drives, you incur a reasonable chance that one or two drives will fail while under warranty, assuming you replace drives as they reach their service life. You will have to ship the drive back to the manufacturer or distributor. But before you do, most manufacturers will require you to get a return authorization or they won't accept the drive back. Then you wait for a new drive. All this usually takes far too long. You can't wait that long to get a server back into service.

There are two alternatives. One is to ask your supplier if they support an early return policy, whereby they will send out the replacement unit as soon as the return is authorized. If you are willing to pay the overnight courier charges, you can have replacements in 24 to 48 hours. Even that fast is not fast enough in many cases, however. The second alternative (to my mind, the only practical one) is to keep spare disks on hand. If you never have a drive fail under warranty, the spare is wasted; but at a few hundred dollars a drive, it's cheap insurance if it saves you hours of downtime in a crisis. If you have a redundant disk arrangement, of course, the 24- to 48-hour delay for a replacement is a reasonable risk in that the statistical likelihood of a second drive failing with 24 to 48 hours of the first is small. Unless, of course, your site has a fundamental problem with cooling or mishandling of drives.

If you deal directly with the drive manufacturer, the warranty you get is clearly the manufacturer's warranty, the terms of which are clearly laid out in the product documentation or the manufacturer's Web site. If you source drives from a reseller, make sure that you know what warranty you are getting. Do not assume that it will be the standard manufacturer's warranty. Drives are often wholesaled by the manufacturer at reduced cost. In this case the manufacturer may decline warranty coverage for them. The reseller in this case provides the warranty, if there is going to be a warranty. The terms of that warranty are entirely up to the reseller, which means *caveat emptor*.

Finally, what warranty coverage will the replacement drive carry? If it is a new drive, will it be covered for the full three- or five-year warranty period from the time of replacement or only until the end of the old drive's warranty period? If the latter and the old drive was close to the end of its warranty, you may want to buy a new drive and use the replacement as a spare. Is the replacement drive even new? It may be a remanufactured unit, in which case you might want to inquire how long the warranty will be. If it is a full three or five years, or even the remainder of the original drive's warranty, then the drive is probably a reasonable risk. It would not be as encouraging if the replacement carries only a 30- or 90-day warranty. Where reliability is concerned, I try only to do business with suppliers who stand behind what they sell, and have a reputation for selling quality goods.

Reliable Cooling

Keeping component temperature down is an effective way to increase the service lifetime of both solid-state and mechanical components. Rising temperatures tend to cause exponential increases in failure rates, but if the temperature can be kept within design boundaries, it should be possible to get the full service life from each component. While some of the largest computers of the 1970s and 1980s resorted to liquid cooling, current servers can be adequately cooled by pushing modest quantities of air through the case. Processor speeds are continually rising, however, and heat generation increases with processor speed. High performance graphics cards and disk drives are also becoming significant heat sources, yet at the same time there is pressure to make server cases smaller rather than larger. All this means that cooling is becoming more complicated than it once was.

CPU Cooling

The single most important cooling task is the CPU, both as it is obviously central to the operation of the machine, and because the CPU is probably the largest single heat source the case. A 1-GHz processor can generate as much as 35 watts of heat energy that needs to be dissipated in some way. While 35 watts may not sound like much, all that heat energy is concentrated into the CPU case. Concentrating even 35 watts of heat generation into an object as small as a CPU case adds up to high temperatures and can be a real problem. A dedicated CPU cooling fan is mandatory. The principle is simple: Blow some air on the CPU to keep it cool. For a slower, cooler CPU the standard fan supplied by the builder of the server is usually sufficient. When entering the realm of the 1+ GHz processor, however, a bit more engineering is advisable. In fact, Intel's Chief Technology Officer stated recently that "Heat is becoming one of the most critical issues in computer and semiconductor design . . . We have a huge problem to cool [future] devices, given normal cooling technologies."

The heat must be drawn out of the CPU case before it can be dissipated, and a good heat sink designed to fit the CPU is crucial to effective cooling. A heat sink is a device designed to help move heat from a small, exposed high temperature area at the top of the CPU case to a larger surface area where the cooling airflow can draw the heat away more effectively. Heat sinks usually take the form of a set of thin metal fins attached to the top of the CPU case. It is worth it to use thermal grease between the heat sink and the CPU case. Doing so significantly improves the heat flow at the boundary between the CPU and the sink. Some processors ship with a heat sink attached. Do not replace it with a different one. The factory heat sink will have been designed for adequate cooling, and replacing it may void the warranty. A nice big CPU fan comes next, as the sink alone cannot dissipate the heat into the case without air movement directly over the fins of the sink. Coolers that have a dual fan are preferred for fan redundancy. Some smaller cases are tight for space above the CPU, and may not allow for a nice large fan. Instead opt for a more spacious case. Some dual processor motherboards mount processors close together, and may require specialized fans to maintain good airflow across both heat sinks, or between the processors.

Peltier Coolers

If you are running a very fast processor and you find that your current heat sink and fan are not able to keep CPU temperatures as low as you might like, you can try a Peltier cooler. This device is a miniature solid-state refrigerator. A refrigerator is more correctly called a heat pump, as it's job is to remove heat from inside the fridge and pump it to the outside, leaving the fridge colder as a result. A Peltier cooler is also a heat pump. It looks like a flat plate with a pair of wires exiting an edge. When you plug it in, it pumps heat from one side of the plate to the other, leaving one side of the plate cold and the other warm. To cool a CPU, the Peltier plate is mounted on top of the CPU, cold side down. A conventional heat sink and fan are then mounted on the warm side of the plate. The low temperature on the cold, CPU side of the plate coaxes the heat out of the CPU, which is then pumped over to the warm topside of the Peltier cooler and dissipated by the heat sink and fan.

A typical Peltier cooler can create a temperature difference of as much as 70 Fahrenheit degrees between the cold and hot sides of the plate, so it can be an effective aid to CPU cooling. There must be a catch, right? Well, the catch is that, like all heat pumps, the Peltier cooler is not 100-percent efficient. In other words, the amount of heat that needs to be dissipated at the top of the plate includes heat created by the operation of the cooler itself in addition to the heat drawn out of the CPU. It turns out that in fact the cooler generates quite a bit of heat. That heat must come from somewhere, implying that the power draw of the cooler could be significant, and it is. The bottom line, then, is that a Peltier plate can definitely keep your CPU nice and cool. But, it draws a significant amount of power that it turns into heat, so that should your cooling fan fail and all that heat can not be dissipated effectively from the heat sink, your Peltier cooler turns into a Peltier heater and can bake your CPU. That doesn't mean you shouldn't use a Peltier cooler, but it does mean that you need to be particularly careful about monitoring the cooling fan if you do. I'll be showing you a way to monitor fan operation and CPU temperature later in this chapter. And don't forget to take into consideration the power draw of the Peltier when sizing the internal power supply.

One last word on Peltier coolers. Humidity is an issue that needs to be watched. If the relative humidity in the room is too high, moisture can condense on the cold side of the cooler, and water on the CPU is not a healthy condition. Also, if the Peltier plate is a bit bigger than the CPU, the overhang will expose a small bit of the cold side to the ambient air, which can cause condensation problems.

In Case Air Flow

A good CPU cooling arrangement can still be ineffective if the heat drawn out of the CPU cannot be exhausted from the case. A good case design has an engineered airflow that passes a good volume of ventilation air from outside of the case, across the CPU, through the rest of the case, and then on out. The widely used ATX form factor case is designed to do this by situating the CPU close to the power supply exhaust fan. In the ATX specification, air is drawn in through the power supply fan, blown out of the power supply onto the CPU, and then exits through vents in the front or side of the case. That means that air warmed in its passage through the power supply is used to cool the CPU. Many system builders have found this to be less than satisfactory, and reverse the airflow, using the power supply fan to exhaust air from the case. In addition, extra fans mounted below the power supply or at the front of the case are often used to assist airflow through the case.

When adding extra fans, keep in mind that the idea of good ventilation is neither to push as much air into the case as possible or remove as much as possible, but to move as much as possible *through* the case. If a fan at the front of the case pushes air in, make sure the fan at the back is sucking it out! Also make sure you do not put an exhaust fan close to an inlet fan, or the air will take a short cut from one to the other and will not pass through the entire volume of the case. Intel's Scalable Platforms (SP) Initiative favors the use of air ducts to control and direct air to specific components that need the cooling, and these may very well become common in future servers. Figure 3.2 illustrates examples of good and bad case cooling airflow.

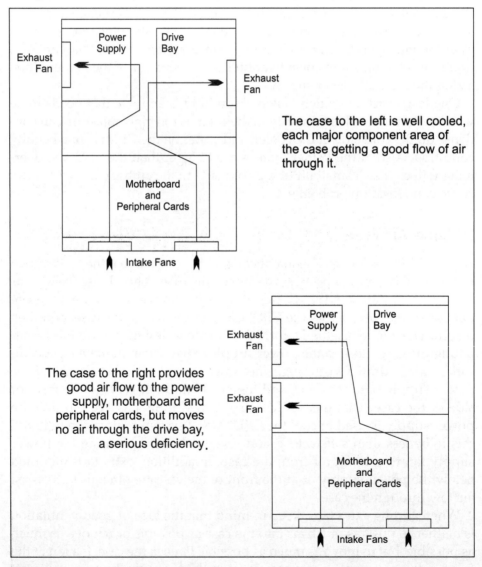

Figure 3.2 Note the difference between good and bad case cooling.

THE INTEL SCALABLE PLATFORM INITIATIVE

The Scalable Platform (SP) project originated in Intel's developer lab in 1999. According to Intel, "Its mission is to ensure Intel Processor Platforms deliver rich, easy-to-access end user benefits." Intel goes on to state, "the mission (SP) encompasses platform capabilities as a whole, not only the microprocessor core. The SP initiative addresses performance solutions in operating system and applications as well as platform elements such as power, thermal, rich graphics, interconnect packaging and printed circuit board designs." The fact that Intel is sponsoring an integrated, platform-based approach promises improvements on both performance and reliability in the next generation of servers. The SP initiative considers factors such as

- Electromagnetic interference
- Acoustic noise
- Delivering more power in less space
- Designing components that interconnect well
- Making the best use of circuit board space
- Good thermal management

One example of the work flowing from the SP initiative is the Thermal Test Board (TTB). This is a standard Intel Pentium 4 processor and chip set motherboard, specially instrumented with a number of temperature probes at key locations on the board. The board can be installed into a test system, and support further probes mounted in temperature sensitive locations such as system memory, expansion slots, drive bays, and the power supply. A separate PC is used to gather and report the temperature data gleaned from the TTB itself. While the end user of a server is unlikely to go to the length of using the TTB in selecting a case design, it is encouraging to know that systems packagers now have sophisticated tools such as the TTB that should assist in ensuring that the rigorous thermal design needed for future servers can and will be done well.

More information on the SP initiative can be found at developer.intel.com.

Exhaust fans that ventilate by pumping air out of the case are rarely fitted with screens. This is good as a non-existent screen can never clog up with dust and block airflow. It does mean, however, that all the dust and dirt in the surrounding room gets sucked into the case. Keeping your servers in a reasonably clean environment and cleaning out the crud every now and again are both good common-sense practices. Case designs that pump air in to the case to ventilate often do have inlet screens that must be checked periodically for clogging.

Drive Bay Cooling

Earlier, in talking about drive reliability I stressed the importance of proper cooling for drives. Keeping a good airflow through the drive bay needs to be a part of the overall air management through the case. Next to the CPU, disks are the next greatest heat producers. If you have several drives, they are usually mounted one atop the other in a cage, and a typical ATA or SCSI drive will draw 10 to 15 watts at idle. That means a cage of four drives could easily produce more heat than the CPU. And, if you read the operating temperature specification for the drives, you will see that the maximum operating temperatures for drives are often higher than the maximum temperatures for the CPU. Those drives need the same attention to cooling as does the CPU.

A good server case needs to integrate drive bay ventilation into the overall plan. This kind of cooling detail is not usually necessary in the average desktop or small ATX case server, but it becomes more important for larger servers. This is particularly the case with a larger server having several drives, either to support larger data entities or disk redundancy. A 1+ GHz CPU and a six-pack of fast SCSI drives will add the best part of 100 watts of heat generation. To manage that kind of heat, you need an engineered cooling solution. Source a case having multiple fans. One fan should pump air into the case and another should exhaust. At least one or more fans should keep a good volume of air flowing through the drive bay, and there should be a good airflow passing across the CPU. The best cases I have seen in this respect conform to the WTX case standard. This was a standard proposed by Intel in 1998 as a heavy-duty server complement to the light duty ATX case. WTX cases are larger than ATX cases, with multiple fans and drive bays. They accept ATX motherboards, as well as a WTX form factor for motherboards that the industry did not widely adopt. WTX cases are not common, but if you want a really well designed server case, they have nearly everything you could want.

If you have multiple SCSI drives, mount them in an external enclosure. Look for an enclosure with good front-to-back ventilation and one that comes with its own power supply (most do). That gives you power supply redundancy and avoids loading the server power supply with the power required by the SCSI disks. If something goes wrong with the server, it also makes the disks a self-contained portable unit that can be moved to a backup system quickly and easily. And last but not least, it removes the heat load of the drives from the server case.

Rack-Mounted Servers

The move to higher density servers has fueled the popularity of the rack-mount case. These cases are much more compact than the standard ATX tower case. Fortunately, though, they are usually well engineered with cooling especially taken into account. What you need to do is to make sure that the server rack gets the airflow it needs. The compact nature of these machines means that a dozen or so rack-mounted servers and some rack mount disk enclosures will generate a significant amount of heat in a pretty small space. The server room needs to have the ventilation to handle it. In fact, it needs more than enough ventilation, as the number of servers in that rack will inevitably grow, not shrink. It may also be useful to use supply ducts to direct the ventilation air to the air intakes on the servers or exhaust ducts to remove the warm air from the room effectively. Be sure that the Heating/Ventilation/Air Conditioning (HVAC) system in the building can supply a sufficient airflow into and out of your server room. You may need to ask your building services staff to rebalance the ventilation airflows to get enough air. If you are setting up in or moving to a new facility, ensure that those who keep the ventilation air flowing in your servers' new home realize the heat load that your equipment will place on the building's system so they and you can plan for it. Buildings whose air distribution system was designed for general office use often have difficulty supplying sufficient fresh air to a room with a high concentration of computer equipment.

Reliable Power

Reliable power supply is clearly fundamental to keeping a server going. I am going to separate power supply into two different issues: external and internal power supply. The power supply chain for a PC starts with a relatively high voltage power source— usually 110 VAC— external to the PC itself. This I call the external power. That high voltage AC must then be converted into low voltage DC, 12 volts for drive and fan motors and 5 volts for digital logic circuits. This conversion is done by the power supply unit inside the server case that I will call the internal power supply.

External Power

The first consideration in terms of external power is to accept that the grid supplying power to your site will at some point fail. It may fail to supply power at all, or fail to maintain power at the normal levels. Power outages could last for only a moment, or for periods of minutes, hours or in the worst case, days. It is also possible to get too much power in the form of a spike. Spikes are as certain as outages, though less noticeable. They have the potential to be worse than outages because the chance of physical equipment damage is greater in the case of a spike than an outage. Although spikes and outages are different problems, the solution to both turns out to be much the same: an uninterruptible power supply.

Uninterruptible Power Supplies

An uninterruptible power supply (UPS) is a device placed between the incoming external power supply and the server's internal power supply. It acts rather like a large sponge. Under normal conditions, power flows from the outside into the sponge and out the opposite end to the server. Should a surge (a mild, short-lived increase in voltage) or a spike (a short, severe increase in voltage) appear at the input to the sponge, it soaks up the excess power and stores it, allowing only the steady flow of power that the server needs to leave the output side of the sponge. Should the input to the sponge experience a sag (a short, mild reduction in voltage), brownout (a sustained reduction in voltage), or blackout (sudden and total failure), the sponge can be squeezed, extracting the energy stored in it to temporarily maintain the power supply to the server until the external power supply is restored.

The sponge in a UPS is in fact nothing more complex than a battery. Batteries, however, can only supply DC voltage, while the input to the server power supply requires AC voltage. In the cases when a UPS must make up a power shortage, it must manufacture AC voltage from the DC supplied by its internal battery by a process of high-speed switching. Unfortunately, this is not as efficient a process as one would like, so even a substantial battery may be able to supply only an hour or two of power to a large server. The battery inside most UPSs is a sealed lead/acid cell and has about the same useful life as a car battery in the range of three to five years. The UPS battery should be tested regularly to ensure that it will be in shape to do the job should the need arise. A record should be kept of the date the battery was installed and the date it is due for replacement. I suggest you write this information right onto the battery itself, and then you won't lose it! Old batteries contain highly corrosive acid and should be disposed of properly and with care.

Some UPSs have a built-in battery test function. If yours does, use it on a regular basis. Some favor doing a periodic acid test; that is, manually removing the external power supply and letting the UPS take over while in production. If it works, great. If something goes wrong, you may not be getting your bonus any time soon. I prefer to keep acid tests for periods of scheduled downtime. Some may think me timid. I prefer to think of it as prudent. If you really want to try it in production, pick a time of the day or week when the server is at its quietest, or the application can be temporarily shut down. There is no need to take unnecessary risks.

Transient Power Problems

Temporary problems like sags or surges are considered transient. They last typically less than a second and are over with. These anomalies are more common than one might think. They are often caused not by some fault of the power supplier but by local factors the supplier has no control over. Large current draws close to a server in the distribution network within a building can cause sags or surges. If the panel that supplies your server is fed from the same phase as the elevator, for example, your server may experience a measurable sag each time the elevator starts upward. In the same way, surges can be generated when a large current draw is suddenly stopped. In effect the current flow has a sort of momentum that must be dissipated somewhere, and if your server is close enough, then each time the heavy-duty coffee machine shuts off, it may cause an upwards blip on the server's power input. Unless you closely monitor incoming line power (and many controlled machine rooms do) you will never notice these mild aberrations. It is difficult to predict, however, the effect they can have on a server. Without any form of protection, the server's internal power supply unit has the ability to smooth out these sags or surges, but it is limited and could, if sustained over a long enough period, affect the service lifetime of the power supply itself. Erratic hardware problems, such as crashes or freeze ups whose cause cannot be traced to software or any detectable hardware defect, are sometimes eventually traced to power problems.

Electrical Noise

Another form of transient problem is noise. These are high frequency fluctuations in voltage caused by electrical signals being picked up by the power distribution network. These can be caused when power supply lines pass through electrical fields such as those created by fluorescent lighting or electric motors, as well as radio frequency data transmissions. Such electromagnetic interference (EMI) or radio frequency interference (RFI) can pass through the server's internal power supply and affect the operation of the server itself. As Moore's Law drives chip densities higher, I have mentioned that heat generation becomes an increasing problem. One of the antidotes to this is to lower the operating voltage of the logic circuits within the chips. This means, however, that the binary logic becomes more sensitive to small fluctuations in voltage. A 5-volt logic circuit will typically interpret anything above 3.5 volts as a binary one, anything below that as a binary zero. In that case I can allow the voltage to dip or rise by as much as a volt and not have problems. (A 1-volt drop would make a healthy 5-volt signal into a 4-volt signal, but that is still greater than 3.5 volts, so it is still interpreted correctly as a binary one.) Newer technologies are dropping logic voltages significantly, however. The new Serial ATA standard, for example, will use logic based on a high signal of only 250 millivolts, or one quarter of one volt. In this case a drop of only a small fraction of one volt would cause chaos. EMI or RFI signals passed in to the server over the incoming power signal could create just this kind of subtle fluctuation and produce serious difficulties.

A UPS is an effective way of eliminating problems with noise. The sponge effect of the UPS serves as an effective buffer to absorb these higher frequency transients. In the case of EMI and RFI, a good quality UPS will add extra circuitry to eliminate any of these signals which might survive the damping effect of the battery. Thus a good UPS will not only even out the sags and surges, but will also clean the power supply to the server as well. This is in itself a valuable aid to reliability, even if you never use the UPS to cover an actual power failure.

Total Power Failure

The UPS really earns its keep, of course, in the case of a complete blackout. In this case the UPS need to be sized to keep the server running for as long as you want it to. How long that is depends on your power outage strategy. I wish I could eliminate all your risks, but unfortunately this is one area where we all have to play the odds. To play this game, you ask this question: In my area of the world, how often do I lose power, and how long does it stay off? You can get historical data from your power supplier, and then place your bets accordingly. If the longest single outage in the last 25 years was eight hours, then you could choose eight hours as a reasonable worst case. I would point out that in my area of the world, central Canada, we experienced an ice storm in the winter of 1998 that not only broke, but obliterated all known historical records. Miles of high-voltage distribution lines were brought down, and some areas were without power for weeks, despite the best efforts of an army of power utility workers drawn from hundreds of miles around. My point is that your strategy must have two phases. In the short term, you can use a UPS to cover and hope that you don't find yourself helping to break any more disaster records. If the worst happens, however, you need to be able to detect when you are reaching the end of your UPS battery capacity and shut down your server cleanly before the juice runs out and it crashes. In order to do that, the server and the UPS have to be able to talk to each other.

The Network UPS Tools Package (nut)

There are several competing Linux packages to manage communication between a server and a UPS. I will focus on *nut*, which is the package Red Hat ships with its distribution. Most UPS units have the ability to report operational information back to the server they support through a dedicated hardware connection, usually an RS-232 serial connection. Using this connection, the server can query the UPS to determine things such as the current state of charge or incoming line voltage. In turn, should the line voltage fail, the UPS will start supplying power from its battery and inform the server that it is now running on battery power. At this stage the server needs to make a decision. How long should it continue to run on battery power before shutting down? If the UPS has sufficient capacity, the server may decide to run for a pre-determined period of time before getting concerned. If the power returns before that time period has elapsed, the UPS will inform the server and operation returns to normal. On the other hand, if the power has not returned and the battery is running low, the server should really use the remaining battery power to cleanly shut down. Although this means downtime, at least the server will not crash and risk data loss or corruption. As soon as line power returns, the server should automatically restart.

How nut Is Structured

nut is designed to be a network aware client server application. The architecture is shown in Figure 3.3. In the illustration, solid rectangles and lines indicate physical components and physical connections; dashed rectangles

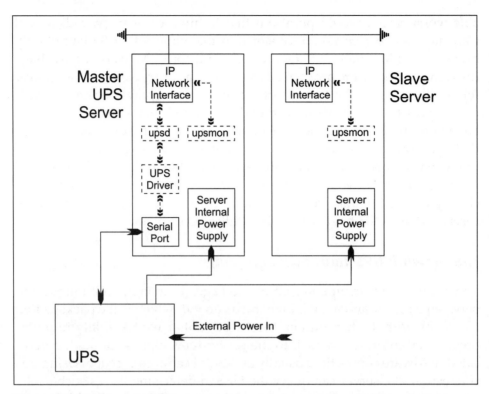

Figure 3.3 In this nut architecture, solid rectangles and lines indicate physical components and physical connections; dashed rectangles and dashed lines indicate software components and communication paths.

and dashed lines indicate software components and communication paths. You can see that one server in the network is physically connected to the UPS hardware monitor line, and normally gets its power from the UPS, also. This is the master power server. Additional servers may also get power through the UPS, but have IP network connections to the power control server. These are clients of the master, but *nut* refers to them as slaves. If, during a supply power outage, the UPS battery gets dangerously low, the master will inform the slaves over the network, allowing the slaves to start shutting down. Once the slaves are shut down, the master shuts itself down and then finally powers the UPS off. The power switches on all servers remain on, so that when power is restored, the UPS will turn on and all the servers will boot back up. Now let's look at the details of how to make this work.

Configuring nut for Red Hat Linux–
The Master Server

The central machine in a *nut* installation is the master server, so let's look at it first. Note that if you have only one machine, you would configure it as a master. My example network is shown in Figure 3.4. The master runs three daemons. The first to be started (the order is important) is the UPS model specific driver.

Finding the Correct UPS Driver daemon

The *nut* package supplies several drivers for some of the more popular commercial UPS units. Unfortunately, *nut* does not include *man* pages, so you will need to go to */usr/share/doc/nut<nut version>* for reference information. The README file in this directory lists the drivers that should be in the package. I have found, however, that the package Red Hat ships is

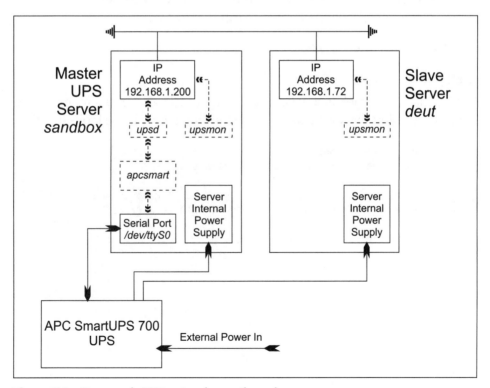

Figure 3.4 Our sample UPS network runs three daemons.

missing some drivers listed in the README. Use this command to list which ones you have:

```
# rpm -ql nut
```

I have an American Power Conversion SmartUPS 700, so my driver is */usr/bin/apcsmart*. This driver is what talks directly to the UPS via a serial port, so when you start it you need to point it to the serial port to which your UPS is connected. One important point to note is that, for security reasons, this driver will not run as *root*, but as *nobody* in the group *nogroup*. On my Red Hat 7 system this creates two problems. One is that there isn't a group called *nogroup*, so I had to create it. Adding this line to */etc/group* should work. If a group number 98 exists, find an unused number.

```
nogroup:x:98:
```

The other problem I had was that serial ports are by default owned by *root*. Consequently the UPS driver running as *nobody* did not have permission to write to it. A change in ownership like this was the fix:

```
# chown nobody:nogroup /dev/ttyS0
```

Configuring upsd

Next is the *upsd*. Its job is to talk to one or more UPS driver daemons. There is a configuration file for the daemon, */etc/ups/upsd.conf*. Mine looks like this:

```
# cat /etc/ups/upsd.conf
 1 # Network UPS Tools: upsd configuration file
 2 #
 3 # This file contains passwords, so you should keep it secure.
 4 # Having it owned by root, mode 0600 should be sufficient.
 5
 6 UPS apc700 /var/lib/ups/apcsmart-ttyS0
 7
 8 # Access Control (ACLs)
 9
10 ACL all 0.0.0.0/0
11 ACL sandbox 192.168.1.200/32
12 ACL deut 192.168.1.72/32
13
14 ACCESS grant master sandbox beach
15 ACCESS grant login deut deutroot
16 ACCESS deny all all
```

Please note the comment at the top concerning passwords. These are *nut*-specific passwords. If an ordinary user gets hold of them, he or she can potentially shut down power from the UPS to the server, so watch the permissions on this file. Line 6 defines my UPS. If this *upsd* were to manage multiple UPSs, there would be a line for each. The string *apc700* in the second field is an arbitrary identifier you invent to identify this UPS. The third field defines the location of the file *upsd* will use to store current data for this UPS. The file will be located in */var/lib/ups* and its name will be made up of the name of the driver you just dealt with and the serial port, separated by a hyphen, as shown in the listing.

Next come the access controls. Slave servers will talk to the *upsd* on the master server through an IP socket, so IP addresses are used to identify these clients. The ACL directive is used to assign a name to a group of IP addresses. Line 10 specifies that the ACL *all* will be used to refer to the set of all possible IP addresses. Lines 11 and 12 are examples of ACLs that include only one IP address. A specific group of addresses could be referenced like this:

```
ACL my_network 192.168.44.0/24
```

The /24 is used in the standard IP fashion to designate that the first 24 bits of the address specified represent the network portion. Hence in this example the ACL *my_network* would include any host whose IP address starts with 192.168.44.

Now lines 14 through 16 use the ACCESS directive to assign privileges to the ACLs just defined. Line 14, for example, grants master privilege to any host in the ACL *sandbox*, provided the host can supply the password *beach*. In this case, there is only host in the ACL *sandbox*, so this line gives master privilege to the host 192.168.1.200, which is the master server itself. You might think it unnecessary to have to specify, as this does, that the machine running *upsd* is the master, but in fact you do. In similar fashion, line 15 grants login privilege to the client host 192.168.1.72, requiring the password *deutroot*. When a request from a client arrives from the network to *upsd*, it will examine these ACCESS directives in the order they appear in the file, and the first one matching the client machine IP address will determine the privilege granted. If the end of the list were reached with no match, the privilege granted would be ambiguous, hence the last ACCESS directive, line 16 ensures that any host making it to the end of the list is explicitly denied any privilege. It is also possible to use the command *drop*. This has the same effect as *deny*, but sends no error message back to the client. This is useful if you want to make the master server appear invisible to clients attempting to contact it. This is a security issue as by default *upsd* listens on (nonprivileged) port 3305 and could fall victim to a port scan if *upsd* revealed its existence by returning an error message.

There are several levels of privilege that determine what the client will get from *upsd*, defined thus:

- base: basic commands, no information retrieval (also allows TCP connections)
- monitor: base plus read only information retrieval
- login: monitor plus login for shutdown sync
- master: login plus forced shutdown abilities for multi-ups client sync
- manager: master plus variable setting plus instant commands
- all: match any level

So, as *sandbox* is attached to the UPS, it gets master privilege, *deut* will need to login to *sandbox* to allow the proper shutdown mechanism, so it gets login privilege. The passwords defined in the final field will be needed by *sandbox* and *deut* whenever they use a *nut* client to talk to *upsd*.

Now we're ready to start the server daemon on sandbox, like this:

```
# /usr/bin/upsd
```

Configuring upsmon on the Master Server

Finally, *upsmon* needs to be configured. This daemon is the one that really does the work. It polls the *upsd* to check the current power status. If the UPS tells *upsd* via the serial control cable that power has failed, *upsmon* learns this at the next poll and initiates shutdown procedures for the machine it runs on, and, if it is the master server, will send a signal to the UPS to turn off at the end of the shutdown. The configuration file for *upsmon* is */etc/ups/upsmon.conf*, and on the master *sandbox* looks like this:

```
# cat /etc/ups/upsmon.conf
 1 # upsmon configuration file
 2 #
 3 # This file contains passwords, so keep it secure.
 4
 5 MONITOR apc700@192.168.1.200 1 beach master
 6 # MONITOR apc700@sandbox 1 beach master
 7 MINSUPPLIES 1
 8 SHUTDOWNCMD "/sbin/init 0"
 9 # NOTIFYCMD /usr/local/ups/bin/notifyme
10 POLLFREQ 30
11 POLLFREQALERT 5
12 HOSTSYNC 120
13 DEADTIME 100
14 POWERDOWNFLAG /etc/powerfail
```

Again, note the comment regarding passwords. The central function of *upsmon* is defined by line 5, which tells *upsmon* that host 192.168.1.200 is the master server connected to the UPS named *apc700*. Once started, *upsmon* polls the *upsd* running on 192.168.1.200 at frequent intervals to determine the current power status. If it is told that the power has failed, *upsmon* immediately begins to shut down the host it is running on. If *upsmon* is running on the master itself, it should behave slightly differently than if it is running on a slave server. If a slave server, the shutdown will start immediately upon notice of the power failure. In this case the last field of the MONITOR line will say slave rather than master. On the master, the shutdown should be delayed until any slaves have had the opportunity to shut down, when the master shutdown commences. This is important as the UPS will be turned off by the master at the end of the master shutdown process, and, without delaying the start of the shutdown on the master, the slaves may not have had time to completely shut down when the UPS power is turned off. The fourth field of the MONITOR line, *beach* in this example, is the password specified in the master server *upsd* configuration file for the ACL this *upsmon* host must be a member of. If the shutdown on any of the slaves hangs up, the master cannot wait forever to shut down or the UPS battery will run out. Line 12 uses the HOSTSYNC parameter to specify in seconds how long the master will wait for the slaves to log out before it starts to shut down anyway.

The third field of line 5, the numeral 1 in this example, specifies the number of power supplies that the UPS on the server 192.168.1.200 supplies on the system running *upsmon*. This would come into play where a server has multiple redundant internal power supplies, each of which is supplied by a separate incoming power line, each protected by separate UPSs monitored by separate master *nut* servers. This type of no single point of failure system is not uncommon for large server installations. A separate MONITOR line would be required for each of the *nut* servers. This parameter will be one where servers have a single incoming power source. The MINSUPPLIES directive at line 7 is related to this, specifying for a multipower supply server the minimum number of supplies necessary to keep the server going.

Note that lines 5 and 6 say in essence the same thing, as *sandbox* is in fact 192.168.1.200. I have commented out the version that has a hostname, however, as otherwise every time *upsmon* polls it will have to do a host name lookup. Of course it is more convenient to use the hostname version in case the IP address ever changes, and you can if you like—just be aware of the extra performance overhead, especially if you decide to poll every two seconds.

Configuring the System Shutdown

When running on the master server and informed of a power failure, *upsmon* first creates an empty file whose name is determined by the POW-ERDOWNFLAG parameter at line 14, then uses the command specified by the SHUTDOWNCMD parameter at line 8 to start the shutdown. (Pay attention to the double quotes around the command string; see the sidebar, "UPS: Notes from The Trenches," for details.) When running on a slave server, *upsmon* uses SHUTDOWNCMD to initiate the shutdown, but does not create the flag file. Why the difference? On the slave servers, it is only necessary to shut down the operating system, after which the power will be cut off when the master server turns the UPS off. On the master server, then, there has to be some mechanism to turn the UPS off at the end of the shutdown, and that is the purpose of the flag file.

Each Linux distribution handles the process of shutting the system down differently. Red Hat uses the SYSVINIT system, derived from the method used by System V UNIX, one of the last AT&T Bell Labs versions produced. In this system the */sbin/init 0* command, as specified at line 8 will result in a series of scripts executed, each of which stops a specific operating system utility. Then, the script */etc/rc.d/init.d/halt* runs to shut down what is left of the operating system. The command to shut off the UPS must be inserted at the end of this script to complete the master server configuration. You will need to add a conditional clause that tests for the existence of the POWERDOWNFLAG file. If that file exists, then the shutdown in process must have been initiated by *upsmon* following a power failure when the UPS needs to be turned off. If POWERDOWNFLAG does not exist, then the shutdown in process was initiated by some other means and the UPS will not be touched. This is what the last lines of */etc/rc.d/init.d/halt* must look like:

```
 1 # Now halt or reboot.
 2 echo "$message"
 3 if [ -f /fastboot ]; then
 4   echo "On the next boot fsck will be skipped."
 5 elif [ -f /forcefsck ]; then
 6   echo "On the next boot fsck will be forced."
 7 fi
 8
 9 HALTARGS="-i -d"
10 if [ -f /poweroff -o ! -f /halt ]; then
11   HALTARGS="$HALTARGS -p"
12 fi
13
14 if [ -f /etc/powerfail ]; then
15   echo "Shutting down UPS now "
```

```
16 /usr/bin/apcsmart -k /dev/ttyS0
17 fi
18
19 eval $command $HALTARGS
```

Lines 14 to 17 (shown in bold) are the lines you need to add. If the test for the existence of */etc/powerfail* at line 14 returns true, the *apcsmart* command at line 16 shuts off the UPS, and the halt or reboot command normally executed at line 19 never has the chance to run. This should be safe, as by this point the only remaining file systems are mounted read-only and would not be damaged by the power off.

UPS: NOTES FROM THE TRENCHES

While testing my UPS network for this chapter, I ran across several challenges that raised noteworthy questions. The first was an issue of version confusion. When the test network (shown in Figure 3-4) was set up, the UPS server (*sandbox*) was running Red Hat v7.0, while the client (*deut*) was a Red Hat v7.1 installation. In a simulated power failure test, the server behaved perfectly. The client seemed to be communicating properly with the server, and when informed that the battery level had gone critical executed its SHUTDOWNCMD. Yet, Linux did not shut down and the still-running machine had its power cut off when the server shutdown finished and turned off the UPS. Researching the problem, I discovered that Red Hat v7.0 shipped version 0.44.0 of *nut*, while v7.1 shipped *nut* version 0.44.1. It turned out that the function that parses the *upsmon.conf* file changed between versions, requiring the text of SHUTDOWNCMD to be a quoted string if contains any blanks. The string in my example was */sbin/init 0*. Without the quotes the newer version of *nut* running on the client dropped the argument 0 from the string, and ran just */sbin/init* as the shutdown command. Unfortunately, the command */sbin/init* alone does nothing.

Each distribution and each version of each distribution will contain different packages at different revision levels. Consequently, if you have problems getting two Linux servers to cooperate, check which distribution and version they are running, then see if, as a result of distribution differences, you are running different versions of the same package. For an rpm-based distribution, you could use this command to determine, for example, what version of *nut* you have:

```
$ rpm -qi nut
```

(continues)

If you do have different package versions, there are two alternatives to resolving the difference. You may be able to retain the different version if you can find out what changed between the two so you know how to configure each machine. Look in the */usr/share/doc* directory for a subdirectory carrying the name and version of the package. For *nut* on my Red Hat 7.1 machine, the directory is */usr/share/doc/nut-0.44.1*. This subdirectory contains all of the documentation shipped with the package. You will commonly find a file called Changes, Changelog, or something similar that details the change history of the package. This was the file that solved my problem with nut. A README file may also contain useful information.

The other alternative is to install the same version of the package on both servers, the later version generally being preferable. If you have a distribution CD that has the rpm for the version you want, use the upgrade option of *rpm* to install the newer version in place of the older one. I could have upgraded my server with this command:

```
# rpm -U nut-0.44.1-5.i386.rpm
```

If you don't have a CD with the rpm for the version you want, the best place to find rpms is at *rpmfind.net*.

Another problem I ran into stemmed from the UPS itself. *nut* relies on the UPS to decide when the battery is critically low. In my testing I was running both servers with monitors and an external SCSI enclosure turned on from the same UPS. It turns out that this is a sufficient load for this UPS to make a poor judgment call on the low battery condition, leaving it so late to sound the critical battery condition alarm that there was not enough left in the battery to keep the UPS going long enough to allow both machines to fully shut down. The UPS simply gave up and turned itself off part way through the server shutdowns, resulting in both of them crashing. A repeat of the test with only one server running worked perfectly. So, know thy UPS. It will make decisions regarding power conditions that may not always make sense. You may feel more comfortable using *upsc* to monitor the actual state of the UPS and making the decision to shut down yourself rather than allowing the UPS to make the decision for you. The only way to know for sure what will work best for you is to test it. Never assume.

Finally, we need to cover a few remaining parameters. Lines 10 and 11 define the polling interval. A POLLFREQ of 30 means *upsmon* polls *upsd* every 30 seconds as long as there is no power outage. If an outage occurs, the polling frequency changes to POLLFREQALERT. In the example, the normal polling is set below the default of five seconds to reduce traffic while in production, but the POLLFREQALERT value is greater than the default to be more sensitive during a shutdown situation. The NOTIFY-CMD line allows specification of an arbitrary command to run when *upsmon* has anything important to say. This could be used to generate a call to a pager, or an internal alarm of some sort. It is not used in this example, so the line is commented out. DEADTIME isolates a dead UPS. If *upsmon* cannot contact the UPS for more than DEADTIME seconds, it concludes the UPS is dead and logs it. If this happens to a UPS that was supplying battery power, *upsmon* will initiate a shutdown.

Starting the daemons on the Master Server

Once they are all configured, three daemons need to be started in proper order at boot time on the master server—first the *apcsmart* driver, then *upsd*, and finally *upsmon*. Red Hat supplies a script to do this, */etc/rc.d/init.d/ups*. You need to add a start link to this in your run-level directory, as usual. For a Red Hat 7 system, this should work for servers booting into run level three (the default run level):

```
# ln -s /etc/rc.d/init.d/ups /etc/rc.d/rc3.d/S99ups
```

Or if your server does a graphical boot, it will be run level five:

```
# ln -s /etc/rc.d/init.d/ups /etc/rc.d/rc5.d/S99ups
```

This UPS startup script uses a configuration file, */etc/sysconfig/ups*, to start the UPS driver daemon. Using the APC UPS, */etc/sysconfig/ups* on the master server will look like this:

```
1 SERVER=yes
2 MODEL=apcsmart
3 DEVICE=/dev/ttyS0
```

The SERVER parameter indicates this machine is the master, the MODEL parameter ensures that the proper driver daemon is started, and the DEVICE parameter specified the serial port the UPS is connected to. Once these last files are in place, reboot the master server and make sure all the daemons are running properly.

In my example I have a second server attached to the same UPS, so I'll need to configure it next.

Configuring nut for Red Hat Linux: The Slave Server

Slave servers need only run the *upsmon* daemon, so the configuration is less complex. On my slave server *deut*, I need an */etc/ups/upsmon.conf* file that looks like this:

```
 1 # upsmon configuration file
 2 #
 3 # This file contains passwords, so keep it secure.
 4
 5 MONITOR apc700@192.168.1.200 1 deutroot slave
 6 # MONITOR apc700@sandbox 1 deutroot slave
 7 MINSUPPLIES 1
 8 SHUTDOWNCMD "/sbin/init 0"
 9 POLLFREQ 30
10 POLLFREQALERT 5
11 DEADTIME 100
12 POWERDOWNFLAG /etc/powerfail
```

And an */etc/sysconfig/ups* file like this:

```
SERVER=no
```

As on the master server, add a run-level directory link to start ups, reboot to ensure that the daemons will start properly . . . and you are finished.

Soft Power Switches

One thing you need to be careful of in any UPS supported server is the so-called soft power switch. These are popular in many ATX case power supplies and can be a problem if you aren't careful. The idea of the soft power switch is to make the hardware power switch controllable by BIOS software. The operating system can talk to the BIOS, so if the BIOS can turn the power off, then this allows the operating system to turn the power off, too. As far as shutting the system down, this poses a problem for the *nut* configuration I have just described because the power needs to be shut off at the UPS, not at the server. If the soft power switch is used to shut off the server, then the server cannot also shut off the UPS, and vice versa! A further problem arises when the power comes back on. In a soft switch system, the user normally needs to physically push a momentary contact switch either on the server case or on the keyboard to switch the power supply on. In a UPS configuration, you want the server to power up automatically as soon as the UPS detects a return of line power. Being physically present to push the switch should not be required.

Fortunately, most systems that use the soft power concept have support in the BIOS to turn it off, or allow you to specify that the power should switch on as soon as power is supplied externally. Make sure you have set these values properly, or your server may not power up following a shutdown. Personally, I prefer to source a power supply that does not bother with soft power at all. That makes one less thing that can go wrong.

Useful nut *Clients*

Once you have your *nut* configuration up and running, there are a few more useful things you can do with it. The *upsc* command is a client of the *upsd*, and can ask *upsd* questions regarding the state of the UPS. The amount of information you get back varies with the model of UPS, but it can include information on the battery condition, the power now being drawn by the server, line voltage, line frequency, and other information all of which is useful for keeping track of the power state of your UPS. For example, here is some sample output from the *upsc* command run on the client host *deut*:

```
# upsc apc700@192.168.1.200
host: apc700@192.168.1.200
MFR: APC
MODEL: SMART-UPS 700
SERIAL: WS9733080979
STATUS: OL
UTILITY: 121.5
BATTPCT: 100.0
ACFREQ: 60.00
LOADPCT: 045.7
BATTVOLT: 26.52
OUTVOLT: 122.2
UPSTEMP: 041.8
UPSIDENT: UPS_IDEN
LOWXFER: 103
HIGHXFER: 132
WAKEDELAY: 000
LINESENS: H
```

The value OL for STATUS indicates that the UPS is operating on line power; if it were running on battery, STATUS would be OB. A BATTPCT of 100 shows the battery is fully charged. ACFREQ shows a 60-Hertz line frequency. LOADPCT at 45.7 indicates that the current being drawn through the UPS at the time of sampling would be 45.7 percent of its capacity running on the battery. Finally, UPSTEMP of 41.8 degrees centigrade is warm, but not hot.

In a general power failure, your server room fresh air supply will almost certainly fail in conjunction with this rise in UPS temperature. If your server room is well cooled, you should weather a short failure all right. If the failure is a long one, your machines will eventually exhaust the UPS, be shut down, and cool off. If, however, the power cycles on and off, and your server room ambient temperature is too hot to begin with, the extra heat load created by the UPS running on its battery has problem potential.

If you want to log this data, you can use the *upslog* command. *upslog* will poll the *upsd* at the specified interval and write the output to a log. I could poll my *apc700* every five minutes with this command:

```
# upslog apc700@192.168.1.200 /var/log/apc700 300
```

Here, */var/log/apc700* is where the log output will be written and the log interval is 300 seconds, 5 minutes. There are a variety of options for formatting the output. Issue the *upslog* command with no arguments for information regarding formatting syntax.

Alternatives to nut

Most UPSs sold today have some form of support software to do the job that *nut* does, and increasingly they are being ported to Linux. My previous example could have used APC's PowerChute software, which they have recently ported to Linux. You can evaluate each alternative on its merits and decide whether you want to go the proprietary software route or stay with a generic, open source package like *nut*. You may choose to include Linux support as a prerequisite when sourcing a UPS, and if you can find one that suits your needs and supports Linux, so much the better. If you don't like *nut*, there are several other open source UPS management packages available. Some are vendor-specific, like *apcupsd* for APC UPSs, while some, like *genpower*, are generic in scope. Visit rpmfind.net to locate current rpms for these packages.

Internal Power

Using a good UPS, you can now rest assured there is reliable supply of power to your server's internal power supply. But what happens if that internal supply fails? If your server has only one internal supply, this is clearly a single point of failure, and a power supply failure typically comes with little or no warning, resulting in a server crash. This is a weakness that has become more pronounced with the current trend to higher power draw processors and disk drives, while at the same time power supply size is being reduced to allow for higher densities in server farms. This leads to smaller components and strain on the designer of the power supply. A colleague of mine who runs a business maintaining business computer networks says that in the last two or three years, power supplies have become the single largest cause of failure in the systems he supports.

The only real solution is to decide that you will live with the risk or invest in a server that has a redundant internal power supply. Hot swap redundant power supplies and cases to fit them are no problem to get in the generic PC hardware market. If you source your server prebuilt from one of the name brand manufacturers, you will find that all of their larger-scale servers now come with redundant internal power either optional or in some cases standard equipment. Make sure that there is some means of detecting a power module failure and that it is Linux supported. Some supply an audible alarm and visible LED failure warning that may be sufficient so long as the server is physically checked at reasonable intervals. Don't skimp on the size of the supply. A dual 300-watt supply will load balance while both modules are working, meaning that neither should be heavily loaded, with an aggregate capacity of 600 watts. Should one fail, the backup has to carry the entire load, which could drive it close to its capacity, therefore, you want to avoid leaving it running that hard for an extended period of time. If you have several servers, it is worth it to keep a spare module on hand, unless you are confident of a reliable source for them close to hand.

Reliable Network Hardware

The only piece of actual network hardware on the server is the network interface card (NIC). In theory there is no reason that you can't install two NICs in a server, using one with the other a warm standby. In the event of a failure of the primary NIC, the spare could be configured with the same IP address as the dead primary, and you're back in business. In practice, however, it's trickier than it looks. The first challenge is: How do you detect that the primary NIC has failed? If you suddenly can't talk to the server, it could be that the NIC has failed, but how do you know it isn't some other problem? It could be that the application you are talking to has run into trouble, or possibly the operating system has crashed. There may be nothing at all wrong with the server, it may be a network break. If you can't contact a server over the network, you need a physical connection to come up with an accurate diagnosis of the problem. You might want to consider keeping an old-fashioned modem around for emergency access, if you can convince the security folks to let you.

Let's assume that you are able to determine by using a physical connection to the server that the NIC, configured as *eth0*, has in fact died. If you had a spare, designated *eth1*, in the server, you should be able to issue:

```
# /sbin/ifdown eth0
# /sbin/ifup eth1
```

and be back in business, and from the server's end, you are. There is a problem at the client side, however, as their *arp* caches will still contain the hardware address of the failed *eth0* NIC. How are you going to get each and every client to flush their *arp* cache? You may be able to get around this by sourcing a NIC for the server that allows the hardware address to be soft configured using the *hw* option to the */sbin/ifconfig* command. That should work since there is no way you could have a duplicate hardware address; the old NIC is dead.

This kind of thing is dealt with in specialized versions of Linux. They are designed to support highly available clusters in which each server monitors the other and acts as a buddy ready to take over should anything die. These clusters have their own special software infrastructure to deal with failure detection and fail over. I'll be talking about them in Chapter 10.

Reliable Backup Hardware

Solid, trustworthy backups are a critical part of any reliable server solution, and so it is worth spending some time choosing the right backup hardware. There are a variety of technologies available to the Linux systems administrator. I'll look at several of them from the reliability viewpoint.

Tape Drive Technology

The traditional form of backup device has been the magnetic tape drive for many years. Tapes have the advantage of being a well-proven and mature technology. They still have the greatest storage capacity of any competing backup solution and are widely supported. I have divided tape technologies into two categories according to the way they store data, using either linear or helical scanning.

Linear and Helical Scanning: What Are They?

The earliest form of magnetic tape storage devices used what is called linear scanning. In this system, the tape is drawn across a stationary recording head that lays down the data onto a linear track running along the length of the tape. In audio tapes, the capacity was doubled by removing the tape at the end, flipping it over, and running it backwards. As the head was mounted a bit off the center of the tape, this allowed a second data track to be laid down on the tape parallel to the first, but running in the opposite direction. Modern linear scan data tapes do essentially the same thing, but they eliminate the need to physically remove and flip the tape by moving the recording head up and down instead. In this fashion, multiple tracks can be laid down in a sort of greatly elongated S shape along the length of the tape. As the tape reaches the end, the head drops down a notch and the tape reverses direction. The procedure is repeated at the opposite end of the tape until the width of the tape has no space for any more tracks. The data path that results is illustrated in Figure 3.5. As the total length of the data path increases, so does the amount of data that can be stored. Clearly then, the longer the tape, the more data. Also, a wider tape will accommodate more reversals, or tracks, thus further elongating the data path and increasing the storage capacity of the tape.

Helical scan tapes lay the data down differently due to the history of the technology. Helical scanning was introduced as a means of storing live video data on tape. Linear scan tape can store video data with no trouble,

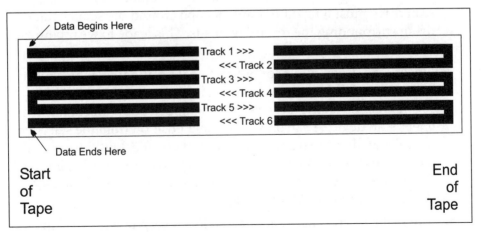

Figure 3.5 Multiple tracks run in an S shape along the length of this linear scan tape.

but a problem arises when slowing down or pausing the video. When slowing the tape speed, the video motion slows, but so does the rate at which I can read the data, so the image quality cannot be maintained. Should I stop the tape entirely, I now have a stationary tape and a stationary head, therefore, I can read no data at all. Clearly I cannot pause the show with a linear scan tape. Helical scanning solves the problem by putting the recording head in constant motion. The heads are mounted to a shaft and spun at constant speed in a small circle. A semicircular wall is erected around the spinning heads, and the tape is wrapped in a spiral around the outside of this wall. While the tape is playing, the head is also spinning, and the speed of the head relative to the tape is appropriate for full motion video. If the tape stops, the head continues to spin and can still read data from the tape, although now it is the same data over and over again, which produces a still picture. As the tape is wrapped in a spiral (or helix) around this semicircular wall, the head actually scans in a diagonal line across the tape, which increases the length of each scan, increasing the volume of data that can be read at each rotation of the head. This technology was the basis of videotape, and it is how any VCR works today.

What Is Better, Linear or Helical Scan?

Each technology of course has its boosters. Those who favor linear scanning technologies argue that

- Linear scan drives are less complex mechanically than helical scan units, and their recording heads tend to last longer, as the contact between the tape and the head is small. By comparison, a helical scan drive must wrap and draw the tape around the semicircular drum surrounding the recording heads. This leads to wear both on the drum and on the tape.

- Linear scan drives allow for bidirectional positioning, which most helical scan drives can not do. By this I mean that if I need to find several files on a tape, I can search the tape in both directions on a linear scan device. I can only accurately position from the start of a helical scan device, so once I have found one file, I need to rewind the tape and start searching for the second file from the beginning. This can make extracting individual files from a helical scan tape slower than from a linear scan device.

- Due to the multi-track structure of a linear scan tape, I can skip quickly through the data stored by simply dropping two or three tracks down, without having to move the tape backwards or forwards. This also leads to faster performance in extracting individual files.

- Future development roadmaps for linear scan technologies allow for larger volumes of data storage than do future helical scan technologies. This is an important consideration, as a backup system is a significant investment, and once you have committed to a technology it would be ideal if you could stay with it for a number of years into the future.

Meanwhile, those who like helical scan drives point out that

- The data transfer rate depends on the head-to-tape speed. Because the heads in a helical scan drive are spinning quickly, high head-to-tape speeds giving transfer rates comparable to linear tape, can be achieved without needing to move the tape nearly so quickly past the heads. This places less stress on the tape thus improving media life and reducing the chances of tape breakage, all of which improves reliability.

- Linear tapes require several tracks laid down on the tape to realize full storage capacity, so to fill a tape it must go back and forth in the drive multiple times. A helical scan tape passes through the drive only once to fill completely. Less wear and tear on the tape in the helical scan drive results in better reliability.

- Due to the lower storage density of linear tape (relative to helical scan tape), the use of single reel cartridges is common in linear tape technologies. This requires a system to draw the tape out of the cartridge and into a take-up reel inside the drive. These mechanisms are prone to failure, necessitating repair to either the drive or the cartridge to allow recovery of the stored data.

I would like to be able to tell you firmly that one is better than the other, unfortunately, there is no clear winner. While I was not impressed with some of the earlier helical scan technologies, much work has been done in recent years to address some of the inherent weaknesses of this technology, and the current crop of offerings competes well against some of the older linear scan drives. When you go shopping for drives, cost may be the factor that tips the balance. You will tend to find that helical scan technologies are less costly for small- to medium-sized data volumes, making them popular in smaller shops. Large-scale backup systems like those associated with mainframe computer sites rely primarily on linear tape technologies that scale well into the terabytes, but can carry hefty price tags.

Next, let's examine the main implementations of both of these technologies so you will know what you are shopping for.

8 mm Tape: The First Helical Scan Drive

The first use of helical scan technology for data storage was introduced by Exabyte in 1987, and was commonly called 8-mm tape. It had a storage capacity of 2.4 GB and supported a data transfer rate of 240 KB/s, using a tape cartridge essentially identical to the Sony 8-mm video cartridge. Exabyte pushed this technology to a capacity of 7 GB and a 1 GB/s transfer rate, before introducing MammothTape, a second-generation 8-mm technology in 1994. MammothTape improved reliability with a new tape handling system, a dynamic head cleaning system, and an improved tape design, increasing capacity to 20 GB at a 3 MB/s transfer rate. Exabyte's current technology roadmap sees this technology supporting future capacities of 200 GB at 20 MB/s transfer rates. Current Mammoth drives use a SCSI interface, with Fibre Channel support optional.

Sony has developed its own second-generation 8-mm helical scan technology called Advanced Intelligent Tape (AIT). Introduced in 1996, AIT currently supports a capacity of 50 GB, at a 6 MB/s transfer rate, with a roadmap projecting capacities to 200 GB at 48 MB/s. AIT introduced a novel idea called Memory-In-Cassette (MIC). Each AIT cartridge has a 64-KB flash memory chip built in. When inserted into the drive, the MIC chip is used to identify the tape and store logs, search maps, and other user definable data. This can be used to overcome some of the problems of slow access due to the unidirectional positioning limitation of helical scan tape. Sony also claims even lower tape tensions than Exabyte's Mammoth technology, and promises longer tape life as a result.

4 mm DAT: The Other Helical Scan Tape

In the 1980s, Sony adapted helical scan technology to the storage of digital audio data, resulting in Digital Audio Tape or DAT. In 1989 they adapted DAT technology to the storage of generic digital data, and the Digital Data Storage (DDS) standard was born. The DDS standard, like DAT, uses a 4-mm tape cartridge. There have been several generations of this standard, the current being DDS-4, with capacity of 20 GB and a transfer rate of 3 MB/s. The basic technology is similar to 8-mm drives, and shares the same characteristics. DDS tapes have the advantage of being smaller than 8 mm, if that is an issue for you.

Quarter Inch Cartridge (QIC): The First Linear Tape Technology

The earliest linear scan tape drives were in fact the first tape drives period, and were originally large open reel tape decks. The first practicable cartridge style linear tape was the QIC standard, introduced by 3M in 1972. Using a tape 1/4 inch wide, the earliest QIC standard used the floppy drive controller as it's interface to the system bus and stored only 40 MB of data. Many years have passed since then, and there are now more than 100 different QIC standards. 3M rationalized this uncontrolled explosion of competing QIC standards into the Travan series of standards, which has become another way of saying QIC. The state of the art in the Travan standards is the TR-5 specification, giving a capacity of 10 GB and a transfer rate of 1 MB/s, with an impending TR-6 standard that should double the TR-5 numbers. Drive units are available with both ATA and SCSI interfaces, and also a few using USB, which is now supported in the new 2.4 kernel.

Digital Linear Tape (DLT)

DLT is a half-inch linear tape similar in principal to the QIC standard, but designed for larger-scale, heavy-duty operation. The current standard is known as Super DLTape and supports a single cartridge capacity of 200 GB at a 20 MB/s transfer rate. The standard is projected to be capable of eventually supporting up to 2 TB per cartridge. DLT is unlike QIC in that it is a single-reel cartridge, requiring all of the tape to be drawn out of the cartridge onto a take up reel inside the drive during operation, with the tape returned to the cartridge before removal. The idea is to maximize the physical storage density of the cartridge itself by eliminating the space otherwise taken up in the cartridge by an empty take up reel. This requires a mechanism that can hook the end of the tape to begin to draw it out of the cartridge after the cartridge is inserted into the drive. The physical mechanism used in older standards sometimes gave trouble in this regard, but the current standard claims a much improved and more robust means of doing this.

DLT is a popular technology in mid-size to large data installations, and has a substantial installed base. DLT drives commonly start at a 40 GB capacity and go up from there, with multiple cartridge tape library units common. The interface is normally some flavor of SCSI, with larger tape libraries edging towards Fibre Channel.

Linear Tape Open (LTO): The New Linear Tape

LTO is a joint development of Hewlett-Packard, IBM, and Seagate. Released in 1998, it is designed to be an open standard, available to OEMs at a nominal cost. The hope is that this new standard can cut across the proliferation of existing linear and helical scan technologies, and perhaps bring some simplification to the field of tape storage. LTO, as the name implies, is a linear tape format, but it has two distinct flavors—one built for speed, the other for capacity. The Accelis version uses a dual reel cartridge, like QIC and the helical scan tapes, but uses a mid-loading design borrowed from IBM's mainframe tape storage products. In this design, the tape is always left exactly halfway through with one half of the total tape length on each reel before it is ejected from the drive. That way, when the tape is inserted, access time to any random point on the tape is minimized, as the tape need not always start from the beginning. Mid-reel loading coupled with the serpentine data path characteristic of linear tape drives allows data to be extracted from the tape quickly, making Accelis well suited to data warehouses using tape storage.

The Ultrium flavor of LTO uses a single reel cartridge, like DLT, and for the same reason, to maximize the storage capacity of each cartridge. To allow for more data tracks, Ultrium tape is a full half-inch wide, compared to Accelis's 8 mm tape width. The first generation Ultrium cartridge has a capacity of 100 GB and supports a transfer rate of 10 MB/s. The Accelis cartridge stores 25 GB and gives the same transfer rate as Ultrium. Ultrium is ultimately slated to support 800 GB cartridge capacities and Accelis, 200 GB with transfer rates in excess of 80 MB/s. LTO drives usually use a SCSI interface, with Fibre Channel interfaces available on tape library units.

One interesting feature of the LTO cartridge is LTO-CM. This is similar to the embedded NVRAM chip featured in Sony's AIT helical scan tapes. Like the AIT chip, the LTO-CM chip stores calibration information, manufacturer's data and initialization information. Unlike AIT, LTO-CM has less capacity, 32 KB versus the 64 KB in the AIT tape, and it uses a passive radio frequency (RF) interface, allowing the chip to be read by a noncontact reader external to the drive itself. Hence tapes can be scanned by an operator prior to insertion, and without taking up a drive in the process. This kind of functionality is clearly directed towards large data installations, where LTO will be a major player. You can track the state of the LTO art at www.lto-technology.com.

Tape Drive Configurations

The smallest tape drive unit is of course a single cartridge drive, typically built into the server case itself. In this case, the capacity of a single cartridge is an important factor in choosing a drive, as data in excess of the capacity of a single cartridge could not be backed up unattended. It is generally preferable to do backups at times of low system load, both to ensure the integrity of the data and to minimize the performance cost of the backup, and in real life this often means during the night. It may well be impractical or economically unfeasible to employ an operator to come in at 3 A.M. just to switch tapes, and then go home! Fortunately, several of the technologies I have reviewed have enough single cartridge capacity to store the kind of data volumes that might be expected on a small-scale single server.

Should a single cartridge drive be inadequate, the next option is a small tape library, or jukebox. Small libraries start at capacities of six cartridges, giving single unit capacities of 400 GB and up. Libraries grow, with the functional upper limit generally being your budget. The largest libraries scale to terabytes and incorporate sophisticated robots to handle the cartridges. If you are buying your first tape storage unit, be careful not to limit your ultimate expansion ability. The volume of data you will have to store in the future will only grow. If you are going to come even close to filling a single cartridge today, invest in a small autoloading library unit, and you will not have to go through a migration process to a new technology a year or two from now.

Tape Drive Compatibility

One thing you will need to be careful about is compatibility. There are so many different tape drive technologies, each of which has a variety of different standards. All of the drive technologies we have reviewed can make use of data compression techniques to pack more data into a tape. There are as many different standards for data compression as there are drives that implement them. My rule is that each time I make a tape, I label it physically, not only with a record of the data it carries, but also the drive it was created in, and all parameters I can think of that might be relevant.

My rule for backups is that every time I make a tape, I test a tape. That is, when I design my backup routine, for each tape generated, I pull a tape from the archive and test it to make sure that it is still readable. Far too many people have war stories about sites that invested in backup systems and operated them for years before discovering in a time of crisis that none of their backups were any good.

Tape and Tape Drive Maintenance

Like any mechanical device, a tape drive needs to be maintained if it is to operate reliably. The single most important issue with all varieties of tape drive is cleaning. Dust and dirt get into tape drives and can adhere to the heads and get caught up in the tape, both of which will cause data errors. Of all the components that benefit from a clean environment, the tape backup unit benefits the most. Another source of contamination is the tape itself. Much work has been done to eliminate the problem of the magnetically sensitive oxides laid down on the surface of the tape flaking off and adhering to the heads and other parts of the tape handling mechanism. Some oxides will also stain the head as they are drawn across it. The current high storage capacities all of the drives give today would not have been possible without the media advances of recent years. In many cases, increases in capacity between generations of a particular drive technology was only possible due to improvements in the media itself. If your drive specifies a particular media type or grade, use it. Saving a few dollars on older, cheaper media is not worth the data loss it can easily cause. If a specific media is necessary, the manufacturer should state it clearly in their documentation.

All tape drives need to be cleaned on a regular basis. This is so basic to reliable operation that some of the newer technologies have incorporated self-cleaning capabilities. Others will inform you using a display on the drive if the drive is due to be cleaned. If your drive does neither, you need to set up a maintenance schedule for the drive that ensures it will get cleaned regularly.

If you source two drives of the same make and model, you would reasonably assume that a tape written in one should be readable in the other. But never assume; always test. Current technology tapes have such high data densities that recording head alignment is crucial. As long as the heads on your two drives are properly aligned, you should have no problem. But if they are new, if one was purchased after the other, or if they have been moved or otherwise disturbed, it is prudent to test the readability on one drive of tapes produced in the other. If there is a problem, the drive can be serviced. This is not a problem you want to discover in the middle of a disaster recovery process.

Tape Storage and Handling

Tapes must be handled and stored properly. You might not think it, but rough handling can make a tape unreadable. I have known tapes that would not read after being accidentally dropped on the floor. One manufacturer actually specifies a particular height from which if dropped its tape should survive. The fact that this testing is being done and advertised indicates that shock is an issue for tape cartridges. It should go without saying that tapes be stored in a clean, dry, and cool location, it is sometimes overlooked that the storage location should be free from magnetic contamination too. All of the major tape storage technologies are based on magnetic encoding; hence any exposure of a tape to a strong magnetic field has the potential for data corruption. The worst of it is, you can't see it happening, and you will not know it has happened until you discover the tape will not read.

Reusing Tapes

Tape media will usually come with a specification for the number of times the media can be re used. Technologies compete with one another for the highest number in this regard, claiming a lower cost of operation the greater number of times you can reuse your tapes. Some people, however, have a policy that says never to use a tape twice. Their reasoning is that the data stored on the tape is worth many times the cost of the tape itself, so much so that it is a false economy to be incurring a greater loss risk by reusing media. In some cases the decision is made for you if there is a requirement, often for legal or tax reasons, to keep the data as an archive record of your companies operations for audit purposes. In that case each backup you make goes into storage and would not be available for reuse for several years (by which time the tape is probably obsolete anyway). Certainly the data corruption risk is minimal if you never re use media, just as certainly media can be successfully re used. It is very difficult to predict at how many cycles the quality of the media begins to become dangerously low. Your best defense is Campbell's Law. It is a choice you will need to make.

Other Backup Technologies

While tape is the most widely used backup solution, and clearly the least expensive on a per-byte stored basis, it is not the only way to do backups.

In the next section I'll look at some alternatives to tape, and where and when they may be a good choice for you.

Compact Disc-Based Backup

The CD is another Sony invention. Like DAT, CD technology was originally applied to digital audio data and later adapted to the storage of generic digital data. Unlike the DDS standards, however, the storage capacity of a single data CD has not changed since its inception, although transfer rates have risen significantly. A data CD still stores only 650 MB of data. Apart from this significant limitation, the CD has much going for it. It offers must faster data location times than tape, and data transfer rates equal to the fastest tapes. Manufactured CD discs, although by no means indestructible, are less sensitive to dirt, humidity and magnetic fields than are magnetic tape media, and so should have longer lifetimes. The CD is also very compact, and is easy to load and unload, as there is no tape threading and transport required. Also, reading a CD involves no contact between the read head and the CD, so there is no wear involved even if the CD is read and reread numerous times.

Compact Discs: CD-ROM, CD-R, and CD-RW

There are several acronyms used to describe data CDs. As they are rather inaccurately used, they benefit from some explanation. CD-ROM literally stands for Compact Disc Read Only Memory, which means that a CD-ROM, once created, can never be altered; it is a read-only media. This is the acronym most often applied to what, for lack of a better term, I call manufactured CDs. I mean a CD many copies of which have been mass-produced in a factory. The data on such a disc is physically and permanently imprinted onto a foil layer on the top of the plastic disc. This process cannot be reversed; hence, once made the CD is clearly a read only media, and as the information is physically stamped into the foil it is very durable, assuming the disc does not get damaged. This is fine when the requirement is to mass-produce many identical CDs and its advantages for software distribution are obvious.

The cost of the manufacturing process, however, makes it useless when a backup requires just one CD, not thousands. To easily create a single unique disc, two technologies, CD-R and CD-RW, were developed. CD-R allows a CD to be made using a generic blank. Instead of physically imprinting the data onto a layer in the CD, a CD-R drive uses a small laser to heat up a layer of dye encased in the blank disc. The heat permanently discolors the dye to store the data. Because the discoloration is permanent, once written the CD also becomes a read-only medium. As the information is held in a dye layer, it is not as robust as the foil layer of a manufactured CD and is, in fact, sensitive to deterioration over time, largely as a result of exposure to light. If stored in a cool, dark location, however, CD-R discs are rated to survive at least as long or longer than the most optimistic storage lifetimes of magnetic media.

A CD-R, then, would seem a possible alternative to tape, if only for smaller data sets. Tape, however, can be erased and reused; a CD-R once burnt stays burnt. Enter CD-RW. A CD-RW disc can be written, erased, and rewritten multiple times. To achieve the erasability, the CD-RW uses phase-change technology, relying on certain curious dyes whose reaction to light can be changed by exposure to different temperatures. Like a CD-R, a CD-RW disc has a dye layer and a CD-RW drive imprints the data on them by using a laser to selectively heat the dye and thus imprint the data pattern. What is different about the CD-RW is that a subsequent operation that heats the dye to a higher temperature will reverse the process, effectively erasing the disc and allowing it to be re written with new data. The CD-RW carries the improved resistance to moisture, wear and magnetic fields offered by a CD-ROM or CD-R, and is erasable, too.

CD, CD-R, and CD-RW offer a good flexibility of durability and functionality, but there is still the 650 MB storage limitation. A CD-based backup solution is a viable alternative to tape for small data sets. Is there a future in it for larger data volumes? For the answer, let's look at DVD.

Digital Versatile Disc

Digital Versatile Disc (DVD) is the newest CD-style data storage media. Its development was driven by the digital video market, but, like DAT and CD, has been subsequently turned towards the task of data storage. Use of the DVD standard for data backup is new, and standards are just emerging. One of the options is the DVD+RW offering from a consortium including Hewlett-Packard, Phillips, Sony, and others. Using the same phase-change technology as CD-RW, DVD+RW supports a double-sided disc storing 9.4 GB available at a transfer rate in the region of 2 MB/s. DVD+RW uses the Universal Disc Format (UDF) file system structure, designated as the successor to the older ISO9660 format used on all CD devices to date. UDF is supported in the 2.4 kernel, so there should be no major obstacles to using DVD+RW in a Linux environment.

With the first generation of this technology already supporting almost 10-GB capacity, and the attractive nature of the media stability and size,

I am inclined to think that for small and medium sized backup applications, these optical devices may give tape a serious challenge. You can follow this technology at www.dvdrw.com. News about other optical storage developments can be found at www.osta.org, home to the Optical Storage Technology Association.

Removable Disks

One final option you may want to consider is a removable disk storage medium. The earliest versions of these devices were typically based on a floppy disk drive, with increased capacity. While the capacity of these drives was usually less than adequate for backing up a whole server, they could be very convenient for backing up small amounts of data or transporting data from machine to machine. The current generation of removable drive has now broken the 1-GB barrier, however, with further increases in capacity promised. While even these higher capacity units are not in the large scale backup market, they might very well be practicable for a small to mid sized server. Iomega have recently introduced their Peerless drive, which has a single cartridge capacity of 20 GB and transfer speeds up to 15 MB/s. As this is primarily intended as a dynamic data storage device rather than an archive device, it supports PC interfaces including USB and IEEE 1394 (better known as FireWire or i.Link), as well as a SCSI option.

Removable disks offer the advantage of fast and convenient access to data, unlike tapes that need to search for a file within an archive and then extract it. Removable drive cartridges are typically more fragile than a tape cartridge, as they contain a modified hard disk, although the current generation of removable disks advertise significant resistance to damage. The USB and FireWire versions would then be hot pluggable, which is a bonus. On the down side, the drive draws power from the host machine, limiting its scalability.

I'm going to finish this section with a summary of the various different backup options I've presented (see Table 3.2). The capacities listed represent the current standard, and the projected capacity as the technology matures.

Reliable Core Hardware

Core hardware refers to the central and most fundamental component of the server, the motherboard itself, and any peripheral expansion cards

Table 3.2 Backup Options

| BACKUP TECHNOLOGY | CAPACITY@TRANSFER RATE | | INTERFACE |
	CURRENT	PROJECTED	
Mammoth 8-mm Helical Scan Tape	20 GB @ 3 MB/s	200 GB @ 20 MB/s	SCSI
AIT 8-mm Helical Scan Tape	50 GB @ 6 MB/s	200 GB @ 48 MB/s	SCSI
DDS 4-mm Helical Scan Tape	20 GB @ 3 MB/s	improvement unlikely	SCSI
QIC/Travan Linear Tape (TR-5)	10 GB @ 1 MB/s	20 GB @ 2 MB/s	ATA, USB, SCSI
DLT Linear Tape	200 GB @ 20 MB/s	2 TB @ 160 MB/s	SCSI
LTO Linear Tape —Accelis	25 GB @ 10 MB/s	200 GB @ 80 MB/s	SCSI
—Ultrium	100 GB @ 10 MB/s	800 GB @ 80 MB/s	SCSI
CD-R, CD-RW Optical disc	650 MB @ 6 MB/s	improvement unlikely	USB, 1394, ATA, SCSI
DVD+RW Optical Disc	9.4 GB @ 2 MB/s	??	SCSI
Peerless Removable Disc	20 GB @ 15 MB/s	??	USB, 1394, SCSI

plugged in to the motherboard. Curiously, although you might think these components, critical as they are to the server, would require a great deal of attention, in fact there is little to say. They are solid-state components having no moving parts and there is nothing to deteriorate or wear in service; consequently, if they work when installed, they rarely fail while in service. Overheating is the greatest danger. It is also preferable to avoid physically disturbing production machines any more than is absolutely necessary as disturbance carries small risks of damage or loosening internal connections.

If a motherboard fails, it is of course catastrophic for the server and will involve completely dismantling the server to repair or replace the failed board. If your risk analysis determines that you are willing to consider some contingency, the only viable defenses that would get a server back in service more or less immediately would be a complete spare server or a server cluster arrangement. This is a case in which data storage structured on the Titanic principle in combination with external storage cabinets will speed the ability to move the application and its data from the failed server to a backup machine. Should you need to replace the board, take in to consideration that it could take some time to source and install a suitable replacement; you may want to consider keeping a spare board on hand.

One another final point about motherboards: In the continuing rivalry between Intel and AMD to produce CPUs, there have been reports of problems encountered in terms of incompatibilities between processors, processor support chip sets, and motherboards, leading to unreliable systems with problems difficult to debug. If you are shopping for a motherboard and find a good candidate or you are sourcing a complete pre-built server unit, ensure that you check the Linux hardware compatibility lists to ensure there are no known problems with the hardware you are considering. The Red Hat hardware compatibility lists found at hardware.redhat. com detail video and sound cards, processors, motherboards, and a number of complete server units by manufacturers such as Compaq, Dell, IBM, and others. Turnkey Linux-specific server packages that should eliminate any question of incompatibility are marketed by all major PC vendors as well as Linux specialists such as Penguin Computing (www.penguin computing.com), Linux Networx (www.linuxnetworx.com), and others.

Hardware Monitoring

Having taken some care in choosing a good CPU cooler and case design, how do I know that they are doing their job and keeping critical temperatures under control? How do I know if a cooling fan has failed, or a heat sink has become blocked and my CPU or drive bay temperatures are climbing? Should a CPU fan slow or stop this can be a nasty thing, because of what happens to the CPU as it overheats. If the CPU simply failed entirely, it would be bad enough. In fact what happens is that the CPU starts to randomly malfunction, but will not necessarily fail altogether. Thus the server can run for some time causing application errors and possibly damaging your data before it eventually crashes the operating system and brings the server down.

The only defense is to continuously monitor the CPU temperature, and for good measure, the fan operation too. Many larger systems purpose built to serve as heavy-duty servers come with this built in. Much of this functionality is proprietary, to varying degrees, however, and support for Linux is not universal. If the server you are considering advertises hardware monitoring, be sure that there is a Linux port of the client software available. If there is no Linux client code, you may still be able to make use of the monitoring hardware, it just takes a bit of work. Even if you have a traditional motherboard, you may also be able to monitor hardware, as many motherboards these days are including monitoring hardware as a standard feature.

Generic Hardware Monitoring: The i2c/SMBus

The generic solution to hardware monitoring involves an implementation of the i2c bus. If your motherboard uses this standard, and many do, Linux can probably monitor it. The i2c bus is a simple two wire serial bus developed by Philips as a generic means of communication between micro controller devices. In a modified form known as the System Management Bus (SMBus) the i2c bus is used as a communications path by certain special function chips on a motherboard. The chips of particular interest from a hardware monitoring point of view are those that either contain, or can be connected to, sensors that measure physical parameters such as voltages, temperatures, or fan speeds. The values returned by these sensors can be monitored by operating system utilities and alarms sounded if danger thresholds are crossed. Support for the i2c bus is built in to the 2.4 kernel, but to monitor your hardware you will also need the *lm_sensors* package, which includes device drivers necessary to support the wide variety of sensor chips in common use.

Configuring lm_sensors

First of all, though, you need to need to ensure that your motherboard has sensors and a sensor chip on it. When examining motherboard specifications, look for references to "health monitor", or hardware monitor capabilities. You need to see support for both the i2c or SMBus itself, and also a sensor chip. The i2c bus support is often provided by the processor chip set, that group of chips designed to support the various I/O requirements of the processor. Sensor chips are not installed on all motherboards, and tend to be associated with higher quality boards. If you think your motherboard has what it needs, the *lm_sensors* package includes a useful script to confirm that the proper chips can be addressed, and help get Linux configured to support them. The first thing to do is to run */usr/sbin/sensors-detect* as root. This should give you a dialog that looks like this. I have shown your input in bold:

```
# /usr/sbin/sensors-detect
This program will help you to determine which I2C/SMBus modules you need to
load to use lm_sensors most effectively.
You need to have done a 'make install', issued a 'depmod -a' and made sure
'/etc/conf.modules' (or '/etc/modules.conf') contains the appropriate
module path before you can use some functions of this utility. Read
doc/modules for more information.
Also, you need to be 'root', or at least have access to the/dev/i2c[-]* files
for some things. You can use prog/mkdev/mkdev.sh to create these /dev files
if you do not have them already.
If you have patched your kernel and have some drivers built-in you can
safely answer NO if asked to load some modules. In this case, things may
seem a bit confusing, but they will still work.
We can start with probing for (PCI) I2C or SMBus adapters.
You do not need any special privileges for this.
Do you want to probe now? (YES/no): YES
```

An answer of YES probes for any i2c or SMBus devices on the system, and loads any kernel modules needed to support the found devices, and that looks like this:

```
Probing for PCI bus adapters...
Use driver 'i2c-viapro' for device 00:04.4: VIA Technologies VT 82C686 Apollo ACPI
Probe succesfully concluded.
 We will now try to load each adapter module in turn.
Load 'i2c-viapro' (say NO if built into your kernel)? (YES/no): YES
Module loaded succesfully.
 Do you now want to be prompted for non-detectable adapters? (yes/NO): NO
 To continue, we need module 'i2c-dev' to be loaded.
 If it is built-in into your kernel, you can safely skip this.
 i2c-dev is not loaded. Do you want to load it now? (YES/no): YES
Module loaded succesfully.
```

So far so good. I have discovered the SMBus support in the VIA 82V686 south bridge motherboard chip and loaded drivers to talk to it. Next the SMBus device is itself probed, searching for sensor chips attached to that bus:

We are now going to do the adapter probings. Some adapters may hang halfway through; we can't really help that. Also, some chips will be double detected; we choose the one with the highest confidence value in that case. If you found that the adapter hung after probing a certain address, you can specify that address to remain unprobed. If you have a PIIX4, that often includes addresses 0x69 and/or 0x6a.

Next adapter: SMBus vt82c596 adapter at e800 (Non-I2C SMBus adapter)
Do you want to scan it? (YES/no/selectively): **YES**
Client found at address 0x00
Probing for 'National Semiconductor LM78'... Failed!
Probing for 'National Semiconductor LM78-J'... Failed!
Probing for 'National Semiconductor LM79'... Failed!
Probing for 'Winbond W83781D'... Failed!
Probing for 'Winbond W83782D'... Failed!
Probing for 'Winbond W83783S'... Failed!
Probing for 'Winbond W83627HF'... Failed!
Probing for 'Asus AS99127F'... Failed!
Probing for 'ITE IT8705F / IT8712F'... Failed!
Client found at address 0x2d
Probing for 'Myson MTP008'... Failed!
Probing for 'National Semiconductor LM78'... Failed!
Probing for 'National Semiconductor LM78-J'... Failed!
Probing for 'National Semiconductor LM79'... Failed!
Probing for 'National Semiconductor LM80'... Failed!
Probing for 'National Semiconductor LM87'... Failed!
Probing for 'Winbond W83781D'... Failed!
Probing for 'Winbond W83782D'... Success!
        (confidence 8, driver 'w83781d'), other addresses: 0x48 0x49
Probing for 'Winbond W83783S'... Failed!
Probing for 'Winbond W83627HF'... Failed!
Probing for 'Asus AS99127F'... Failed!
Probing for 'Genesys Logic GL518SM Revision 0x00'... Failed!
Probing for 'Genesys Logic GL518SM Revision 0x80'... Failed!
Probing for 'Genesys Logic GL520SM'... Failed!
Probing for 'Genesys Logic GL525SM'... Failed!
Probing for 'Analog Devices ADM9240'... Failed!
Probing for 'Dallas Semiconductor DS1780'... Failed!
Probing for 'National Semiconductor LM81'... Failed!
Probing for 'Analog Devices ADM1025'... Failed!
Probing for 'Analog Devices ADM1022'... Failed!
Probing for 'Texas Instruments THMC50'... Failed!
Probing for 'ITE IT8705F / IT8712F'... Failed!
Client found at address 0x2f
Probing for 'National Semiconductor LM78'... Failed!
Probing for 'National Semiconductor LM78-J'... Failed!
Probing for 'National Semiconductor LM79'... Failed!
Probing for 'National Semiconductor LM75'... Failed!
Probing for 'Winbond W83781D'... Failed!
Probing for 'Winbond W83782D'... Failed!
Probing for 'Winbond W83783S'... Failed!

```
Probing for 'Winbond W83627HF'... Failed!
Probing for 'Asus AS99127F'... Failed!
Probing for 'Dallas Semiconductor DS1621'... Failed!
Probing for 'ITE IT8705F / IT8712F'... Failed!
Client found at address 0x49
Probing for 'National Semiconductor LM78'... Failed!
Probing for 'National Semiconductor LM78-J'... Failed!
Probing for 'National Semiconductor LM79'... Failed!
Probing for 'National Semiconductor LM75'... Success!
    (confidence 3, driver 'lm75')
Probing for 'Winbond W83781D'... Failed!
Probing for 'Winbond W83782D'... Failed!
Probing for 'Winbond W83783S'... Failed!
Probing for 'Winbond W83627HF'... Failed!
Probing for 'Asus AS99127F'... Failed!
Probing for 'Dallas Semiconductor DS1621'... Success!
    (confidence 3, driver 'ds1621')
Probing for 'ITE IT8705F / IT8712F'... Failed!
```

Wow, that's a lot of output—and it seems most everything failed. This doesn't look promising. Never fear, it isn't as bad as it looks. The probe is looking for a whole bunch of possible sensor chips at a whole bunch of possible bus addresses. It is normal that most of them fail. All you really need is one success for at least one functional sensor chip. This may be all you need, as one chip will normally support multiple inputs. In this case, a Winbond 83782D was apparently found. This is suspicious as the specifications for this motherboard indicates it has a different sensor chip installed, an AS 99127F, which wasn't detected. This is where the confidence level comes in. Notice in the output that each detected chip shows a confidence level. This is because hardware detection is often a challenging task. The degree to which these chips are documented varies. Chips that documentation is available for, or which behave in an unambiguous fashion can be detected with a high confidence level, but others are less certain. In my case, I compare what I know the board has to what is being detected and I see a discrepancy. The confidence level is high, though, so I will go with it for now, and see what happens. It may be that these two chips speak the same language and can be considered interchangeable. Two other chips were apparently also detected, an LM75 and a ds1621, but they show a low confidence level of 3, and as we shall see, the detection routine later concludes that these should be disregarded.

Next, sensors-detect goes on to probe the ISA bus. Now, as my motherboard does not have an ISA bus, this is a neat trick. In fact, current motherboards still have ISA buses; they just don't have ISA slots. The bus is implemented in the processor chip set for the benefit of devices that may at one time have been ISA cards but long ago were integrated into the motherboard support chip infrastructure. Some sensor chips fall into this category, so they are probed next:

```
Some chips are also accessible through the ISA bus. ISA probes are
typically a bit more dangerous, as we have to write to I/O ports to do
this.  Do you want to scan the ISA bus? (YES/no): YES
Probing for 'National Semiconductor LM78'
  Trying address 0x0290... Failed!
Probing for 'National Semiconductor LM78-J'
  Trying address 0x0290... Failed!
Probing for 'National Semiconductor LM79'
  Trying address 0x0290... Failed!
Probing for 'Winbond W83781D'
  Trying address 0x0290... Failed!
Probing for 'Winbond W83782D'
  Trying address 0x0290... Failed!
Probing for 'Winbond W83627HF'
  Trying address 0x0290... Failed!
Probing for 'Winbond W83697HF'
  Trying address 0x0290... Failed!
Probing for 'Silicon Integrated Systems SIS5595'
  Trying general detect... Failed!
Probing for 'VIA Technologies VT 82C686 Integrated Sensors'
  Trying general detect... Success!
    (confidence 9, driver 'via686a')
Probing for 'ITE IT8705F / IT8712F'
  Trying address 0x0290... Failed!
```

This probe does find a VIA 82C686, another of the processor support chips, and as noted this chip does have some integrated sensors that the motherboard manufacturer might choose to use, so a module should be loaded for this chip. All of the detection is now finished, and the output wraps up with a summary of what was found, and the drivers that should be loaded at boot time:

```
Now follows a summary of the probes I have just done.
Just press ENTER to continue:
Driver 'w83781d' (should be inserted):
  Detects correctly:
   * Bus 'SMBus vt82c596 adapter at e800' (Non-I2C SMBus adapter)
     Busdriver 'i2c-viapro', I2C address 0x2d (and 0x48 0x49)
     Chip 'Winbond W83782D' (confidence: 8)
Driver 'lm75' (may not be inserted):
  Misdetects:
   * Bus 'SMBus vt82c596 adapter at e800' (Non-I2C SMBus adapter)
     Busdriver 'i2c-viapro', I2C address 0x49
```

```
      Chip 'National Semiconductor LM75' (confidence: 3)
Driver 'ds1621' (may not be inserted):
  Misdetects:
   * Bus 'SMBus vt82c596 adapter at e800' (Non-I2C SMBus adapter)
     Busdriver 'i2c-viapro', I2C address 0x49
     Chip 'Dallas Semiconductor DS1621' (confidence: 3)
Driver 'via686a' (should be inserted):
  Detects correctly:
   * ISA bus, undetermined address (Busdriver 'i2c-isa')
     Chip 'VIA Technologies VT 82C686 Integrated Sensors' (confidence: 9)
 I will now generate the commands needed to load the I2C modules.
 Sometimes, a chip is available both through the ISA bus and an I2C bus.
 ISA bus access is faster, but you need to load an additional driver
module
 for it. If you have the choice, do you want to use the ISA bus or the
 I2C/SMBus (ISA/smbus)? ISA
```

Finally, I get a summary of the modules I will need to load at boot time to be able to read my sensors:

```
WARNING! If you have some things built into your kernel, the
below list will contain too many modules. Skip the appropriate ones!
To load everything that is needed, add this to some /etc/rc* file:
#----cut here----
# I2C adapter drivers
modprobe i2c-viapro
modprobe i2c-isa
# I2C chip drivers
modprobe w83781d
modprobe via686a
#----cut here----

To make the sensors modules behave correctly, add these lines to either
/etc/modules.conf or /etc/conf.modules:
#----cut here----
# I2C module options
alias char-major-89 i2c-dev
#----cut here----
```

Rather ambiguously, I am advised to add several driver load lines to some */etc/rc** file. But which one? In a Red Hat system, I use */etc/rc.d/rc<run-level>.d/S99local*, the script normally used for machine specific local customization. I use a default run level of 5, so I add the four *modprobe* commands exactly as shown at the end of the *sensors-detect* output to the end of */etc/rc.d/rc5.d/S99local*. Finally I need to edit */etc/modules.conf* as directed, adding the alias for the i2c device. Then I reboot.

In my case, I have what might be called a qualified success. The system boots fine and the modules load, but the system gives a continuous audible alarm and flashes the power light! Evidently the drivers I have loaded are doing something wrong. There is nothing in the *man* page about this, so the next thing to do is to talk to the developers. I go to the home of the *lm_sensors* project, www.netroedge.com/~lm78, and post a trouble ticket explaining my problem. Fortunately for me, the ticket is resolved the next day with the information that, as I had suspected, the AS 99127F is commonly misidentified by the probe routines. The w83781d driver the probe suggested is the proper driver, but it needs to be told specifically that there is an AS 99127F, so I need to add a force option to my *modprobe* command, like this:

```
modprobe w83781d force_as99127f=0,0x2d
```

I make the necessary changes to */etc/rc.d/rc5.d/S99local*, and reboot. This time everything loads fine, and I can verify it by looking at the boot log, where I see:

```
# dmesg
 1 Linux version 2.4.2-2 (root@porky.devel.redhat.com) (gcc version 2.96
20000731 (Red Hat Linux 7.1 2.96-79)) #1 Sun Apr 8 20:41:30 EDT 2001
 2
 3 <some output removed here>
 4
 5 i2c-core.o: i2c core module
 6 i2c-viapro.o version 2.5.5 (20010115)
 7 i2c-core.o: adapter SMBus vt82c596 adapter at e800 registered as
adapter 0.
 8 i2c-viapro.o: vt82c596 bus detected and initialized
 9 i2c-isa.o version 2.5.5 (20010115)
10 i2c-core.o: adapter ISA main adapter registered as adapter 1.
11 i2c-isa.o: ISA bus access for i2c modules initialized.
12 sensors.o version 2.5.5 (20010115)
13 w83781d.o version 2.5.5 (20010115)
14 i2c-core.o: driver W83781D sensor driver registered.
15 i2c-core.o: client [AS99127F chip] registered to adapter
[SMBus vt82c596 adapter 16 at e800](pos. 0).
17 i2c-core.o: client [AS99127F subclient] registered to adapter
[SMBus vt82c596
18 adapter at e800](pos. 1).
19 i2c-core.o: client [AS99127F subclient] registered to adapter
[SMBus vt82c596
20 adapter at e800](pos. 2).
21 via686a.o version 2.5.5 (20010115)
22 via686a.o: sensors not enabled - upgrade BIOS?
23 via686a.o: No Via 686A sensors found.
```

Lines 5 to 8 show the 82c596 SMBus adapter being successfully initialized, and lines 9 to 11 show the ISA bus driver loaded. The sensors.o module noted at line 12 is the module that will read the sensors, and the w83781d module noted at line 13 is the driver for the sensor chip. The output at lines 14 to 20 show the effect of my added module load flag as the AS99127F is successfully recognized as a client of the vt82c596 SMBus controller, using the W83781D driver. Finally the vt82c686a sensor chip is recognized, but no sensors are found. This is consistent with the specs for this board. The 686a chip is a part of the processor chip support set chosen by the manufacturer. It happens to include environmental sensors, but this manufacturer has chosen not to use them, substituting instead the AS99127F sensor chip. Hence it makes sense that the BIOS has no support for the 686a sensors.

Accessing lm_sensors Information

Well, it looks as if everything is working, so how do I read the sensor values? For this I use the *sensors* command. It takes no options or arguments, and gives output that looks like this:

```
# sensors
 1 as99127f-i2c-0-2d
 2 Adapter: SMBus vt82c596 adapter at e800
 3 Algorithm: Non-I2C SMBus adapter
 4 VCore 1:    +1.71 V  (min =  +1.61 V, max =  +1.77 V)
 5 VCore 2:    +2.48 V  (min =  +1.61 V, max =  +1.77 V)
 6 +3.3V:      +3.52 V  (min =  +3.13 V, max =  +3.45 V)
 7 +5V:        +4.99 V  (min =  +4.72 V, max =  +5.24 V)
 8 +12V:      +11.89 V  (min = +10.79 V, max = +13.19 V)            (beep)
 9 -12V:       -1.81 V  (min = -10.78 V, max = -13.18 V)            (beep)
10 -5V:        -1.37 V  (min =  -4.74 V, max =  -5.24 V)            (beep)
11 fan1:      2812 RPM  (min = 3000 RPM, div = 2)
12 fan2:         0 RPM  (min = 3000 RPM, div = 2)
13 fan3:         0 RPM  (min = 3000 RPM, div = 2)                   (beep)
14 temp1:     +26.0ÁC   (limit = +60ÁC, hysteresis = +50ÁC)
15 temp2:     +35.2ÁC   (limit = +60ÁC, hysteresis = +50ÁC)
16 temp3:    +127.7ÁC   (limit = +60ÁC, hysteresis = +50ÁC)        (beep)
17 vid:       +1.70 V
18 alarms:    Chassis intrusion detection                          (beep)
19 beep_enable:
20           Sound alarm disabled
```

Lines 1 to 3 are consistent with what we have just seen. Line 4 (Vcore), line 6 (+3.3 volt), line 7 (+5 volt), line 8 (+12 volt), line 11 (fan1), line 14 (temp1), and line 15 (temp2) all correspond to values I can read if I bring the machine down and go directly in to the BIOS. The other readings in this output may or may not be useful, but as they are not supported in the BIOS, I would like to remove them from my sensors output. I also know by comparing the values from the BIOS to the values received from *sensors* that the labels describing what the values represent are correct for the voltages, but that fan1 is the CPU fan, while temp1 is the motherboard temperature and temp2 is the CPU temperature. To control the output of sensors to ignore readings that I do not want and change the labeling, I edit */etc/sensors.conf.* like this:

```
 1 chip "as99127f-*"
 2
 3    label in0 "VCore 1"
 4   ignore in1
 5    label in2 "+3.3V"
 6    label in3 "+5V"
 7    label in4 "+12V"
 8   ignore in5
 9   ignore in6
10
11    label temp1 "Board"
12    label temp2 "CPU"
13
14    compute in3 ((6.8/10)+1)*@ ,   @/((6.8/10)+1)
15    compute in4 ((28/10)+1)*@  ,   @/((28/10)+1)
16
17 # set limits to  5% for the critical voltages
18 # set limits to 10% for the non-critical voltages
19 # set limits to 20% for the battery voltage
20    set in0_min vid*0.95
21    set in0_max vid*1.05
22    set in1_min vid*0.95
23    set in1_max vid*1.05
24    set in2_min 3.3 * 0.95
25    set in2_max 3.3 * 1.05
26    set in3_min 5.0 * 0.95
27    set in3_max 5.0 * 1.05
28    set in4_min 12 * 0.90
29    set in4_max 12 * 1.10
30
31 ignore fan3
32 ignore temp3
33 ignore vid
```

Line 1 matches my sensor chip. You will find that the default file is much longer than this, with sections for a variety of sensor chips. Once you know which chip you have, you can safely delete all the others. Lines 3 to 12 either determine the label given a value or tell sensors to ignore the value. The identifiers in0, in1, in2, and so on refer to input 0, input 1, input 2, and so forth on the sensor chip. The only way you can tell what sensor is connected at what input is by comparing the output of *sensors* to the values given by the BIOS, or if the motherboard manufacturer supplies this information in their reference documentation. Lines 14 and 15 apply a calculation to the raw data value returned by the sensor chip to produce a real value. The formulas given here were copied from the default configuration file, and gives values that are identical to those from the BIOS. The syntax for these formulas is discussed in the man page for *sensors.conf*. The limits set in lines 17 to 29 govern the range each value must stay within or generate an alarm, and lines 31 to 33 ignore several other irrelevant values.

Having edited the configuration file, I must run *sensors -s* as root to cause the new values to be read, and my finished sensors output now looks like this:

```
# sensors
as99127f-i2c-0-2d
Adapter: SMBus vt82c596 adapter at e800
Algorithm: Non-I2C SMBus adapter
VCore 1:    +1.69 V  (min =  +1.61 V, max =   +1.77 V)
+3.3V:      +3.52 V  (min =  +3.13 V, max =   +3.45 V)
+5V:        +4.99 V  (min =  +4.72 V, max =   +5.24 V)
+12V:      +11.97 V  (min = +10.79 V, max =  +13.19 V)          (beep)
fan1:      2793 RPM  (min = 3000 RPM, div = 2)
fan2:         0 RPM  (min = 3000 RPM, div = 2)
Board:     +26.0°C   (limit = +60°C, hysteresis = +50°C)
CPU:       +35.2°C   (limit = +60°C, hysteresis = +50°C)
alarms:    Chassis intrusion detection                         (beep)
beep_enable:
           Sound alarm disabled
```

The final thing to do is to incorporate this output into a monitoring script that will pick up any out of range values and do something about it. I'll be talking about showing how to do that in Chapter 6, "Monitoring Linux in Production."

Hardware Maintenance

After investing time and care selecting and installing a solid reliable hardware platform, maintaining it properly is equally important. Every server room should have a maintenance schedule posted and adhered to. Here are some maintenance suggestions:

Install a minimum-maximum thermometer in the server room. These register the maximum and minimum temperatures observed between resetting the unit. This will tell you how well the ventilation system is keeping ahead of the heat load. A rising temperature trend can be spotted by the thermometer faster than you might feel it. It is also useful evidence in discussions with the building's operations staff if your perception of the temperature in your office areas differ from theirs. If you think humidity is an issue, install a recording humidistat, too. If you are using hardware monitors, your servers should be recording motherboard and CPU temperatures so you can track trends and build experience concerning acceptable in-case operating temperatures.

There is little to mechanically maintain on most servers except cleaning fan screens. Unfortunately as there is really nothing else to maintain, this important job is often neglected. Establish a schedule to clean filters as frequently as your server room conditions require.

Keep records. Note, for example, power outages. Over time this will help you to determine quantitatively what your power failure risk is. This is especially useful if you have multiple sites, as you can build a picture of which sites have reliable power supplies. If you want, you can extend this record keeping to include any incidence of server outage. This allows you to build accurate historical data on the risks your site is experiencing. Using this data that is specific to your operation, you can do more accurate risk analysis. If you have multiple sites, you can use the data to compare and contrast their operations, learning from what is working well at the more reliable locations to assist those with poorer records.

When hardware needs replacement, make sure to log the details of any changes that were necessary to accommodate the new hardware. A new drive may be a different make, model, or type, or be a different size than its predecessor, requiring configuration changes. Make sure those changes are tracked in case the entire server needs replacement at a later date and the old information is used to order replacements. If you keep spares on hand, make sure an inventory count is maintained to ensure that a replacement will be there if needed. In my house, if someone takes the last box of crackers from the pantry, that person puts crackers on the shopping list. The same principal applies to your pantry of spare component parts.

Finally, pay attention to your servers. Once installed and running quietly, it is all too easy to let them fade into the background. Make it a habit to visually check them periodically for anything out of the ordinary. If a new noise appears, be attentive. The best way to deal with failure is to see it coming and stop it before it happens.

The following action list is based on the different issues raised in this chapter and should help lead you through the process of building your server hardware platform. If you act on all of it, you should have a solid server hardware foundation.

What You Can Do Now

1. Look at Table 3.1 again and assess your hardware against the list of potential hardware failures, considering which of the listed defenses you want into place.

2. Begin to build your servers on paper. Start by comparing your disk storage requirements with the capabilities of ATA, SCSI, and FC disks. Factor in the reliability issues of each of these technologies to come up with a detailed disk storage configuration. Keep in mind that software RAID is an option (see Chapter 5.)

3. Source a case for your server. Consider proper cooling, whether you want internal power supply redundancy, and the form factor. Do you want a traditional tower case or would a rack mount work better for your space and future expansion requirements?

4. Consider how you will supply power reliably to your server. Start by evaluating the quality of the external power supply to your site and choose a UPS accordingly. Can this UPS be integrated into the Linux software environment using *nut* or a similar utility so that power failovers will be automated?

5. Choose a suitable backup hardware solution. Make sure it supports not only your current need, but also your future needs. Budget for the development of a backup plan that ensures regular, complete backups will be made automatically. Include provision for off-site backup storage, fully documented backup, especially recovery procedures, and regularly scheduled backup drills.

6. As you source each hardware component, make sure it is listed as Linux supported and compatible. Does it support dynamic monitoring of critical operating parameters? Does it integrate hardware failure notifications into the Linux operating environment using

lm_sensors or a similar utility? Consider the merits of some of the excellent turnkey Linux server offerings on the market.

7. Consider what kind of home you will build for your server. If you already have a formal machine room environment, so much the better. If you don't, consider modifying a room in your current office to give your servers a secure, protected, and comfortable environment. Set up a maintenance schedule in the server room and plan to monitor and record both the operating environment and operational events of interest, in particular those that involve failures or downtime.

Installing and Configuring
for Reliability

"The first blow is half the battle."
—Oliver Goldsmith

The previous chapter concentrated on hardware reliability. This chapter looks at what can be done from an operating system software point of view to make Linux as robust as possible. Are there decisions that can be made when installing Linux that could help (or hurt) its reliability? What kernel version and distribution is best? How should disk storage be laid out when installing Linux? What about installing applications? How about reliability issues in the many configuration options available in Linux? How can boot failure problems be avoided? Read on . . . .

Which Linux Kernel Should You Use?

After a hardware configuration has been chosen for the base server, the next important decision is the version of the kernel to run. Although the Linux kernel is the product of countless developers all over the world, Linus Torvalds still centrally coordinates the official kernel release process, which has a well organized structure. Kernels are identified by a three-digit identifier, as shown in Figure 4.1. The first digit of the number is the primary release, which changes slowly. The first ever Linux kernel was numbered 0; the current primary release is 2. The second digit determines whether this is a stable or a development kernel. There are always

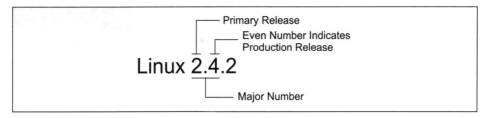

Figure 4.1   The Linux kernel uses a three-digit identifier.

two current versions of the kernel in this respect. One is the latest, cutting edge version actively being developed. It is available primarily for testing and debugging purposes, and is not considered to be production stable. It is indicated by an odd-numbered digit. An even-numbered second digit indicates that this kernel contains the newest available code to have undergone sufficient testing and debugging to be considered production stable. This is important because you should never run a development kernel on a production server. This digit changes relatively slowly over the life of a primary version. The current stable release is the 2.4 kernel; the current development release is 2.5. In this case, 2.4 is considered the *major number*.

The last digit represents the *revision number*. It is the most volatile element and represents a further subdivision of the current release. It changes rapidly on the development kernels. New revisions on the development side largely reflect a combination of new alpha- or beta-quality functionality and bug fixes. This digit can increment weekly, or even daily in the development kernel. In a production kernel, the revision number changes at a more sedate pace and usually indicates additional bug fixes or new functionality that has been in the development kernel long enough to be considered stable and ready for prime time. All three digits together define a specific kernel version, such as v2.2.18, or v2.4.3. In theory, each successive revision should be an improvement on the preceding one; but historically, some have been better than others and are favored for production servers. A visit to www.kernel.org will tell you the current version of both production and development kernels.

The general rule is never to run a development kernel on a production machine. It is also useful to see if your application vendor has a preference for a certain kernel version. If so, don't be surprised if it is an older version. Tried and true is the name of the game when you want reliability and stability.

All about Distributions

You will find, however, that when looking for Linux, you will not be able to choose a kernel version directly. Instead, your choice will be between distributions, otherwise referred to as *distros*. A distro is a packaging together of a particular kernel version along with the hundreds of utilities necessary to implement a functional Linux installation and support a variety of optional functionality.

Some of these distros are put together by commercial companies, such as Red Hat and Caldera, while some are produced by volunteer effort, such as the Slackware or Debian distros. Each distro has its own version numbering scheme, which doesn't necessarily have anything to do with the kernel version it is built around. The installation process of each distro varies, as does the version release level of the various utilities included in it. Servers running different distros can look surprisingly different from an administration point of view. Unless you have expertise in all of the peculiarities of one distro over another, it is preferable to pick one and stick with it. Too many different servers with different sets of idiosyncrasies will not keep your life simple or make for stable production.

You will find that the commercial distros choose production kernel versions known for stability, and they tend to stay with them, even as they fall behind the leading development edge. Stability is favored over support for the latest gadgets, especially if uptime is a priority. In choosing a distro for a production server, I look for an emphasis on stability, ease of installation and software management, and good online support. In particular, a good mechanism for alerting me to newly discovered bugs or other problems with the distro that I should know about is critical. Along with this, a quick and easy path to getting and installing any fixed or upgraded code is mandatory.

Commercial distros also offer various forms of telephone or e-mail customer support, while the volunteer distros rely more on newsgroups or mailing lists. Much is made of the fact that Linux is free, and it certainly is. Support for Linux is of course another matter. You have to make your own decisions as to whether you will buy support, and how much. You also get the opportunity to evaluate the quality of the support you get. Some will argue that the quality of support available from the community through mailing lists and newsgroups is as good as any of the commercial support channels. In its childhood, when Linux lived primarily in the academic community, my experience of this public forum support was very positive. I cannot think of any situation in dealing with a proprietary operating system in which I was able to ask a question and have an answer returned to me personally by the actual author of the source code. This happens daily in the open-source world. On the other hand, as Linux enters the commercial arena, it remains to be seen how the public forum support model will hold up.

This book doesn't recommend one distribution over another. You should, however, go shopping armed with a checklist of what to look for in a good distro. As you shop, you may find Eric Raymond's *Distributions HOWTO* useful. It summarizes the features of all the major (and some minor) distros and includes contact information for the distributors. Eric tries to keep it up to date, and takes it out of circulation periodically to overhaul it.

RPMs: Aren't They for Car Engines?

A Linux installation involves thousands of data files. Each distro uses some type of system for organizing these files into groups for software management purposes. Files are grouped according to the function they implement. Specific programming projects, which contribute a utility or group of utilities to a distro, normally drive the grouping. An example of a utility is *lilo*, the Linux boot loader, or *dhcpd*, the Distributed Host Control Protocol (DHCP) server daemon. In a distro, each utility is typically packaged into some type of compressed archive file. A selection of these archives, which you choose to make up your system are then uncompressed and installed into the proper file system locations during the installation process. Each archive file is flagged with a version level of the code in it and, if necessary, cross references information in other archives upon which it may depend. This functionality is commonly termed package management. The terms package and utility are essentially synonymous.

Red Hat (and most of the other commercial distros) use RPM, the Red Hat Package Manager. RPM was developed by Red Hat, based on an earlier package management system developed by Doug Hoffman, Kevin Martin, and Rik Faith for BOGUS Linux, one of the first Linux distros. RPM is significant in that it goes beyond the task of simply organizing files for installation purposes. It actually tackles the problem of managing the source code, the binary code that stems from that source, the compilation procedure that produces the binaries from the source, and any other auxiliary files such as documentation or sample configuration files. In the open-source world, each function, service, or application is developed by a separate group of developers. Sometimes more than one implementation of a necessary function may be available. Without some kind of system to standardize a process amongst hundreds of projects and thousands of developers, mayhem would ensue.

How RPM Works

Here is how RPM tackles distros. Let's say I have written a new utility for Linux that I want to package for distribution. I use the *rpm* command, supplying it with my source code, any patches required to the source, and an RPM spec file. This spec file defines everything necessary to build the utility (including any necessary commands to patch, build, and install the finished binaries), descriptive information about the utility, and a list of all the files associated with the utility. The output of this *rpm* command will be two files, one called a source RPM (or SRPM) and the other called the binary RPM. These files are in an RPM-specific binary format. The *rpm* command takes the source, patch, and build information and packages them inside the SRPM. Then, it compiles all the binaries for the utility and packages them inside the binary RPM, along with the file lists and the descriptive information. As a developer, I now release my new RPMs on the world.

If you want to use my utility, you need only download the binary RPM. You will use the same *rpm* command I used to build the package, but you will ask *rpm* to install rather than build. This will extract the binary, configuration, and documentation files from the binary RPM and install them where the spec file used to build the RPM directs. To keep track of installed packages, *rpm* manages a database of all installed packages on your server, to which my utility will now be added. You can now use *rpm* to make queries on this database and keep track of which packages at what revision level are, or are not installed on your system. Should a new revision of an installed package become available, possibly implementing new functionality (or more likely fixing bugs, but of course this will never happen for my package), you download the new binary RPM and use *rpm* to update the installed package.

Should you want to see the source code for the package, you would download the SRPM and install it. This gives you all of the source code files necessary to build the distro along with any patch or other build information. You can now hack my distro to your heart's content, use *rpm* to build a new SRPM and binary RPM, and distribute them. Of course, if my distro had become popular, you would consult with me about your alterations. Assuming I see your point of view, I would include your revisions in my own RPM distribution (giving you proper credit in the README file, of course).

USING *rpm*

As a system administrator, you can use *rpm* to see what packages you have installed and their revision level. You can add or remove packages, or upgrade existing ones, with a single, standard command syntax. Here is the command to query all installed packages along with a few lines of sample output:

```
$ rpm -qa
filesystem-2.0.7-1
glibc-2.1.92-14
XFree86-libs-4.0.1-1
Xfree86-xfs-4.0.1-1
...
```

I see that I have the package *filesystem* installed, at a revision level of 2.0.7-1. I may want to know more about this package. So I can ask like this:

```
$ rpm -qi filesystem
Name         : filesystem          Relocations: (not relocateable)
Version      : 2.0.7               Vendor: Red Hat, Inc.
Release      : 1                   Build Date: Fri 21 Jul 2000 11:26:37 AM EDT
Install date: Sun 21 Jan 2001 11:17:54 AM EST Build Host:porky.devel.redhat.com
Group        : System Environment/Base  Source RPM: filesystem-2.0.7-1.src.rpm
Size         : 368688              License: Public Domain
Packager     : Red Hat, Inc. <http://bugzilla.redhat.com/bugzilla>
Summary      : The basic directory layout for a Linux system.
Description :
The filesystem package is one of the basic packages that is installed on
a Red Hat Linux system.  Filesystem  contains the basic directory layout
for a Linux operating system, including the correct permissions for the
directories.
```

If I want to see what specific files the RPM contains, I can query like this:

```
$ rpm -ql filesystems
/bin
/boot
/etc
/etc/X11
/etc/opt
...
```

The *rpm* database itself is held in */var/lib/rpm*, which should be backed up on a regular basis on any essential production server.

RPM and Reliability

So, what has this got to do with reliability? Well, I have yet to see a perfect, 100 percent bug-free operating system. Even the most vocal supporters of the quality of open source code are not unrealistic enough to call it perfect. So, when a bug is discovered, what is the mechanism for dealing with it? In the case of an RPM package, the volunteer maintainer of the code receives bug reports and manages bug fixes. If the package is being maintained as an RPM, a new version will be released incorporating bug fixes. Inside the RPM, those bugs and fixes should be documented. Most RPMs will install a subdirectory under */usr/share/doc* containing any documentation associated with the package. The subdirectory will have the same name and revision level as the package itself. Look there for a file titled README, CHANGES, BUGS, or possibly NEWS. If the bug fix is considered critical for security or reliability, the manager of the distro may announce the new RPM version through the distro's support channels. Red Hat announces all critical updates to its distros through its home page, www.redhat.com.

If you experience a problem on a production server, which you suspect to be a bug, first determine the version of the package you are running:

```
$ rpm -qi <package>
```

Next, check with the manager of your distro to see if there are any related bugs. Also, check the documentation provided with your current version. If these steps don't explain the exhibited behavior, contact the maintainer of the package and file a bug report.

Practice Safe RPM

Where server stability is critical, it is important to get your RPMs from a reliable source, normally your distro CD-ROM. All RPM files include in the spec information who created the RPM and may optionally include a PGP (Pretty Good Privacy, an open source data security package) digital signature to verify authenticity. In addition, file mode information and MD5 checksums are stored in the RPM. These can be used to verify the integrity of the files of the RPM at any time after they have been installed, should you become concerned that any files have become corrupted or have been tampered with. This is highly useful functionality that in the past could only be achieved by using an external security scanner, such as *COPS* or *tripwire*.

Try

```
# rpm -V <package>
```

to verify integrity and

```
# rpm --checksig <package file>
```

to check PGP signatures. For scripting purposes, *rpm* will return nonzero if any checks fail.

The development of *rpm* has created a standardized means of tracking and controlling those hundreds of packages from thousands of developers into an organized, maintainable structure. Most of the commercial versions of Linux have adopted *rpm* as a de facto standard. This kind of consistency is good for ease of management, and ease of management supports stability and reliability. There are other good package management systems in Linux distros that do the same job as *rpm*. I would neither choose nor reject a distro solely on the basis of its package management system, but it should be a significant factor in your decision making process

Document What Works

Once you have put together a stable server, it is a good idea to document the combination of installed packages that works for you. This can help in building other servers, and can save time in the event that you have to rebuild a dead server from scratch. I know you'll never have to do that, but it doesn't hurt to be prepared, just in case, right? Run

```
# rpm -qa | sort
```

to generate an alphabetically sorted list of installed packages and redirect the output to a file stored online as well as offline. Keep the listing up to date by creating a new list each time you install or update a package.

Installation Dos and Don'ts

Now that you have decided on the hardware base you wish to build your server on and chosen your distro, it's time to install Linux. Each of the Linux distributors has written its own installation utility. Some are considered more user-friendly, while some require more technical knowledge. Red Hat's install utility requires practically no technical knowledge to perform a default installation, but this default install may not be ideal for a reliable server installation. Fortunately, the Red Hat installer has a great deal of flexibility, and imposes few limitations on you.

About Partitioning and File Systems

The first major decision you are faced with in the installation process concerns partitioning. Red Hat offers three different broad options early on in their installation, a workstation, server, or custom install. Both the workstation and server installs make assumptions regarding disk layout and installed packages. The custom option allows you to partition the disk yourself, and decide which file systems will go in which partition. To do this, you need to know where specific information is located in the Linux directory tree and what partitioning layout will minimize your data liability.

The Titanic Principle

The simplest possible Linux installation involves only two disk partitions. One is required for swap space and one for everything else—operating system files, applications, and data files. If you choose the server installation option when installing Red Hat Linux, however, you will find that the installed system has several disk partitions. A separate partition is created for the contents of /, /boot, /usr, /home, and /var. Why? It's what I call the Titanic principle. The RMS Titanic was constructed using a series of watertight compartments so that if any one compartment were to be holed, the watertight doors could be closed and the flooding restricted to only that local compartment. Any equipment in that compartment would be at risk, but the remainder of the ship would be protected.

In the same way, dividing the operating system into sections and placing each of them in a different disk partition prevents a file or directory from growing uncontrollably, absorbing all of its available disk storage, and thus causing a crisis for the operating system. Each of the individual partitions is still at risk. However, if any one of them fills, the operating system or application function using that partition will be affected, but the operating system should remain functional.

That, anyway, is the theory. Tragically, history reminds us that the theory did not successfully translate into practice in the case of the Titanic. What went wrong? A consecutive series of compartments flooded simultaneously, one overflowing into the next, drawing the ship down to its death. In the case of disk partitioning, it is impossible for data to overflow from one partition into another, should a partition become full. This is good, and it would appear that the Titanic principle should keep us safe from disaster.

Unfortunately however, certain partitions are more important and vulnerable than others by virtue of the data stored in them. Should any one of them fill, they could render the server effectively useless, and for all intents and purposes, sink the ship.

Understanding Red Hat Server Install Partitions

In order to see which are the important ones and why, consider the output of this *df* command:

```
$ df -k
Filesystem        1k-blocks      Used  Available  Use% Mounted on
/dev/hda8           256667      37773     205642   16% /
/dev/hda1            23302       2596      19503   12% /boot
/dev/hda6          1683960         44    1598372    1% /home
/dev/hda5          1683960     394984    1203432   25% /usr
/dev/hda7           256667       9197     234218    4% /var
```

This output comes from a machine installed by choosing the server installation option, which automatically divides the disk into these five partitions seen in the listing. Looking at this output, it is important to realize that there is an emerging standard for the layout of directories and their contents on a Linux system, the Linux Standard Base (LSB) project. Visit www.linuxbase.org and the objective is revealed: "The goal of the Linux Standard Base is to develop and promote a set of standards that will increase compatibility among Linux distributions and enable software applications to run on any compliant Linux system." The LSB is supported by Red Hat as well as all of the other major Linux distributors, both commercial and noncommercial. Hence, distributions produced by any of the LSB partners would be expected to follow the standard as closely as is viable.

A major component of the LSB is the Filesystem Hierarchy Standard (FHS). The FHS is a project that originated back in 1993 as an effort to reorganize and develop a standard for the directory structure of a Linux installation. Currently, the FHS project includes not only Linux, but also contributors from BSD UNIX variants, and the goal is to generate a standard for anything calling itself open source UNIX. The FHS is intended to specify "a standard file system hierarchy for FHS filesystems by specifying the location of files and directories, and the contents of some system files." The current version is FHS 2.1, and can be found at www.pathname.com/fhs. I'm going to look at each of the file systems in the *df* listing in turn. As Red Hat Linux does claim to support the FHS, I will use the FHS standard itself as a guide to the contents of each file system.

The root File System

The first partition in the listing is mounted at the root directory of the logical file system, and is termed the root file system. According to the FHS 2.1 standard: "The contents of the root file system should be adequate to boot, restore, recover, and/or repair the system. To boot a system, enough must be present on the root partition to mount other file systems. This includes utilities, configuration, boot loader information, and other essential start-up data. */usr*, */opt*, and */var* are designed such that they may be located on other partitions or file systems. To enable recovery and/or repair of a system, those utilities needed by an experienced maintainer to diagnose and reconstruct a damaged system should be present on the root file system. To restore a system, those utilities needed to restore from system backups (on floppy, tape, and so on) should be present on the root file system."

The root file system is usually implemented as a small partition. There are several arguments in favor of a small root file system. From a reliability standpoint the most compelling are that in an emergency recovery case I may have to mount the root file system from removable media, hence the smaller the better. Ideally, it should fit on a floppy, which it usually does. Also, as the root file system contains system critical files (such as the kernel itself, boot loader information, and most of the operating system configuration files) data corruption in the root file system can cause havoc. The smaller the file system structure, the less prone it will be to corruption in case of a crash.

You should be conscious of what goes in the root file system and what does not. You want to keep it small, and focused on booting the operating system only. Let me give you some examples. The FHS defines the subdirectories of the root file system thus:

/	The root directory
/bin	Essential command binaries
/boot	Static files of the boot loader
/dev	Device files
/etc	Host-specific system configuration
/home	User home directories (empty)
/lib	Essential shared libraries and kernel modules
/mnt	Mount point for mounting a file system temporarily (empty)
/opt	Add-on application software packages (empty)
/root	Home directory for the root user

/sbin Essential system binaries

/tmp Temporary files

/usr Secondary hierarchy (empty)

/var Variable data (empty)

Keeping in mind these directories, here are some root file system dos and don'ts:

If you want to automate the process of recovering the system from a backup in case of emergency, you will need to write a script. I'll talk about such scripts in Chapter 7, "Backup and Recovery Strategies." The best place to store that script would be in */sbin*. Then make a boot diskette that contains the root file system and your recovery script. The Bootdisk HOWTO outlines procedures for creating such a boot/root diskette. There are also some generic rescue disk images in the public domain; one of the more popular ones, tomsrtbt, was built by Tom Oehser. You can get it from www.toms.net/rb. It is based on an older 2.0 series kernel, but should still work fine in a rescue context. Add your own restore scripts to this rescue diskette and you can boot and restore the machine to a new disk using only the boot/root diskette and a backup tape.

Many administrative scripts need to run with *root* privilege. If one of these scripts generates output, it is tempting to direct the output to a file in *root*'s home directory. As *root*'s home directory is normally located in the root file system, doing this is a bad idea. Logs of any sort have a nasty habit of growing, and growing files in the root file system are not good. The root file system is small, and, if it fills, the operating system can be seriously affected. The proper place for logs is in the */var* file system, as shown shortly.

You will notice that several of the directories in the root file system are flagged as empty (specifically, */home*, */mnt*, */opt*, */usr*, and */var*). These exist purely to be mount points for other file systems and no data should be stored in them. If one of these other file system mounts fail for any reason, it is possible for processes to write to the directory anyway, placing the data in the wrong disk partition and potentially filling the root file system.

The default Red Hat server install includes */tmp* in the root file system. Many administrators, myself included, like to see */tmp* placed in a separate partition. All too often I have run across applications that demand substantial amounts of space in */tmp* for all sorts of reasons.

They really should use /var, but they don't. You have two choices. You can create a separate file system for /tmp, or you could make /tmp a symbolic link to /var/tmp. The FHS defines /var/tmp as temporary storage space that survives a reboot, where data in /tmp is not guaranteed to survive a reboot. If this distinction is important to you, then go with a separate partition for /tmp. In a Red Hat installation you need to use the custom install option, as the server install does not give you the option of creating your own partitions. The server install is fine if you want to make /tmp a link to /var/tmp, although strictly speaking that would violate the FHS standard.

The /boot *File System*

The next file system to be mounted after root is /boot. According to the FHS, "This directory contains everything required for the boot process except configuration files and the map installer. This may include saved master boot sectors, sector map files, and other data that is not directly edited by hand." Why the separate file system? The FHS goes on to comment, "On some i386 machines, it may be necessary for /boot to be located on a separate partition located completely below cylinder 1024 of the boot device due to hardware constraints."

The hardware constraint they speak of is the limitation in the ability of older BIOS firmware code to address anything beyond block 1024 of a disk. This is primarily an ATA disk issue, as Linux has supported larger SCSI disks for a long time now. The kernel is stored in /boot, and during the boot process the BIOS needs to be able to read all of the data blocks of the kernel from disk into real memory, before the kernel actually begins to run. If the BIOS can only address up to block 1024, then you must ensure that no part of the kernel is stored above that point on the disk. The standard way to do that is to make a separate partition for /boot, and make it the first partition on the drive. If you look at my *df* output, you will see that the server install has done just that, creating /boot on /dev/hda1, the first partition on the disk.

There is quite a history to this, which Andries Brouwer has done an excellent job explaining in his *Large Disk HOWTO*. The short story is that this is largely an issue with older machines. In most cases involving modern BIOS firmware (I define modern in this case as after January 2000), an up-to-date kernel (2.2.14 or later, use *cat /proc/version* to determine your running kernel version), and *lilo* (version 21.4 or later, *lilo -V* reports your *lilo* version), it should *not* be necessary to create a separate /boot partition. These current code levels use a disk-addressing scheme independent of the actual physical geometry of the disk, which is where the old limitations lie.

This geometrically independent addressing scheme is selected by the *lba32* option in your */etc/lilo.conf* file, as in this sample:

```
boot=/dev/hda
map=/boot/map
install=/boot/boot.b
prompt
timeout=50
message=/boot/message
lba32
default=linux

image=/boot/vmlinuz-2.2.16-22
        label=linux
        read-only
        root=/dev/hda2
        append="mem=256M"
```

If you already have *lilo* installed, make sure you reinstall it (just issue the *lilo* command as root) after you edit */etc/lilo.conf,* and then reboot to make sure it is working. I trust it goes without saying that this would be a good time to have your boot/root diskette handy, just in case it isn't.

If the BIOS, kernel, and *lilo* are all up-to-date, and you are using linear addressing for the boot map, the only remaining problem you could see concerns ATA drives larger than 33.8 GB. In some cases, even fairly recent BIOS code cannot boot from these drives, though Linux itself has no problem with them. If in doubt, contact the manufacturer of your motherboard and ensure that its BIOS will support booting from these large ATA drives.

Having said all this, if you have an older machine with an ATA boot disk, it certainly does not hurt to create a separate */boot* partition, though it may not actually be necessary. It shouldn't prevent you from using the Red Hat server install, if the convenience of that option works for you.

The /home *File System*

Next to be mounted is */home*. The FHS definition for the content and usage of */home* is so loose as to hardly be a specification at all. It reads,

> */home* is a fairly standard concept, but it is clearly a site-specific file system. The setup will differ from host to host. This section describes only a suggested placement for user home directories; nevertheless we recommend that all FHS-compliant distributions use this as the default location for home directories. Different people prefer to place user accounts in a variety of places. Therefore, no program should rely on this location.

According to this, the standard for *home* can differ from server to server, and cannot be relied upon. Doesn't seem like much of a standard to me! The problem the authors of the FHS have run up against here is one of history. The directory location for home directories has been different in just about every major UNIX variant. I have seen */u*, */usr/home*, */usr/users* used as well as */home* in systems I have worked with in the past. It seems that the authors of the FHS can only hope that their standard will be picked up. I for one am all for it, and where I have a choice I will use */home*!

Perhaps a more important issue surrounding */home* is not so much where the data gets stored so much as what gets stored in a user home directory. Strictly speaking, the */home* file system is personal storage space for users. User, however, does not necessarily mean flesh and blood login user. It can be that a user account is required by an application, which uses the users home directory to store either the applications binaries (rare) or its data (not so rare). Also, accounts may be necessary to support application or database developers and maintainers. Those users may use their home directories to store no end of interesting things, up to and including entire test versions of an application or sample databases. (Remember Campbell's Law of Disks, "user data expands to fill the space available for its storage.") This can quite easily become a substantial disk space requirement. In short, if there isn't a well-defined place for data to go, it often ends up in a home directory. Remember this when setting aside space for */home* in your disk budget.

Finally, remember from the discussion of the root file system earlier I noted that root's home directory is not */home/root*, but */root*, placing it in the root file system rather than the */home* file system. As the primary administrative account, *root* can at times generate large amounts of log or debugging data that has to get written somewhere. Do not get into the habit of writing such output into *root*'s home directory, as it risks filling the root file system, and that is a *bad thing*.

The /usr *File System*

The FHS defines */usr* thus: "*/usr* is shareable, read-only data. That means that */usr* should be shareable between various hosts running FHS-compliant [sic] and should not be written to. Any information that is host-specific or varies with time is stored elsewhere."

Read-only data implies that none of the data stored in *usr* changes while the operating system is running. The FHS specifies the following subdirectories under *usr*:

SUB-DIRECTORY	DESCRIPTION
bin	Most user commands
games	Games and educational binaries
include	Header files included by C programs
lib	Libraries
local	Local hierarchy (empty after main installation)
sbin	Non-vital system binaries
share	Architecture-independent data
src	Source code

This adds up to the majority of the operating system installation, with the exception of the ambiguous definition for */usr/local*. As */usr* contains only read-only data, you should be able to mount */usr* as a read-only file system, which you can. This is a plus for reliability, as it prevents both filling the file system as well as tampering, deliberately or accidentally, with any of the data in it. To mount */usr* read only, you will need to edit the file system table, */etc/fstab*. Your default entry in */etc/fstab* for */usr* will be similar to this:

```
LABEL=/usr   /usr    ext2    defaults   1 2
```

Add the read only option like this:

```
LABEL=/usr   /usr    ext2    defaults,ro   1 2
```

Now */usr* will be mounted read only at the next boot. If you do this, it does mean that in order to install, uninstall, or patch any packages having files under */usr* you will need to remount the file system read-write, like this:

```
# mount -o remount,rw /usr
```

After you have done your maintenance, remount it read-only like this:

```
# mount -o remount,defaults,ro /usr
```

This should not affect running production processes, as they should never be trying to write to */usr* anyway. But, do reboot and thoroughly test your applications to make sure that a read-only */usr* will not break anything. Just because applications are not *supposed* to write into */usr* doesn't mean they don't. For example, the default Red Hat install rebuilds the *whatis* database each night. Since the *whatis* database files are held in */usr*, mounting */usr* read only will result in errors mailed to *root*, as the *makewhatis* command will return a write error. To fix this, remove the *makewhatis.cron* scripts from */etc/cron.daily* and */etc/cron.weekly* directories. If you find *whatis* useful, and you still want it updated, or there is some other functionality you need that requires */usr* to be writeable, you can always temporarily remount it read write, as I have shown.

WHAT IS *whatis* ANYWAY?

The *whatis* database is created by extracting the description line from the NAME section of each man page. The descriptions are collated into a single file, */usr/share/man/whatis*. This file can then be searched by keyword to locate man pages that may be appropriate to the keyword. The search is performed by the commands *man -k*, *apropos*, or *whatis*. All three commands are equivalent.

For example, if I want man pages concerning mounting file systems, I could try one of the following:

```
$ man -k mount
$ apropos mount
```

Either of them gives this partial output:

```
free            (1)  - Display amount of free and used memory in the system
mklost+found    (8)  - create a lost+found directory on a mounted Linux
second extended file system
mount           (2)  - mount and unmount filesystems
mount           (8)  - mount a file system mounted with ncpmount
rpc.mountd [mountd]  (8)  - NFS mount daemon
rpc.mountd [rpc]     (8)  - NFS mount daemon
showmount       (8)  - show mount information for an NFS server
sleep           (1)  - delay for a specified amount of time
smbmnt          (8)  - helper utility for mounting SMB filesystems
smbmount        (8)  - mount an SMB filesystem
smbspool        (8)  - mount an SMB filesystem
smbumount       (8)  - umount for normal users
umount          (8)  - unmount file systems
usermount       (1)  - A graphical tool to mount, unmount and format
filesystems
```

The bracketed number represents the volume number in the inline manual. For instance, in the case of the *mount* command, there are two man pages, one in volume two, documenting the source code mount function call, and the other in volume eight, documenting the command line directive to mount a physical file system. To read the volume two entry, I would issue

```
$ man 2 mount
```

Either of the following will give you the volume eight page:

```
$ man 8 mount
$ man mount
```

The default volume section search order is given by the *MANSECT* directive in the file */etc/man.config*.
In these days of hypertext everything, this may seem crude, but it just plain works and there are few days that pass when I don't still use it at least once or twice. It can be especially helpful if you are in a bind trying to get a machine up and running and that machine either doesn't have a graphical interface, or you are trying to fix it.

When you budget disk space for */usr*, leave room for expansion. It is certain that you will be adding something there next week. Something always crops up that needs to be installed. Patches for a certainty are one. If there is insufficient space in the */usr* file system, the partition */usr* resides in will need to be expanded, requiring the adjacent partition to be equally reduced in size. That may in turn constrain the space available for the file system in the adjacent partition. This domino effect usually escalates into something pretty close to an operating system reinstallation—obviously not good for uptime.

It would be wonderful if there were some way of dynamically extending a partition. Fortunately, there is. It's called Logical Volume Management (LVM). It's in the v2.4 kernel and is discussed in Chapter 8, "Logical Volume Management." If your server disk requirements, operating system, application binaries, and data lie below the 30–50 GB range, however, you can build a reasonably reliable system without going into the extra complexity of LVM. LVM is nice, though, and once you've used it, you may have trouble living without it.

The vaguely defined */usr/local* will conclude our discussion on */usr*. The FHS defines */usr/local* to contain local hierarchy. Traditionally, */usr/local* is where most non-operating system application code (and sometimes also configuration files) is installed. It is also where many system administrators will locate their own local administrative shell scripts. If /usr is implemented within a single-disk partition, this leads to operating system code and application code getting stored together on the same drive, weakening the positive effect of the Titanic principle.

To help with this issue, the FHS defines /opt as follows: "/opt is reserved for the installation of add-on application software packages. A package to be installed in /opt shall locate its static files in a separate /opt/<package> directory tree, where <package> is a name that describes the software package."

This means that /opt becomes to applications what /usr is to the operating system. Like /usr, /opt should be static and predictable in size. It also allows you the option of creating /opt as a separate file system, which can be mounted read only, and maintained independently of /usr. This allows for a nice separation between the application and the operating system. With /opt on a separate drive from the rest of the operating system, you could remove the application drive from a server with a failed operating system and easily move it to a backup server. Additionally, each package is nicely organized into its own subdirectory tree, which would allow you to further subdivide storage, should you so desire, and make applications individually portable. It is my fond hope that the application code that today goes somewhere under /usr/local should in the future increasingly be found in /opt, as distros and application packagers adopt the FHS standard.

The /var File System

The last file system in my listing is /var. According to the FHS, "/var contains variable data files. This includes spool directories and files, administrative and logging data, and transient and temporary files."

So, /var holds volatile data such as incoming mailboxes, application data cache files, log and print spool files. You need to consider the fact that production mishaps are likely to cause any of these files to balloon in size. If a physical printer were to fail, for instance, queues serving that printer might continue to accept jobs. With today's Postscript and PCL files, that can quickly add up to a lot of data. Because Web content also tends to be volatile, the default Apache Web server installation places the html content it serves in the directory /var/www. So, If I were to set up a Web server that supports a printer and someone uploads hundreds of MPEGs to the Web site, /var could fill, preventing the processing of print jobs. In this case, something that went wrong on the Web server had an effect on printing, an entirely unrelated service. Though strictly speaking the machine is not down, nobody can print or upload additional files to the Web server, so the Web server is not fully functional, either.

How can I protect myself? If there is substantial print and Web content, I might want to create a separate disk partition for each data category. I would have to prepare a disk budget to estimate how much space the printer and Web server would need, and then project how that requirement will grow with time. Preparing an initial estimate is usually not too hard, and of course disk space today is cheap. 40 GB and larger drives are becoming commonplace on home computers, never mind commercial server machines, and it is tempting to simply buy a big disk and assume you will never run out of space. But never say never. It is amazing how fast a disk can fill.

Consider monitoring disk usage by users. This can be done using disk quotas. Separately, you can provide individual users or groups a quota of disk space on a per-file-system basis. The operating system then monitors usage and prevents users and groups from exceeding this quota. Maintenance of this system is not burdensome, and the processing doesn't require excessive overhead. Where quotas are placed on application disk usage, it is possible to cause problems for the applications, but it is usually preferable to running out of space entirely. Chapter 6, "Monitoring Linux in Production," describes how to implement disk quotas.

Logs are an important category of growing files that reside in */var*. Many system logs reside in */var/log* and need proper management. If the concern

---

DISKS: IS BIGGER REALLY BETTER?

Large disks can pose a threat to reliability. Although it may not seem reasonable at first, one of the cornerstones of server reliability is that many pieces of hardware are preferable to a few. The more hardware, the more likely there will be failures. However, whether there are 5 pieces of hardware or 50, you *will* have a failure over time. If your business relies on only five pieces of hardware, you will lose at least one fifth of your capacity when one of them breaks—quite possibly more if there is a domino effect on the remaining hardware. If the same processing load were spread over 50 pieces of hardware, you would lose only one fiftieth of you processing capability. If those pieces of hardware involved some redundancy, such as RAID arrays, you may in fact lose none of your capacity, which is much more encouraging. So, never use one disk when you can use two.

The downside of this appears as disks get larger, and you buy far more disk space than needed to achieve the advantage of physical device redundancy.

is to avoid filling the file system, you could choose to reduce or eliminate logging altogether. This would avoid filling a partition with logs, but it would also throw away one of the most important tools for trouble diagnosis, and the ability to fix problems quickly and efficiently is clearly central to keeping a server reliably up.

The solution is to enable logging and manage the resulting log files properly. Linux provides the *logrotate* utility to do this. The man page for *logrotate* reads: "It [*logrotate*] allows automatic rotation, compression, removal, and mailing of log files. Each log file may be handled daily, weekly, monthly, or when it grows too large."

In a Red Hat installation, a script in */etc/cron.daily* runs a *logrotate* command once every 24 hours. Yet, you will find that logs are not necessarily rotated daily. The rotation criteria as well as other *logrotate* options are governed by the configuration file */etc/logrotate.conf*. There is an excellent explanation and example of this file in the man page for *logrotate*. I can't improve on it, so I'm not going to try. In short, the configuration file is used to tell *logrotate* how often to rotate specifically named log files. It also allows for rotation based on size rather than age, as well as compressing the old logs, automatically naming them sequentially, mailing them to a user, running an arbitrary pre- or post-rotation script, as well as a number of other more obscure options. There isn't much you can do with a log file that isn't covered.

The default */etc/logrotate.conf* file looks like this:

```
# see "man logrotate" for details
# rotate log files weekly
weekly

# keep 4 weeks worth of backlogs
rotate 4

# send errors to root
errors root

# create new (empty) log files after rotating old ones
create

# uncomment this if you want your log files compressed
#compress

# RPM packages drop log rotation information into this directory
include /etc/logrotate.d

# no packages own lastlog or wtmp -- we'll rotate them here
/var/log/wtmp {
```

```
        monthly
        create 0664 root utmp
        rotate 1
}

# system-specific logs may be configured here
```

Notice the line *include /etc/logrotate.d*. This directory contains files in *logrotate.conf* syntax. Each file is part of an *rpm* package that produces logs that need managing. This allows the packager to ensure that their logs are properly managed. This is generally a *good thing* for server reliability. It also allows you a standard framework to control these logs yourself, if you need to alter the default log management. As the system login record */var/log/wtmp* turns out not to be owned by any *rpm*, a stanza to handle this file needs to go into */etc/logrotate.conf*. If you have applications whose logs need managing, and which are not packaged as an *rpm*, or their *rpm* does not include a *logrotate* configuration file to go into */etc/logrotate.d*, then you will need to add a stanza or stanzas as necessary at the end of */etc/logrotate.conf*.

At the end of the previous section on */usr* I told you about the */opt* directory. The FHS also defines a */var/opt* directory, like this,

> Variable data of the packages in */opt* should be installed in */var/opt/<package>*, where *<package>* is the name of the sub tree in */opt* where the static data from an add-on software package is stored.

This centralizes application data into one standard location, retrieving it from */home* and the various other places where it can be found on many servers today. Dynamic data is well suited to the */var* file system, as I already know to manage the contents of */var* as dynamic, transient data. Also, like */opt*, the use of the *<package>* subtree structure allows me to separate data from one application cleanly from another, allowing me the option of implementing */var/opt/<package x>* and */var/opt/<package y>* in separate partitions, or even separate drives altogether.

Dealing with File System Mounting Errors

What can you do if a problem arises mounting a file system? When you boot a server, typically all of the file systems the server will be using get mounted as part of the boot process. Also, any applications that will run on the server start up as part of the boot process. What would happen if a data file system needed by an application failed to mount, but the application started up anyway? At best, the application would crash, or not work properly. Either of these possibilities would be obvious enough to alert you that something was wrong and to start investigating, although this has already cost you downtime. What if, however, the application doesn't crash, but continues to run, and, as critical data is missing, causes damage? It could, for example, generate large amounts of error messages. It could loop trying to access the missing data and effectively tie up all of the CPU resource on the server. In the worst case, a weakly coded application could decide to print 12,000 blank invoices.

Although it may seem logical, it does not necessarily follow that an application that will run on a server should be started automatically on boot. If you do want an application to start automatically, it is a good idea to ensure that the script starting them carefully checks each resource the application needs. Whether it be a mounted data file system, network connectivity, or whatever, check that the required resources are available before the application is started. Although it may seem inconvenient, some server administrators make this a manual process. You will need to ensure that all application data that needs to be restored has been restored before starting the application. After a crash there may be some other manual operations that have to be performed on the data before the application can safely use it.

Here is a *bash* script fragment you can use to test for the existence of a mount of partition */dev/sdb2* before starting your application:

```
1 mount | grep "/dev/sdb2" > /dev/null 2>&1
2 RETVAL=$?
3 if [ $RETVAL -eq 0 ]
4 then
5    <command(s) to start your application goes here>
6 else
7    echo "Partition /dev/sdb2 not mounted, cannot start application"
8 fi
```

The return code from the pipe at line 1 (assigned to *RETVAL* at line 2) will be a success if *grep* can find the string */dev/sdb2* in the output from the *mount* command. The return code is tested at line 3. If it is successful, your application will be started; otherwise, any nonzero return code results in an error message. If you need to test the availability of another server on the network, say a machine called *tux*, you could use this fragment:

```
1 ping -c1 tux > /dev/null 2>&1
2 RETVAL=$?
3 if [ $RETVAL -eq 0 ]
```

```
4 then
5    <command(s) to start your application goes here>
6 else
7    echo "Server tux not responding, cannot start application"
8 fi
```

This fragment is similar in operation to the previous one. If the *ping* at line 1 is successful, *RETVAL* will equal zero and the *if* clause will start your application; otherwise, an error message results. Note, this assumes that if the machine responds to a ping, then the required service is on that machine and is available. That may not necessarily be so. If the kernel is running enough to support IP, then the machine will ping. There may still be serious problems elsewhere on the machine that make it incapable of anything much other than pinging. If you need to determine for certain that your application is available, you need to replace the ping with an appropriate command that will return success if your application is working.

What can you do if the file system cannot be mounted because it contains errors? This situation could arise as a result of a crash in that the default Linux *ext2* file system is not fault tolerant. That is, should a system crash occur while there were file system transactions in process, both the file systems data or metadata can be damaged, possibly irreparably. In this case the file system checker, *e2fsck,* must be run on the file system. Normally, the *mount* command will detect this situation when it tries to read the primary file system superblock (see the following sidebar for more about superblocks) and automatically run *e2fsck*. If this happens, either you will have a few minor errors that are not fatal or the file system will be significantly corrupted and likely not worth the time to salvage.

**THE *ext2* FILE SYSTEM UNDER THE HOOD:
DATA, METADATA, AND SUPERBLOCKS**

While the *ext2* file system was developed by and for the Linux community, it is based on the file system structure developed in the earliest days of UNIX. It uses the concept of an i-node table to index data into files and directories. An i-node is a small (128-byte) data entity. Each file is assigned an i-node, which contains all the data the file system needs to store concerning the file, including ownership, permissions, date stamps, and the logical addresses of the data blocks that hold the actual data content of the file. The data held in the i-node is not truly part of the data of the file itself, yet it is essential if the file system is to manage the file. Such data is called metadata.

Along with the i-node table, another metadata object is the superblock. This contains summary information about the file system. Several parameters can be set in the superblock that have a bearing on uptime. First, you need to use the *dumpe2fs* command to look at the current superblock, like this:

```
# dumpe2fs /dev/hda5
dumpe2fs 1.18, 11-Nov-1999 for EXT2 FS 0.5b, 95/08/09
Filesystem volume name:    /boot
Last mounted on:           <not available>
Filesystem UUID:           bf94ffe0-14ad-11d5-9b64-c81790a1523f
Filesystem magic number:   0xEF53
Filesystem revision #:     1 (dynamic)
Filesystem features:       filetype sparse_super
Filesystem state:          not clean
Errors behavior:                   Continue
Filesystem OS type:        Linux
Inode count:               5688
Block count:               22680
Reserved block count:              1134
Free blocks:               19478
Free inodes:               5661
First block:               1
Block size:                1024
Fragment size:             1024
Blocks per group:          8192
Fragments per group:       8192
Inodes per group:          1896
Inode blocks per group:    237
Last mount time:           Thu Mar 22 08:51:40 2001
Last write time:           Thu Mar 22 08:51:43 2001
Mount count:                       3
Maximum mount count:               20
Last checked:                      Mon Mar 19 09:50:16 2001
Check interval:                    15552000 (6 months)
Next check after:                  Sat Sep 15 10:50:16 2001
Reserved blocks uid:               0 (user root)
Reserved blocks gid:               0 (group root)
First inode:               11
Inode size:                128
```

Note the lines in bold. The Errors behavior parameter controls what the kernel will do should it detect a file system error. The default is simply to log the error, but continue to write to the file system. You may want a higher degree of protection for a critical file system by changing this to cause the kernel to remount the file system read only or cause a full-scale kernel panic. If desired, use the *tune2fs* command to change this parameter as follows:

```
# tune2fs -e remount-ro /dev/hda5
```

The superblock also keeps track of the number of times the file system has been mounted, with the objective of forcing a file system check after either a set number of mounts, or after a defined period of time has elapsed. Hence in my example, mount count of 3 indicates that this file system has been mounted three times since the last check, and maximum mount count of 20 indicates that when the mount count reaches the 20th mount, a check will be forced. Notwithstanding the mount count, the check interval determines that checks shall be performed every six months, as seen in the last checked and next check after parameters.

How does this affect reliability? Some conservative administrators like to check a file system every time it is mounted, or at frequent time intervals. While there is no clear argument proving the utility of frequent checks, it certainly cannot hurt. The other issue can affect booting. If the file system is large, a check can take several minutes, measurably delaying the boot process. If you have lost track of the mount count, this can take you by surprise. Also, if there is any problem found, the check will by default prompt you at the console for direction as to how to proceed, which will completely hang the boot until someone responds. You can change these parameters with the *tune2fs* command also. To set the maximum mount count to 10, for example

```
# tune2fs -c10 /dev/hda5
```

To set the check interval to 14 days, use

```
# tune2fs -i14d /dev/hda5
```

Finally, to protect the file system from filling completely, which can result in metadata corruption when processes continue to try to write to a full file system, a number of data blocks are set aside as reserved blocks. When all but these blocks have been used, the *df* command will indicate the file system to be 100 percent full, and no further allocation will be possible. The only user who can access these reserved blocks is the one listed in the superblock as the reserved blocks uid-root (uid=0) by default. The reserved block count parameter indicates how many blocks have been reserved, the default is 5 percent of the total number of blocks. This is a small price to pay to protect the file system from exhausting all disk space. The following command reserves 100 blocks:

```
# tune2fs -r100 /dev/hda5
```

If there was any significant amount of activity in the file system at the point of the crash, it is almost certain that you will have lost all of the data held in the file system buffer cache, as well as having to deal with metadata inconsistencies leading to orphaned file data blocks and other often irrecoverable inconsistencies. Because you usually have little way of knowing what files may have had pending writes at the time of the crash, or what metadata changes may have been underway, it is impracticable to determine which files may have been corrupted by the crash. In short, no file can be trusted any longer. It hurts, but the only real solution is to restore the entire file system from a backup. You can run *e2fsck* and it will clean up the file system metadata structure, but as you cannot trust the data integrity of the files, it would be dangerous to put that file system back into production. You could wind up causing more problems than you solve.

There is a way to protect yourself in such cases through the use of journalling file systems rather than the *ext2* file system. Chapter 9, "Alternative File Systems," presents several options for a Linux journal file system.

Sample Server Scenarios

Now, let's draw this together with some examples. So far, I've been using the partition structure from a standard Red Hat server type install. If I move beyond this and implement some other options, what would be the results?

Small Single-Disk Example

First, let's look at the case of a smaller server. In this scenario, you have been asked to build a Samba file and print server for a group of Windows clients. The server also functions as the network gateway for these clients to the Internet. To reduce the bandwidth requirement for the Internet connection, the server implements a caching proxy Web server, which will store and then locally serve frequently accessed Web pages to reduce the amount of traffic on the outgoing network.

A disk budget indicates that there is currently 5 GB of user data that the Samba file server needs to support. Statistics from the current print server indicate that at peak usage the printer turns out two pages per minute. The pages are graphics intensive, however, and on average each page represents 250 KB of data. If the printer should go down for an hour at this peak time, then, the print server needs to have at least 60×250 KB $\times 2$ (30 MB) of spool space to cope. You are not really sure how much cache space you should allow for the Web server, as this is a new thing and no historical data is available. You guess at 10 MB, but want to leave extra space in case you find in production that more would be useful.

RELIABLE PRINTING

My single-disk example includes printing as a server function. This is a common, if not the most common, function required of a network server. With the addition of Samba to support Windows clients, Linux makes an excellent print server. Back in the early days of UNIX at Berkeley, a network printing communication protocol was developed called *lpd*. This protocol became a de facto standard, eventually codified in RFC 1179. Linux distros today commonly include some version of this original print spooler code. A great deal of water has passed below the bridge since this code first saw the light of day, however, and what you get today varies widely. Grant Taylor in his *Printing HOWTO* writes "There are a large number of LPD sources floating around in the world. Arguably, some strain of BSD UNIX is probably the official owner, but everyone implements changes willy-nilly, and they all cross-pollinate in unknown ways, such that it is difficult to say with certainty exactly which LPD you might have."

Later on, he describes the code base for *lpd* as "frightfully haphazard." As you can imagine, this tends not to lead to a stable print server.

You may want to consider two alternatives. The *lpd* standard is very widely implemented, and most client platforms, Windows included, supply *lpd* clients. If for these reasons you wish to stick to the *lpd* standard, consider the *LPRng* package.

Taylor writes "*LPRng* is a far better implementation of the basic LPD design than the regular one; if you must use LPD, consider using *LPRng* instead. There is far less voodoo involved in making it do what you want, and what voodoo is there is well documented."

In my observation, one of the strengths of *LPRng* is that it has far better logging than the stock *lpd*, and that has served me well in diagnosing production problems. And the voodoo is definitely better documented in *LPRng*. *LPRng* also provides a more secure service. It has no SUID binaries and supports authentication using PGP. If you use the Red Hat distro, you will find that at v7.0 Red Hat replaced their old *lpd* package with *LPRng*. If you are using a different distro, *LPRng* can be found at www.lprng.com.

Another option is an implementation of the new Internet Printing Protocol (IPP). IPP is an HTML-like protocol designed to replace *lpd*. It is defined in RFC2910, RFC2911 and various drafts. This is a new protocol (the current version of pertinent RFCs were published in late 2000), so it remains to be seen

> where it will go. It may gain momentum from the Simple Web Printing (SWP) protocol being developed by Microsoft and Hewlett-Packard. SWP is based on the same model and semantics as IPP, but is described as a "leaner subset" of a full IPP implementation. The only implementation of IPP I know of in the Linux world is the Common UNIX Printing System (CUPS) package, available from www.cups.org. Should SWP and IPP become more widely used, and should CUPS or some other IPP implementation gain an established track record in production, these may be the print servers to watch for in the future.

You have been given a server that is two years old and a budget to purchase a new, large disk. Shopping for disks, you discover that the smallest ATA drive you can source is 20 GB, which should be more than adequate. Table 4.1 suggests how you can partition that drive.

A /boot partition of 25 MB is more than adequate and 100 MB is sufficient for the root file system, so long as you are implementing all the other major file systems in separate partitions. Allowing 2 GB for /usr should allow for plenty of expansion beyond the applications you'll need at the outset. You should allow at least 40 MB of storage in /var to cover print spooling and Web caching. Allocate 2 GB to /var mostly because of a large drive relative to the storage needed to get the job done. The major block of storage is the 5 GB worth of samba data, which still leaves 16 GB available, adequate to satisfy normal data growth for several months at least. Finally, allocate space for swap space.

Table 4.1 Sample Single-Disk Server Disk Partitioning

PARTITION	SIZE	MOUNT POINT	OPTIONS	COMMENTS
/dev/hda1	25 MB	/boot	defaults	Must be the first partition on the drive
/dev/hda5	100 MB	/	defaults	
/dev/hda6	2 GB	/usr	defaults, ro	Need to add the ro option to /etc/fstab
/dev/hda7	2 GB	/var	defaults	httpd cache and logs
/dev/hda8	15.8 GB	/home/pcguest	defaults	Samba data storage
/dev/hda9	125 MB	swap	defaults	

Let us assume you create a *pcguest* user to own the samba data, which is commonly done in a Samba environment. You may also choose to have separate accounts for Windows users, allowing each of them to own files in */home*. In that case the separate file system for */home/pcguest* could be replaced by a */home* file system. You could then use disk quotas to control each user's disk usage.

What is to prevent the Web cache from filling */var*? Do you need to place some sort of quota on the *httpd*? If you use the Apache Web server, you will find that the size of the cache is controlled by the server's own configuration (note the *CacheSize* directive in */etc/httpd/conf/httpd.conf*). This is an example of a well-behaved application that can be trusted to manage its own data entities.

Be on the watch for less graceful applications that simply ask for more space until the operating system denies it, at which point the application may quit or crash. Whatever you decide in terms of space allocation, it is imperative that you monitor disk usage to ensure that you are not approaching the point of filling a disk partition, particularly in the case of the root file system. Scripts built around commands such as *df* and *du* will do that job, I'll be talking about them in Chapter 6.

It is useful to note that in this example you could use the Red Hat server install option. That would give you separate file systems for /, */boot*, */home*, */usr*, and */var*. The install divides the majority of the disk space between */usr* and */home*, which would work reliably since you could use disk quotas on */home* to control the disk used by your Samba users.

Larger Multidisk Example

In this example you have been asked to implement a large Web server. It will support up to 100 virtual Web sites. The owners of these sites will use *ftp* to upload content to their respective sites, but you need to be able to limit the total amount of space each site gets. Of the 100 sites, 75 are limited to 25 MB each, while the remaining 25 get 200 MB each. In addition, the machine will host an anonymous *ftp* server for a large archive of data, currently 15 GB in total. This is not a free archive: Customers must pay for the information they download. To manage this, your company has contracted a developer to write an application to handle accounting and billing for the downloaded data. That application needs to produce printed statements monthly for some 5,000 customers, whose profiles are managed in a database 200 MB in size, and growing.

For performance reasons you would be well advised to consider a SCSI disk for this machine. As a starting point, consider the three-drive layout shown in Table 4.2.

Table 4.2 Sample Multidisk Partition Layout

PARTITION	SIZE	MOUNT POINT	OPTIONS
Drive sda	**8 GB**		
/dev/sda1	150 MB	/	defaults
/dev/sda5	2.5 GB	/usr	defaults,ro
/dev/sda6	125 MB	swap 1	
/dev/sda7	2 GB	/home	defaults,usrquota
/dev/sda8	1 GB	/tmp	defaults
/dev/sda9	725 MB	/var	defaults
/dev/sda10	1.5 GB	/var/spool/lpd	defaults
Drive sdb	**12 GB**		
/dev/sdb1	1 GB	/var/opt	defaults
/dev/sdb2	10 GB	/home/virtuals	defaults,usrquota
/dev/sdb3	125 MB	swap 2	
/dev/sdb4	500 MB	/opt	defaults,ro
Drive sdc	**30 GB**		
/dev/sdc1	30 GB	/home/ftp	defaults

Again, the table proposes a small root partition on the first disk, *sda*. Now with a SCSI disk, the need for a */boot* partition at the beginning of the disk is eliminated as SCSI does not have the same BIOS limitations as ATA disks in this respect. Size *sda* as an 8 GB drive, which is reasonable, even small for a modern SCSI drive. With that amount of space available, allow 2.5 GB for */usr*. This should be enough for a Red Hat 7 installation, even if you install absolutely everything in the distribution. Take the precaution of creating a separate, generous partition for */tmp*. There is a fair amount of data on this machine and there is a good chance someone will want or need to shift it around one day. A separate file system for */tmp* allows for temporary scratch space without the risk of filling the root file system.

Separate */var* across two partitions, keeping in mind the print server requirement. If the worst happens and the printer crashes at the beginning of 5,000 month-end invoices, I want ample spool space in */var/spool/lpd* to allow the print server to spool those print jobs, letting the application continue undisturbed while I fix the printer. There is still space enough left to leave 725 MB for */var*, which should be plenty for logs and such, and keep the printing and logging space in separate compartments.

I hope I have enough pull with the developers to convince them to go with the FHS standard for data storage, hence the partition for */opt*, which you may note will be mounted read only. I would position */opt* on the second drive, *sdb*, along with the data. This completely separates the operating system and the application and makes *sdb* a portable, functional implementation of the entire application. This allows *sdb* to be moved to a backup server in case the operating system disk on this server fails. Keep in mind that this application depends on the anonymous *ftp* server provided by the operating system, so you need to ensure that the backup server has a properly configured *ftp* server.

Separate the data stored below */home* into three sections. General home directory storage resides on *sda*, while storage for the virtual Web sites will be under */home/virtuals* on *sdb*, so as to keep the production data off the operating system disk. Finally, */home/ftp* is for the 15 GB of anonymous ftp data, as anonymous ftp servers typically store their data in the *ftp* user's home directory */home/ftp*. This I have placed on *sdc*, a separate 30 GB drive, so as to allow room for the inevitable expansion of the ftp archive. Note the *usrquota* option in */etc/fstab* for */home/virtuals* to implement disk quotas to enforce the virtual Web site storage limits. Also on *sdb* is */var/opt*, where the database application stores its customer database.

Finally, *sdb* has a second swap space. This is for performance reasons—a trade-off. As a general rule, what you do to improve performance has a nasty habit of increasing failure vulnerability. The reverse also applies in that improved availability configurations often have a performance cost. In this case the improved performance of the dual swap spaces increases the liability in the case of disk failure. With dual swaps, if either *sda* or *sdb* fail, the kernel may crash. Only *sdc* is not a single point of failure. If performance is an issue, I may have to take this risk, unless I can find the budget to buy more real memory, with the aim of reducing or eliminating the need for the kernel to page at all.

Configuring Operating System Services

You now have an installed operating system with a disk layout designed for reliability. Other than that, all of the other configuration choices (and in any UNIX-based machine, there are many choices) still reflect the default values set by the installation process. When your server boots, a number of services are started that provide the basic support for running applications.

Which services should your server run, and are there any configuration parameters for these services that should be changed to reduce downtime liability? In the next few pages I am going to review several of the more commonly used operating system services, and look at how they can be configured to reduce downtime liability.

Understanding Run Levels

Just before I start, though, I want to make the point that a standard Red Hat installation will install and start services like *sendmail*, *portmap*, *lpd*, *identd*, *xfs* (the X font server), and others, depending on the packages you chose. Many of them may not be necessary for the functions your server needs to perform; running them anyway adds unnecessary, unproductive complication to the system and introduces more things to monitor and more things to go wrong. If you don't really need any of these utilities, don't run them. If you run a Red Hat distro, to control what runs or doesn't, you have to understand run levels.

The Red Hat distro makes use of the concept of operating system run levels derived from the original AT&T versions of UNIX. While this differs from the way that Berkeley UNIX works, and some argue it to be overly complicated, I prefer it in a production server as it enforces an order and discipline in the process of booting. It may seem complicated at first, but once you understand it, you have a standardized system for installing, starting, and stopping any operating system utility in a controlled order, which is useful when building a reliable server. Let's see how it works.

When the kernel boots, the first process started is process id #1, known as *init*. *init* has a configuration file, */etc/inittab*, in which there will be a line like this:

```
id:3:initdefault:
```

The 3 indicates that this system will boot into run level 3. To see what that means, go to the directory */etc/rc.d/rc3.d*. Note the 3 in that last subdirectory name. There are several other subdirectories at the same level, *rc1.d*, *rc2.d*, and so on, each corresponding to a different possible run level. If you examine the contents of these directories, you will see that they contain a group of symbolic links, similar to this:

```
# ls -l /etc/rc.d/rc3.d
lrwxrwxrwx    1 root     root     15 Apr 13 19:48 K01pppoe -> ../init.d/pppoe
lrwxrwxrwx    1 root     root     14 Apr 13 19:43 K05innd -> ../init.d/innd
lrwxrwxrwx    1 root     root     14 Apr 13 19:55 K10ntpd -> ../init.d/ntpd
lrwxrwxrwx    1 root     root     16 Apr 13 19:55 K15mysqld -> ../init.d/mysqld
```

```
lrwxrwxrwx   1 root    root    14 Apr 13 19:56 K15pvmd -> ../init.d/pvmd
lrwxrwxrwx   1 root    root    15 Apr 13 19:56 K16rarpd -> ../init.d/rarpd
lrwxrwxrwx   1 root    root    20 Apr 13 19:52 K20bootparamd -> ../init.d/bootparamd
lrwxrwxrwx   1 root    root    13 Apr 13 19:47 K20nfs -> ../init.d/nfs
lrwxrwxrwx   1 root    root    16 Apr 13 19:48 K20rstatd -> ../init.d/rstatd
lrwxrwxrwx   1 root    root    17 Apr 13 19:48 K20rusersd -> ../init.d/rusersd
lrwxrwxrwx   1 root    root    16 Apr 13 19:48 K20rwalld -> ../init.d/rwalld
lrwxrwxrwx   1 root    root    15 Apr 13 19:48 K20rwhod -> ../init.d/rwhod
lrwxrwxrwx   1 root    root    15 Apr 13 19:56 K25squid -> ../init.d/squid
lrwxrwxrwx   1 root    root    13 Apr 13 19:39 K28amd -> ../init.d/amd
lrwxrwxrwx   1 root    root    16 Apr 13 19:55 K30mcserv -> ../init.d/mcserv
lrwxrwxrwx   1 root    root    19 Apr 13 19:51 K34yppasswdd -> ../init.d/yppasswdd
lrwxrwxrwx   1 root    root    15 Apr 13 19:53 K35dhcpd -> ../init.d/dhcpd
lrwxrwxrwx   1 root    root    13 Apr 13 19:48 K35smb -> ../init.d/smb
lrwxrwxrwx   1 root    root    18 Apr 13 19:39 K45arpwatch -> ../init.d/arpwatch
lrwxrwxrwx   1 root    root    15 Apr 13 19:40 K45named -> ../init.d/named
lrwxrwxrwx   1 root    root    15 Apr 13 19:50 K50snmpd -> ../init.d/snmpd
lrwxrwxrwx   1 root    root    13 Apr 13 19:56 K54pxe -> ../init.d/pxe
lrwxrwxrwx   1 root    root    16 Apr 13 19:56 K55routed -> ../init.d/routed
lrwxrwxrwx   1 root    root    18 Apr 13 19:46 K60mars-nwe -> ../init.d/mars-nwe
lrwxrwxrwx   1 root    root    14 Apr 13 19:56 K61ldap -> ../init.d/ldap
lrwxrwxrwx   1 root    root    16 Apr 13 19:54 K65kadmin -> ../init.d/kadmin
lrwxrwxrwx   1 root    root    15 Apr 13 19:54 K65kprop -> ../init.d/kprop
lrwxrwxrwx   1 root    root    16 Apr 13 19:54 K65krb524 -> ../init.d/krb524
lrwxrwxrwx   1 root    root    17 Apr 13 19:54 K65krb5kdc -> ../init.d/krb5kdc
lrwxrwxrwx   1 root    root    13 Jun 28 12:06 K74ups -> ../init.d/ups
lrwxrwxrwx   1 root    root    15 Apr 13 19:53 K75gated -> ../init.d/gated
lrwxrwxrwx   1 root    root    14 Apr 13 19:55 K80nscd -> ../init.d/nscd
lrwxrwxrwx   1 root    root    16 Apr 13 19:51 K84ypserv -> ../init.d/ypserv
lrwxrwxrwx   1 root    root    14 Apr 13 19:43 K96irda -> ../init.d/irda
lrwxrwxrwx   1 root    root    15 Apr 13 19:46 S05kudzu -> ../init.d/kudzu
lrwxrwxrwx   1 root    root    18 Apr 13 19:39 S06reconfig -> ../init.d/reconfig
lrwxrwxrwx   1 root    root    18 Apr 13 19:43 S08ipchains -> ../init.d/ipchains
lrwxrwxrwx   1 root    root    17 Apr 13 19:39 S10network -> ../init.d/network
lrwxrwxrwx   1 root    root    16 Apr 13 19:39 S12syslog -> ../init.d/syslog
lrwxrwxrwx   1 root    root    17 Apr 13 19:47 S13portmap -> ../init.d/portmap
lrwxrwxrwx   1 root    root    17 Apr 13 19:47 S14nfslock -> ../init.d/nfslock
lrwxrwxrwx   1 root    root    14 Apr 13 19:39 S16apmd -> ../init.d/apmd
lrwxrwxrwx   1 root    root    16 Apr 13 19:52 S18autofs -> ../init.d/autofs
lrwxrwxrwx   1 root    root    16 Apr 13 19:39 S20random -> ../init.d/random
lrwxrwxrwx   1 root    root    15 Apr 13 19:39 S25netfs -> ../init.d/netfs
lrwxrwxrwx   1 root    root    16 Apr 13 19:47 S35identd -> ../init.d/identd
lrwxrwxrwx   1 root    root    13 Apr 13 19:40 S40atd -> ../init.d/atd
lrwxrwxrwx   1 root    root    16 Apr 13 19:45 S45pcmcia -> ../init.d/pcmcia
lrwxrwxrwx   1 root    root    16 Apr 13 19:39 S50xinetd -> ../init.d/xinetd
lrwxrwxrwx   1 root    root    14 Apr 13 19:47 S55sshd -> ../init.d/sshd
lrwxrwxrwx   1 root    root    20 Apr 13 19:39 S56rawdevices ->
../init.d/rawdevices
```

```
lrwxrwxrwx   1 root    root    16 Jun 16 15:51 S60arkeia -> ../init.d/arkeia
lrwxrwxrwx   1 root    root    13 Apr 13 19:46 S60lpd -> ../init.d/lpd
lrwxrwxrwx   1 root    root    18 Apr 13 19:40 S75keytable ->
../init.d/keytable
lrwxrwxrwx   1 root    root    14 Apr 13 19:43 S80isdn -> ../init.d/isdn
lrwxrwxrwx   1 root    root    18 Apr 13 19:48 S80sendmail ->
../init.d/sendmail
lrwxrwxrwx   1 root    root    13 Apr 13 19:43 S85gpm -> ../init.d/gpm
lrwxrwxrwx   1 root    root    15 Apr 13 19:39 S85httpd -> ../init.d/httpd
lrwxrwxrwx   1 root    root    15 Apr 13 19:39 S90crond -> ../init.d/crond
lrwxrwxrwx   1 root    root    13 Apr 13 19:39 S90xfs -> ../init.d/xfs
lrwxrwxrwx   1 root    root    17 Apr 13 19:39 S95anacron -> ../init.d/anacron
lrwxrwxrwx   1 root    root    15 Apr 13 19:50 S97rhnsd -> ../init.d/rhnsd
lrwxrwxrwx   1 root    root    19 Apr 13 19:46 S99linuxconf ->
../init.d/linuxconf
lrwxrwxrwx   1 root    root    11 Apr 13 19:39 S99local -> ../rc.local
```

You can see that each link has a similar naming format. The name begins with either S or K followed by a number and a service name. An S means that this service will start at this run level; the K ensures that the service will be killed, that is, inoperative at this run level. Each link points to a file in the directory */etc/rc.d/init.d*. These files are the scripts that will start or stop a particular operating system function defined by the service name.

Here is an example. */etc/rc.d/rc3.d* has a link called *S50xinetd* (shown in bold in the previous listing). That link points to */etc/rc.d/init.d/xinetd*, which if you look at it is a shell script containing a case statement that will start, stop, or restart the network super server daemon *xinetd*. If I want to start *xinetd*, I can issue that script with a command line argument *start*, like this:

```
# /etc/rc.d/init.d/xinetd start
```

A few lines below the initdefault line I just showed you in */etc/inittab* is this line:

```
l3:3:wait:/etc/rc.d/rc 3
```

This line tells *init* that when the run level is 3 (matching the second field), then run the script */etc/rc.d/rc*, passing it the argument 3. This script will descend into */etc/rc.d/rc3.d* (not *rc1.d* or *rc2.d* because the run level is 3, not 1 or 2), and sequentially execute each command in that directory in alphabetical order. Now we come to the significance of the S. If the link in *rc3.d* starts with an S, then the command run by */etc/rc.d/rc* will be passed the argument *start*; if the link begins with a K, it will be passed the argument *stop*. The result is that *init* issues this command:

```
# /etc/rc.d/rc3.d/S50xinetd start
```

But, I have shown that */etc/rc.d/rc3.d/S50xinetd* is really only a link to */etc/rc.d/init.d/xinetd*, so the command that is really being issued is

```
# /etc/rc.d/init.d/xinetd start
```

and you have already seen that this will start the *xinetd* daemon. Had the entry in */etc/rc.d/rc3.d* been called *K50xinetd*, then this command would have resulted:

```
# /etc/rc.d/init.d/xinetd stop
```

The only remaining question is, what about the 50? Why is there always a number in the name of the links in the run level subdirectories? Remember that when */etc/rc.d/rc* processes the run level directory, it does it in the alphabetical order that the links would sort to. Thus, the numbers can be manipulated to control the order in which services start or stop. This can be very important in some cases where one service depends on another. In the case of *nfs*, for example, it is critical that the *portmap* service starts before *nfs*, and so the order of the links must be crafted to ensure this. If you get this wrong, your server may not start necessary services, which equals downtime.

Conventionally, run level 3 is the run level used for normal server operations, including all applications that are expected to run on the server. Run level 5 normally starts the same services as run level 3, with the addition of a graphical environment started on the console. These are the most commonly used levels, although there are a few others defined at the beginning of */etc/inittab*. You can alter the conventional usage for any run level as desired. It is possible to switch between run levels while the server is running by issuing the command *init*, passing the desired run level as an argument. The *runlevel* command will tell me the previous and the current run levels. Here is an example:

```
# runlevel
N 3
# init 5
INIT: Switching to runlevel: 5
Starting X Font Server:                                    [  OK  ]
< other services stop or start here >
# runlevel
3 5
# init 3
INIT: Switching to runlevel: 3
Stopping X Font Server:                                    [  OK  ]
< other services stop or start here >
```

```
# runlevel
5 3
#
```

Run level 0 means stop everything, so the fastest safe way to bring the operating system down is to issue *init 0*. This does not, however, give logged-in users any warnings or time to complete work and it will halt the operating system entirely when the shutdown process is complete. You may prefer to use the *shutdown* command instead, which allows you to schedule the shutdown for a future time, broadcasts repeated messages to users warning of the impending shutdown, and can be directed to shut down to run level 1, if desired. Run level 1 is called single-user or maintenance mode. In this run level, only the core operating system kernel is running; there is no network connectivity and virtually no other services. This run level is useful for maintenance such as backups or repairing file systems.

Different run levels can be used as a means to start or stop applications. For instance, if the start scripts for you application are flagged with an S for run level 4 and a K for run level 3, then issuing *init 4* while in run level 3 would start the application, and could be followed by *init 3* to stop it.

To manage all of this structure reliably, the *chkconfig* command is provided. *chkconfig* can be used to list at what run levels each service will run and can be used to change the configuration. For example, using the *--list* flag returns a summary of the current configuration. With no further arguments, *chkconfig* will summarize all services and run levels, like this:

```
# chkconfig    --list
syslog        0:off   1:off   2:on    3:on    4:on    5:on    6:off
crond         0:off   1:off   2:on    3:on    4:on    5:on    6:off
netfs         0:off   1:off   2:off   3:on    4:on    5:on    6:off
network       0:off   1:off   2:on    3:on    4:on    5:on    6:off
random        0:off   1:off   2:on    3:on    4:on    5:on    6:off
rawdevices    0:off   1:off   2:off   3:on    4:on    5:on    6:off
xfs           0:off   1:off   2:on    3:on    4:on    5:on    6:off
amd           0:off   1:off   2:off   3:off   4:off   5:off   6:off
xinetd        0:off   1:off   2:off   3:on    4:on    5:on    6:off
reconfig      0:off   1:off   2:off   3:on    4:on    5:on    6:off
anacron       0:off   1:off   2:on    3:on    4:on    5:on    6:off
httpd         0:off   1:off   2:off   3:on    4:on    5:on    6:off
apmd          0:off   1:off   2:on    3:on    4:on    5:on    6:off
arpwatch      0:off   1:off   2:off   3:off   4:off   5:off   6:off
atd           0:off   1:off   2:off   3:on    4:on    5:on    6:off
named         0:off   1:off   2:off   3:off   4:off   5:off   6:off
keytable      0:off   1:off   2:on    3:on    4:on    5:on    6:off
gpm           0:off   1:off   2:on    3:on    4:on    5:on    6:off
innd          0:off   1:off   2:off   3:off   4:off   5:off   6:off
```

ipchains	0:off	1:off	2:on	3:on	4:on	5:on	6:off
irda	0:off	1:off	2:off	3:off	4:off	5:off	6:off
isdn	0:off	1:off	2:on	3:on	4:on	5:on	6:off
pcmcia	0:off	1:off	2:on	3:on	4:on	5:on	6:off
kdcrotate	0:off	1:off	2:off	3:off	4:off	5:off	6:off
kudzu	0:off	1:off	2:off	3:on	4:on	5:on	6:off
linuxconf	0:off	1:off	2:on	3:on	4:on	5:on	6:off
lpd	0:off	1:off	2:on	3:on	4:on	5:on	6:off
mars-nwe	0:off	1:off	2:off	3:off	4:off	5:off	6:off
nfs	0:off	1:off	2:off	3:off	4:off	5:off	6:off
nfslock	0:off	1:off	2:off	3:on	4:on	5:on	6:off
sshd	0:off	1:off	2:on	3:on	4:on	5:on	6:off
identd	0:off	1:off	2:off	3:on	4:on	5:on	6:off
portmap	0:off	1:off	2:off	3:on	4:on	5:on	6:off
postgresql	0:off	1:off	2:off	3:off	4:off	5:off	6:off
pppoe	0:off	1:off	2:off	3:off	4:off	5:off	6:off
rstatd	0:off	1:off	2:off	3:off	4:off	5:off	6:off
rusersd	0:off	1:off	2:off	3:off	4:off	5:off	6:off
rwalld	0:off	1:off	2:off	3:off	4:off	5:off	6:off
rwhod	0:off	1:off	2:off	3:off	4:off	5:off	6:off
smb	0:off	1:off	2:off	3:off	4:off	5:off	6:off
sendmail	0:off	1:off	2:on	3:on	4:on	5:on	6:off
snmpd	0:off	1:off	2:off	3:off	4:off	5:off	6:off
rhnsd	0:off	1:off	2:off	3:on	4:on	5:on	6:off
ypbind	0:off	1:off	2:off	3:off	4:off	5:off	6:off
yppasswdd	0:off	1:off	2:off	3:off	4:off	5:off	6:off
ypserv	0:off	1:off	2:off	3:off	4:off	5:off	6:off
autofs	0:off	1:off	2:off	3:on	4:on	5:on	6:off
bootparamd	0:off	1:off	2:off	3:off	4:off	5:off	6:off
ciped	0:off	1:off	2:off	3:off	4:off	5:off	6:off
dhcpd	0:off	1:off	2:off	3:off	4:off	5:off	6:off
gated	0:off	1:off	2:off	3:off	4:off	5:off	6:off
kadmin	0:off	1:off	2:off	3:off	4:off	5:off	6:off
kprop	0:off	1:off	2:off	3:off	4:off	5:off	6:off
krb524	0:off	1:off	2:off	3:off	4:off	5:off	6:off
krb5kdc	0:off	1:off	2:off	3:off	4:off	5:off	6:off
mcserv	0:off	1:off	2:off	3:off	4:off	5:off	6:off
mysqld	0:off	1:off	2:off	3:off	4:off	5:off	6:off
nscd	0:off	1:off	2:off	3:off	4:off	5:off	6:off
ntpd	0:off	1:off	2:off	3:off	4:off	5:off	6:off
ups	0:off	1:off	2:off	3:off	4:off	5:on	6:off
ldap	0:off	1:off	2:off	3:off	4:off	5:off	6:off
pvmd	0:off	1:off	2:off	3:off	4:off	5:off	6:off
pxe	0:off	1:off	2:off	3:off	4:off	5:off	6:off
rarpd	0:off	1:off	2:off	3:off	4:off	5:off	6:off
routed	0:off	1:off	2:off	3:off	4:off	5:off	6:off
squid	0:off	1:off	2:off	3:off	4:off	5:off	6:off
vncserver	0:off	1:off	2:off	3:off	4:off	5:off	6:off
vmware	0:off	1:off	2:off	3:off	4:off	5:on	6:off
arkeia	0:off	1:off	2:on	3:on	4:on	5:on	6:off

```
xinetd based services:
        amandaidx:      off
        amidxtape:      off
        finger: on
        linuxconf-web:  off
        rexec:   off
        rlogin: on
        rsh:     on
        swat:    off
        ntalk:   off
        talk:    off
        telnet: on
        tftp:    off
        wu-ftpd:        on
        comsat: off
        imap:    off
        imaps:   off
        ipop2:   off
        ipop3:   off
        pop3s:   off
        eklogin:        off
        gssftp: off
        klogin: off
        krb5-telnet:    off
        kshell: off
```

Using *xinetd* (shown in bold in the output) as an example, this listing tells us that the *xinetd* service will start at run levels 3, 4, and 5 and will be inoperative at run levels 0, 1, 2, and 6. Notice at the end of the listing that *chkconfig* also tells us what services *xinetd* is supporting; we'll be looking at *xinetd* again shortly and you will see the significance of this. To ensure that *xinetd* starts at run level 6, use this command:

```
# chkconfig --level 6 xinetd on
```

To confirm that this worked, issue this command:

```
# chkconfig --list xinetd
xinetd          0:off   1:off   2:off   3:on    4:on    5:on    6:on
```

Or, to confirm it directly from the run level directory, use

```
# ls -l /etc/rc.d/rc6.d/*xinetd
lrwxrwxrwx  1  root  root 16 Jul 25 13:59 /etc/rc.d/rc6.d/S50xinetd ->
../init.d/xinetd
```

Finally, this scheme of run levels and the */etc/rc.d* run level script tree are not the only ways to do it. The convention in Berkeley UNIX was to use a script */etc/rc* to start the basic operating system's functions, and then */etc/rc.local* to do anything else. Unfortunately, over time this idea has been modified and today almost every Berkeley UNIX grandchild has a slightly different approach. There is also nothing to prevent using both the AT&T */etc/rc.d* way as well as an */etc/rc.local* script or any other script for that matter to start or stop any operating system service or application server. You will need to find out how your application chooses to do it and work with it as best you can. When I have a choice, I make the application conform to the */etc/rc.d* structure, as it is then consistent, and less prone to error.

Task Scheduling: *at* and *cron*

Regular upkeep is a critical part of keeping a server working reliably, and the ability to automatically schedule maintenance tasks at specific times is a basic tool in your toolbox. There are two commands available to do this: The *at* command schedules a one-time execution at the specified time, while *cron* allows for the repeated execution of a command at a regular interval. Both *at* and *cron* rely on daemons, the *atd* and *crond* respectively, which need to be started at boot time. Maintenance tasks that have significant performance overhead, such as creating backups, weeding out outdated space-wasting files, or application-related maintenance are the sort of thing you do not want to do at peak production times. Consequently, it is common to want to run them at off times, like in the middle of the night, when you have no desire to be there. Administrative tasks that need to run with *root* privilege also fall into this category, as giving a night operator *root* privilege simply to run such routine tasks is clearly an unacceptable solution.

In such cases, *at* or *cron* may be of use. You could write a script to clean up outdated data from a file system at 2:00 A.M. tomorrow with this *at* command:

```
# at 2am tomorrow < /usr/local/clean.out.the.old.files.sh
```

You can also specify a particular day. To run the job at 4:00 A.M. on December 20, issue

```
# at 4am Dec 20 < /usr/local/clean.out.the.old.files.sh
```

To specify a time in the relative sense, such as three hours from now, use

```
# at now +3 hours < /usr/local/clean.out.the.old.files.sh
```

Once the jobs are scheduled, you can view them with the *atq* command, like this:

```
# atq
4         2001-04-10 02:00 a root
5         2001-12-20 10:00 a root
6         2001-04-10 01:51 a root
```

Finally, to remove a scheduled job before it runs, use the *atrm* command —referencing the job with its number, the first field in the *atq* output, like this:

```
# atrm 6
```

It is important to realize that any of the commands you specify in the script file will run in the default */bin/sh* shell. Unless you redirect output in your script, all output will be mailed back to the user who scheduled the job. The shell environment the job will run in is the same as was in effect at the time the job was scheduled. If any of these things will prevent your script from running properly, you will have problems, so check it out.

It may be that you want to run your script not just once, but at regular intervals, say every Saturday at 2:00 A.M., or every weekday at noon. In that case you need the repeating version of *at*, which is *cron*. A *cron* job is defined by adding the name of the script to be executed and the execution time information to a *crontab*. Each user may have a private *crontab*. *crontabs* are managed with the *crontab* command, using the *-e* flag to edit, the *-l* flag to view, and the *-r* flag to remove the *crontab*. A typical *crontab* looks like this:

```
# crontab -l
# DO NOT EDIT THIS FILE - edit the master and reinstall.
# (/tmp/crontab.8676 installed on Tue Feb 20 13:10:51 2001)
# (Cron version -- $Id: crontab.c,v 2.13 1994/01/17 03:20:37 vixie Exp $)
10 5 * * 0 /usr/local/bin/backup.tux.weekly
30 2 * * * /usr/local/bin/backup.tux.daily
```

The *crontab* is stored by the system as a file in */var/spool/cron* (another directory in the */var* file system that needs to be included in you backup policy). Each uncommented line in the *crontab* represents one task. Of the six fields in each line, the first five specify the time of execution, while the last specifies the name of the script or command to be executed. The five time fields represent the minute, hour, day, month, and day of the week. An asterisk in any field implies all possible values, and the days of the week number from 0 to 6, starting with Sunday. *cron* runs once every minute, so the most frequently you could run a *cron* job would be once every minute (which you would specify with an asterisk in the first field). Thus, the first uncommented line in the previous example implies that the script */usr/local/bin/backup.tux.weekly* will run at 10 minutes past 5:00 A.M. on any day of the month and in any month of the year, but only if the day is a Sunday. The last line of the example determines that */usr/local/bin/ backup.tux.daily* runs at 2:00 A.M. every day. You can also specify ranges or lists of values. It's all in the *man* page. Just ensure that you look at the volume 5 page (*man 5 crontab*), which is the page for the *crontab* file, rather than the default volume 1 page (*man crontab*), which is for the *crontab* command.

In addition to user-specific *crontabs*, *cron* also processes a global *crontab* defined by */etc/crontab*. The default Red Hat */etc/crontab* points *cron* to a set of four directories: */etc/cron.hourly*, */etc/cron.daily*, */etc/cron.weekly*, and */etc/cron.monthly*. The directives in */etc/crontab* tell *cron* to examine each of these directories hourly, daily, weekly, and monthly, respectively. A shell script called */usr/bin/run-parts* is called that executes in sequence each of the scripts in the directory being processed. Thus, there is a pre-existent framework supplied by the default install to automatically perform maintenance tasks on a variety of intervals. As a system administrator, you can now tie into this by simply adding your own scripts to the hourly, daily, weekly, or monthly directory, as appropriate.

So far, then, each user, *root* included, can define their own *crontab*, and global administrative tasks can be scheduled using */etc/crontab* or the */etc/cron.hourly*, */etc/cron.daily*, */etc/cron.weekly*, and */etc/cron.monthly* directories. As if this weren't enough choice, you need to know that *cron* also recognizes the directory */etc/cron.d*, which can contain any number of system *crontabs* that *cron* will process, should they exist. The default Red Hat install places one lone *crontab* in */etc/cron.d*, and it drives only one task, a sweep of installed kernel modules looking for unused modules that can be removed from the running kernel. This sweep runs every 10 minutes, too frequently for */etc/cron.hourly*, so it goes into */etc/cron.d*.

Unlike *at*, the environment a *cron* task runs in is determined by environment variable settings in the script itself. If you are having problems getting your *cron* jobs to run reliably, try explicitly setting every environment variable the script references. It is possible to specify environment variables directly in the *crontab* with lines having the format *name = value*, but I prefer to set all my variables in the script. That way each script is self standing, and I do not set a value for some environment variable at the beginning of the *crontab* that may not work properly for all of the scripts in the *crontab*. Like *at*, script output is mailed back to the owner of the *cron* job, unless it is specifically redirected inside the script.

Missed Jobs: *anacron*

A problem arises with both *cron* and *at* in the case where the execution time is missed. Should the machine be down when a job should run, neither *at* nor *cron* has a mechanism to determine that the job was missed during the downtime and assess whether it should run when the system comes back up. This problem can also arise during a time change, such as when the system clock is readjusted, or in the hour lost or gained in the transition to or from Daylight Savings Time. If this is not taken into account, important scheduled jobs will be missed, and that can cause unnecessary downtime.

There is a third utility devised to address this problem, and that is *anacron*. While *at* and *cron* rely on daemons, *anacron* is simply a single process that, when it runs, scans a configuration file and runs the jobs specified therein. When each job runs, however, *anacron* notes the date the job ran in a time stamp file in the directory */var/spool/anacron*. The next time *anacron* runs, it scans its configuration file and compares the frequency each job is expected to run at, and the last time the job ran, according to the time stamps recorded in */var/spool/anacron*. If the definition for a job in */etc/anacrontab* were to specify a daily execution, but the time stamp indicates that the last time the job ran was two days ago, *anacron* would conclude that the job had been missed and would run it. Note that the *anacron* time stamps record only the date, not the time of execution, and so *anacron* cannot be used to handle jobs whose frequency is less than at least one full 24-hour day.

The default */etc/anacrontab* looks like this:

```
# /etc/anacrontab: configuration file for anacron

# See anacron(8) and anacrontab(5) for details.

SHELL=/bin/sh
PATH=/usr/local/sbin:/usr/local/bin:/sbin:/bin:/usr/sbin:/usr/bin

# These entries are useful for a Red Hat Linux system.
1       5       cron.daily      run-parts /etc/cron.daily
7       10      cron.weekly     run-parts /etc/cron.weekly
30      15      cron.monthly    run-parts /etc/cron.monthly
```

Note the environment variable assignments, which are global to the commands processed by *anacron*. The first field of each job entry is the frequency, in days, with which the job should run. The second field is a delay in minutes from the time *anacron* is started to the time the job will be started. The third field is the identifier used in the time stamp file to identify this job, and the rest is the command to be executed.

Now, the final issue is, how do we put *anacron* and *cron* together to ensure that *anacron* will pick up any jobs missed by *cron* as a result of downtime or missing hours errors? The answer lies in a flag to *anacron*, the -*u* flag. This tells *anacron* to process /etc/anacrontab, but not to execute any jobs, only update their time stamp value, as if *anacron* had executed them. Then, all of the jobs listed in any *crontab* that we wish *anacron* to back up must also be listed in /etc/anacrontab. By default, the /etc/cron.daily, /etc/cron.weekly, and /etc/cron.monthly directories are all listed in /etc/ anacrontab. Having done that, we then direct *cron* to run *anacron -u* from the /etc/cron.daily directory, before any of the other *cron* jobs. Thus, so long as *cron* is working, *cron* will run the jobs that need doing, and ensure that each time *cron* runs those jobs, the *anacron* time stamps are brought up-to-date, giving *anacron* a record that *cron* has successfully run all necessary jobs. Then we include *anacron* in the boot process. Now, should the machine go down and miss *cron* jobs, the boot *anacron* process will deal with them.

Here is an example to show how it unfolds. Say the machine goes down at 10:00 P.M. December 7, remaining down until 11:00 A.M. December 9. According to /etc/crontab, all of the jobs listed in /etc/cron.daily should have run on December 9, but with this downtime, they will be missed. The last time those jobs did run successfully was at 4:02 A.M. December 7, and as the *anacron -u* command would have run at that time also, the *anacron* time-stamp will read December 7. When the machine boots on the morning of December 9, *anacron* will run (from /etc/rc.d/init.d/anacron) and observe that it is December 9, yet the timestamp values indicate that the jobs flagged *cron.daily* last ran December 7, one day too long ago. Consequently, *anacron* will run those jobs now. The second field in the /etc/anacrontab allows for a delay before *anacron* actually starts issuing commands, to let the boot process complete. Normally, *anacron* will go into the background, emerging only to start the next job (should there be more than one defined by /etc/anacrontab) and finally terminating after the last job completes. When this is all done, the *anacron* time stamp will read December 9, and everything will be caught up.

Realize that the next time a machine boots after an outage may not be the best time to recover missed *cron* jobs. In some cases, there may be no point in recovering a job; in others, the machine may not yet have fixed enough from the first reboot after the outage to be able to run the missed *cron* job.

In these cases, you may need to review the default */etc/anacrontab* and add or remove jobs from it accordingly.

System Logging: *syslogd*

The *syslogd* is an operating system daemon that provides a logging service for running applications. It is also used as the primary means for the operating system itself to log normal and abnormal activity. As such it is a critical element in a reliable server, providing essential monitoring information. The *syslogd* configuration file is */etc/syslog.conf*. A typical line from it looks like this:

```
mail.info                           /var/log/maillog
```

There are three pieces of information in this and every line of the file. In this example, mail is the name of the *syslog* facility. A facility is typically a daemon or internal operating system function that may want to generate log messages at some point in time. The string *info* is the priority. There are eight priority levels, ranging up from *debug* to *emerg*. The level specified in the configuration file implies to log all messages generated by the facility that are at the specified level or any higher level. Finally */var/log/maillog* is the name of the log file to be used.

One rather neat thing you can do with *syslog* is to tell it to forward log messages to another machine on the network also running *syslogd*. In this way you can set up a log server, a central machine collecting log information from multiple network servers. This can be a useful tool if you manage multiple servers. Using the earlier example, I could log mail messages locally as well as forwarding them to a log server called *watchman* with these lines in */etc/syslog.conf*:

```
mail.info                           /var/log/maillog
mail.info                           @watchman
```

You may need to alter the *syslog* start script in */etc/rc.d/init.d* to make this work. By default, newer versions of *syslogd* do not accept log messages from remote machines. You need to add the *-r* flag in the *start* stanza of the start script. Mine looks like this, note the added *-r* in bold:

```
start() {
        echo -n "Starting system logger: "
        # we don't want the MARK ticks
        daemon syslogd -m 0 -r
        RETVAL=$?
        echo
```

```
            echo -n "Starting kernel logger: "
            daemon klogd
            echo
            [ $RETVAL -eq 0 ] && touch /var/lock/subsys/syslog
            return $RETVAL
    }
```

It is possible—indeed common—for applications to use their own *syslog* facility to customize logging for that application. Consequently, when an application is installed, its installation script may automatically try to edit */etc/syslog.conf*. Although, more commonly, information concerning the facility name the application will use is available in a README file or other application documentation. It is very important to make sure that you do set up logging for any application that supports it, as this can be a lifeline to debugging operational problems that can lead to down time. Some applications may generate large logs as a normal part of their operation. In this case, you may want to place those logs in a separate partition, or subject them to quota checking.

If you have edited */etc/syslog.conf*, you must send a hang up (HUP) signal to *syslogd* to make it read its configuration file again; it will not do it on its own. Issue the following command to do so:

```
# killall -HUP syslogd
```

Finally, *syslog* is not the only option for logging. Some applications simply directly write their own log files. In that case *syslogd* configuration is irrelevant, instead consider putting large logs in their own partition or quota-limiting them.

Hardware Configuration: *kudzu*

The *kudzu* utility is the closest thing to plug and play in Linux. It is designed to detect and configure new or changed hardware. If you have a hardware failure and the replacement hardware is comparable, but not identical to the old hardware, *kudzu* can be useful. *kudzu* relies on the ability of the hardware to be detected by kernel code probes, usually at boot time. Any hardware detected is compared to a reference listing in the file */etc/sysconfig/hwconf*. If there are any discrepancies between what was detected and the reference database, *kudzu* will attempt to configure the new or altered device. Configuration usually involves adding lines to */etc/modules.conf*, to ensure the appropriate kernel driver modules are loaded at boot time, or when the device is needed.

I strongly suggest you consult the hardware compatibility lists available from Red Hat (or which ever distro you may use) before sourcing any hardware. If you are running a Red Hat release, Red Hat has a hardware certification program called Red Hat Ready that puts hardware through a test suite to ensure full compatibility with Red Hat Linux. You may pay a premium for the certified hardware, but you can save an awful lot of expensive time otherwise wasted fiddling with marginally supported hardware. Further information on Red Hat certified hardware and supported hardware lists for Red Hat distributions can be found at hardware.redhat.com.

UPS Monitoring: *upsd*

A variety of options are available to implement an uninterruptible power supply on a Linux server. If you do use a UPS, you need a utility to determine when the UPS is supplying power and to monitor its battery level. See Chapter 3, "Choosing the Right Hardware," for a fuller discussion about UPSs.

Network Services Configuration

If your server is a network server—and few servers today are not—then the stability and reliability of the network services provided by the server are usually as critical to the availability of the application as the availability of the server machine itself. The following sections review a number of common network services and give you some pointers on configuring them with reliability in mind.

Electronic Mail: *sendmail*

Configuring *sendmail* is a whole vocation in itself, and entire books have been written on the subject. I'm not going to attempt that here. It is such a commonly needed application, however, that I need to say at least something about it. *sendmail* is an implementation of the Simple Mail Transfer Protocol (SMTP). The simple part of SMTP refers to the fact that all of the relevant information needed by mail servers to address and route mail messages around the internet is included in plain ASCII text at the head of each mail message. SMTP servers read and append to this header as mail travels about the net so that it is simple at any time for a human to read a mail header and discover all there is to know about a mail message.

Unfortunately, it turns out that there are quite a number of variables involved in the process of handling mail, and in this regard SMTP is anything but simple.

From a reliability standpoint, here are some basic pointers:

If you don't need it, don't run it. Strangely enough, you may not need *sendmail* to send mail. Many mail client applications can generate an SMTP mail message and send it along to a *sendmail* server for forwarding entirely on its own. What *sendmail* does is to forward mail from one mail server to another. It is properly termed a mail forwarding agent. If you have a Post Office Protocol (POP) client on your server, you do not need *sendmail* to receive mail either. Mail forwarded to a host running *sendmail* would be held there for pickup. The hosts running *sendmail* would also run a POP daemon, allowing you to collect your mail from it.

If you need to run *sendmail*, make sure it is configured to make minimum use of *root* privilege. The original version of *sendmail* ran as *root*, which created an exposure that led to a long string of security exploits. Current versions of *sendmail* do not have to run entirely as *root* and should be configured accordingly.

If you are running a large mail forwarder, put your mail spool directory in its own file system, and monitor it. If you lose your outbound network connection, *sendmail* will continue to accept and queue mail from local clients until the connection returns, in which case you may need significant spool space to hold that outbound mail.

Address Resolution Protocol: *arpwatch*

The *arpwatch* utility tracks Ethernet hardware address and IP address pairs. It mails *root* when any of three things happen: The first is the case in which the IP address associated with a hardware address changes, as that could be a security violation known as IP spoofing. Second, it looks for the reverse, IP addresses that suddenly appear with a different hardware address. This could simply mean the network card in that host was replaced, or that someone configured a machine with the wrong IP address, but it could also mean someone is illegally borrowing an IP address. Third, *arpwatch* reports a change of IP address for a host name. To do this, *arpwatch* keeps a database of IP addresses, hardware addresses, and host names in */var/arpwatch/arp.dat*.

arpwatch is primarily intended as a security monitoring tool, and as good security is important in maintaining a reliable server, it could also be considered a reliability tool. It can also be a means of discovering a configuration error, or an unexpected configuration change. As such, it can be a useful debugging tool. Good debugging tools also improve reliability.

The Network Services Super Server: *xinetd*

xinetd is the network super server daemon and is an updated version of the older *inetd* daemon. According to the man page for *xinetd*, "*xinetd* performs the same function as *inetd*: It starts programs that provide Internet services. Instead of having such servers started at system initialization time, and be dormant until a connection request arrives, *xinetd* is the only daemon process started and it listens on all service ports for the services listed in its configuration file. When a request comes in, *xinetd* starts the appropriate server."

xinetd differs from the older *inetd* in that "*xinetd* takes advantage of the idea of a super server to provide features such as access control and logging." This improves security, and whatever keeps a server more secure is generally also good for reliability. It is important to note, however, that increased security tends to involve increased complexity, so it is particularly important to get the new security configuration right.

The main configuration file for *xinetd* is */etc/xinetd.conf*. It is modeled on the syntax of the Apache Web server configuration files. It is also possible to include further configuration files by using the *includedir* directive in */etc/xinetd.conf*. In fact, the default Red Hat installation includes this line in its default *xinetd* configuration:

```
includedir /etc/xinetd.d
```

An examination of the */etc/xinetd.d* directory shows it to contain several further *xinetd* configuration files, each for a specific service. Each of these files will be processed by *xinetd* when it starts or is signaled to re-read its configuration.

Earlier, while discussing run levels, you were introduced to the *chkconfig* command. You can use it to track the services started by *xinetd*, too. Issue the command *chkconfig --list*. The *xinetd* services will be found at the end of the output. The two major and very common services normally managed by *xinetd* are *ftp* and *telnet*, both of which have default configuration files in */etc/xinetd.d*.

There are several other services also started by default, however, that are questionable in a production server—specifically, *finger*, *ntalk*, *rlogin*, *rsh*, *talk*, and *tftp*, (and possibly others, depending on your distro). While there may be a justification in specific circumstances for one or more of these services, several pose significant security risks, and in most cases all of them should be disabled. This can be done by editing the files, commenting out lines, or simply deleting the file from */etc/xinetd.d*. After your changes, make sure that you either stop and restart *xinetd*, like this:

```
# /etc/rc.d/init.d/xinetd stop
# /etc/rc.d/init.d/xinetd start
```

Or, you may use signals like this:

```
# killall -USR2 xinetd
```

Notice in the last case that, unlike many other daemons, *xinetd* will not re-read its configuration on receiving a HUP signal, rather it listens for a USR1 signal, which is a soft reset (servers running at the time of reset do not terminate), or for a USR2 signal for a hard reset (servers for services no longer available as a result of the reset are terminated, a more secure option and thus preferred).

One of the useful things about *xinetd* is that it can be configured for logging. The *log_type* directive in an *xinetd* configuration file can specify logging either via *syslogd*, or to a specific named log file. As always with logging, care must be taken to make sure that the log file does not grow large enough to cause problems. One nice feature of *xinetd* is the ability to control the size of the log file right in the *xinetd* configuration. For example,

```
service telnet
{
        flags            = REUSE
        socket_type      = stream
        wait             = no
        user             = root
        server           = /usr/sbin/in.telnetd
        log_on_failure   += USERID
        log_type         = FILE /var/log/telnet.log 10000 11000
}
```

This file, placed in */etc/xinetd.d*, would set up logging for each successful *telnet* session, logging to the file */var/log/telnet.log*. When the log exceeds 10,000 bytes in size, a soft error is returned to *syslogd* at an alert priority, and should the log continue to grow, its size will be absolutely capped at 11,000 bytes. This is good for protecting against disk space over runs, but realize that you still need to clear or archive this log at regular intervals or, once the log hits the upper limit, no new log entries will be generated.

Firewalls: *ipchains*

If you want to implement a firewall on a server, you will likely use *ipchains*. Note that *ipchains* is not a separate daemon that needs to be started or stopped; rather it is an inherent part of the kernel. If you do nothing to configure it, it will by default do no examination or filtering of network traffic. If you do want to implement a firewall using *ipchains*, you need to develop a set of firewall rules. These are logical statements that determine which incoming and outgoing network packets are examined and if they will be accepted or rejected. The decision to accept or reject is based on source or destination addresses. A typical firewall will have a number of these rules, some of which take some time to develop, particularly in the case of less common or proprietary applications. The rules are loaded into the actual kernel firewall using the *ipchains* command. Once loaded, they can be queried using *ipchains -L*, but the entire rule set does not get stored on disk anywhere, consequently after a reboot, the rules must be redefined from the command line. Each rule requires one *ipchains* command to define it to the kernel firewall. There are usually a number of rules, so it would be reasonable to store them in the form of a firewall startup script that can be run as a part of the boot process and backed up for recovery purposes.

If you choose to use the */etc/rc.d/init.d* boot scripts as supplied with a Red Hat distribution to start your firewall, however, you need to know that the script supplied to start *ipchains* makes use of an *ipchains* option, allowing the firewall rules to be read from an ASCII text ruleset file rather than running a series of *ipchains* commands from the script. This ruleset file can be generated from a running firewall or hand edited. Using the ruleset file is an acceptable alternative to a firewall boot script; however, it has a danger: If you manually modify your firewall by adding a new rule from the command line, this new rule will not be added to the ruleset file unless you ask for the ruleset file to be updated, like this:

```
# /etc/rc.d/init.d ipchains save
```

If you miss saving a new ruleset file, your firewall will not come back with the proper ruleset during a reboot. This can be dangerous, as it may not be obvious that your new rule failed to get defined. You would have to dump the current ruleset and look through it to discover the problem. If the new rule was designed to close a potential hole in the firewall, you may only be examining the ruleset as a part of a post mortem on the security breach that cost your server major downtime, and that is what you want to avoid. It probably goes without saying that if you are depending on a firewall, then you are regularly running intrusion tests from the outside to ensure that it is working properly. If you are doing that, then your missing rule would get detected.

Red Hat Network Services: *rhnsd*

The *rhnsd* is the Red Hat Network Services daemon. According to the documentation, "this is a daemon which handles the task of connecting periodically to the Red Hat Network Services servers to check for updates, notifications and perform system monitoring tasks according to the service level that this server is subscribed for." Currently Red Hat Network is capable of storing a hardware and software profile of your system and automatically informing you of any applicable operating system updates relevant to your server. Software updates can be automatically downloaded and installed, as you wish. The intent of the service is to improve the reliability of a server by ensuring that important fixes get quickly and automatically installed. If you are not a user of this service, there is no need to run the daemon. If you want to know more about this service, go to www.redhat.com/network.

The Secure Shell: *sshd*

According to the *sshd man* page, "*sshd* (Secure Shell Daemon) is the daemon program for *ssh*(1). Together these programs replace *rlogin* and *rsh*, and provide secure encrypted communications between two untrusted hosts over an insecure network." *ssh* is commonly used as a secure means of allowing remote login sessions. It is also possible to direct other protocols such as *ftp* to use an encrypted *ssh* session, although it is beyond the scope of this book to get into that. Applications that require secure communications may choose to use this protocol, in which case problems with *ssh* will lead to application downtime. Although *sshd* can be started from *inetd* or *xinetd*, the nature of the encryption key exchange that takes place at the creation of an *ssh* connection makes it awkward to use the super server daemon approach. Consequently, the *sshd* is normally started at boot time from an */etc/rc.d/init.d* startup script.

   Global startup configuration of the *sshd* is done in */etc/ssh/sshd_config*. Note that *sshd* will refuse to start if there is no configuration file. Among many other things, the *syslogd* log facility and level is configured in this file. Depending on your configuration, there are several other files that may be necessary for *sshd* to operate properly, specifically, */etc/ssh_known_hosts*, files in */etc/ssh*, and files in user home directories in the *.ssh* subdirectory. Make sure that these files are properly backed up and will be restored in case of need so that *sshd* will work properly after the restore.

Network Monitoring: *rstatd, rusersd,* and *rwhod*

These daemons collect and make available over the network information concerning performance (*rstatd*), currently logged-in users (*rusersd*), and current system usage (*rwhod*). They are conveniences; none are really necessary. Unless you wish to monitor this kind of information over a network, you can safely do without them. Should you decide not to use them, check to make sure none of your applications rely on the information they provide. It is unlikely that they do, but not impossible.

Broadcasting Messages: *rwalld*

This daemon allows console messages to be broadcast across a network to multiple servers. It may be necessary to support an application that wishes to use it for messaging purposes. Otherwise, you can live without it. If you do need it, the actual server is */usr/sbin/rpc.rwalld*, and it is normally invoked from *inetd* or *xinetd*.

The X Font Server: *xfs*

X Windows is the graphical environment common to most UNIX environments and the X Font Server daemon (*xfs*) supplies font information to X Windows display servers. If you want to use a graphical environment at the console of your server, you should run *xfs*. If you have client machines that will run an X desktop, but will look to your server for their font information, than you will also need to run *xfs*. If neither case applies to you, you can safely simplify your server by not running *xfs*.

xfs is normally started at boot from an */etc/rc.d/init.d* script, and takes its configuration from */etc/X11/fs/conf*. Like much X Windows traffic, *xfs* uses an unprivileged port (port 7100/tcp by default). Make sure that if you need to run X Windows traffic over a firewall, the firewall rules can accommodate traffic on these ports.

Domain Name Service: *named*

The *named* daemon implements the Berkeley Internet Name Domain service, more commonly known as just Domain Name Service, or DNS. This is the distributed machine name to IP address mapping databases used universally on the Internet to match up host names, like www.wiley.com, to a specific IP address. Run *named* when you have a registered Internet domain and choose to operate your own name server. You may also run a name server for domains for which you are a host. Making sure that *named* is running can be central to server uptime as nothing much happens on the Internet without name resolution services. You may have an entire server devoted to just name service. If you are not serving a domain, accessing the Internet requires being a DNS client.

In the case of a server, the *named* daemon will be started from the boot script */etc/rc.d/init.d/named*. The default configuration file is */etc/named.conf*, and the default location of the DNS database itself is typically */var/named*. As DNS data is really more static than dynamic, and is (hopefully) not transient, */var* is not the place you should expect to find it, yet that is where it commonly is found. Your backup facility needs to be aware of this to make sure the DNS database gets backed up properly.

If you do serve any domains, you should certainly supplement your primary server with at least one secondary server, preferably located on a different physical network. When you are updating the primary server database, never forget to increment the serial number in the forward resolution file, or your secondary servers will not download the changes. This can cause serious problems if your secondary server functions primarily as a backup (as opposed to load sharing). In that case, should your primary server go down, your secondary may be running just fine, but with a completely outdated data base, making it quite possibly worse than no backup at all.

If you are implementing your own servers, it is a good idea to dedicate machines to the purpose. It doesn't take a particularly large or fast machine to make a modest DNS server, and there is very little to go wrong. In fact, almost all of the data can be read-only on such a machine, excepting logs. That way your DNS servers will not be affected by any other application issues on the same machine, and you can locate them on physically different networks to reduce the chances of a network failure making the DNS service unavailable.

Even if you do not need to run a DNS server, there is a performance advantage to running what is known as a caching only name server. This type of server holds no database and has to forward all the requests it gets to an upstream server, but once it has the information it caches it locally, reducing the traffic to the external server. If you repeatedly look up the same host names, this can represent a useful performance improvement, and tends to reduce your dependence on the external server, especially if it tends to be slow at times, which many DNS servers are. Red Hat supplies an *rpm* package just for this, called *caching-nameserver*, and the procedure to set it up is well documented, as are most other DNS issues, in the DNS HOWTO. In this case, the machine running the caching nameserver will list its loopback in */etc/resolv.conf* as its first choice of nameserver. Do remember to include at least one other downstream server, however, just in case the caching only server goes wrong for any reason.

If your server will not serve name resolution information, it will need to be able to function as a DNS client to function reliably on most networks. If you will be a DNS client, it is necessary to edit */etc/resolv.conf*, and make sure there is an entry for your local DNS primary and secondary name-servers. Secondary nameservers are implemented to improve name resolution reliability by acting as backups in case the primary nameserver fails. If you do not list the secondary nameserver in */etc/resolv.conf*, the client has no way of finding it on its own, and you might as well not have a secondary at all, as far as that client is concerned.

A typical */etc/resolv.conf*, would look like this:

```
domain foo.bar.com
nameserver 192.168.1.200      # your primary local DNS
nameserver 192.168.3.200      # your secondary local DNS
nameserver 1.2.3.4            # offsite upstream DNS
```

This also suggests that you should avoid changing the IP address of a DNS server, if at all possible, as all clients would have to be informed of the change, as well as any secondary servers. Those kinds of changes have a high probability of causing confusion and downtime, and should be avoided. It will also be necessary to register any nameserver address change with the master Internet domain registry, or the rest of the world will not be able to see your new server. There is a time lag for this kind of change to propagate to the DNS root servers. A period of 12–24 hours is typical, which should be considered when the changeover of a nameserver address is unavoidable.

If you do not operate your own DNS servers, then ask your service provider for at least two DNS server addresses that they operate. If the provider does not have two servers, consider finding a better service provider. Also find a DNS server above your local provider, in case both of their servers fail. This may seem unlikely, but many smaller service providers locate both primary and secondary DNS servers in the same location, where a site loss would knock them both out. In that case you may well lose your connection, in which case an upstream server address is useless, but it doesn't hurt to have it in your configuration anyway. Even if you operate your own primary and secondary DNS servers (in which case they will both be included in a client's */etc/resolv.conf* file), still include an upstream server address from your provider. If for any reason your servers should go down, your clients will then still be able to at least resolve host names outside of your domains, and that may be enough to keep them in production.

Network File System (NFS): *nfsd, biod, mountd, statd, lockd, rquotad,* and *portmap*

NFS is a network file server utility originally developed by SUN Microsystems in the mid-1980s. Since then it has become a de facto standard in the UNIX world. Several different versions of NFS are available. Probably the most widely used is version 2, which has been implemented in the Linux kernel for a number of years. Version 3 offers a number of improvements, particularly in the area of performance, but is only supported in kernels 2.2.18 or later. There is a version 4 in development, which incorporates improvements from other network file systems such as the Andrew File System (AFS) and the Coda file system. NFS 4 shows promise, but it is in the early stages at this point in time for use in a reliable production server. If both client and server will support it, NFS 3 is the best choice. Unfortunately, although the current Linux kernel supports NFS 3, not all NFS clients or non-Linux servers support version 3. As the saying goes, your mileage will vary.

It is a common practice to distribute production applications across several servers, but centralize file storage on a dedicated server. If NFS is the application chosen to support the network access to that file server, then keeping NFS running properly will be essential to all your application servers. From a reliability standpoint, there are several issues to consider. The first is, what will happen to a client process and its data should they be in the process of writing to an NFS server and the server fails? If the file system is mounted by the client with the *hard* option, which is the default, the client process will wait until the server has acknowledged that the data has been sent to its local file system before continuing processing. Note that the data is not necessarily written to disk at this point, as all writes to a file system are buffered in memory before they are written to disk. A disk crash at this critical point could cause data loss. This risk can be reduced by specifying the *sync* option in the */etc/exports* file on the server, which forces the buffered data to be written to disk following each NFS write operation. This reduces the loss risk, but can cause a significant performance hit on a busy server.

A more efficient option would be to use a RAID disk array, to cover the possibility of a disk crash. In the event that the server crashes, there really is no completely risk-free method to ensure that the data in transit from the client to the server will survive if the client lets go of the data before it has been completely committed to disk at the server. A journalling file system would help to protect the integrity of the file system metadata, but does not ensure file system data integrity, as I will show in Chapter 9.

While a *hard* mount is preferable in terms of data security, a server outage still causes the client process to hang indefinitely until the server returns and completes the transaction. This can be avoided by mounting the file system with the *soft* option, in which case the client will give up after a period controlled by the *timeo* mount option. The *soft* option, however, risks the possibility of data loss should the writing application be relying on NFS to ensure that the data is safely written, so it is not an acceptable choice where reliability is an issue. A compromise is found in the *intr* option. If the file system is mounted with both *hard* and *intr*, then the client application can be interrupted with a signal. In this case the client knows that the data did not make it safely to the server and can respond accordingly. But, some mechanism still needs to generate the interrupt signal to the client process and deal with the fact that the data was not written to disk. In addition, the data now has nowhere to go, and the application might hang anyway.

All this highlights the risk of using a network file server for production data. Anything that goes wrong on the network now has the potential to disrupt any production server that is a client of the file server, and the file server has become a single point of failure for all its clients. If possible, keep application data storage local to the application server itself. Use network file servers for read-only data that can be replicated across multiple servers, and for non-production-critical maintenance tasks such as backups and system monitoring.

Should the data on the server be read-only information, then the *soft* option is fine. A server outage will return read errors, but they will time out and nothing will hang. Of course, if the data required from the mount is critical to the application running on the client, you are still out of production. You can plug this reliability gap by setting up a redundant NFS server for the same read-only data and using the NFS *automounter* to specify more than one server for a particular mount, in which case the *automounter* would automatically fail over to the secondary server if the primary were to fail. There is a mini HOWTO for *automounter* configuration available at www.linuxdoc.org.

You should be aware also that Linux NFS servers use the */etc/hosts.allow* and */etc/hosts.deny* files to place security restrictions on client access. If clients or servers change addresses during a fail over or reconfiguration, these files may have to be adjusted to get NFS services running properly again. Good security also dictates that you restrict which clients can mount a file system from a server by listing each NFS client in the server's */etc/exports* file. Otherwise, the directory can be mounted by any client that can get a mount request to the server. That is weak security, and weak security does not support strong reliability. Again, make sure that if you add or change IP addresses, those changes are properly reflected at the NFS servers. Remember that if you edit */etc/exports*, you need to issue an *exportfs -rav* command to re-export the directories. If you wish to change client side mount options, you need to unmount and remount the file system with the new options.

Let me summarize this with an example. Say I have an NFS server called *earth* (IP address 192.168.1.200, netmask 255.255.255.0) and a client host named *moon* (IP address 192.168.1.1, netmask 255.255.255.0). *earth* exports two directories to *moon*, */var/opt/application_data* which is exported read write and */usr/doc/application_manual* which is exported read only. First I need to ensure that NFS is running on *earth*. The server normally boots to run level 3, so check the entry in the run level:

```
# cd /etc/rc.d/rc3.d
# ls -l *nfs
lrwxrwxrwx   1 root    root       13 Jan 21 11:28 S20nfs -> ../init.d/nfs
```

That will make sure NFS starts at the next boot. If NFS is not running now, then start it manually:

```
# /etc/rc.d/init.d/nfs start
```

Next, make the following entries in */etc/exports*:

```
/var/opt/application_data        moon(rw)
/usr/doc/application_manual      moon(ro)
```

As NFS is already running, re-export all exports:

```
# exportfs -ra
```

NFS makes use of the *portmap* daemon to provide a look-up service. Briefly, *portmap* provides a service similar to *xinetd*, in that it knows which IP service ports the various NFS function calls can be accessed through. NFS does not use *xinetd* for this mostly for performance-related reasons. Clients need to be able to access *portmap* on an NFS server for their NFS calls to work. If you are security conscious, and you should be as NFS has a nasty history of security exploits, you will put the following entries in two host access control files. First, in */etc/hosts.deny*:

```
portmap: ALL
lockd: ALL
statd: ALL
mountd: ALL
rquotad: ALL
```

These entries establish a default policy that shuts off all access to *portmap* and other NFS functions for all hosts. Now you need to add the legitimate client to */etc/hosts.allow*:

```
portmap: 192.168.1.1
lockd: 192.168.1.1
statd: 192.168.1.1
mountd: 192.168.1.1
rquotad: 192.168.1.1
```

If you wanted to allow all hosts on the local subnet 192.168.1.0, the entries would look like this:

```
portmap: 192.168.1.0/255.255.255.0
lockd: 192.168.1.0/255.255.255.0
statd: 192.168.1.0/255.255.255.0
mountd: 192.168.1.0/255.255.255.0
rquotad: 192.168.1.0/255.255.255.0
```

You might be tempted to use a host name in these files rather than an IP address. In the specific case of the *portmap* entry, this is not a good idea. The *portmap* daemon is also used by Network Information Services (NIS), which may be used for host name lookups. In that case, resolving a host name in */etc/hosts.allow* could require a call to *portmap*, which would require resolving a host name, which would require a call to *portmap*, which would require resolving a host name. I think you get the idea? It is not necessary to signal any daemons after you edit these access control files, as they are read dynamically at each attempted access.

While we are talking about *portmap*, we must ensure that it starts at the next boot:

```
# cd /etc/rc.d/rc3.d
# ls -l *portmap
lrwxrwxrwx   1 root    root    17 Jan 21 11:29 S13portmap -> ../init.d/portmap
```

There is an important point here: Because of the way *portmap* and NFS work together, *portmap* must start before NFS. It is critical to ensure that the number following the S in the link entry in the */etc/rc.d/rc3.d* directory guarantees that *portmap* will start *before* NFS. If you are doing this manually and you have already started NFS, you must stop NFS, start *portmap*, and then restart NFS, like this:

```
# /etc/rc.d/init.d/nfs stop
# /etc/rc.d/init.d/portmap start
# /etc/rc.d/init.d/nfs start
```

That completes the job at the server end, next is the client. You will want both directories mounted at boot, so put these entries in */etc/fstab*:

```
earth:/var/opt/application_data   /application_data   nfs rw,hard,intr 0 0
earth:/usr/doc/application_manual /application_manual nfs ro,soft      0 0
```

Make sure that the mount point directories exist or the mounts will fail. Test by manually mounting the file systems first, then if possible, do a reboot just to make sure.

Finally, you should know that there are several performance issues with NFS that can reduce throughput enough to cause stability or reliability problems in a busy NFS environment. There are issues regarding optimum data block sizes, network device drivers, the number of NFS daemons to run, and several others. Getting all of these right can make the difference between a functional NFS server and one that is slow enough to be a cause of real trouble. Section 5 of the NFS HOWTO details each of these issues and is well worth the time to read.

Network Information Service (NIS): *ypbind, yppasswdd, ypserv,* and *portmap*

NIS is a client/server utility that allows centralized management of several key configuration files, primarily those defining the user database, */etc/passwd* and */etc/group*. An NIS client still holds copies of these files locally, but they only contain a few entries. If a user attempts a login to the client and their user id does not appear in the client's local */etc/passwd*, the client makes a call to its NIS server, which looks up its */etc/passwd* file to validate the user login. In this fashion, a single user account definition can be easily shared between a number of clients of the same NIS server. NIS can also be used to share other configuration files that you may want to be held in common by a group of machines. These include, for example, */etc/services* and */etc/hosts*, as well as several others. A group of clients all sharing the same set of files from a server make up an NIS domain. The server is said to be the master server for this domain, and for reliability purposes there should be at least one slave server also configured. A slave server holds copies of the central configuration files that it gets from the master, so that it might act as a server also, in order to balance load and provide redundancy in case the master fails.

In the same way that NFS provides centralized file sharing convenience, NIS provides centralized configuration convenience. In the same way, too, that NFS introduces dependencies of one machine upon another (as well as the connecting network) and therefore more points of failure, so does NIS. On the other hand, centralizing configuration information greatly improves the reliability of change management, making it easier to ensure that every server gets up-to-date and consistent configuration information. There is a trade off to be made. In the case of managing user login accounts, it is useful to note that most client/server application software today does not need a large number of user accounts. Usually, actual login accounts on the server are only needed for administrators of the operating system and the application. Client users typically submit requests for service through a network service connection that does not require a login. It is not unusual for even large application servers to have no more than 20 or 30 login accounts, in which case there may be little advantage to using NIS.

If you decide not to use NIS, but you do want to use NFS, then it is very important that the */etc/passwd* file on both the NFS client and server be the same, at least in terms of the numeric user id assigned to each account, as NFS uses the numeric id (the second data field in each */etc/passwd* line entry, often called the UID) to identify the remote user, not the user name. Referring to my earlier NFS example, if there were an account for *iain* on client host *moon* having a UID of 500, and an account for *bettina* on the NFS server *earth* with the same UID, then *iain* would get access to *bettina*'s files, should they be made available to *moon* via NFS. If you were using NIS, with *earth* as the NIS server, this would not happen, as *earth*'s */etc/passwd* file would also be used by *moon*, and the UID numbers would be consistent.

If your application server is a client in an NIS domain, the nature of the *ypbind* daemon is that it will broadcast a client request and bind to whichever NIS server responds. Should the NIS server go down, the application server will perform another broadcast hoping to find another server. You should have slave servers set up, one of which will respond and the application will then be bound to the new slave server. Thus, the fail-over for NIS is automatic. What happens, though, if no NIS servers respond? In that case your application server will be without any of the NIS databases it may be relying on. To protect yourself in this case, you may want to leave certain key host name resolutions in the clients */etc/hosts* file. Likewise, you may want to leave certain critical administrative accounts defined in */etc/passwd*. Each server should certainly define *root*'s account locally, in */etc/passwd* for example; otherwise, logging in as *root* can become dependent on NIS.

If you are using NIS, there are three daemons involved: The *ypserv* daemon will run on both master and slave servers, and responds to client requests. The *yppasswdd* runs only on the domain master, and takes care of managing passwords on the master server, allowing client users to change their central password. *ypbind* runs on all NIS clients, and has the task of locating (by a network broadcast) an active server, master or slave, that the client will use. A server can be a client of itself, or another server, so it's quite possible to see all three running on one machine.

In the case of servers, master or slave, *ypserv* would normally be started from a boot script, and takes its configuration from */etc/ypserv.conf*. There are several security options that must be correct in this file. It is possible, for example, to restrict clients that can get service from this machine to specific addresses or address ranges. For example, the entry

```
10.1.1. : * : port : no
```

prevents non-root users on any client on the network 10.1.1/24 from using the *ypcat passwd* command to list encrypted user passwords. This improves security as access to encrypted passwords gives a hacker the raw material for a brute force password guessing attack. In addition to */etc/ypserv.conf*, there is also another file, */var/yp/securenets*, which determines which networks are allowed to request map information from this server.

In a reliable NIS environment, you must have at least one slave server, if not two or three, for redundancy. Ideally, each physical network segment should have at least one slave server on it, to cover the possibility of both master server loss and network connectivity loss. Each of these configuration files needs to be consistent on all servers, master and slaves, for your NIS environment to work properly. And of course, both files need to be included in server backups in order to ensure that a restored server will operate properly.

Change Management

There is a saying: Nothing is so constant as change. Certainly in the course of day-to-day operations, various aspects of any server's configuration will need to change. Unfortunately, as soon as you disturb a running server, you risk causing problems. A systems administrator once remarked to me that in his experience a significant source of server downtime was poorly managed changes in hardware and software configurations. Ideally, you should never change anything, but that is clearly impossible. How then can you manage necessary changes and still control downtime? Here are some suggestions:

Avoid changes that stray from established standards or common practice at your site. You may know what you are doing, but may not have to deal with the problem tomorrow. I knew a programmer who wrote marvelous code that worked brilliantly. The problem was that is was so marvelous it took other less brilliant programmers days to figure it out when they had to revise or modify it later in the product cycle. Standards like the FHS may seem to be a nuisance to comply with, but the common standard they set is designed to improve consistency and predictability, and these attributes support improved reliability.

Always fully document everything you do. It may not be you who has to take this server the next step along the road. If you isolate and fix a problem, but don't document it, the next person may end up having to deal with the problem all over again, which would be wasted effort. Even if it is you who returns to the machine later, will you remember what you did six months ago, and why you did it? It's bad enough to have downtime to fix a problem once; documenting the solution will ensure that you don't have a second round of downtime to fix the problem again.

Make heavy use of comments in configuration files. Most configuration in a Linux machine is done in ASCII text flat files. When you edit any of those files, put plenty of comments in the file, explaining what was changed and why. Include your name and a keyword like CHANGE, HACK, or DEBUG so that later you can use *grep* to quickly find any changes.

Attach a date to everything. So much in today's client/server world involves interconnected machines that the chronology of change can be important in debugging problems. Say server A starts to give problems on March 12, but the nature of the problem means that it does not become apparent until the month-end reports are run on April 1. It may be that you have changed several things in the last month on that server, or other servers that may be involved in the whole structure. Which change caused the problem? More than likely the one dated March 11. This can be a shortcut to a solution that will save you downtime.

Wherever possible, allow yourself a path to revert to the previous configuration if your change backfires for some reason. Otherwise, it could cost you significant downtime trying to reconstruct the old working configuration. Always keep a backup of the previous version of the configuration file you are editing. If you don't want to manage multiple old copies, comment out the old code and add the new.

Be mindful of the possible fallout effect of changes to configuration data on application data. For example, if you change a configuration file and, upon putting the application back into production, discover that your new configuration was in error, you may lose or corrupt a significant quantity of production data. Keeping a backup copy of the old configuration file will not bring the damaged production data back to life.

In a Linux environment, changing a configuration file often requires a server daemon to be stopped and restarted; be mindful of the effect this may have on clients of the server, and prepare yourself accordingly. Restarting a server that has active clients can cause the clients to hang or crash, especially if the server comes back up with some different configuration. The fix may be to simply restart the client, but if the client is on the other side of the world, there are 342 clients, or restarting the client will result in data loss, downtime may result and your situation will not be a happy one.

Avoid making changes at critical times, like the day before month end or the day the boss brings around the venture capitalists. I know you're confident that it is a minor change and it will work, 100 percent guaranteed. Alas, nothing is 100 percent guaranteed. Time your changes for off-peak and noncritical times. That way any downtime you incur as a result of the change will have minimal effect on operations. The boss will get her funding and you will keep your job.

Don't change anything unless the change is clearly necessary or useful. Changing the oil in your car on a regular basis is good for motoring reliability; on the other hand, changing the operating system revision every six months requires scheduled downtime and can introduce new problems where there were none before. Only if there is a clear benefit in increased functionality or reliability in the upgrade should you consider it. If it ain't broke, don't fix it.

If you need to implement a change in a limited time frame, such as a scheduled downtime window, invest some time in planning how you are going to manage the downtime window efficiently. Make sure you have all the information you need, as well as any media or hardware. If something is missing when the day comes, carefully consider the risks of proceeding anyway and balance them against rescheduling the downtime window to a later date. Make the most of the downtime by having a list of extra changes that would be helpful (though not production critical) that you can do if you have extra time left in the scheduled window after the essential jobs have been done.

In the Linux world, make full use of the advantages offered you by the user community. Use mailing lists or discussion groups to describe the change you need to implement and ask others what they think. You may be able to reap the benefit of others' experience at no cost to you. The Linux user community is a valuable resource, but unfamiliar to those who have not experienced this way of operating. Don't underestimate it.

Let me conclude this chapter with the following war story, which was a learning experience for me. Once upon a time, longer ago now than I like to admit, I worked in a university research center where we used a pair of PCs as a firewall. These machines ran in the corner of an empty, lights-out room. Now the university went on a power conservation kick, so of course, someone who didn't realize what these firewall machines did walked into the room one day and simply turned them off, reasoning that some energy wasting scoundrel had left them going by mistake. Within moments heads began popping out of offices. The heads rapidly concluded that there was a fundamental problem and formed a delegation, aimed straight at the little dark room. When we got there it was easy enough to see what had happened. The fix was another matter. We simply turned the machines back on, waited till they had come up and returned to our offices to pick up our gopher searches (yes, it was that long ago), where they had died. The problem was, we were still down. The firewall machines had booted fine, but the firewall software wasn't doing the job. It turned out that the administrator who set the firewall up had not taken care to ensure that the proper configuration files were up-to-date, nor had he documented anything. The icing on the cake was, he had left his job only a week or so previous, so the whole burden of reverse engineering his broken firewall fell to the new administrator. He was a very good administrator, but it still took him several days to get everything working properly again.

Apart from the importance of documenting, which I have already talked about, the lesson I learned that day was what I call the Extra Boot principle. Any time I alter the configuration of a running machine and that alteration needs to survive a reboot, I always consider what would happen if the machine were rebooted when I am teaching a class three time zones away. I am close to paranoid about checking that any configuration file or script that needs to be altered gets checked and double checked to make sure that the machine and its applications will come up properly on a reboot. Then, if at all possible, I always do the acid test, a reboot, before I leave the site. I fondly think of it as kicking it one last time before I go. When the system comes up correctly without having to place my hands on anything, I know I'm not likely to be getting unhappy calls. Production requirements may not always allow that reboot. In that case, I try to schedule a test reboot when I am going to be close by so that I am on the spot to determine what the problem is.

What You Can Do Now

1. Using my criteria and your own experience, evaluate and choose a Linux distribution that you feel comfortable with. As you look at distros, observe which kernel version is most commonly used by the commercial distros, as it is probably the most stable at the time.

2. Evaluate the applications you need to serve, and their data, and work out a disk partition layout.

3. Install Linux. After installing Linux, but before installing any applications or data, review the operating system configuration. Remove anything that is not obviously needed, and check the configuration for required services.

4. Install your applications and data, and test them thoroughly. Testing may reveal operating system configuration problems or bugs. Get them worked out now, before you go into production.

5. Simulate a power failure and make sure your UPS is working properly. Also, do a reboot and make sure everything comes back up, working properly.

Now that you have a working system, document it and back it up. If you need to recover in a disaster, you have a golden image to recover from. This backup can then form the foundation for other servers.

Building Reliable
Disk Storage

"Two may keep counsel when the third's away."

—Shakespeare (Titus Andronicus, Act IV, Scene ii)

So far in our server construction we have sourced a hardware platform designed to yield the best stability and reliability possible. We have also installed an operating system on that platform that will be reliable. Is there anything else that can improve the reliability of our server before it is production ready?

As disk storage is one of the prime failure risks, you should consider using a RAID to reduce your disk failure liability. The originators of the RAID acronym and the concept were researchers at the University of California, Berkeley, who introduced the phrase as *redundant array of inexpensive disks* in a 1988 paper. Since then, many have replaced "inexpensive" with "independent." Either way, a RAID is a means of introducing redundancy to disk storage to reduce the liability to the server in the event of a disk failure. RAID is what this chapter is about. I start by going through the theory of RAID and show you how the different RAID levels work. Then I provide a hands-on tour of the software RAID functionality of the 2.4 Linux kernel.

RAID Theory

RAID is, strictly speaking, an inaccurate acronym, in that it includes the term *redundant,* implying that any RAID incorporates some form of redundancy. This is not the case. The RAID concept is to collect two or more pieces of disk storage and combine them into one virtual storage entity. The manner in which these pieces are combined may incorporate redundancy, if fault tolerance and hence improved reliability is the objective. On the other hand, these multiple pieces of storage space may also be combined in a manner that improves disk performance or simply makes it easier to manage the overall disk storage picture. I will show you how each of these methods works, but I'll concentrate on those RAID configurations that truly incorporate redundancy in the hands-on section at the end of the chapter, since the focus of this book is primarily server reliability.

The Basic Building Block

Any RAID is an *array*, or group, of two or more contiguous pieces of disk space. A piece of disk space in this context could be an entire physical disk or a single partition within a disk. No rules say that each of the pieces must be the same size, that each of the pieces must be implemented on the same disk technology (for example, ATA or SCSI), or even that the pieces must reside on different disks. The size and location of the pieces depend on the nature of the RAID being built and the RAID's purpose.

In the Linux RAID implementation, this basic building block takes the form of a standard disk partition, created and managed in the same way as any other disk partition. If you want a RAID consisting of three drives, you create a single partition on each of the drives, each partition using the entire drive. Any standard disk partitioning command such as *fdisk* may be used to create the partitions.

A second thing to understand about RAID is that it operates below the level of logical storage entities (such as file systems). Once configured and operating, a RAID appears to be a physical storage device to any higher-level data structure that uses it. In other words, I could create a 10-GB RAID that consists of pieces carved from four different physical disk drives that incorporate redundancy so that, if any of the drives were to fail, the RAID would still be fully functional. Once configured, I may choose to use the RAID to store files and build a file system metadata structure in it. To that file system, the RAID will appear to be a single 10-GB storage device irrespective of how many actual disks are in it or how much actual storage space was required to build it. When the file system reads and writes from the RAID, it has no idea that its data is spread around several drives, possibly in duplicate. The file system thinks it is writing into a single, contiguous 10-GB disk partition. This layered approach is a great advantage because no code or application using a RAID needs alteration in any way to work in a RAID environment.

Software Raid versus Hardware RAID

Combining more than one physical device to appear to be a single device can be implemented in two ways. You could design a special hardware device that contains multiple drives internally, but has firmware and purpose-built hardware inside the box that makes these multiple drives appear to be one physical drive to the server the box is attached to. Such a device is a hardware RAID and usually has only one data connector (typically ATA or SCSI) to attach it to the server. Each of these hardware RAID devices will have its own operating parameters and features. Since they appear to the operating system as a single drive, they are treated no differently from any other drive from a Linux standpoint.

There can be a good cost benefit for you to use a hardware-based solution rather than the software RAID presented in this chapter, but implementing hardware RAID is a vendor product-specific issue that falls outside of the range of this book. Hardware RAID units often come in the form of a disk controller card modified with extra hardware to perform the disk mirroring and checksum calculation required by the various RAID levels. If this is the type of hardware RAID you are considering, you will need to ensure that there is a kernel driver for the card you choose. To be sure, check with the vendor of the card for the availability of Linux support and check the hardware compatibility lists for your distribution. You can find the Red Hat compatibility list at hardware.redhat.com.

The second way a RAID can be built is to use the way the operating system already knows how to talk to disks. Within the operating system, an extension is built so that the concatenation of disks or partitions into RAID devices can be done within the operating system software. Thus, a RAID can be built using standard disk devices and disk hardware. This is termed a software RAID. This capability has been available in the Linux kernel for several years, but has undergone revision and improvement for the current 2.4 kernel release. This chapter talks about software RAIDs.

What about ATA Raid?

Motherboards are commonly available with as many as four on-board ATA controllers. Each ATA controller supports one master and one slave device so, in theory, such a board could support eight devices. If one of them were a CD-ROM, that would leave room for seven disks. Unfortunately, there are two problems. One is that performance is poor when concurrently writing to an ATA master and its slave, and the nature of RAID arrays is that they constantly do just that. Consequently, it is only practical to put one RAID drive per controller. If the CD is not frequently used, you could safely have four RAID drives. As 40-GB drives are now common and cost effective, that could give you a practical 120-GB RAID5 array. If your server motherboard has only two to four ATA controllers but you require more, ATA controller peripheral cards are widely available.

The other problem is that when one of the drives fails, you need to bring the server down and power it off to safely replace the failed ATA drive. The ATA standard does not support *hot swapping* (the ability to remove or add a device to the bus while it is powered on).

About Hot-Swap Disk Hardware

If you decide to build a software RAID array, you will want to consider hot-swap disks. After all, the whole idea of a RAID is to have, if at all possible, no server downtime when a disk fails. It defeats the purpose to some extent if you build a RAID using disks that cannot be physically replaced without bringing the server down. Hardware RAID arrays use hot-swap disks as a matter of course.

The SCSI bus is better suited to hot-swap RAIDS. Any of the various SCSI standards support at least seven drives per bus, and hot-swap SCSI hardware is widely available, in many cases in engineered prepackaged server configurations. While SCSI hot-swap hardware solutions are available and are a mature technology, Linux kernel support for hot-swap SCSI devices is a work in progress. At the time of writing, support in the kernel SCSI code is in the experimental stage. It is possible for this code to determine that a device has been hot plugged. The challenge that remains is mapping device driver entries consistently. If one drive fails, it is necessary to ensure that the hot-plug replacement appears to the operating system as the same device as the failed drive; otherwise serious confusion ensues. Look for this support in the near future. At the moment, it may be necessary to use a proprietary extension to the public kernel code to fully support hot-plug SCSI devices.

The more popular and less expensive ATA bus unfortunately has fewer hot-swap options. Units containing a pair of hot-swap drives are available that plug in to a standard ATA controller. However, they are generally pre-configured to function as two-drive hardware RAID1 arrays. There is a standard for hot-swap PCI (Peripheral Connection Interface, the hardware bus that is the de facto standard in today's PC) devices called CompactPCI, which is designed primarily for the industrial PC market. It does have the advantage that it supports hot swapping whole PCI cards, one of which could be an ATA controller. CompactPCI hardware is also built to higher standards than regular hardware and should be very durable. There is of course a cost premium. Further information about CompactPCI can be found at www.picmg.org. Compaq has developed a proprietary hot-swap PCI standard they call PCI Hot-Plug. Even better, there is a Linux driver for this technology; better still, it was developed for the current 2.4 kernel.

Understanding RAID Levels

I touched briefly on the subject of RAID levels in Chapter 2, "Risk Analysis." Here, I expand on this topic and give you a more complete description of the five different RAID levels supported by the 2.4 kernel. These levels are summarized in Table 5.1 and further detailed in the following sections. As the primary focus of this book is reliability, you will see that in the third column I have noted which RAID levels support a measure of disk redundancy.

A RAID is made up of two or more contiguous pieces of disk that are in fact traditional disk partitions. There is no rule that says each of these partitions must take up the entire disk, although that is common for several good reasons, which I'll talk about in turn. To keep the text simple, however, for the rest of this chapter I'll use the term *disk* to mean one discrete

Table 5.1 RAID Levels

LEVEL	FEATURES	REDUNDANCY
Linear	Disk partition concatenation	No
0	Data striping	No
1	Data mirroring	Yes
4	Data redundancy, achieved using checksums	Yes
5	Data redundancy, achieved using distributed checksums	Yes

storage piece of a RAID. I would prefer to be more technically correct and call it a partition, but disk is the terminology most commonly used in the documentation and I would rather use the common terminology than create my own. Further information on RAID levels and other aspects of RAID in general can be found at www.raid-advisory.com.

Linear RAID

The benefit of a Linear RAID is an increase in storage management flexibility. One of the classic challenges in managing storage is to be able to predict and deal with disks that become full. It would be convenient if the volumes of data we deal with shrunk as often as they grew. Unfortunately, this has not been my experience. The English satirist C. Northcote Parkinson formulated Parkinson's Law, which states that work expands to meet the time available for its completion. I suggest a corollary: Data expands to meet the space available for its storage. With this in mind, prudent systems administrators will do their best to guess how much storage space is needed for an application in the future. As the space allotted approaches fill, the administrator has to prepare for a storage restructuring weekend in which new disks are installed; new, more spacious partitions and file systems are made; and the old data is moved into its larger quarters. If the file system could be extended beyond the size of the disk, it would be really useful if two or more disks could be concatenated to provide the storage for such an enlarged file system, and that is possible using a Linear RAID.

Each successive disk in a linear mode RAID is written to serially, as illustrated in Figure 5.1. By this I mean that if there were three disks in the array, writing would start at the beginning of the first and only spill over to the second when the first is completely full, and so on to the third or more. Note that I have illustrated the array as it would look immediately after four new files have been created in a new file system, so the files are not fragmented. As files are deleted, added, and edited, they will become more and more fragmented; the Linear RAID will not do anything to stop this natural process of file fragmentation. You can see that there is no storage redundancy in a Linear RAID.

There may be a marginal performance improvement once data has spread to more than one device. For example, if two pieces of active data find themselves stored on different disks, operations on the data would be performed in parallel, to the best extent to which the hardware is capable. The size of the disks in the array need not be similar, or even close to similar.

There are other terms commonly used to describe what Linux calls Linear RAID. You may hear it referred to as disk spanning, or by the acronym

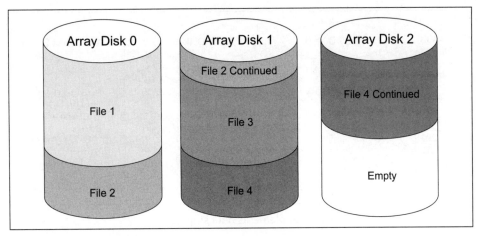

Figure 5.1   Each successive disk in a Linear RAID is written to serially.

JBOD, for *Just A Bunch of Disks*. Do not confuse Linear RAID with Logical Volume Management (LVM). While the idea of a Linear RAID is somewhat similar to the idea of a logical volume, LVM goes a great deal beyond Linear RAID as a disk management scheme. Chapter 8, "Logical Volume Management," presents LVM in detail.

RAID Level 0

RAID0 implements data striping. This is similar to linear mode RAID in that two or more disks are concatenated into a single storage space, and that there is no redundancy built in to the array (when you think RAID0, think zero redundancy). What is different about RAID0 compared to linear mode RAID is the way the data gets distributed across the disks in the array. On a write operation, a RAID0 array will assign a chunk of data to be stored on each disk of the array. The chunk size is a configurable parameter of the array. Using a 4 KB chunk size, for example, a write of 16 KB to a three-disk RAID0 would result in the first 4 KB written to the first disk, the second 4 KB written to the second disk, and a third 4 KB written to the third disk. This set of assignments—one chunk on each disk of the array—is termed a *stripe*. Once the first complete stripe is written, the assignment then loops around and begins a second stripe, writing the final 4 KB chunk of the file back on the first disk, as shown in Figure 5.2. The key, as far as RAID0 is concerned, is that these operations are done in parallel to the best extent the hardware allows. This parallel distribution of data flow across multiple devices yields significant performance gains in most circumstances, which

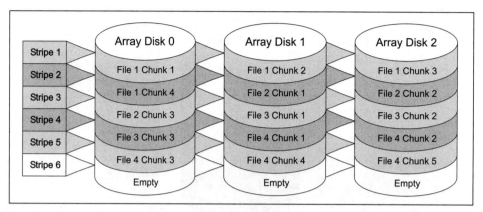

Figure 5.2   A RAID Level 0 array implements data striping.

is the design intent. The chunk size also affects the performance of the array, the ideal size varying depending on the nature of the data being written with 32 KB considered a reasonable starting point for experimenting.

In an N disk array, each disk of which can sustain B KB per second, a RAID0 array would in ideal conditions give N * B KB per second throughput. In practice, operating system overhead and congestion on the data bus supporting the disks will reduce this performance. Bus congestion is usually the greatest source of the performance reduction. A well-designed RAID0 would use a bus having a bandwidth well in excess of each disk on it, or spread its disks across multiple buses. Though not a requirement, it is preferable for all of the disks in a RAID0 to be the same size. Otherwise, as the smaller disks fill, fewer disks are available for new data storage. Thus, the size of the array effectively becomes smaller, and with it the degree to which operations can be parallelized, resulting in poorer performance. Since performance is why you build a RAID0, this is clearly counterproductive.

RAID Level 1

RAID1 implements disk mirroring. This is the simplest way to achieve redundancy in a RAID, with all disks in the array maintained by the RAID driver as exact duplicate copies of one another, as shown in Figure 5.3. Clearly, in this case if any disk in the array fails, any other disk can supply the required data. The level of redundancy is as deep as the number of disks you add to the array. An array with three disks has a double level of

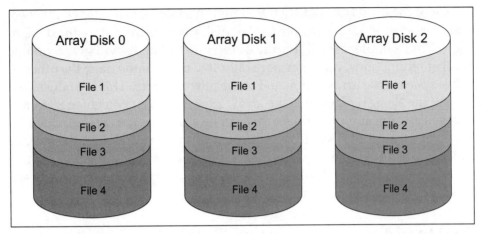

Figure 5.3   A RAID Level 1 array is the first level to support data redundancy.

redundancy, allowing any two disks to fail simultaneously and maintain data availability.

The Linux RAID driver allows construction of a RAID1 array having disks of different size, although this makes no logical sense as the usable size of the array is limited by the size of the smallest disk. Write performance on a RAID1 tends to be slightly less compared to a non-RAID disk because the amount of data written to disk exactly doubles for a two-disk array, triples with three disks, and so on. As with RAID0, however, the writes are done in parallel and, barring serious bus congestion, the added overhead should not be substantial.

Reads on a RAID1 can see a performance improvement as the first available data copy from any disk in the array should be served first. After a failed disk is replaced, a replacement disk is inserted into the array and the kernel RAID driver will rebuild the mirrored data from the existing good disk. Be aware that this mirror rebuilding can involve substantial amounts of data to be written. A RAID1 made up of 40 GB disks, if they were full, would involve writing 40 GB of data to a replacement drive. To ensure that this large write requirement does not drown the server, the RAID driver throttles the speed at which the recovery occurs, effectively spreading it over enough time to ensure the server can still do its regular work without much impairment. This carries a risk, as a second failure during the rebuilding of a two-disk array could result in irrecoverable data loss, but it does allow the server to stay in business. It is a classic example of the trade-off between production performance and reliability.

One of the drawbacks of RAID1 is that to achieve redundancy it is necessary to at least double the amount of disk space used to store the data, or more. For example, a RAID1 array of three 10-GB disks will give a double level of redundancy, yet it can store only 10 GB of unique data; the other 20 GB of space in the array is devoted to the mirror copies. This introduces the idea of the *storage efficiency* of the array. Expressed as a percentage, storage efficiency is the amount of data that can be stored in the array divided by the total amount of disk storage devoted to the array. Hence, the storage efficiency of a RAID1 array is at best 50 percent—less if more than a single level of redundancy is desired. The three-disk array would have a storage efficiency of only 33 percent.

RAID Level 4

The next RAID level supported in Linux is RAID4. A RAID4 array must have at the least three disks and is the first RAID level to make use of parity checksums to provide storage redundancy. In a RAID4 array, data is striped across all but one of the disks, as it is at the RAID0 level. The RAID4 array then calculates a checksum of each stripe written and writes these checksum values (themselves a chunk in size) to the last disk in the array, as shown in Figure 5.4.

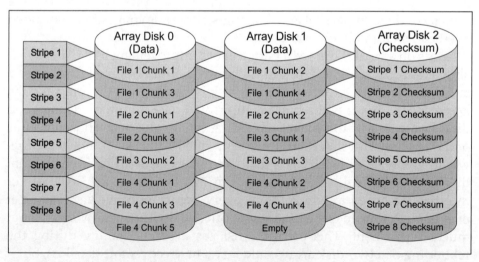

Figure 5.4 A RAID Level 4 array introduces the use of checksums to implement redundancy with better storage efficiency than a RAID1 array.

Now, if any of the data drives fails, the missing chunks stored on that disk can be dynamically recreated by the RAID driver by reading the surviving chunks and the checksum chunk, using the same calculation that produced the checksum in reverse to infer the contents of the missing chunk. On its own, RAID4 thus gives only a single level of redundancy. If that were as far as we could go, it would be no better from a reliability standpoint than RAID1. So to increase the basic RAID4 degree of redundancy, the Linux RAID drivers introduce support for the use of spare disks. A spare disk is one installed, powered on, and identified as a member of the RAID; but until a drive failure, it is unused, acting as a hot spare. If a drive fails, the RAID driver automatically starts using the spare. Thus, you can increase the level of redundancy in the array to the extent of the number of spare disks you allocate. Remember also from the discussion of hardware in Chapter 3, "Choosing the Right Hardware," that support for hot-swap disks is not universal in the Linux world. Without hot-swap disk hardware you cannot safely replace the failed disk without bringing the server down, and that means unscheduled downtime. Thus, subsequent to a disk failure in an array having only a single level of redundancy, you would be forced to operate with no redundancy until you can replace the failed disk. A spare disk will keep the array going and still maintain redundancy until you can schedule down time in an acceptable window.

The advantage of RAID4 over RAID1 lies in improved storage efficiency. You have seen that the storage efficiency of a RAID1 is at best 50 percent. By comparison, all but one of the disks in a RAID4 array hold data, barring any spare disks. An array of four 10-GB disks used in a single mirror copy RAID1 configuration would store 20 GB of data, while the same four drives in a RAID4 would hold 30 GB of data, with the same degree of redundancy. This RAID4 array thus gives the same level of redundancy as the RAID1 but with an improved storage efficiency of 66 percent. If you were to expand to an eight-disk array, the storage efficiency climbs to seven data disks out of eight, or 87.5 percent. You could even add a spare disk to this array and see the data efficiency drop to 78 percent, still better than the four-disk array. Compare this to a three-disk RAID1 array that gives the same double redundancy but with an efficiency of only 33 percent. This sounds wonderful. Is there a catch? Well, there usually is, and in this case it comes in the area of performance, specifically performance while the array is running in a degraded state. A degraded state means that the array has a failed drive, and data reads of any missing chunks are being satisfied by a reverse checksum calculation. This calculation has a significant CPU overhead that needs to be taken into consideration for a production environment. Until recently this calculation overhead was considered too heavy a burden to be placed on the operating system CPU, and checksum protected RAID arrays relied on special RAID controllers that did these calculations in hardware. Modern 1 GHz and faster CPU speeds mean that there is often a good supply of processing cycles available, in which case the increased computing overhead of running in a degraded state may not cause problems. On the other hand, it is a significant overhead, and you would be well advised to do some testing to determine whether your server can handle it. Otherwise, consider bearing the extra disk cost of a RAID1 array, or seek a hardware-based RAID4 solution.

WHAT HAPPENED TO RAID2 AND RAID3?

You will notice that I skipped from RAID1 straight to RAID4. You may also have heard of RAID6 or even RAID7 and you are curious to know what happened to the missing levels. The original Berkeley paper defined five RAID levels, numbered 1 through 5. Since then three more levels, 0, 6, and 7 have been added to the list. I have concentrated on levels 0, 1, 4, and 5 in the main text because they are the most popular and are supported by the Linux RAID drivers. Here are the others:

- RAID2 used a bit level checksum calculation similar to the ECC (Error Correcting Code) calculations used internally by disk controllers and real memory storage banks. RAID2 required large numbers of disks and complex controllers to implement, yet yielded little substantial benefit in either redundancy or performance over other less complex RAID levels. Consequently, it was never widely used.

- RAID3 is almost the same as RAID4, except that the chunk size is much smaller, typically under 1 KB. The performance characteristics of the small chunk size favor sequential reads of large data files, but not much else, and most find RAID5 a better all around performer.

- RAID6 closely resembles RAID5, but calculates two checksum values for each data stripe. Thus, a RAID6 array can survive the simultaneous loss of two devices. Note that this is better than a RAID5 with a spare disk, which could not survive the loss of a second disk until after its spare disk has been populated with the data from its first failed disk.

- RAID7 is not a recognized generic RAID level, rather it is a proprietary solution offered by the Storage Computer Corporation. It is a variation of RAID4, making heavy use of cache hardware to overcome the checksum disk bottleneck.

RAID4 has another performance related drawback. Any write operation requires the alteration of at least one data chunk, which in turn requires the writing or rewriting of the checksum chunk. As all of the checksum chunks are written to the same disk, this disk can become a performance bottleneck unless the array happens to consist of several slow data disks and one fast checksum disk. Chunk size will also affect performance; but as with the RAID0, there is no one ideal chunk size. Whatever the size, the checksum chunk has to be calculated and written to that one disk. The best chunk size for your server depends on a number of variables and is best determined by experiment. A chunk size of 128 KB is a reasonable starting point. The next RAID level, RAID5, is designed to address this checksum bottleneck.

RAID Level 5

RAID5 is similar in almost all respects to RAID4, with the advantage that instead of writing the checksum chunks to one drive, the RAID5 array distributes them among all drives in the array, as shown in Figure 5.5. This eliminates the bottleneck potential of the checksum disk, giving RAID5 generally better performance characteristics. This is the most popular RAID level in production servers. Like RAID4, RAID5 requires at least three disks per array, but can and often does contain more than that to improve storage efficiency. The upper limit on the number of disks in the

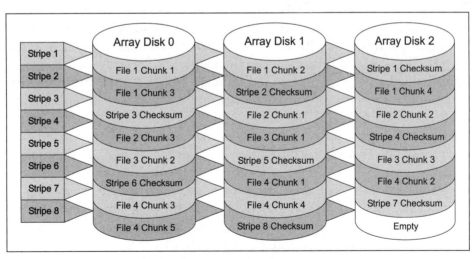

Figure 5.5 RAID Level 5 gives a good balance between storage efficiency and performance.

array is driven by the data storage requirement and the size of disk available. The number of buses is also a factor, as it is with any RAID, because it is easy to fall into the trap of overloading a bus with too many disks.

A RAID5 array still gives only a single level of redundancy. It is no different from RAID4 in that respect, and like RAID4 Linux, supports the use of spare disks if you want to reduce your risk level further. The same factors bearing on storage efficiency and CPU overhead when running in a degraded state for RAID4 apply equally to RAID5.

Combining RAID Levels

It is possible to combine more than one RAID level in a single device. One possibility, for example, is to combine performance and redundancy using a combination of RAID0 and RAID1. The concept is really quite simple. In a two-stage procedure, first you create two RAID0 arrays, and then combine them as a two-disk RAID1. The minimum number of disks for such an array is four. Figure 5.6 illustrates a six-disk example.

This combined array gives good performance combined with redundancy and with the same 50-percent space efficiency of a RAID1 array alone. Consequently, it is probably the most commonly seen combined level array. You could create a similar six-disk array but in the reverse order, first creating three RAID1 mirror pairs and using them as three disks in a RAID0, as shown in Figure 5.7.

As the RAID1 is created first, this array I termed RAID 1+0. So what is the difference between RAID 1+0 and the previous example, which I termed RAID 0+1. The difference, as it turns out, is significant. Look at the two figures and consider the effect of a single disk failure. If any disk in the RAID 0+1 array fails, one of the two three disk RAID0 arrays will be out of commission because there is no redundancy within each of the three disk stripe sets. Thus, the RAID 0+1 array has only a single level of redundancy. On the other hand, if any disk in the RAID 1+0 array fails, there must be a mirror for it, and the array continues to function. Notice that a second disk could now fail. However, as long as it was not the mate of the first failed disk, the array would survive the second failure and continue to function. In fact, as many as three disks could be dead at the same time, as long as there is only one bad disk in each RAID1 mirror pair. This is playing the odds to some extent, but it yields something better than a single level of redundancy and with no cost in space efficiency over a simple RAID1.

It is also possible to combine the striping performance of RAID0 with the checksum redundancy scheme used by RAID4 or RAID5. A RAID 0+5

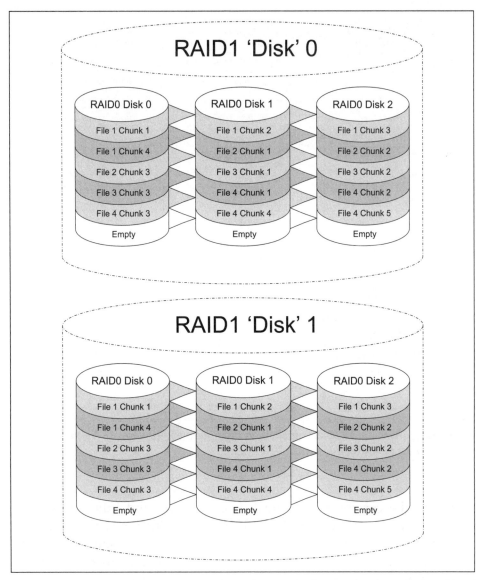

Figure 5.6   This RAID Level 0+1 array shows how multiple RAID levels can be combined in one array.

array, for example, could be made by combining three or more disks, each disk being itself a RAID0 array. This combination gives more or less the same level of redundancy and probably slightly worse performance than a RAID 0+1 combination, but gives better space efficiency—as much as 86 percent or better if the arrays are large enough. As this space efficiency is

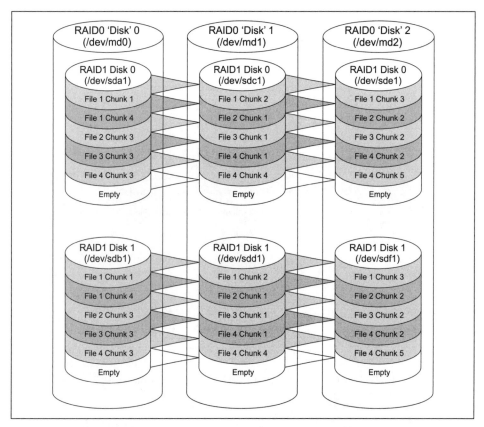

Figure 5.7 Changing the level combination order in this RAID Level 1+0 array improves redundancy over a RAID Level 0+1.

gained at the cost of a great deal of complexity and little substantive improvement in redundancy, the RAID 0+5 combination is not common.

Another combination to consider is the RAID 1+5 matchup. Although complex and poor in space efficiency, this "seat belt and airbag" approach gives the best redundancy of all, combining the mirroring redundancy of RAID1 with the checksum technique of RAID5. Figure 5.8 illustrates a six-disk RAID 1+5 made up of three RAID1 mirrored pairs, combined into a three-disk RAID5. Note that there is a double level of redundancy; that is, this array can always survive the simultaneous loss of any two drives. If each of the two failed drives is half of two different mirror pairs, then the RAID1 mirroring will take care of the failure. If both drives in a single mirror pair fail, the RAID5 sees that as the loss of one of its disks and uses the checksum calculation to recreate the lost data. The level of redundancy

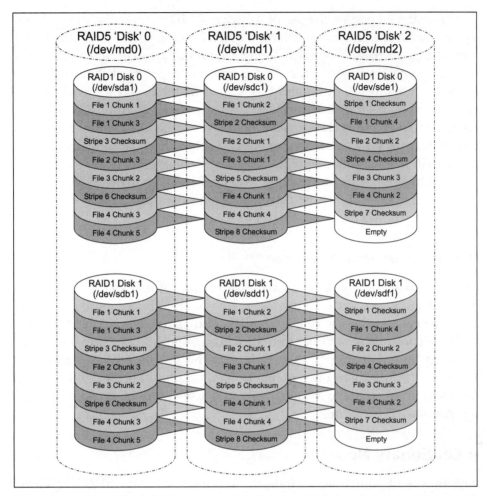

Figure 5.8 This RAID Level 1+5 array maximizes fault tolerance, but at a cost in storage efficiency.

improves again. However, if you consider that if one of the mirror pairs fails, the RAID5 will recover and that one drive from each of the surviving mirror pairs could then also fail, with the RAID1 mirroring covering those failures. Thus, if the right drives fail, as many as four out of the six total drives in the combined array could fail with no data loss! This availability comes at a cost, however, in that the space efficiency of this array is only 33 percent, with four of the six disks devoted to either checksums, mirrored data, or mirrored checksums, not to mention the complexity of the configuration. This combination is supported by the Linux RAID drivers. The next section provides a configuration example.

As mentioned earlier, the use of software RAID is a relatively new thing, especially for the checksum-oriented RAID4 and RAID5 levels, due to the computing overhead required. Today's servers, however, have such substantial processing power that this is becoming practical. You will find, however, that most discussions of combined RAID levels often include references to combining hardware and software RAID solutions to get these combined levels to work. The assumption is that to ask the operating system to bear the burden of not one but two sets of RAID redundancy, operations will have an unacceptable computational overhead cost. Using the Linux software RAID, for example, you could use a hardware-based solution to create several mirrored disk pairs, and then provide these disks to the software RAID to form a RAID4 or RAID5 array.

Partial versus Total Redundancy

One final point to consider in the construction of a RAID is how much redundancy you want to implement. I have already compared different RAID levels and the use of a spare disk. You also need to consider using multiple controllers, not only to reduce bus congestion performance problems, but to eliminate points of failure. Some people will also go to the length of placing disks on separate power supplies. Figure 5.9 illustrates the maximum extent to which you could use RAID to protect yourself against hardware failure.

A Cautionary Note

One important point that I cannot stress enough is that *no RAID is infallible*. Do not fall under the misconception that because you have stored your data on a RAID, you need not be concerned about backups. There are plenty of risks that can destroy an entire RAID. Examples include an application that malfunctions, accidental or deliberate erasure of data by an employee, and the loss of an entire server for whatever reason. Although rare, it is even possible for a single disk to fail in such a fashion that it brings down other devices on the bus with it. If there is more than one disk on the same bus, your RAID will almost certainly be destroyed. Also, if more than one disk in any RAID is on the same controller, then a controller failure will also destroy the RAID. A RAID significantly reduces the liability of data loss due to the failure of a single disk, and that is definitely useful enough to use a RAID, but it is not perfect. There is no replacement for reliable backups.

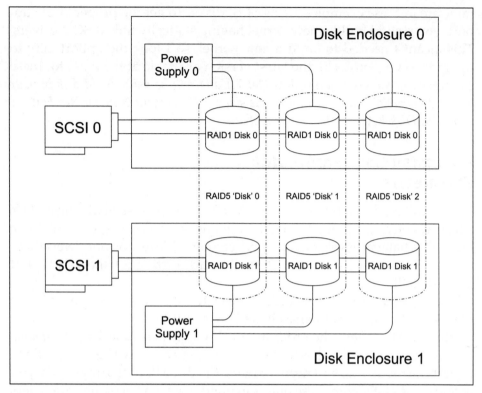

Figure 5.9 In this arrangement, redundant hardware is employed to build a RAID with no single point of failure.

Having briefed you on the theory of the different RAID levels, I'll now show you how to implement them using the Linux 2.4 kernel. Note that the RAID drivers are also available as patches to the 2.2 series kernel. For further information on using RAID in an older kernel or other questions, you may want to join the linux-raid mailing list at vger.kernel.org.

Configuring Linux Software RAID

This section leads you through the configuration requirements for the major RAID levels listed in Table 5.1 as well as two examples of combined RAID levels. To begin, I need to make an important point concerning the kernel I used for purposes of this section. The stock Red Hat 7.1 kernel is a version 2.4.2 kernel, having its SCSI driver support implemented as loadable modules. This can cause problems if your RAID arrays are built, as mine are in these examples, using SCSI disks. To get the proper SCSI support, you should build a new kernel having statically linked SCSI drivers. This meant I needed to build a new kernel, so I took the opportunity to upgrade to version 2.4.5, (the latest version available at the time) for these examples. *If you are running Red Hat 7.1 and will be using SCSI disk in your RAID, be sure to read the details in the sidebar "Important Note for Red Hat 7.1 and SCSI Disk RAID" later in this section.*

Understanding */etc/raidtab* Parameters

The central configuration file for all RAID arrays on a server is */etc/raidtab*. All arrays on a server are defined within this one file, however many there may be, whatever level they may be, combined levels or not. Everything happens in this file, so this is where I'll start. Listing 5.1 shows a typical */etc/raidtab* file.

It is important to note the order in which the parameters appear in the file, as the function that parses it is picky about this. Also, if you want to combine RAID levels, the order in which the arrays appear in */etc/raidtab* has to make sense. That is, if you want to create a RAID5 using three RAID1 mirror arrays, you need to define the three RAID1 arrays *before* you define the RAID5. With these points in mind, here is a list of the parameters and their meaning.

- **raiddev.** Each RAID definition starts with a *raiddev* parameter, as seen at lines 6 and 20. The name of the device is arbitrary, but the convention is */dev/md0* for the first array, */dev/md1* for the second and so on.

- **raid-level.** This is self-explanatory, valid values for *raid-level* being linear, 0, 1, 4, 5, as I described previously.

- **nr-raid-disks.** This parameter defines how many disks will be in the array. Currently 12 disks are supported as a maximum, but this number has already been extended to 256 in development kernels.

- **nr-spare-disks.** If you want to include spare disks, *nr-spare-disks* defines how many there will be in the spare disk array. Note that spare disks are only supported at RAID levels 1, 4, and 5.

- **persistent-superblock.** Not to be confused with the metadata superblock object in an ext2 file system, this superblock is RAID metadata. It is a small data block placed at the end of each RAID array device. It contains all of the information necessary to start the

```
 1 # sample raid config file
 2 # i campbell july 2001
 3
 4 # first array is a two-disk RAID1
 5
 6 raiddev /dev/md0
 7      raid-level              1
 8      nr-raid-disks           2
 9      nr-spare-disks          0
10      persistent-superblock 1
11      chunk-size              4
12
13      device                /dev/sdb1
14      raid-disk             0
15      device                /dev/sdc1
16      raid-disk             1
17
18 # next array is a five-disk RAID5
19
20 raiddev /dev/md1
21      raid-level              5
22      nr-raid-disks           5
23      nr-spare-disks          1
24      persistent-superblock 1
25      parity-algorithm        left-symmetric
26      chunk-size              128
27
28      device                /dev/sdd1
29      raid-disk             0
30      device                /dev/sde1
31      raid-disk             1
32      device                /dev/sdf1
33      raid-disk             2
34      device                /dev/sdg1
35      raid-disk             3
36      device                /dev/sdh1
37      raid-disk             4
38
39      device                /dev/sdi1
40      spare-disk              1
```

Listing 5.1   This is a typical `/etc/raidtab` RAID configuration file.

RAID based on the contents of */etc/raidtab*. It is there so that at boot
time the kernel can make sure that no disks have been moved since
the RAID was last used. This could well be the case if you choose to

restructure your disk storage such that the partition that was once */dev/sda1* becomes */dev/sdc1* by virtue of its parent disk having been moved to a different SCSI address or controller. In this case there would be a discrepancy between the RAID superblock, which would list */dev/sdc1* as the first disk in the array, and */etc/raidtab*, which may list */dev/sdc1* as the third disk in the array, for example, or even as a disk belonging to a different array. This is useful to prevent disk mix-ups doing serious damage to a RAID; consequently the value of *persistent-superblock* should always be set to 1. A copy of the entire RAID superblock is on each device in the array to ensure redundancy. It is also important when you create disk partitions destined to be elements of a RAID that you flag them as type 0xfd. This ensures that the kernel will look for this RAID metadata at boot time.

- **parity-algorithm.** This parameter is only applicable to RAID5 arrays and controls the way in which the data checksums are written to disk. There are several possible patterns for laying out both the data blocks and the checksums across the disks of the array, and there has been a substantial amount of research into the subject dating back ten or more years. The authors of the current RAID drivers suggest that in general the best one is *left-symmetric*. You may want to experiment with other choices for performance reasons; in any case, the algorithm chosen should not affect data redundancy.

- **chunk-size.** The value of *chunk-size* determines the amount of data written to each disk before moving on to the next disk. This is also commonly called the stripe size. Don't confuse this with the term stripe width, which is the number of disks in the array. Look back to Figure 5.5. If this RAID5 had a chunk size of 128 KB, then one data stripe would include 128 KB on each of the two data chunks, and 128 KB of checksum on the checksum chunk; hence, one stripe holds 256 KB of application data. The stripe size for this array would be 128 KB. The stripe width would be three. The *chunk-size* parameter matters to all RAID levels except linear. It still is necessary to include a *chunk-size* value when defining a Linear RAID to keep the RAID driver happy. However, its value is meaningless because a Linear RAID does no data striping. The *chunk-size* parameter is expressed as a number of kilobytes, it must be a power of two, and has a maximum value of 4,096. Values in the range 4 to 128 are reasonable. Like the *parity-algorithm* parameter, trying different values of *chunk-size* can improve performance, but will not significantly affect redundancy.

■ **device.** This parameter is used to define the disk devices in the array. As explained earlier, a device in this context is a regular disk partition, tagged with the 0xfd type flag. Immediately following each device line must be a line describing the part this device will play in the array. There are four possible parameters here:

  ■ *raid-disk* specifies that the drive just defined will be an active disk in the array being defined. The value given to *raid-disk* indicates the position in the array, starting to count at 0.

  ■ *spare-disk* is supported as described in earlier sections for RAID levels 4 and 5.

  ■ *parity-disk* is valid only for a RAID4 array. A device can be specified as a *parity-disk*, which forces it to the end of the array where it would become the checksum disk.

  ■ *failed-disk* flags a disk as failed. This is an interesting option, allowing the construction of a RAID in a degraded state. This can

---

IMPORTANT NOTE FOR RED HAT 7.1 AND A SCSI DISK RAID

The kernel version shipped with Red Hat 7.1 includes support for SCSI disks, but it is compiled as a module to be loaded into the kernel at boot time. This causes problems for autodetecting RAID superblocks. The kernel code that looks for the 0xfd flag in a partition indicating that partition to be part of a RAID occurs in the boot sequence *before* any modules are loaded. Thus if your kernel supports SCSI as a module, RAID superblocks residing on any SCSI disk will *not* be detected at boot. To work around this, Red Hat includes an alternate means of starting such arrays by including in the boot script */etc/rc.d/rc.sysinit* an *if* clause that uses the */etc/raidtab* file in conjunction with *raidstart* to start all of your arrays. This will work fine so long as no disks in an array have failed and the current SCSI disk identifiers are consistent with the array definitions in */etc/raidtab*. If you have experienced a disk failure, neither of these conditions is necessarily true, however, and the script method of initializing the arrays can fail. The intent of the designers of the RAID driver was to let the RAID superblock gracefully handle these issues. This is the way it should be done.

Consequently, you should do two things to your stock 7.1 installation. First, you need to build a new kernel that statically links into the kernel the appropriate SCSI driver for your SCSI controller. Building kernels is beyond the scope of this book. If necessary, consult the Kernel-HOWTO or your favorite Linux systems administration book. Once you have your new kernel, you should then comment out the *if* clause in */etc/rc.d/rc.sysinit* that attempts to start the RAID arrays. Look in the script for the comment "Add raid devices."

be useful to define and start to use an array, but at the time you
do not have all of the disks that are intended to be in it.

Sample RAID Configurations

Now let's look at some sample * /etc/raidtab* files for the standard RAID levels, and then some combined levels. Listing 5.2 shows the configuration for
a three-disk RAID0 striped array. There are no *parity-algorithm* or *spare-disk*
keywords since they are irrelevant at the RAID0 level.

Listing 5.3 is for a RAID1 array having three disks. The *parity-algorithm*
parameter is missing, of course, as RAID1 does not use checksums.

Listing 5.4 is for a four-disk RAID4 array with a spare disk. Although
RAID4 does use parity checksums, no *parity-algorithm* parameter is neces-

```
 1 raiddev /dev/md0
 2      raid-level             0
 3      nr-raid-disks          3
 4      persistent-superblock  1
 5      chunk-size             32
 6
 7      device                 /dev/sda1
 8      raid-disk              0
 9      device                 /dev/sdb1
10      raid-disk              1
11      device                 /dev/sdc1
12      raid-disk              2
```

Listing 5.2   Here is a sample `/etc/raidtab` for a RAID0 configuration.

```
 1 raiddev /dev/md0
 2      raid-level             1
 3      nr-raid-disks          3
 4      persistent-superblock  1
 5      chunk-size             32
 6
 7      device                 /dev/sda1
 8      raid-disk              0
 9      device                 /dev/sdb1
10      raid-disk              1
11      device                 /dev/sdc1
12      raid-disk              2
```

Listing 5.3   Here is what `/etc/raidtab` looks like for a RAID1 configuration.

```
 1 raiddev /dev/md0
 2      raid-level            4
 3      nr-raid-disks         4
 4      nr-spare-disks        1
 5      persistent-superblock 1
 6      chunk-size            32
 7
 8      device               /dev/sda1
 9      raid-disk            0
10      device               /dev/sdb1
11      raid-disk            1
12      device               /dev/sdc1
13      raid-disk            2
14      device               /dev/sdd1
15      raid-disk            3
16
17      device               /dev/sde1
18      spare-disk           0
```

Listing 5.4   Here is a sample `/etc/raidtab` for a RAID4 configuration.

sary to specify the layout of the checksum information in the array, as by definition all of the checksums in RAID4 go on the last disk of the array.

Listing 5.5 shows the configuration for a four-disk RAID5 array, which is almost identical to the RAID4 configuration except for the addition of the *parity-algorithm* parameter.

```
 1 raiddev /dev/md0
 2      raid-level            5
 3      nr-raid-disks         4
 4      nr-spare-disks        1
 5      persistent-superblock 1
 6      parity-algorithm     left-symmetric
 7      chunk-size            64
 8
 9      device               /dev/sda1
10      raid-disk            0
11      device               /dev/sdb1
12      raid-disk            1
13      device               /dev/sdc1
14      raid-disk            2
15      device               /dev/sdd1
```

Listing 5.5   This `/etc/raidtab` is for a RAID5 configuration.

```
16      raid-disk               3
17
18      device                  /dev/sde1
19      spare-disk              0
```

Listing 5.5 This /etc/raidtab is for a RAID5 configuration. (continued)

Now let's see how you can configure combined RAID levels. Listing 5.6 shows the configuration file for the RAID 1+0 configuration illustrated in Figure 5.7.

```
 1 raiddev /dev/md0
 2      raid-level              1
 3      nr-raid-disks           2
 4      persistent-superblock   1
 5
 6      device                  /dev/sda1
 7      raid-disk               0
 8      device                  /dev/sdb1
 9      raid-disk               1
10
11 raiddev /dev/md1
12      raid-level              1
13      nr-raid-disks           2
14      persistent-superblock   1
15
16      device                  /dev/sdc1
17      raid-disk               0
18      device                  /dev/sdd1
19      raid-disk               1
20
21 raiddev /dev/md2
22      raid-level              1
23      nr-raid-disks           2
24      persistent-superblock   1
25
26      device                  /dev/sde1
27      raid-disk               0
28      device                  /dev/sdf1
29      raid-disk               1
30
31 raiddev /dev/md3
32      raid-level              0
```

Listing 5.6 Combining RAID levels results in this /etc/raidtab for a RAID 1+0 configuration.

```
33      nr-raid-disks         3
34      persistent-superblock 1
35      chunk-size            32
36
37      device                /dev/md0
38      raid-disk             0
39      device                /dev/md1
40      raid-disk             1
41      device                /dev/md2
42      raid-disk             2
```

Listing 5.6 Combining RAID levels results in this `/etc/raidtab` for a RAID 1+0 configuration. (continued)

Finally, Listing 5.7 shows what the configuration file for the RAID 1+5 array shown in Figure 5.8 would look like; you'll notice that it is almost identical to the RAID 1+0 configuration.

```
 1 raiddev /dev/md0
 2      raid-level            1
 3      nr-raid-disks         2
 4      persistent-superblock 1
 5
 6      device                /dev/sda1
 7      raid-disk             0
 8      device                /dev/sdb1
 9      raid-disk             1
10
11 raiddev /dev/md1
12      raid-level            1
13      nr-raid-disks         2
14      persistent-superblock 1
15
16      device                /dev/sdc1
17      raid-disk             0
18      device                /dev/sdd1
19      raid-disk             1
20
21 raiddev /dev/md2
22      raid-level            1
23      nr-raid-disks         2
24      persistent-superblock 1
25
26      device                /dev/sde1
```

Listing 5.7 Similar to the previous listing is this `/etc/raidtab` for a RAID 1+5 configuration.

```
27        raid-disk            0
28        device               /dev/sdf1
29        raid-disk            1
30
31 raiddev /dev/md3
32        raid-level           5
33        nr-raid-disks        3
34        persistent-superblock 1
35        parity-algorithm     left-symmetric
36        chunk-size           32
37
38        device               /dev/md0
39        raid-disk            0
40        device               /dev/md1
41        raid-disk            1
42        device               /dev/md2
```

Listing 5.7 Similar to the previous listing is this `/etc/raidtab` for a RAID 1+5 configuration. (continued)

Managing RAID Arrays

You now know the theory of the different RAID levels and how to configure them. This final section talks about the commands you will need to initialize and manage your RAID arrays once you have them configured, including procedures for replacing failed disks. Please note that these examples are based on the RAID drivers for the 2.4.5 kernel release level. If you are working with a different kernel, some of the commands and log output will almost certainly have changed, as, like many elements of Linux, the RAID tools are under constant revision and improvement.

Initializing Your Array

Having partitioned your drives and created an /etc/raidtab defining the RAID you want, the next step is to initialize the array. This ensures that all of the disks in the array are available, writes RAID superblock information to the disks as necessary, and, if mirroring or checksums are involved, makes sure that any data that needs synchronization gets it. The command that does the task is *mkraid*. You will pass *mkraid* as an argument the name of the array in /etc/raidtab that you want initialized. This is what it will look like in the case of a simple one-pair RAID1 mirrored array.

```
# mkraid /dev/md1
handling MD device /dev/md1
analyzing super-block
disk 0: /dev/sdc1, 208813kB, raid superblock at 208704kB
disk 1: /dev/sdd1, 205808kB, raid superblock at 205696kB
```

Note that in this case the RAID disks are slightly different in size. The two drives this RAID is built on were made by different manufacturers and have different physical disk geometries; hence, the partitions will not be exactly the same size. One of the beauties of software RAID is that this doesn't matter. The array will work just fine anyway. This is an advantage when replacing failed drives since there is no requirement to replace a failed drive with an identical replacement unit. The rule is that the replacement unit must be as large or larger than the failed unit.

When partitioning, watch for slight differences in partition size due to differences in cylinder size. The concept of the disk cylinder stems from the early days of hard disks when the drive was divided into allocation blocks built around the number of actual read/write heads inside the drive and the number of pie-shaped data sectors laid out on the media platters. This can get complicated because ATA and SCSI drives deal with this issue differently. (Good references include the Linux Partition HOWTO and the Large Disk HOWTO.)

The analyzing superblock message could be misleading, as it implies that there is a superblock to analyze. As you are creating the array, no RAID superblock currently exists. The two following lines inform you that new superblocks have been written to the RAID disks at the locations noted. It is possible, however, that one or the other of these drives is already a member of an array (specified in *etc/raidtab* in error) or was

---

UPCOMING CHANGES

The examples in this chapter use commands such as *mkraid* and *raidhotadd*. These commands are a part of the *raidtools* user tools package for the RAID kernel drivers. Like much of Linux, the authors of these tools are always striving to expand and improve upon the state of the art. These tools are currently undergoing a revision, introducing a new management command, *mdadmin*, that will make use of kernel functionality not yet fully realized by the current *raidtools* package. *mdadmin* promises the ability to create arrays from a command line interface rather than using the */etc/raidtab* file, allowing better direct access to the data stored in the RAID superblock. If this tool proves useful, there is every likelihood that it may be included in future releases of the *raidtools* package.

previously a member of an array. In either of these cases, there will be a RAID superblock at the end of the partition. If you run *mkraid* against such a partition, you would see this:

```
# mkraid /dev/md1
handling MD device /dev/md1
analyzing super-block
disk 0: /dev/sdc1, 208813kB, raid superblock at 208704kB
/dev/sdc1 appears to be already part of a raid array -- use -f to
force the destruction of the old superblock
mkraid: aborted, see the syslog and /proc/mdstat for potential clues.
```

If you are sure that you have not made an error, the creation of the array can still be forced using the *-f* flag to *mkraid*, as noted in the error message.

The next thing you will want to do is to create a file system in your array. If you decide on the standard Linux *ext2* file system, you would create it using the *mke2fs* command no differently than if you were making a file system in a regular disk partition. In fact, the layered nature of the RAID driver means that the *mke2fs* command actually has no idea that it is creating the file system in a RAID array. It will think that */dev/md1* is a single contiguous partition. That implies that, in theory, you should be able to use any Linux supported file system in a software RAID. Chapter 9, "Alternative File Systems," talks about some reliable file system alternatives to the *ext2* file system, which you might want to consider for implementation in a RAID. Making the *ext2* file system looks like this:

```
# mke2fs /dev/md1
mke2fs 1.19, 13-Jul-2000 for EXT2 FS 0.5b, 95/08/09
Filesystem label=
OS type: Linux
Block size=1024 (log=0)
Fragment size=1024 (log=0)
51584 inodes, 205696 blocks
10284 blocks (5.00%) reserved for the super user
First data block=1
26 block groups
8192 blocks per group, 8192 fragments per group
1984 inodes per group
Superblock backups stored on blocks:
        8193, 24577, 40961, 57345, 73729, 204801

Writing inode tables: done
Writing superblocks and filesystem accounting information: done
```

Finally, you can mount the new file system wherever you want to use it, for example by:

```
# mount /dev/md1 /opt/data
```

Mounting a file system that resides in an array can be done by including an entry in */etc/fstab* in the normal way:

```
/dev/md1          /opt/data          ext2    defaults      1 1
```

As you flagged the partitions making up the array as type 0xfd, the kernel will detect early in the boot process that each flagged partition is part of a RAID and ensure that the array is running before */etc/fstab* is processed. When the server shuts down, the RAID will be gracefully stopped; there are no additional commands needed to stop arrays before a shutdown is initiated.

Monitoring RAID Arrays

The primary monitoring tool for any RAID is the file */proc/mdstat*. Like many of the */proc* file system files, you simply use *cat* to dump the file to the screen. Before you initialize any RAID arrays, the output will look like this:

```
# cat /proc/mdstat
Personalities : [linear] [raid0] [raid1] [raid5]
read_ahead not set
unused devices: <none>
```

Examining */proc/mdstat* immediately after a *mkraid* command for a two disk RAID1 gives output similar to this:

```
# cat /proc/mdstat
Personalities : [linear] [raid0] [raid1] [raid5]
read_ahead 1024 sectors
md1 : active raid1 sdd1[1] sdc1[0]
     205696 blocks [2/2] [UU]
     [=>.................] resync =  7.9% (16496/205696)
finish=1.9minspeed=1649K/sec
unused devices: <none>
```

This output indicates that the mirror is currently being built. As you will see, this is similar to the output you see when the mirror is being rebuilt following replacement of a failed disk. Once the mirror is built, the status output should look like this:

```
# cat /proc/mdstat
Personalities : [linear] [raid0] [raid1] [raid5]
read_ahead 1024 sectors
md1 : active raid1 sdd1[1] sdc1[0]
     205696 blocks [2/2] [UU]

unused devices: <none>
```

So long as everything is working properly, this is the output you would normally expect to see. What will it look like if a disk fails? If */dev/sdc1* were to fail, the output would look like this:

```
# cat /proc/mdstat
Personalities : [raid1]
read_ahead 1024 sectors
md1 : active raid1 sdd1[1] sdc1[0](F)
      205696 blocks [2/1] [_U]

unused devices: <none>
```

The [2/1] and [_U] entries indicate that there is only one of two disks running, and the sdc1[0](F) indicates that it is */dev/sdc1* that has failed. An examination of */var/log/messages* confirms this diagnosis.

```
scsi0 channel 0 : resetting for second half of retries.
SCSI bus is being reset for host 0 channel 0.
SCSI disk error : host 0 channel 0 id 2 lun 0 return code = 26030000
I/O error: dev 08:21, sector 0
raid1: Disk failure on sdc1, disabling device.
Operation continuing on 1 devices
raid1: sdc1: rescheduling block 0
md: recovery thread got woken up ...
md1: no spare disk to reconstruct array! -- continuing in degraded mode
md: recovery thread finished ...
dirty sb detected, updating.
md: updating md1 RAID superblock on device
sdd1 [events: 00000002](write) sdd1's sb offset: 205696
(scsi0:0:3:0) Synchronous at 10.0 Mbyte/sec, offset 15.
(skipping faulty sdc1 )
raid1: sdd1: redirecting sector 0 to another mirror
```

Replacing a Failed Disk

Note that so far you have lost no data and the server is running just fine on the remaining good drive. At the next convenient opportunity, you bring the server down, replace the failed drive, and reboot. Your server should boot fine as you still have one good data copy. If you were to look at */proc/mdstat* just after boot, it would look almost the same as it did after the failure.

```
# cat /proc/mdstat
Personalities : [linear] [raid0] [raid1] [raid5]
read_ahead 1024 sectors
md1 : active raid1 sdd1[1]
      205696 blocks [2/1] [_U]

unused devices: <none>
```

Notice that the entry for *sdc1* has disappeared, whereas before the reboot it was there marked as failed. A look in */var/log/messages* is informative on this point. Starting at the end of the file and searching back for the string autodetecting RAID arrays, my server had these entries:

```
 1 autodetecting RAID arrays
 2 (read) sdd1's sb offset: 104320 [events: 00000006]
 3 autorun ...
 4 considering sdd1 ...
 5    adding sdd1 ...
 6 created md0
 7 bind<sdd1,1>
 8 running: <sdd1>
 9 now!
10 sdd1's event counter: 00000006
11 md0: former device sdc1 is unavailable, removing from array!
12 md0: max total readahead window set to 124k
13 md0: 1 data-disks, max readahead per data-disk: 124k
14 raid1: device sdd1 operational as mirror 1
15 raid1: md0, not all disks are operational -- trying to recover array
16 raid1: raid set md0 active with 1 out of 2 mirrors
17 md: updating md0 RAID superblock on device
18 sdd1 [events: 00000007](write) sdd1's sb offset: 104320
19 md: recovery thread got woken up ...
20 md0: no spare disk to reconstruct array! -- continuing in degraded mode
21 md: recovery thread finished ...
22 .
23 ... autorun DONE.
```

Because the *sdd1* partition is unharmed and flagged for autodetection, its RAID superblock is read, as seen at line 2. At line 11, the autodetect code realizes it is missing *sdc1*. How did it know that *sdc1* is supposed to be a member of the array *md0*, when at this point in the boot process the root file system has not been accessed and consequently the information in */etc/raid-tab* is not available? Remember that the superblock on each disk of an array contains information for the entire array, so all that is required is one good superblock for the autodetection code to obtain all the information it needs. The good superblock from *sdd1* will tell the autodetect code that *md0* is a RAID1 array, and as there is one good disk, by line 16 the code can conclude that the array can be made active with one good disk, running in degraded mode.

The next thing you need to do is partition your new drive. This is where your hard copy system configuration information will come in handy, as you will need to know how large the partition needs to be. In many cases, it will be the entire drive, but not necessarily. In this case there is one good disk. So you can also use the *fdisk* command to examine the current size of /dev/sdd1, like this:

```
# fdisk -l /dev/sdd
Disk /dev/sdd: 255 heads, 63 sectors, 131 cylinders
Units = cylinders of 16065 * 512 bytes

    Device Boot    Start      End    Blocks   Id  System
/dev/sdd1              1       13    104391   fd  Linux raid autodetect
```

Once the new /dev/sdc drive is partitioned, use the *raidhotadd* command to add it back into the array, like this:

```
# raidhotadd /dev/md0 /dev/sdc1
```

If you examine /proc/mdstat shortly after you add the new disk to the array, you should see something like this:

```
# cat /proc/mdstat
Personalities : [linear] [raid0] [raid1] [raid5]
read_ahead 1024 sectors
md0 : active raid1 sdc1[2] sdd1[1]
      104320 blocks [2/1] [_U]
      [=>.................]  recovery =  9.8% (11108/104320)
finish=1.5min speed=1009K/sec
unused devices: <none>
```

This indicates that the mirror is being rebuilt on the new disk. The procedure for replacing a failed disk in a RAID4 or RAID5 array is identical; the only difference is the appearance of the /proc/mdstat output.

What You Can Do Now

1. Based on your risk analysis, decide whether the extra cost of a RAID is worth the benefit of increased protection from disk failure. List how much data you want to protect.

2. Decide which RAID level you want to use. The two main factors in your decision should be better storage efficiency versus lower CPU requirement.

3. Consider whether a RAID0 array may be indicated for performance-critical data. Consider the possibility of using a combined level RAID1+0 array for a combination of performance and reliability.

4. If you want a high level of redundancy, consider using a RAID1+5 array, or a RAID1 array with three or more disks.

Make sure your kernel autodetects your arrays properly. If your storage is in a removable enclosure for ease of portability to a backup server, make sure the backup server can read the RAID superblocks at boot time. Make sure to test the switchover.

Monitoring Linux in Production

"Come, Watson, come. The game is afoot!"

—Arthur Conan Doyle's Sherlock Holmes

Once you have installed and configured your server, the job has just begun. Now that it is in production, it must be watched to ensure that everything continues to function normally and that no resource limits are being approached. Monitoring must be automated because random checking of a few critical values will not ensure high up times.

This chapter gives you two approaches to monitoring. You may want to write your own monitor scripts. In this case, you will need to know what to watch and how. I'll lay out a basic framework for what you need to watch and supply sample scripts suitable for you to customize to your own needs and create your own monitor package. Alternatively, you may choose not to write your own monitors, but source a system-monitoring software package. Several are available. I'll review some of them at the end of this chapter to enable you to see how they might fit into your system. No matter what approach you choose, however, you need to start by considering what should be monitored.

What to Watch?

You should be concerned about two basic areas: resource exhaustion and errors. Resource exhaustion means situations in which a system resource (such as disk space, real memory, or CPU capacity) is approaching the point at which it is exhausted. While this may not bring the server down, it will affect the server's ability to function properly. If the situation is not addressed, it will affect other tasks in other areas. Eventually, it can escalate into a serious problem. Some people may see this as a performance issue rather than a reliability issue, but performance issues left unattended eventually become reliability issues. Why not solve them sooner? Then you get both better performance and good reliability.

The other area of concern is actual errors that can be either software errors or hardware errors. The primary tool in this case is log buffers and log files. Watching, then, involves examining logs. Of course an error that doesn't get logged is a difficult error to find in a log, so the first thing to do is to make sure the right events are being logged. Then, the next challenge is watching the logs. Short of hiring an army to pore over pages of logs daily, you want some kind of automated way to examine logs with an eye to picking out what matters.

The bulk of many log files contains information on the normal functioning of a hardware or software component. Often the secret to seeing what matters in a log is to be able to pick out the exception, what is not usually in the log. The key to this is to build some form of intelligence into an automated log checking system. You may be able to do this yourself, if you know specifically what you are watching for.

When in the process of debugging a problem, it is often valuable to be able to write a simple script that will search for a specific log entry. On an ongoing basis, you may write a more complex script, or you may choose to use one of several prebuilt log monitor packages available. In the case of a specific software log, the application may itself come with a log monitor specific to that application. For generic applications like the Apache Web server, there are also packages available that understand the particular ins and outs of Apache logs.

When a script discovers an error worthy of note, it needs to have a means of alerting you. This could be an online alert such as a broadcast message or an e-mail. This, however, is little use if you are away from the machine. A good log monitor must be able to generate a page. Ideally, it will page reasonably. That is, it will not page for trivial problems, but needs to be loud when it really matters.

When to Watch?

Ideally, a production server should be under constant scrutiny, 7 days a week, 24 hours a day. What may not be so obvious is time counted in a different sense. Many administrators tend to overlook logging and log checking for a system that is running well. So long as it continues to run well, that may seem fine, but what happens when it starts to go wrong? Now you increase your logging activity and start watching logs carefully. You discover errors and you address them, but the problems persist. You begin to realize that although the machine seemed healthy enough, you had overlooked underlying problems because they had not yet caused any noticeable disruption in system operation.

In some cases, error log entries are normal. By this I mean that some software will in the normal course of correct operation write entries into an error log. Sometimes this is just a poorly built internal error checking mechanism that reports what may technically be an error, but in fact will not cause trouble. Sometimes there are historical reasons, for example a condition that would have caused problems for an older version of the code but that has been fixed in the current version. The error messaging may still persist, for the benefit of those still using the older version. The point is that not everything in an error log is necessarily a real problematic condition, and part of the Tao of error monitoring is developing a feel for what is serious and what can be safely ignored.

Finally, you need to see that the time to set up logs and start monitoring them is when the system is working well. In that case, there is no pressure and you can budget time to set things up well. This investment pays dividends when the problems arise, as you have in place a system to catch real error conditions. More importantly, you have established a baseline for normal operation, which is important as a tool. You can use this baseline to establish exceptions to the norm.

Where to Watch?

Obviously, you have to watch for errors on the server itself. But, if you want to be paged when the server goes down, it is little use setting up the server to do the paging. Some vendors supply specialized hardware capable of retaining some basic communications abilities in the case of a server crash, but these solutions are generally proprietary and may not be supported in an open source context. Consequently, a second machine is usually necessary to act as a watchdog. This implies a network-capable log monitoring system so that the logging and reporting machine can remotely monitor its servers and blow the whistle as necessary. If you have several servers, this one watchdog machine should be able to handle all of the necessary monitoring. Don't forget to set up a monitor on one of the other servers to watch the watchdog.

How to Watch?

You may want to source a package that will tackle the job of system monitoring or you may prefer to roll your own. I'll start by showing the basics of creating your own system-monitoring tool. If you decide to go this route, you can use these sample scripts as the basis for your package. When you have it built, you may even choose to release it to the rest of the open source world.

Even if you don't build a fully functional monitor structure, these samples are useful for occasions when you may want to put together a small monitor on a temporary basis for troubleshooting purposes or to monitor something that a prebuilt package just doesn't do the way you want it done. If you prefer to source a package, I finish this chapter with an overview of some available free and commercial packages.

Writing Your Own Monitor

Your monitor package needs to watch several areas. You should keep track of disk usage, so you need to monitor all of the file systems in use and be alerted if they exceed threshold values. Those thresholds need to be tunable on a file-system-by-file-system basis. You also want a report of the largest files on the system and of the user owning the most files so you can see where the disk space is going. It would be a bonus if you could get graphs of disk usage in the output.

You should keep track of CPU and memory usage, being alerted for dangerously high usage levels, and maintain a history so you can be proactive in heading off any imminent shortages. There are always key daemons that must be kept running, so you should track those, too. There will almost certainly be other servers or network devices that you need to be able to make contact with. If you lose touch with them, you need to know about it. You need a tool to watch error logs for anything that looks serious, and if your hardware supports it, you will want to monitor for hardware operational parameters falling outside of safe limits.

Summarized, here are seven components that would make up a comprehensive system monitor:

- Disk usage monitor
- File monitor
- CPU and memory usage
- Daemon monitoring
- Other network servers
- System log monitoring
- Hardware monitoring

In all cases, you want to be able to sound an alarm if any of my monitors registers a dangerous condition. As this functionality is common to all of the monitors, I'll tackle it first.

Sounding an Alarm

The first decision to make is: What kind of alarm? Local to the server itself, the most common forms of alarm are sending an e-mail, broadcasting a message to the system console, or, if the console is a graphics console, popping up an alert window. You may also want to generate an alarm to an external device, possibly a watchdog monitoring server or a pager.

Listing 6.1 provides a script to handle these possibilities. It is designed to be called from a monitor script to generate an alarm. When the monitor script detects the alarm condition, it calls the alarm script, passing it two arguments—an alarm method and a character string describing the alarm condition. The alarm script looks like this:

```
1 #!/bin/ksh
2
3 # script to generate alarms
4 #
5 # syntax: sound_alarm <alarm method> <alarm description>
6 # where:
7 # alarm method = "mail"      for internal e-mail notification
8 #              = "broadcast" for broadcast on the local host
```

Listing 6.1   sound_alarm

```
 9 #              = "window"    to open an alert window on the console
10 #              = "watchdog"  to forward an alarm to another server
11 #              = "pager"     to send an alarm to a pager
12 #
13 # alarm description = a character string describing the cause of
14 #                     the alarm
15
16 # simple input filter
17 if [ $# -ne 2 ] ; then
18    echo "$0: Bad Args : $*" >&2
19    exit 1
20 fi
21
22 # define local vars
23 alarm_method="$1"
24 alarm_description="$2"
25 mail_recipient=root
26
27 # do it
28 case "$alarm_method" in
29 mail)      echo "$alarm_description" | mail -s "** ALARM **" root ;;
30 broadcast) wall "** ALARM ** : $alarm_description" ;;
31 window)    xmessage -display :0.0 -center -geometry 200x200 \
32                                                              \
33 "'date'
34
35 $alarm_description" ;;
36
37 watchdog)  logger -p local6.info "** ALARM ** : $alarm_description" ;;
38 pager)     snpp -m "$alarm_description" admin ;;
39 *)         echo "$0:Error :Unknown alarm method > $alarm_method <"
40            exit 1 ;;
41 esac
42
43 exit 0
```

Listing 6.1   sound_alarm (continued)

I have included a simple input filter at lines 16 through 20. This filter is
quite simple and is mostly there to make the point that you should do some
kind of input filtering. You should do something more robust, unless you
are confident that the calling script will be good at passing the proper arguments to this one. I have hardcoded *root* as the recipient of a mail alarm.

When you modify this sample for your environment, you may want to change this to your administrative account e-mail or pass an extra argument to allow mailing to any arbitrary user.

The main body of the script is a simple case statement that branches based on the value of *alarm_method*. If you are working in the KDE desktop, you will find that the *wall* command used in line 30 to implement the broadcast alarm will result in a nice graphical popup window that date stamps the output as well as keep a buffer of previous *wall* messages, which is handy. The *window* alarm at line 31 should work in any generic X-Windows installation that includes the *xmessage* client. As *xmessage* does not include a date stamp, I have added the *date* command output as shown in line 33. Unfortunately the *xmessage* client does not interpret the \n convention for a newline; hence, the carriage return must be hard coded inside the double quotes, as shown. Either the script looks ugly, or your output looks ugly; take your pick.

Writing Alarms to a Log

The option to log the alarm to a remote server is implemented by the *logger* command at line 37. This is a problem, however, as *logger* can only log to the local *syslogd*. There is no client utility to log directly to a remote *syslogd*. What can be done, though is to log to the local *syslogd*, and configure the local daemon to forward that entry to a remote machine. To make my alarm script work, then, I must also modify the local *syslogd* configuration. Noting that in the alarm script I logged to the facility *local6*, I need to add this line to my local */etc/syslog.conf*, assuming that the remote monitor machine has host name *watchdog*:

```
local6.info                    @watchdog
```

Don't forget to configure *syslogd* on *watchdog* to accept remote input. You will need to add the *-r* flag to the *syslogd* startup script, as shown in Chapter 4, "Installing and Configuring for Reliability."

Remote logging done this way is easy, but there are some things to watch for. In the event that an outage prevents clients from resolving host names, then your client *syslogd* would not be able to send to *watchdog* as it would be unable to determine *watchdog*'s address. You could hardcode the IP address in the *syslogd* configuration file, but that makes things less portable. An alternative would be to put *watchdog*'s address in the client's */etc/hosts* file, allowing reliable local name resolution.

The same problem applies at the remote server. Incoming log messages carry only the IP address of the sender, and *syslogd* on *watchdog* will try to resolve these addresses to host names when it writes them to its local log.

Watch for logjams. Overly verbose logging or a logging mechanism that runs away can flood logs and cause problems. If you use remote logging, the problem has the potential to multiply over the network. Also, once the remote *syslogd* has been configured to accept remote entries, it has no internal means of deciding who is sending it messages. This could be considered a security loophole, leading to the possibility of a denial of service attack. You may wish to consider protecting the remote *syslogd* by using a firewall and filtering input to the *syslogd* port 514/UDP.

Alarming to a Pager

The final alarm type is *pager*. In a perfect world, there would one simple way to generate pager messages. But we live in a far from simple world. There are in fact a variety of different ways you can page, as discussed in the accompanying sidebar, "A Pager Primer." My example uses the *snpp* command, which comes as a part of the *sendpage* package mentioned in the sidebar. The *-m* flag allows inclusion of the text to be sent to the pager from the command line, otherwise *snpp* reads from standard input. The last argument to *snpp*, *admin*, is an identifier that needs to be set up in the *send-*

A PAGING PRIMER

Pagers can vary widely, from the simple "you call my pager and leave your number and I'll call you back some time" variety to the current crop of alphanumeric, two-way pager cum e-mail client cum Web client models. Probably the most useful type in the server management field are the alphanumeric pagers that allow a character string message to be sent, describing the problem for the recipient of the page. These pagers use the Telocator Alphanumeric Protocol (TAP) protocol, published by the Personal Communications Industry Association (PCIA). This is an ASCII-based protocol usually implemented over a serial communications line between the server originating the page and a paging terminal operated by the pager vendor. A page generated by a server using a TAP session is the automated equivalent of you calling a pager number and sending a numeric, alphanumeric or voice message page. Once the page has been sent, it is routed through their network of paging terminals to the one closest to the pager itself, from where it is finally broadcast to the pager.

To enable your server to automatically create a page, you need a TAP client. There are several open source TAP clients, including Beepage, QuickPage, and Sendpage. In addition to being a TAP client, QuickPage and Sendpage also implement the Simple Network Paging Protocol (SNPP) as defined by RFC1861. An SNPP client uses SNPP to send the page to an SNPP server via the local network. That server has the outgoing modem connection and uses TAP to send the pages it received via SNPP to the paging terminal, from whence it traverses the paging company's network to the pager itself. The advantage of using SNPP between the originator of the page and the modem is that it allows for pages to be collected from multiple clients, which can be distributed across a local network and then queued for transmission from a single modem.

The next generation of pagers will commonly offer two-way paging. The next generation protocol, Telocator Network Paging Protocol (TNPP), can handle this type of communication. Watch for Linux TNPP clients in the future.

More information on paging can be found at www.pcia.com and www.refreq.com. You can find QuickPage at www.qpage.org and Sendpage at sendpage.cpoint.net.

page configuration file. It would point to a pager telephone number and, if necessary, the PIN of the person to be paged.

Now you have a standard means of sounding an alarm in the event that a monitor detects a dangerous condition. The next thing to do is to write some monitors.

Monitoring Disk Usage

The sample script in Listing 6.2 watches disk usage by file system and generates an alarm when thresholds values are exceeded:

```ksh
 1 #!/bin/ksh
 2
 3 # script to monitor filesystems
 4 # this script is designed to be run hourly from /etc/cron.hourly
 5 #
 6 # syntax: monitor_filesystems
 7
 8 alarm_threshold=70
 9 page_threshold=90
10 typeset -RZ4 usage_with_percent_sign
```

Listing 6.2   monitor_filesystems

```
11
12 df -P | tail +2 | while read foo
13 do
14     usage_with_percent_sign=$(echo $foo | awk '{print $5}')
15     usage=${usage_with_percent_sign%%%}
16     fs=$(echo $foo | awk '{print $1}')
17     mount=$(echo $foo | awk '{print $6}')
18     if (( usage > alarm_threshold )) ; then
19         /usr/local/bin/sound_alarm broadcast \
20             "File system $fs mounted at $mount is $usage % full"
21     fi
22     if (( usage > page_threshold )) ; then
23         /usr/local/bin/sound_alarm pager \
24             "File system $fs mounted at $mount is $usage % full"
25     fi
26
27 done
```

Listing 6.2   monitor_filesystems (continued)

As noted on line 4, this script could be run easily from */etc/cron.hourly*, or more frequently from a *crontab* if desired. The script takes no arguments and scans all local mounted file systems. Line 8 defines the alarm threshold; 70 representing any file system greater than 70 percent full. A higher value for the threshold at which a page will be sent is established at line 9 to avoid unnecessary paging. Any monitor that sends too many pages can fall victim to the Never Cry Wolf syndrome. You recall the story of the boy who cried wolf for fun when there was no wolf, but fell into deep trouble when the wolf appeared and nobody would listen to his cries for help. By then, his credibility was shot. Too many pages for minor problems greatly increase the chances that an important page will be treated lightly. These threshold values could be read in as arguments, if desired, or possibly from a configuration file.

The *typeset* at line 10 is required to define a variable to temporarily hold the value of the percentage of the file system used that will be obtained from a *df* command. The *RZ4* right justifies with leading zeroes added into a 4-character field, three for the actual number and the last for the percent sign, which will later be chopped off. The *df* command at line 12 is piped into *tail* to chop the column headers off and then to a *while* loop that will iterate all of the lines of the *df* output. At line 14, *awk* extracts the file system usage value, which is the fifth field in the *df* output. For those unfamiliar with the Korn shell, line 15 will remove the trailing percent sign from *usage_with_percent_sign* and assign the result to *usage*. This is necessary because *usage* will shortly be used in a numeric comparison. Lines 16 and 17 extract the file system and mount point so that the alarm message can be reasonably informative. Finally, the *if* test at line 18 determines whether the file system is over the threshold and sends an alarm appropriately. If this alarm goes unheeded and the condition worsens, the *if* test at line 22 will eventually send an additional alarm to a pager.

The kind of monitoring this script does is important to inform you about disk usage. Unfortunately, while it can alert you that the disk is filling, it cannot actually do anything itself to stop the disk filling. What would be ideal is a proactive monitor that automatically controls assignment of storage space to a process at the time the space is requested. That sort of system could automatically keep the file system usage in check so that your monitor needs to come into play only if this automatic control malfunction. This automatic control system is known as disk quotas. We'll look at this next.

Configuring ext2 *File System Quotas*

Disk quotas can be enabled on some or all local file systems. Disk quotas are a standard feature of the *ext2* file system, but are not configured by default. If you would like to use disk quotas, here are the configuration steps:

1. Mark the file system as active for quotas in */etc/fstab* by adding the quota flag, like this:

```
/dev/hda6          /home        ext2  defaults,usrquota    1 1
```

   The *usrquota* flag allows quota checking on a user-by-user basis. You can also use *grpquota* to check usage by groups, or you can do both. Each file system you want to enforce quotas for must be flagged. Once */etc/fstab* has been edited, you must remount each of the file systems you enabled quotas for, like this:

```
# mount -o remount /home
```

2. Next you need to create the quota data files using the *quotacheck* command, like this:

```
# quotacheck /home
```

3. You now need to turn quota checking on with the *quotaon* command, like this:

```
# quotaon /home
```

Having set quotas up, by now you would think this would happen automatically. But there is a good reason for the necessity. If there is a *quotaon* command, there must be a *quotaoff* command, right? Yes, there is, and it is important, as there are some operations you may want to do that will be affected by quotas. It is necessary to be able to temporarily disable quota checking on a file system to accommodate these situations.

4. Next, you need to set up the quota limits themselves using the *edquota* command. Passed a user ID as an argument, *edquota* will open an interactive edit session. If the user has never had a quota set, the initial state of the quota file will look like this:

```
Quotas for user iain:
/dev/hda6: blocks in use: 1952, limits (soft = 0, hard = 0)
        inodes in use: 38, limits (soft = 0, hard = 0)
```

The only numbers you edit are the ones in the parentheses. There are two quotas, one on disk space, expressed in terms of blocks (in this context a block is 1 KB), and the other the number of inodes. As one inode is required for each file, the inode quota in effect controls the number of files the user may create. This is as important a quota as disk space itself as there are a finite number of empty inodes available to allocate to new files in any file system. If they are used up, it is impossible to create a new file even though there may be ample disk space available in the file system. Recall that empty files and symbolic links both use an inode, but neither use any disk space. A simple, but effective denial of service attack involves creating empty files until the inode table is full and the file system is essentially out of commission. The inode quota protects against this.

If the user exceeds the soft limit for either space or inodes, a grace period timer starts. If the user is still over his or her soft limit at the end of the grace period (seven days by default) the soft limit becomes the hard limit, the hard limit being the point at which further attempts at allocations will fail. You will want to edit the quota values as appropriate to your server so that they look something like this:

```
Quotas for user iain:
/dev/hda6: blocks in use: 1952, limits (soft = 50000, hard = 65000)
        inodes in use: 38, limits (soft = 3000, hard = 4000)
```

Note that, rather counterintuitively, a value of 0 represents unlimited usage, as opposed to no allocations allowed. Once you have edited the quotas for all users, you can get a report using *repquota* as follows:

```
# repquota -v /dev/hda6
*** Report for user quotas on /dev/hda6 (/home)
                        Block limits              File limits
User              used    soft    hard  grace    used  soft  hard  grace
root        --  182948  200000  250000          20111     0     0
iain        +-    1952    1000    2000  7days       38  3000  4000
```

In this report the second field of *iain*'s entry contains a + sign, indicating that *iain* is over the soft limit for data storage and has seven days of grace remaining to fix the problem. This example also appears to place a quota on *root* usage. This will not be enforced, even if the hard limit is exceeded.

5. Make sure this will all come back after a reboot. Setting the quota flag on a file system in */etc/fstab* will not ensure that quota checking is turned on at boot time. You need to add the *quotaon* command to a boot script that will run after the file systems to be monitored have been mounted. You should also run a *quotacheck* command at boot as well as periodically, such as every night, to ensure that the quota records are up-to-date. If quota checking is turned off and then on again, any changes while checking was turned off will not be reflected in the current quota figures. I prefer to add these quota commands to the end of the local rc script, */etc/rc.d/rc.<run level>/S99local*.

Disk quotas are based on usage by a specific user or group rather than the space taken up by a particular directory or used by a specific application.

EXT2 SUPERBLOCK LIMITS

If you do not want to go to the trouble of setting up quotas for a file system, there is a simpler way to protect against filling a file system that may serve your purposes. It is a feature of the *ext2* file system that a proportion of the disk space and also the inode table can be reserved for the exclusive use of *root*. By default, 5 percent of any *ext2* file system is reserved in this fashion. Consider this *df* output from a default Red Hat 7.1 installation:

```
Filesystem      1k-blocks       Used     Available    Use%    Mounted on
/dev/hda1        2869900    2183612        540500     81%     /
```

If you add up the number of blocks used and the number available, you will find that the sum is 5-percent short of the total number of blocks in the file system. That missing 5 percent is reserved for the exclusive use of *root*. Once the file system is 95-percent full, *df* will report it as 100 percent and non *root* users will get an error if they request more space. You can alter this default using the *tune2fs* command. For example, to increase the reserved proportion to 10 percent, use the following command:

```
# tune2fs -m 10 /dev/hda6
```

You can also allow a user other than root access to the reserved space with the *-u* option. For example, *iain* would be given access to the reserved space with this command:

```
# tune2fs -u iain /dev/hda6
```

If you are not sure what the current state of affairs is, you can query it with the *dumpe2fs* command, like this:

```
# dumpe2fs /dev/hda6
```

I would be remiss if I did not draw your attention to this remark from the *tune2fs man* page: "WARNING: Never use tune2fs to change parameters of a read/write mounted filesystem! Use this utility at your own risk. You're modifying a filesystem!" The proper procedure is to unmount the file system, alter the superblock values, and remount.

Note that this is a simplistic approach to disk space limits. It will allow one user an advantage over all others, but any of the others can still be faced with what to them will be a full file system. In the case where you have one user that is really important, such as the user that owns your application data and you want to ensure that the user has priority on space, this will work well so long as all of the other users will not be adversely affected if the nonreserved proportion of the file system fills up. Be aware also that there is no reservation of inodes, only data blocks. Anyone can still write a loop to create empty files or soft links that exhausts the inode table.

Quotas work well if you can establish your limits on a user account basis. If your application, however, owns all of its data files, quotas are not useful in controlling the amount of storage that might be assigned to the application by the actions of one of its users if that user's identity is not carried through to ownership of actual disk files. Also, applications that must run as *root* are able to get around quotas. Of course, an application that insisted all its data files be owned by *root* would be a poorly written application and should be avoided if at all possible.

Monitoring Files

Monitoring file systems and establishing quotas can prevent the problem of file systems filling up with adverse consequences. Another problem that can arise is the issue of what is filling them. It may be that your monitor pages you with an alarm that a file system normally running at 60 percent is suddenly 90-percent full. It may be that space in a file system thought to be more than adequate for the purpose is becoming scarce. Where did the space go? I find it helpful to watch a server for the largest files in each file system and the largest users of disk space to see if there are any trends, either up (usually) or down (rarely) in disk usage. It is also useful to periodically clean up space wasters such as old core dumps or old data that could be archived to free up online disk space.

The key to this is the *du*, or *disk usage* command. *du* recurses a directory and reports how many disk blocks are allocated to each file. The command also can provide a summary of the total taken up by a particular directory tree. What you need is a script that runs periodically and uses *du* to create usage summaries for each file system. Listing 6.3 provides an example you can base yours on.

```
1 #!/bin/ksh
2
3 # script to monitor files
4 # this script is designed to be run daily from /etc/cron.daily
5 #
6 # syntax: monitor_files
7
8 # open output file
9 exec 3>/var/log/file_monitor.$(date -I)
10
11 # print file header
12 print -u3 "File Monitor Report - $(date -I)"
13
14 # Find and report top 5 files in each local file system
15 df -l | tail +2 | while read foo
16 do
17     fs=$(print $foo | awk '{print $6}')
18     dev=$(print $foo | awk '{print $1}')
```

Listing 6.3 monitor_files

```
19      print -u3 "\n\nLargest files in $dev mounted at $fs \n"
20      find $fs -xdev -type f -exec du -k {} \; 2>/dev/null \
21          | sort -nr | head -5 >&3
22 done
23
24 # Find and report top 5 files owned by each user
25 print -u3 "\nLargest files owned by each user\n"
26 cat /etc/passwd | cut -d: -f1 | while read user
27 do
28      print -u3 "\nLargest files owned by $user\n"
29      find / -user $user -type f -exec du -k {} \; 2>/dev/null \
30          | sort -nr | head -5 >&3
31 done
32
33 # Find space wasters
34 print -u3 "\nCore dumps that can probably be deleted\n"
35 find / -name core -type f -exec ls -l {} \; 2>/dev/null >&3
36
37 print -u3 "\nOld and big files you can probably do without\n"
38 find /var -atime +200 -size +150k -exec ls -l {} \; 2>/dev/null >&3
```

Listing 6.3   monitor_files (continued)

The script starts out opening a file for output at line 9, using file descriptor 3 and including a POSIX format date in its name. The date is also
included in the header printed at line 12. The *-u3* flag to the *print* command
points output to file descriptor 3. The first report is a listing of the five
largest files in each local physical file system. The *-l* option to the *df* command at line 15 restricts output to only local file systems, excluding NFS
mounts. A recursive search through each file system is necessary to find the
largest files, which is not the sort of thing you want to do over the network.
Even worse, if you use the same script on several clients of the same server,
you will end up doing the same recursion multiple times on the server,
each search initiated by a different client. The *tail* command strips off the
column heads, and then passes each line of the *df* output into the *while* loop
as the variable *foo*.

Once inside the loop, *awk* strips the mount point and disk partition from
foo, assigning them to *fs* and *dev* at lines 17 and 18. These values are used at
line 19 to print a comment to the output file so you will know what you are
reading.

Now comes the real work. The *find* command at line 20 searches each file
system, with the *-xdev* and *-type f* options restricting the recursion to find

only ordinary files (no directories) in the physical file system in which the start point of the search resides. For each file, the *du -k* command is executed to determine the size of the file in KB. That output is then piped to *sort*. The *-nr* options ensure this is a numeric sort in reverse order; hence the largest files come first. Finally, the *head* command passes only the top five results, and that listing is redirected to the output file.

The next report lists the largest files owned by each user. At line 26, *cut* extracts the user name from the first field of */etc/passwd* and passes it into a *while* loop as the variable user. At line 29, a *find* command similar to the previous loop reports the largest five files owned by each user examined. Note that this involves multiple recursions of the entire logical file system, so you may choose to limit this search to only some users. You may also want to restrict the start point of your search to only users' home directories; otherwise, system files owned by *root* and other administrative users or application binaries would turn up repeatedly in your report.

The last thing to do is to look for space wasters. The *find* at line 35 looks for core dumps and lists them. The find command could also be used to delete them by adding an *-exec rm {}\;* clause, but any form of automated deletion is risky. It is better to list them in a report so you can make a judgment as to whether they can be safely deleted. The final *find* at line 38 looks for and lists files larger than 150 KB that have not been accessed for more than 200 days. The argument is that any file that has not been accessed for that long is likely to be redundant and is just wasting space. Again, the *find* command could be used to automatically delete these files, but that is risky; list them instead. This *find* also starts from a different location, */var*, than the root directory. That is done because applications can include files that may be rarely, if ever used, and would show up in this report as wasted space. Deleting any file that is a part of an application is risky, and it is preferable to waste a bit of space than incur the danger of causing potential problems for the application in case the application one day needs the file that was deleted. As noted at line 4, this script could be run daily from */etc/cron.daily*, although you may be happy running this as a weekly report.

Trending File System Usage

The last thing to do is trending. It is useful to track the usage of a file system in case there is an upward usage trend. That way you can predict when the file system will become dangerously full and have a plan in place to handle the situation before the disk fills and panic sets in. The easiest way to do this is to keep a historical record of usage and graph it over time.

Monitoring on a file system basis is useful, as is monitoring the total space occupied by the data set of an application or the space used by each user. In many cases the application will have an associated user who owns the application data, so tracking the user's data allocation is also tracking the application's data allocation.

Listing 6.4 provides a sample script to trend disk usage for local file systems. It runs daily, determining how full the file system is each day, and writes the result to an output file. Only the most recent 30 days are tracked so that the file does not grow forever.

```
 1 #!/bin/ksh
 2
 3 # script to trend local file systems usage
 4 # this script is designed to be run daily from /etc/cron.daily
 5 #
 6 # syntax: trend_filesystem_usage
 7
 8 # make sure the data file exists, if not, create an empty one
 9 if [ ! -f /var/log/fs_trend_data ]
10 then
11     # open a new data file as fd 3
12     exec 3> /var/log/fs_trend_data
13
14     # print the header, hostname on first line
15     #    local filesystems on second line
16     print -u3 "$(hostname)"
17     num_local_fs=0
18     df -l | tail +2 | while read foo
19     do
20         print -u3 -n "$(print $foo | awk '{print $6" "}')"
21     done
22     print -u3 ""
23
24     # fill the rest of the file with zeroes
25     count=1
26     num_local_fs=$(df -l | tail +2 | wc -l)
27     while ((count <= 30))
28     do
29         count2=1
30         while (( count2 <= num_local_fs ))
31         do
32             print -u3 -n "0 "
```

Listing 6.4   trend_filesystem_usage

```
33              (( count2 += 1 ))
34          done
35          print -u3 ""
36          ((count += 1))
37      done
38      exec 3>&-
39 fi
40
41 # append today's usage to the data file, and roll
42 #   the data file over, keeping only the last 29 days data
43 #     first copy the current data file to a tmp file
44 cp /var/log/fs_trend_data /tmp/fs_trend_data
45
46 # now rebuild data file, header first
47 head -2 /tmp/fs_trend_data > /var/log/fs_trend_data
48
49 # now add the current values
50 df -l $fs | tail +2 | awk '{print $5}' | while read foo
51 do
52    usage=${foo%%%}
53    print -n "$usage " >> /var/log/fs_trend_data
54 done
55 print " " >> /var/log/fs_trend_data
56
57 # finally append the historic data from the tmp file
58 tail +3 /tmp/fs_trend_data | head -29 >> /var/log/fs_trend_data
59 rm /tmp/fs_trend_data
```

Listing 6.4 trend_filesystem_usage (continued)

The script in Listing 6.4 appends output to an ASCII text data file that will be read by the *gnuplot* plotting package to generate a graph of file system usage. The first line of the output file contains the host name of the machine under observation, while the second line lists the file systems being trended. Each line in the rest of the file contains a set of values representing the percentage full value for each file system at the time of sampling. The sample script is designed to be placed in */etc/cron.daily*, where it will take one sample a day, so each line in this case represents a day. Output is capped at 30 samples, at which time a plot is made of the values using the plotting script I'll provide in a moment.

The first *if* clause, starting at line 9 and running to line 39, checks to ensure that there is an output file. If this is the first time the script runs, there will not be a data file and one will be created having the proper header with 30 lines of zeroes for output. For the data to be in a convenient order for plotting, the script will record new samples into the file in chronological order, newest values first. To do this, a temporary copy of the current file is made at line 44. Now the data file will be rebuilt by drawing the header back from the temporary file at line 47, adding the current sample data with lines 50 through 55, and finally adding the previous 29 entries from the temporary file to make 30 samples. Thus, each day one new value appears at the top of the file, just below the header, while a 30-day-old value is dropped off the end. The finished product for a host named *deut* having two local file systems mounted at / and */RH71* will resemble the sample shown in Listing 6.5.

```
deut
/  /RH71
38 15
37 15
37 15
37 15
37 15
37 15
38 15
38 15
38 15
38 15
38 15
37 15
37 15
37 15
37 15
37 15
37 15
37 15
37 15
37 15
37 15
36 15
36 15
33 15
33 15
31 15
30 15
30 15
30 15
30 15
```

Listing 6.5   Sample `/var/log/fs_trend_data`

Plotting Data Trends

Now that we have a means of collecting the raw data, how can we see any trends in the data? The easiest way to relate to trends is to plot the data. Fortunately, the *gnuplot* package is included with a Red Hat distribution, which is a simple and quick way to produce data plots. To produce a plot with *gnuplot*, you need a data file and a *gnuplot* control file. The control file contains the *gnuplot* commands that define the appearance of the plot. To completely automate the process, Listing 6.6 provides a script that produces a *gnuplot* control file and uses it to plot the file system data.

```
 1 #!/bin/ksh
 2
 3 # script to plot file system usage
 4 #
 5 # syntax: plot_filesystem_usage
 6 #
 7 # can be run at any time to plot the last 30 days of
 8 #    file system usage
 9
10 # open gnuplot control file
11 exec 3>/tmp/gnuplot_control_file
12
13 # get host from log file header
14 host=$(head -1 /var/log/fs_trend_data | awk '{print $1}')
15
16 # strip header and write raw data to tmp plot data file
17 tail +3 /var/log/fs_trend_data > /tmp/fs_trend_data
18
19 # ask for a title and label the axes
20 print -u3 "set title \"Disk Usage for Local File Systems on "\
21            "Host $host - $(date -I)\""
22 print -u3 "set xlabel \"Days Ago\""
23 print -u3 "set ylabel \"Percent Full\""
24 print -u3 "set terminal jpeg"
25
26 # now plot the data
27 print -u3 -n "plot [29:0] [0:100] "
28 count=1
29
30 # need to know how many fs to plot
31 num_local_fs=$( tail +2 /var/log/fs_trend_data | head -1 | wc -w )
32
33 # add one plot command for each fs
```

Listing 6.6 *plot_filesystem_usage*

```
34 for fs in $(tail +2 /var/log/fs_trend_data | head -1 )
35 do
36   print -u3 -n "/tmp/fs_trend_data\" using 0:$count\
37     title \"$fs\" with lines"
38   (( count += 1 ))
39
40   # add comma only if not the last fs to keep gnuplot syntax OK

41   if (( count <= num_local_fs ))
42   then
43     print -u3 -n ", "
44   fi
45
46 done
47 print -u3 ""
48
49 # generate the plot
50 gnuplot -persist -gray /tmp/gnuplot_control_file\
51     > /var/log/filesystem_usage.$(date -I).jpeg
52
53 # clean up the temp files
54 rm /tmp/fs_trend_data
55 rm /tmp/gnuplot_control_file
```

Listing 6.6 *plot_filesystem_usage* (continued)

You will want to do some reading on *gnuplot* if you want to go any further than what this script will do for you, but this should give you a useful introduction to it. To help you see what this script is doing, Listing 6.7 is what the plot control file that the script in Listing 6.6 produces (*/tmp/gnuplot_control_file*) looks like.

Let's follow through the process. Keep in mind the three files we are dealing with. The raw data file is */var/log/fs_trend_data* (Listing 6.5), the

```
1 set title "Disk Usage for Local File Systems on  Host deut - 2001-06-11"
2 set xlabel "Days Ago"
3 set ylabel "Percent Full"
4 set terminal jpeg
5 plot [29:0] [0:100] "/tmp/fs_trend_data" using 0:1 title "/" with lines,
    "/tmp/fs_trend_data" using 0:2 title "/RH71" with lines
```

Listing 6.7 *gnuplot* control file

script to generate the plot control file is *plot_filesystem_usage* (Listing 6.6) and the plot control file itself is */tmp/gnuplot_control_file*. (Listing 6.7).

The script that drives the process is *plot_filesystem_usage*, so I'll start there, at line 11 in Listing 6.6, where the control file is opened for output. At line 14, the host name is drawn from the data file header. Line 17 strips the data out of the data file and writes it to a temporary file, from where it will be plotted. Lines 20 to 23 generate lines 1 through 3 of the control file, which will create a title for the plot and labels for the axes. The result of line 24 is line 4 of the control file, which will cause *gnuplot* to output the plot in the form of a Joint Photographic Experts Group (JPEG) format graphic image file. This is handy as you can then write a script to gather these images together into a Web page. Put that page up on your Web server and you can view your file system graphs from anywhere on the Web.

If you prefer to print the graphs, you can ask for PostScript format output by replacing line 24 with this:

```
24 print -u3 "set terminal postscript eps 22"
```

The following version of line 24 will give you PCL5 (Hewlett-Packard's Printer Control Language, as implemented by the LaserJet III and similar printers) output:

```
24 print -u3 "set terminal pcl5"
```

You will probably also want to change the file name extension at line 51 to match whichever file format you choose.

The last line of the control file is the most complex and must be generated in pieces. First, line 27 of the plot script defines the scale for the axes of the plot. The rest of the line consists of comma-delimited groups of parameters, each of which defines a single line to plot. Looking at the first parameter group, we see the data file to be read (*/tmp/fs_trend_data*), the data from the file to be plotted (using 0:1, which means the first value on each line of the data file), the title for the line (title "/"), and the type of plot (with lines, as opposed to curves, bar graph, or other plot styles).

Line 31 determines how many file systems we need to plot and therefore how many parameter groups there will be. The *for* loop in line 34 through 46 then fills in the parameter group values for each file system. Line 47 finishes off line 5 of the control file with a carriage return. Finally, line 50 calls *gnuplot* to produce the plot, and lines 54 and 55 clean up the temporary files. The finished plot is shown in Figure 6.1.

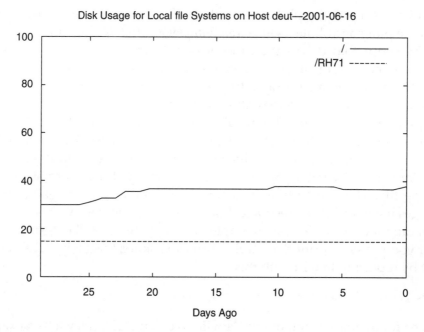

Figure 6.1 A finished file system usage trending plot.

Monitoring CPU and Memory Usage

Monitoring CPU and real memory usage is generally more associated with performance management than server reliability. However, unusual or excessive use of any system resource can also be an indication of trouble that can lead to an outage. An application that malfunctions can easily begin to consume huge amounts of CPU time and effectively bring down a server.

Another application-related problem that on occasion crops up is memory leakage, when as a result of a coding error an application requests increasingly larger amounts of memory in proportion to the amount of time it has been running rather than the volume of work it is doing. This can eventually exhaust real memory, pushing the virtual memory manager to make increasing use of swap space. This results in performance degradation, and if the swap space is exhausted, eventually processes will return failure for requested memory allocations and start to crash. Clearly, this needs to be avoided and a memory usage monitor can do that.

Listing 6.8 provides a script to watch CPU usage.

```
 1 #!/bin/ksh
 2
 3 # script to monitor CPU usage
 4 #
 5 # syntax: monitor_cpu
 6 #
 7 # script runs as a daemon on a 1 minute cycle and alarms on same
 8 #    pid being over a CPU high usage threshold for 5 consecutive
 9 #    monitor cycles
10 #
11 # script runs as a daemon and can be started at boot
12
13 # set a high CPU usage threshold of 60%
14 cpu_threshold=60
15 count=0
16
17 # loop forever
18 while true
19 do
20
21    # determine top CPU process
22    foo=$(ps -eo pid,%cpu,command --sort %cpu | tail -1 )
23    current_top_cpu=$(print $foo | awk '{print $2}')
24    current_top_cpu=${current_top_cpu%%.*}
25    current_top_pid=$(print $foo | awk '{print $1}')
26
27    # if top cpu is over the limit, keep track
28    if (( current_top_cpu > cpu_threshold ))
29    then
30
31       # if top cpu is the same as last time, count it
32       if (( current_top_pid == bad_pid ))
33       then
34          (( count += 1 ))
35
36          # if top cpu has been on top an even multiple of 5 cycles
37          #    it's time to let someone know
38          if (( (count % 5) == 0 ))
39          then
40             /usr/local/bin/sound_alarm window \
41                "Process $bad_pid over $cpu_threshold % CPU threshold"
42          fi
43       else
44          bad_pid=$current_top_pid
45          count=0
```

Listing 6.8 *monitor_cpu*

```
46        fi
47    else
48        count=0
49    fi
50
51    # cycle every minute
52    sleep 60
53 done
```

Listing 6.8 *monitor_cpu* (continued)

It is simple to use the *ps* command to determine the most intensive CPU process. It would be easy if one could conclude that if the top CPU user were using greater than, say, 75 percent of CPU, there must be something wrong. Unfortunately, it is not as simple as that. A legitimate process can momentarily use large amounts of CPU cycles without necessarily indicating a malfunction. What you need to look for is a process that consistently and continuously uses large amounts of CPU cycles. To do this, our monitor script will look for a process that has been in excess of a threshold CPU usage for several consecutive sample cycles. We start out by establishing a high CPU usage threshold of 60 percent at line 14. If there is one single process that constitutes most of what your server does, this could be low; however, in practice it is rare for all of the work of an application to be done by a single process. You want to know if any single process is using greater than 60 percent of CPU cycles on an ongoing basis.

The rest of the script is an open *while* loop that iterates every minute. At line 22, the *ps* command determines the most active CPU process. Line 23 captures the CPU usage to the variable *current_top_cpu* and line 24 removes the percent sign from that value. Line 25 assigns the PID of the top CPU process to *current_top_pid*. The test at line 28 sees if the CPU usage is high enough to be concerned about. If it is, the test at line 32 will see if the *current_top_cpu* process is the same PID as it was at the last iteration, in which case it is assigned to *bad_pid*. If this test succeeds (that is, returns a value of 0), a counter is incremented at line 34 indicating that *bad_pid* has been bad for *count* successive monitor cycles. Every five cycles, the test at line 38 generates an alarm, unless *bad_pid* drops below the threshold value or is not the top CPU user for at least one monitor cycle, in which case *count* is reset to 0 at line 45. This script can be run as a daemon, started from */etc/rc.d/ rc.local* or an equivalent.

Monitoring Real Memory and Paging Space

It is also useful to monitor real memory usage. As Linux implements virtual memory management, running out of real memory is not a problem as such, so long as there is sufficient swap space to accommodate the virtual memory required by all of the current running processes. But things get critical when you run low on swap space. Actually running out of swap space will cause fatal memory allocation failures whose effects on the system are unpredictable. To all intents and purposes, you can consider this a form of crash because you cannot predict which processes will fail.

The script in Listing 6.9 uses memory and swap usage figures available from the */proc* file system. It will mail *root* if real memory runs out. If swap space gets low, a console window pops up, and someone gets paged if the swap space gets dangerously full.

The entire script in Listing 6.9 is an open *while* loop iterated each minute. Figures for total memory, free memory, and swap space are read from */proc/meminfo* and assigned to variables at lines 18 through 25. The test at line 28 catches a low memory situation, but only advises if the situation has persisted for 10 successive iterations to reduce the volume of mail. The test at line 48 pops up a window immediately if swap space runs over 80 percent. A page is generated by the test at line 55 if swap space tops 90-percent full.

```
 1 #!/bin/ksh
 2
 3 # script to monitor memory
 4 #    low memory results in mail to root
 5 #    low swap results in console popup window
 6 #    *REALLY* low swap and some one gets paged
 7 #
 8 # syntax: monitor_memory
 9 #
10 # script runs as a daemon and can be started at boot
11
12 count=0
13
14 # loop forever
15 while true
16 do
17    # query /proc for memory info
```

Listing 6.9 *monitor_memory*

```
18    total_memory=$( cat /proc/meminfo | grep MemTotal \
19              | awk '{print $2}' )
20    total_swap=$( cat /proc/meminfo | grep SwapTotal \
21              | awk '{print $2}' )
22    free_memory=$( cat /proc/meminfo | grep MemFree \
23              | awk '{print $2}' )
24    free_swap=$( cat /proc/meminfo | grep SwapFree \
25              | awk '{print $2}' )
26
27    # if memory is low, advise but do not panic
28    if (( free_memory < (total_memory / 10) ))
29    then
30
31      # only advise every 10 minutes, otherwise root gets
32      #    hundreds of annoying e-mails - even at 10 minute
33      #    intervals this may be too much for a server
34      #    chronically low on memory - adjust the value of
35      #    count accordingly
36      (( count += 1 ))
37      if (( count == 10 ))
38      then
39        /usr/local/bin/sound_alarm mail \
40         "Warning - Low memory"
41        count=0
42      fi
43    else
44      count=0
45    fi
46
47    # if swap is low, tell someone now
48    if (( free_swap < (total_swap / 5) ))
49    then
50      /usr/local/bin/sound_alarm window \
51         "*WARNING* - Running low on swap"
52    fi
53
54    # if swap is *REALLY* low, scream
55    if (( free_swap < (total_swap / 10) ))
56    then
57      /usr/local/bin/sound_alarm pager \
58         "*ALARM* - Dangerously low on swap"
59    fi
60
61    # re check every minute
62    sleep 60
63 done
```

Listing 6.9 *monitor_memory*

Monitoring Daemons

Linux, like all variants of UNIX, relies on the concept of the daemon process. A daemon is a process that runs all the time and supplies a basic functionality, either at the operating system or application level.

A problem that on occasion arises is that a daemon process for some reason dies and cannot be restarted. Consequently the service the daemon provides is not available, which has a domino effect on any other application that needs that service. (A daemon can also enter a race condition in which it runs out of control, consuming memory or CPU at rates hurtful to the rest of the system. That condition would be caught by the CPU or memory monitor I just presented.) A monitor for daemons can assist in ensuring that the daemons you need to see are there and inform you should anything be missing. As daemons are processes, this monitor will watch the process table, as shown in Listing 6.10.

The name of the daemon and its owner are passed as arguments on the command line and are assigned to variables at lines 13 and 14 of Listing 6.10. The rest of the script is an open *while* loop that scans the process table (line 21) to ensure the daemon is still there. If the daemon isn't present, the test at line 25 generates an appropriate alarm.

```
 1 #!/bin/ksh
 2
 3 # this script monitors and reports on specified daemons
 4
 5 # syntax: monitor_daemon <daemon name> <daemon owner>
 6 #    note: <daemon name> must be as it will appear in a ps listing
 7
 8 # script runs as a daemon and can be started at boot
 9 #    NB: each invocation monitors only one daemon, so multiple
10 #        invocations will be necessary to monitor multiple daemons
11
12 # assign input to vars
13 daemon="$1"
14 owner="$2"
15
16 # loop forever
17 while true
18 do
19
20     # look for the daemon in the process table
21     foo=$(ps -eo user,command | grep "$owner" | grep "$daemon"\
```

Listing 6.10 *monitor_daemon*

```
22              | grep -v "$0" | grep -v grep )
23
24      # if the daemon is missing, alarm
25      if [[ X"$foo" = X ]]
26      then
27         /usr/local/bin/sound_alarm window \
28             "*ALARM*: daemon $daemon is MIA"
29      fi
30
31      # check every minute
32      sleep 60
33 done
```

Listing 6.10 *monitor_daemon* (continued)

Monitoring Other Servers

Any distributed computing client server network always has a degree of reliance by one server on services provided by another. Examples are file or print servers, or perhaps an Internet Domain Name Service (DNS) server. This is a two-edged sword. On the positive side it divides the overall functionality of the system among several discrete units so that the failure of any one server does not constitute an entire system failure. On the other hand, some services may be critical to the ability of the whole to function; consequently, the server providing that function becomes a potential single point of failure for the whole system. Care must be taken to either design these servers to be highly reliable, or, better still, ensure that there are available backups in place to keep things running when (think when, not if) the main server fails. In many failure scenarios it is useful to have a monitor in place that will inform you as soon as possible if any network service or connection becomes unavailable.

Ideally, no client reconfiguration should be necessary in the event of a server failure, which should be the goal of the perfect fault tolerant server network. In the case of a failure in a server cluster, for example, the backup server should completely take over the identity of the primary server so that the change is invisible to any running clients. Unfortunately, this is not always possible. In some cases the running application poses a problem. This is true, for example, in the case of an NFS server. When multiple NFS clients depend on a single server, it is prudent to have a backup for the server that could take over the disk storage needed by the clients in the event the primary server fails, and this can be done easily enough. When the primary server fails, however, it will leave its clients holding file handles that will be useless to them when they need to make NFS requests from the backup server. In this case, the clients will have to take action to establish fresh file handles with the new server in order to continue. The recovery in this case requires action on the part of both client and server. Thus, the client needs to have some way of either monitoring for a server failure or the server must be responsible for determining who were the clients of the failed server and informing those clients there has been a server fail-over. This kind of client server interaction forms a good part of what is necessary to build the highly available server clusters and is discussed in Chapter 10, "Server Clustering."

If it is possible to engineer a server failure that is transparent to the client, it is of course still necessary to ensure that someone knows that the primary server has failed so the server can be repaired and placed back in service. Normally the backup server would report the fail-over. This assumes, however, that you have control over both the primary and the backup server, and that you can configure them to report what you want to know. In some cases you may not have control over the services of one or the other of those servers, as is the case with DNS servers when you opt to pay your ISP (Internet Service Provider) to operate and maintain your DNS database.

Another possible failure issue is the loss of a network connection. The server on the other end of the broken wire may be running just fine; but if you cannot get to it, then it is useless. Thus, redundant network connections are just as important as redundant servers. It is critical that these redundant connections follow different physical paths. This may seem obvious, but it is surprising how this can be overlooked. If you rely on external services such as an ISP, ensure that they too have redundant connections. Hal Stern in his book, *Blueprints for High Availability*, (John Wiley & Sons, 2000) recounts the story of a company that sourced Internet connectivity from two different service providers to guarantee that a failure at the service provider would not put the company out of service. Unfortunately, it turned out that both ISPs were resellers of service from the same upstream ISP. When that upstream ISP went down, both of the lower-level ISPs were down too, and Hal's client was cut off.

It is also a good idea to mix and match network hardware. There is a fair history of network hardware problems such as router software or hardware bugs causing problems. If all of your networks depend on the same or even similar make and models of router, a single bug that surfaces in that router could have a catastrophic affect on your entire operation. This is also why upgrades of existing code or migrations to new code should be done progressively rather than all at once, if possible. Upgrading one

---

CALL BEFORE YOU DIG

A news item several years ago illustrated the importance of physical paths. A contractor was excavating a ditch at the edge of the site of a large corporate office in Toronto and severed a conduit. It turned out that the entire communications infrastructure for the building had been channeled through this one conduit to the outside world. It took the telephone utility several days to repair the multiple cables severed in the accident and restore full communications to the office. Business today has become so reliant on communications channels that this kind of outage can be quite costly. Realize that you have little control over this kind of accident. The equipment being used to do the digging was not particularly large and the work was being done off the company's property, so it was not directly involved in what was happening. In short, it was an honest mistake. To protect itself, the company should have had a second service entry point to its building removed a reasonable distance from the first so that this kind of accident would be unlikely to affect both entry points.

---

device to a new software version that turns out to have a bug will affect only that one device, and only one device has to be returned to the previous software revision to repair the problem.

First Failure Messaging

In any case in which one server relies on another, it is typically redundant to implement a specific monitor for the other server. If one server goes down, the loss of the service it supplies will provide clear notification of trouble. It is important, however, that there is a reporting mechanism so that you will be informed of the loss of the service as soon as possible. In today's multi-layered software architectures, failures at one level can be masked and, without proper reporting, it can take some time to drill down through multiple servers to locate the real problem.

The principle of first failure notification is useful here. Consider a system of three servers, A, B, and C, in which those servers depend on each other serially. Server A provides a service needed by B, which in turn provides a service needed by C. Server C serves the end user, consequently it is at C that problems will first become apparent. If server A fails, that will cause a domino effect through B to C, which will be unable to do their jobs and will report an error to the end user. The question is, will it be clear in the error messaging presented to the end user at C that it is not in fact server C that really is the problem, or even server B, but that the source of the problem is actually server A?

The idea of first failure notification dictates that when server B fails to receive the service it needs from A, that information will be passed on to any servers down stream of B. As a result, the error message that eventually appears to the user at C will be multi-layered, saying that C could not do its job as a result of an error in B, and that B failed as a result of an error at server A. Thus, the system administrator can shortcut directly to a root problem at the beginning of a server dependency chain, based on the error messaging from the end of the server chain.

It would be useful if this kind of messaging is standard practice. Unfortunately it isn't yet. If you are in a position to influence the architecture of a multi-server system, this is an excellent question to ask your developers. If you are sourcing a layered server solution, ask your solution provider what can be built into your system along these lines.

Network Monitoring

When you are reliant on a network of servers, routers, and other network devices, it would be convenient if there were a tool you could use to monitor the availability of each of these parts of your overall infrastructure. To build such a monitor on your own can rapidly get complicated, and this is a case when you would be well advised to source an existing package. Fortunately, there are a number of packages available to do this sort of monitoring. Here are some you can investigate:

MRTG. The Multi Router Traffic Grapher is a tool to monitor the traffic load on network links. MRTG generates HTML pages containing GIF images that provide a live visual representation of this traffic. MRTG also indicates when services are unavailable. MRTG is based on Perl and C, and works under UNIX and Windows NT. It will keep up to two years of historical data and can typically monitor several hundred network devices. MRTG was originally released in 1995. It has matured well since then and remains widely used. It is distributed under the GNU General Public License. You can find MRTG at www.mrtg.org.

Cricket. It's developers describe Cricket as a high performance, flexible system for monitoring trends in time-series data. Cricket was developed to help network managers visualize and understand the traffic on their networks, but it can be used for other jobs, too. Cricket has two components, a collector and a grapher. The collector runs from *cron* every five minutes by default and stores data into a data structure managed by RRD Tool. When you want to analyze the data you have collected, you can use a Web browser to view graphs of the data. Cricket reads a set of configuration files called a config tree, which expresses everything Cricket needs to know about the types of data collected, how to get it, and from which targets it should collect data. The config tree minimizes redundant information, making it compact and easy to manage, and preventing mistakes caused by cut-and-paste errors. Cricket is written in Perl and is distributed under the GNU General Public License. Cricket was developed on Solaris, but runs on Linux and other versions of UNIX. It has also been run on Windows platforms, although they are not officially supported. The underlying database Cricket uses, RRD Tool, was written by the author of MRTG. Both Cricket and RRD Tool can be found from SourceForge at cricket.sourceforge.net.

Sysmon. The Sysmon Web page says that Sysmon is a network-monitoring tool that provides high performance and accurate network monitoring. Currently supported protocols include SMTP, IMAP, HTTP, TCP, UDP, NNTP, and PING tests. Sysmon is distributed under the GNU General Public License and can be found at www.sysmon.org.

Xni. If you are willing to spend some money or prefer a commercial product, look at Xni. Fastlane Systems presents Xni as a product designed to allow customers to develop profit centers from their network through effective usage billing. By providing visualization of traffic, Xni enables analysis of usage of internal and Internet resources, application tracking, response time, deployment of quality of service metrics, confirmation, and monitoring of service level agreements. Fastlane also claims that Xni facilitates effective troubleshooting, anticipation of network problems in real-time, projection of the impact of network growth and new applications, and the creation and monitoring of appropriate usage policy. Xni has a fine reporting granularity and keeps permanent records of network events for security and analysis. Further information and a demo version can be found at www.xni.com.

Monitoring System Logs

If any component of a system runs into trouble, the system will typically log an error. Unfortunately, much of what gets written to logs is not necessarily errors. In many cases log entries are made for events in the normal operation of the system. Also, there is no one single consolidated log; rather, logging is spread out over a number of different files. So, you can end up reviewing multiple log files, some of which can be large, sorting out the important from the trivial, to draw any serious conclusions. This is inefficient and, worst of all, slow. After all, if a problem crops up in a log, you want to know about it as fast as possible, not tomorrow when you have the time to print the logs and search through them.

What you need is an automated tool to sift through multiple logs looking for significant entries and alerting you to the problem quickly. Because of the volume of logging common to a production system and the variety of possible error messages to search, this can rapidly become a significant challenge. You could write your own monitor, but in this case I recommend that you consider investing in a prebuilt utility. The authors of these utilities have invested their time examining all sorts of logs and coming up with reasonable things to watch for—and useful ways to inform you.

Log monitor utilities are available free from open source providers. Among the choices are LogCheck/LogSentry from Psionic, available at www.psionic.com. This is a part of the Abacus tool kit produced by Psionic primarily for security monitoring purposes, but it is a generic package that can be told to look for any arbitrary information in log files that you want. The gnu folks offer Xlogmaster, available at www.gnu.org/software/xlogmaster. This tool has technically been superseded by the more ambitious GNU AWACS Advanced Monitoring and Control Structure. GNU AWACS is, however, in the early stages at this point, making Xlogmaster still a current item. Brandon Zehm offers another alternative in the LogDog package, available from marvin.criadvantage.com/caspian/Software/LogDog.

Monitoring Hardware

Your monitor depends on your hardware. If you source hardware with a proprietary hardware monitor capability, make sure that there is a Linux supported software interface. Ensure that it does real-time monitoring and can make measured values, such as voltage levels and temperatures, available to a shell process, from where they can be written to a file or examined by a script. Packages that offer only graphic interfaces may look impressive, but are of limited use in a production environment unless you can afford to hire someone to sit in front of a screen and watch for the warning icons.

If you have hardware supported by the generic Linux *sensors* package described in Chapter 3, "Choosing the Right Hardware," then you can use the *sensors* command to capture real-time values that can be checked against safe threshold levels. A script similar to the CPU monitor script in

Listing 6.8 can be used to generate an alarm if any of the parameters remain above allowable limits for an extended period.

Monitor Software Packages

This chapter has focused on the building blocks to construct your own monitor package. But you may prefer not to write your own monitor, in which case you will be in the market for a prebuilt package. However, you will find that several of these packages rely on local data gathering scripts that you will need to write. Also, there will always be servers for which a prebuilt monitor cannot do everything you want and you will appreciate the ability to quickly put together a monitor script of your own.

There are a variety of system monitor packages available for Linux in both free and commercial form. Each has its pros and cons, and you need to evaluate them in terms of your own requirements. Here are some packages you may wish to investigate. I'll start with the free packages and then move to the commercial ones.

MON, The Service Monitoring Daemon. MON is written entirely in Perl to ease portability. It makes use of monitor scripts that can be written independently of MON itself, making it easily customizable. There are a large number of prewritten monitors included in the distribution that watch common services such as SMTP, FTP, NNTP, HTTP, POP-3, DNS, and LDAP. There are also monitors for local disk usage as well as hardware monitors for Foundry routers, Brocade Fibre Channel switches, and Compaq Presario servers. MON also supports Simple Network Management Protocol (SNMP), a remote systems management protocol used by large-scale commercial tools such as Hewlett-Packard's OpenView. MON supports a sophisticated alert function, allowing a variety of options concerning how and when to alert the proper people, including pager support. There is also a two-way pager interface and several World Wide Web interfaces to the central monitor server, allowing remote server status and history queries. MON can be found at www.kernel.org/software/mon.

Big Sister. Big Sister is a rewrite of Big Brother (discussed later in this section), a popular commercial package. Like MON, Big Sister is written in Perl for portability. It uses a central monitor server to collect and collate data provided by monitored clients running the Big Sister monitor daemon, *uxmon*. This daemon can monitor local parameters, such as disk and CPU usage, as well as including a generic log file monitor. *uxmon* can also monitor a variety of network services and supports SNMP polling, being designed to play well with Hewlett-Packard's OpenView. The central monitor collects this data and makes it dynamically available in the form of Web pages as well as storing and trending historical data. To serve larger or geographically isolated sites, the central monitors can be cascaded into a large scale tiered structure, each central monitor forwarding selected data to its higher-level monitor. Alarms can be generated based on configurable thresholds at all levels of the reporting hierarchy. Big Sister does not directly include pager support, but relies on the *sendpage* package mentioned in the earlier sidebar in this chapter, "A Paging Primer." Big Sister can be found at bigsister.graeff.com and at source-forge.net/projects/bigsister.

NetSaint. According to NetSaint's Web page, NetSaint monitors hosts and services on your network. It has the ability to e-mail or page you when a problem arises and when the problem gets resolved. NetSaint is written in C and is designed to run under Linux, although it should work under most other UNIX variants. It can run either as a normal process or as a daemon, intermittently running checks on various services that you specify. The service checks are performed by external plug-ins that return service information to NetSaint. Several CGI programs are included with NetSaint to allow you to view the current service status, history, and so forth through a Web browser. NetSaint also supports a WAP interface and can be found at www.netsaint.org.

Bluebird. Written by OpenNMS, Bluebird is a new package designed to take on the task of network management starting with a clean sheet. Bluebird is an open source, distributable, scalable network and systems management platform. Bluebird is being developed using open technologies such as Java, XML, and XSL, the idea being to create a platform that will always be open to further development and integration of new open technologies as they are developed. As of this writing, Bluebird hasn't had a production release, but an early adopters' version is in beta testing. This beta version supports functionality such as automated performance monitoring, paging, and e-mail notification of critical events, Web-based reporting, a cross-platform graphical user interface, service level monitoring, a graphical rule builder, polling via SNMP, out-of-the-box support for service pollers that monitor Web, e-mail, FTP, SSH, DNS, and database servers, and a graphical configuration interface. A production release designed to scale to mid- and larger-sized networks (500 or more hosts) is slated for late 2001. More about Bluebird can be found at www.opennms.org.

GNU AWACS. The Free Software Foundation's contribution to system monitoring comes in the form of GNU AWACS, a slightly inaccurate acronym for Advanced Monitoring and Control Structure. Designed as the next generation to the well-established Xlogmaster package, at this writing AWACS is in the early development stage and does not offer a stable production release. It promises to rival the functionality of packages such as MON and Big Sister, but time will tell whether this package will gain ground. You can keep track of AWACS at www.gnu.org/software/awacs.

Next are some commercial packages. You will find when you move into the commercial realm that, with the exception of Big Brother, which is strictly a system monitor, the rest of the commercial offerings are based on a wider view of systems management. Most of these packages go beyond simply monitoring and move into full-scale networked systems management. This typically includes managing software installation and support, network configuration, and printer management as well as remote application installation, maintenance, and management. System monitoring becomes just an element in the overall functionality of these packages. This kind of approach is generally suited to the mid- to larger-sized operations. If that is you, then these packages are for you. In some cases you may already have such a system in place, in which case the question you need to ask is how to integrate your new Linux servers into that preexisting management infrastructure.

Big Brother. The smallest and least complex of the commercial packages is Big Brother, the package that Big Sister was based on. Big Brother uses its own IP monitoring protocol that has been assigned by the IANA (Internet Assigned Numbers Authority) to port 1984. (What other port would Big Brother use?) The functionality offered by Big Brother is similar to that described previously for Big Sister, except that Big Brother also supports Windows NT clients, and because it is a commercial package, offers several support options varying from e-mail to telephone and direct login support. Big Brother has been favorably compared in the trade press to larger and more expensive enterprise management systems, and has a significant user community that provides plug-ins and mailing list support. Big Brother is watching you from his Web home at maclawran.ca/bb-dnld.

eEMU. This package is similar in scale and functionality to Big Brother. According to the developer, Jarrix Systems of Australia, eEMU is a flexible and integration-ready event management tool developed under Linux and consisting of a manager and agents. It integrates monitoring and event manager into one program. Agents are simple scripts invoked by *cron*. These scripts are run at regular intervals of the user's choice. Each run scans the resources it monitors, comparing their thresholds against a configuration file. If a threshold is exceeded, a message is sent to the manager. eEMU uses a TCP-based messaging protocol called *emsg2* that allows the product to scale to multi-tiered internetwork architectures and supplies both text and GUI management interfaces. More on eEMU can be found at www.eemuconcept.com.

Volution. Volution is a new network management tool offered by Caldera. It is designed more to be a network management package, incorporating monitoring as one element in a broader range of functionality. As such, it is placed to compete with the large-scale products discussed later in this section, but has its feet firmly placed in the Linux world, having been written by one of the major vendors of Linux systems. Using Volution, Caldera claims that administrators can manage their systems effectively through hardware and software inventory, software distribution, health monitoring of systems, printer configuration, and scripted scheduled actions. If you are looking for a mid-range systems management and monitoring solution for a primarily Linux environment, this is a contender. More about Volution can be found at www.caldera.com/products/volution.

Finally, if you are approaching management of multiple networked servers from a broader approach than just monitoring system functionality, consider management tools that centrally manage every aspect of server operation, including software management, user database and security management, data storage, and other functions. Several well-known and long established products will do this for you. But be aware that these are large-scale, top-down, structured products that are designed to scale to the largest enterprises and involve a substantial implementation effort and cost. The major products in this market are

- Tivoli from IBM at www.tivoli.com
- Unicenter TNG from Computer Associates at www.cai.com/unicenter

- OpenView from Hewlett-Packard at www.openview.com
- Patrol from BMC Software at www.bmc.com/products/unix

What You Can Do Now

1. Using your network topology diagram, list each server you need to monitor and examine how each server may be dependent on another. Look for servers that are a single point of failure for another server or service, and consider how you may be able to introduce a redundancy to eliminate that single point of failure. Also, look for single points of failure in services such as network connectivity and power supply, and work to implement alternate services or providers in these cases, too.

2. Using the list of servers to be monitored, make a list of what needs to be monitored on each of the servers.

3. Decide how to monitor each of the parameters you listed in step 2. You may choose to write your own monitor, or have a look at one of the prebuilt ones I reviewed.

4. Write or install your monitor and then configure and test it.

5. Go home, relax, and engage in your favorite recreational activity, safe in the knowledge that should anything go wrong, you will be notified appropriately.

Backup and Recovery Strategies

**The wind said
You know I'm the result of
forces beyond my control.**

—A. R. Ammons

It is a reality of life that we must be prepared to deal with forces beyond our control. So far, I have shown you a variety of means to assess your risk level and put into place defenses against loss. None of these tools are perfect; however, and you must consider that forces beyond your control will some day ruin even your most carefully built, properly configured, well-monitored, redundant hardware server. In that case you need to have a backup. No form of hardware redundancy or software data duplication should ever be considered so reliable as to eliminate the need for a data backup. Never say it will never happen to you.

Causes of Data Loss

In building a backup strategy, you need to consider the ways that you will lose data and build your defenses accordingly. Here is a list of the possible loss causes that frame the rest of the chapter:

> **Data lost or damaged as a result of accidental or deliberate action on the part of a legitimate or possibly illegitimate end user.** Also, data loss as the result of a malfunction of an application. In either case, this loss can occur without any hardware failure or operating system

failure. Often this involves the loss of a single file or local group of files and there is no hardware problem with either disk or tape devices. So although the loss of the data can cause problems, it should be straightforward to recover the lost data from a well-organized backup.

Data lost as a result of a storage hardware failure inside a server. While using RAID and other redundancy strategies (described in Chapter 5, "Building Reliable Disk Storage") can reduce the risk of this type of loss, it is still possible for the RAID itself to fail. Using RAID does *not* eliminate the need for backups. In this case, the recovery involves replacing the failed hardware as well as recovering data from a backup.

Data loss or application availability loss as a result of a total server failure due to something like an internal power supply or motherboard failure. Using fault tolerant hardware redundancy can reduce this kind of risk. Your risk analysis may not be able to cost justify a heavily fault-tolerant system, however, and a complete and fast backup system may be acceptable as an alternative.

Data lost as a result of a complete site loss, most likely as a result of a natural disaster. Recovery in this case involves reproducing the lost site in a different physical location, possibly using a third-party disaster recovery service as well as recovering your entire operation from backups.

You need to build a backup strategy that can recover the data lost in each of these cases. This chapter examines each of these four cases to build a definition of what a good backup system needs to do. I then turn that definition into a to-do list that illustrates what you will need to do to build your own backup system.

Recovering Files Lost by Accident

Generally, the first challenge in recovering a lost file is to determine which file is lost. That may seem obvious, but in some cases, if the files were deleted accidentally or deliberately with purpose to damage, it may not be clear which files are actually missing. In this case a list of the files that did exist at the time the last backup was made will be useful. Such a list is not itself data; rather it is metadata, that is, information useful or necessary to make data available. When a backup is made, a list of the files included in the backup needs to be made and included as a part of the backup. That list then needs to be quickly accessible so you will know which tape to look on for the files you need. It can be argued that the Linux commands you use to produce a tape archive can list the files in the archive directly from the archive itself, and this is true. The problem with that is that the entire archive must be read from beginning to end to produce the list of files. Once you have determined which archive the files you need are in, you then need to return to that archive and search through it again to extract the files. This is time consuming, which is not good if the data loss is causing you downtime. Extracting data from tape tends to be slow at best, without adding the overhead of having to search tapes for the files you need first. The bright side of this data loss issue is that the application and the operating system are still operative. Thus the application may be able to indicate through error messages or logs which files it is having trouble either using or finding, and all of the operating system utilities necessary for searching and extracting from a tape are still working.

You cannot predict when a file may be lost or when a disk will crash. Consequently, a good backup system should keep data as up-to-date as possible. If a file is lost and the backed up copy of the file is a month old, it may be of marginal value if most or all of the data in the file changed over the past month. Also, you want your backup system to be as automated as possible. Programmed machines are much better at remembering to do a backup every night without fail than are people.

Recovering from Storage Hardware Failure

Loss of a disk usually translates into the loss of one or more entire physical file systems. Thus, it makes sense to structure your backups such that each tape archive file contains a complete physical file system. In the early days of UNIX, people commonly backed up physical devices, so that each tape archive represented a backup of a single disk. If you are working with a kernel that does not support Logical Volume Management (LVM), (discussed in Chapter 8, "Logical Volume Management"), this is reasonable because such a kernel requires that a physical file system must reside entirely within a single partition, which in turn must be contiguous and contained entirely within one disk. Thus, a file system must reside entirely within one disk, so a backup of a disk will always contain a complete copy of all of the file systems on that disk.

The problem with backing up by disk, however, lies on the restore side. In the case of a disk failure, the replacement disk may not be identical to the failed disk. If the new disk is larger, this is usually not a problem. If the replacement disk is smaller, however, your backup may be useless, since it needs to be streamed entirely onto one device. It is a much better idea to backup the self-contained data structure of the physical file system. Then the limitation on restore is simply that the replacement disk or disks must be large enough to contain each of the file systems archived on the tape rather than the contents of the entire tape. If you choose to use a LVM system, backing up by file system is mandatory as the physical storage becomes completely disconnected from the file system data structures. In effect, a physical file system can become distributed in pieces across multiple physical disks.

Dealing with Data Damage

If the disk loss causes either the application or the operating system to crash, it is possible—even likely—that your application data will suffer some degree of damage. At the time of the crash, a database may have been writing data that needs to be consistent in more than one location, or possibly updating an index.

If the disk that crashes does not contain any of this dynamic data, you may think that you should be okay after you have replaced the operating system or application binary disk that died. Unfortunately, because the interruption to the application was an ungraceful one, even if no application data was actually lost, the state of the data may be inconsistent enough to cause the application trouble when you restart it. In this case either you hope that the application has a built-in recovery mechanism for this situation (and some do) otherwise you may find it necessary to restore your last good application data backup as well to fully recover from the loss.

Recovering from a Total Server Loss

If a server suffers a physical loss such as a power supply failure, there are several possible responses. You can treat it the same way as an operating system disk loss by moving the application data to a backup server and restarting the application. This assumes that the operating system installation on the backup server supports your application. In this situation the value of good change management shows through. In the ideal case, every server should run an identical operating system image, maximizing the interchangeability of each server and making it possible for each server to run any of the applications in the shop. In the real world, it may be difficult to get by with only one operating system installation for all of your applications; but if you keep it as a goal, then you will avoid the opposite extreme, in which each server is unique and nothing is interchangeable. That situation reduces your fail-over options rather than improving them.

On the other hand, it may be less work to replace the failed power supply in the original server than shift your application around. And, if your risk analysis indicates that you want downtime on this server to be measured in seconds or minutes rather than hours or days, you may want to consider a high availability server cluster, or at the least an identical redundant standby server you could migrate the application to as quickly as possible.

You hope that the nature of the failure does not cause damage to any disks, but if the cause of the failure was a power surge, for example, you may not be that lucky. Also, if the server crashes, the resultant application crash could well damage or destroy the application data. Thus, it is still necessary to have a full backup of both the application and operating system so that you have the capability to completely recreate the server from scratch as necessary.

Recovering a Lost Site

The final case to consider is that of the loss of a complete operational site. This could be as a result of a local problem, such as a fire, or it could be the result of a natural disaster. A natural disaster can also vary in scale. A tornado can be terribly destructive, but on a local scale. Your building could be flattened, while another building a few hundred feet away may be undamaged. On the other hand, a disaster such as a hurricane or large flood can affect hundreds of square miles in a drastic way. You will need to assess the risks inherent to your location and make plans accordingly.

Clearly in the case of a site loss on any scale you will need a backup of both the operating system and application stored in a safe off-site location. You also need an alternate operations site, in the event that the disaster puts your site out of commission for an extended period of time. Finally, you need a plan. In the case of disaster, the situation can be confusing. People may be scared, panicky, and not functioning normally. You may not have all of your own staff available. You need to have an operational means of recovering your business function as quickly as possible under these challenging conditions.

Backup System Requirements

Having examined the four data loss cases you need to be prepared for, let's summarize the requirements for a backup system capable of coping with

Table 7.1 Backup System Requirements

DATA LOSS CASE	REQUIREMENTS
Accidental data loss	A quickly accessible list of the files that existed at the time the last backup was made. Backups must happen automatically. Backups must be as frequent as practicable to minimize data loss, and business process recovery time.
Loss due to storage hardware failure	Backups must back up complete physical file systems. Backups must maintain consistency of dynamic data. Requires procedure to recover operating system disk.
Loss due to total server failure	Redundant server for fail over. Complete backup of operating system and application.
Total site loss	Complete backup of operating system application stored off-site. A comprehensive plan to restore operations either at a repaired primary site or an alternate backup site.

the demands of each of these cases. Table 7.1 lists the four loss cases on the left and the major requirements on the right.

The next thing to do is to consider how to build a backup system that meets these requirements. I'll sketch how you could build your own system and then review some prewritten packages. I'll introduce some basic UNIX archiving tools that you will need to use if you choose to write your own backup system. This information is still useful even if you source a prewritten package because a prewritten package generally makes use of the same basic routines.

As a starting point for building a backup system I'll restructure the requirements column of Table 7.1 into a to-do list. Our goal will then be to build a system that can cover all the points on the list:

- The system must create lists of the files backed up, including their sizes and date stamps, and identify which tape each file is stored on. This data must be available quickly in a recovery situation.

- The system should backup complete physical file systems.

- The system must support backups able to deal with dynamically changing data with a minimum of operational down time.

- The system must make backups happen automatically, as frequently as is practicable.

- The system must include a plan for recovering an operating system disk.

- The system should support redundant servers to maintain production in the case of a complete failure of a server.

- The system must maintain a full set of current data backups off-site, along with all of the data and procedures required to rebuild the site in a suitable backup location.

To get started building a backup system, you need to know about some basic UNIX archiving tools. If you have dabbled a bit already with *tar*, *dump*, and *restore*, you can skip the next section. If you are newer to UNIX, the next section will ground you in the most common use of these basic commands.

Basic Archiving Tools

I'll cover three utilities that have a long history in UNIX. *tar*, a contraction of tape archiver, is probably the best known. It takes a list of files and concatenates them into a single archive file that may be written to tape, disk, or any other type of storage media. Most Linux distributions include the GNU version of *tar*, which has enhancements over older traditional versions, so this is the one I will be presenting. Then I'll look at *dump* and *restore*, a pair of utilities designed to archive and restore entire *ext2* physical file systems. None of these basic utilities is sufficient to be a backup system on its own, but you need to know about all of them as they form the basic building block of a complete backup system.

tar: The Tape Archiver

tar is a basic tool and cannot be considered anything more than a low-level building block for a backup system. It simply collapses a group of files into single flat file archive. For many years, however, it has been a standard tool for backing up data and is so pervasive in the UNIX world that you will need to know about it at some point. Much of the open source software distributed across the Internet is packaged in the form of *tar* archives (or tarballs, as they are commonly called). The simplicity of tar also comes into play in recovery situations in which you may not have sophisticated tools available. Let's see how it works.

Any *tar* command must include either the *-c*, *-x* or *-t* options, indicating that you are creating an archive, extracting files from an archive, or asking

CAMPBELL'S LAW OF BACKUPS

Whatever command you choose to use to backup your data, you would be well advised to consider Campbell's Law of Backups, which states, "For every backup tape you make, take a previous one off the shelf and test it." I always marvel at the number of people I have run across who have a story to tell about a site they knew of that put in place a backup system and used it religiously. Then, when something failed and it was necessary to do a restore, it was discovered that for some reason the backups were no good. In some of these stories, backup systems had been running for years and no one had ever thought to test the backups after they were made to ensure that they were actually good!

I argue that each time your backup system completes an archive, it should choose a tape containing a previous archive and perform a test to ensure that it is readable. Realize that in doing this the idea is not just to test that the actual backup command worked, but also to test the durability of the tape. Diamonds, according to James Bond, are forever; unfortunately, the same cannot be said for magnetic storage media. Temperature, humidity, exposure to magnetic fields, and just plain time affect the viability of a data tape. Just dropping a tape on the floor can ruin it. Should you replace a tape drive, the tapes made on the old drive may not necessarily be reliably readable on the new one, especially if the new drive implements a new technology. Backward compatibility can be a significant problem in the particular case of tape drive technology. Stored in the proper conditions, tapes can and should last for years, but there is no harm in keeping tabs on how yours are holding up.

for a table of contents of the archive, respectively. The archive device is specified by the *-f* option, the archive device being the device where the archive is to be written to or read from. Hence the following command writes a *tar* archive of my home directory to the first SCSI tape drive (*/dev/st0*). The *-v* option tells *tar* to echo back to *stdout* the filenames as they are written to the archive, which is useful to meet the first requirement on our to-do list:

```
# tar -cvf /dev/st0 /home/iain
```

Naming a directory as an argument to *tar* implies that the directory will be recursed. I can exclude files or directories from the recursion with the *--exclude* option. The following command archives all of *iain*'s home directory with the exception of the */home/iain/junk* subdirectory:

```
# tar -cvf /dev/st0 --exclude /home/iain/junk /home/iain
```

You may also wish to use the -*l* option to restrict the recursion to files within a local file system. Otherwise, an archive starting at /, for example, would include all files in the entire logical file system structure. For example, this command would create an archive of only the root file system:

```
# tar -cvlf /dev/st0 /
```

This will help meet the second requirement on our to-do list, although as you will see shortly *dump* does a better job of dealing with whole file systems than *tar*.

You can make multi-volume archives with the -*M* option. I find this handy for moving a small number of files between machines using a floppy drive. It will also work fine for tape drives. If the data will fit on a practical number of floppies, you could do it with this command:

```
# tar -cMvf /dev/fd0 /home/iain
```

You should be careful to label the floppies or tapes as there is no way to easily determine from the data in the archive itself which volume number a particular diskette or tape is or how many volumes make up the entire set.

If you are having trouble getting your data to fit your media, you can take advantage of the *gzip* compression algorithm (see the accompanying "What about *gzip*?" sidebar) by asking for it with the -*z* option, like this:

```
# tar -cvzf /dev/st0 /home/iain
```

Note that you used compression to make this archive, so you will need to include the -*z* option also when you restore the archive. If your tape drive does compression in hardware, it is unlikely you will gain much benefit from compressing at both the *tar* level and the hardware level. It is probably better to let the drive do the compression and avoid loading up the server CPU.

Once you have your archive made, you can get a table of contents using the -*t* option, like this:

```
# tar -tvf /dev/st0
```

If you obey Campbell's Law of Backups, you need a way to test a *tar* archive. Unfortunately, there is no specific option that will do this. It is necessary for *tar* to read the entire archive to complete the table of contents, and if *tar* can complete this operation without error, it is likely that the data of the files themselves will also be intact. This is commonly accepted to be a reasonable test of a *tar* archive. It is not certain, however; so if you have the time, you may want to do a restore to the bit bucket, like this:

```
# tar -xvf /dev/st0 > /dev/null
```

Without the redirection to */dev/null*, the *-x* option would cause the entire content of the archive to be restored to the logical file system structure. Just where it gets written can be an issue you need to be careful about. The earlier examples of creating archives used the directory */home/iain*. By default, GNU *tar* will strip the leading / from this absolute path and store all of these files in the form *./home/iain*. This means that when I extract from the archive, the files will be written relative to the current directory at the time I issue the command to extract. Consider the following series of commands:

```
# cd /root
# tar -cf /dev/st0 /home/iain
# tar -xf /dev/st0
```

The final *tar* command to extract the archive would be relative to the current directory, */root*, resulting in the archive being restored to the directory */root/home/iain*, which is probably not what I want. If you want the file stored with full absolute path names, use the *-P* option.

dump: The File System Backup Tool

dump is a command specifically designed to backup an entire *ext2* file system. As such it is perfect fit for the second requirement on our to-do list. What is unique to *dump* is that not only does it include the data files themselves in the archive, but it also includes the data held in the inode table. Thus, *dump* backs up both the data and the metadata of the file system. As the inode table defines the directory structure of the file system, this allows the archive to be examined interactively as if it were a live file system. This

---

WHAT ABOUT *GZIP*?

While *tar* is probably the most common archive tool in the UNIX world, it is being challenged by the newer *gzip* utility. *gzip* was developed by the GNU people as an updated version of *tar*. *gzip* is functionally equivalent to *tar*, but is argued to be better as it automatically compresses the data files before placing them into the archive. It uses the Lempel-Ziv algorithm, the best of the commonly available data compression algorithms. You will often see files distributed as a tar archive that has been "gzipped" to reduce its size for transmission across a low bandwidth network connection. The common convention in this case is to give such a file a suffix of *.tgz*, indicating it is a *gzip* compressed tarball. To extract such an archive, use *gunzip* to uncompress the archive, and then use *tar* to list or extract the files.

gives a fairly satisfactory solution to the first requirement in our to-do list. As we shall see, *dump* has even more functionality. Here is the basic command to back up a file system:

```
# dump -f /dev/st0 /dev/hda5
```

Like *tar*, the *-f* flag to *dump* specifies the output device to receive the archive. If you are backing up to the first SCSI tape, as shown in the example, it is actually unnecessary to use the *-f* flag, as the default output device is usually */dev/st0*. Notice that the file system to be backed up is identified by specifying the name of the disk partition rather than a mount point. This is consistent with the way *dump* works. In this case *dump* will go to the beginning of the partition and start reading the inode table for the physical file system that resides in that partition. It will then recurse that inode table and back up all of the data files in the file system. It will not move beyond the specified physical file system. Consider an example in which a mount table looked like this:

```
# mount
/dev/hda5 on / type ext2 (rw)
/dev/hda1 on /RH71 type ext2 (rw,usrquota)
/dev/hdb1 on /home type ext2 (rw,usrquota)
/dev/hdc1 on /home/iain/data type ext2 (rw)
```

I issue this *dump* command:

```
# dump /dev/hda5
```

Only the data stored in the */dev/hda5* partition is dumped. The recursion would *not* carry over to the data in the file system in */dev/hda1* or */dev/hdb1*, as they are separate physical file systems. The name of the mount point of a file system can also be specified. Using the same mount table as the previous example, the following two commands are equivalent:

```
# dump /dev/hda1
# dump /RH71
```

It is also possible back up only part of a physical file system by specifying a directory part way down the tree for that file system. Again using the mount table of the previous two examples, the following command archives beginning at */home/iain* and recurses until the end of the directory tree for the */dev/hdb1* partition. Data in the file system in partition */dev/hdc1* mounted at */home/iain/data* would *not* be included in the archive.

```
# dump /home/iain
```

Incremental dump *Backups*

Probably the most significant feature of *dump* is that it supports incremental backups. Incremental backups ensure that only data that has changed since the last backup is included in the current backup. This involves a metadata object that lists date stamps for files at each backup so that successive backups can compare the current state of the data to the state at the time of the last backup and so determine which files have changed and so need to be backed up. In a file system in which a minority of the files account for the majority of the data change, this can significantly reduce the amount of data to be backed up and so speed up the process. Be aware that your mileage will vary in the case where your application uses a few large data files, as, for example, some databases do. Even if only a small amount of real data has changed, the date stamp on the data base file will still change, causing the incremental utility to back up the whole data base file.

Although incremental backup can significantly improve performance, it carries a burden of complexity that must be properly managed. Consider that an incremental backup routine must start by a complete backup of all the files in the file system. Once this is done, successive tapes then record only the changes. If you run your backup routine nightly, then each night a new tape will result in 24 hours of changes. If you experience a failure four days from now, you can rebuild your data by first recovering the full backup reference, then recovering the four intermediate tapes in sequence. Thus your file system gets rebuilt in something like a live replay of days' worth of activity. Clearly, however, you cannot do this forever. After a year you would have 365 tapes, each of which would have to be recovered in exact sequence to restore your data to the state it was in at the time of the most recent backup!

In practice, an incremental system will run a full backup reference typically between once per week and once per month, with incrementals occurring daily or weekly between. One common arrangement is to run a full backup once per month, with a weekly backup each weekend and a further daily backup each night. The backup utility can be directed to capture only changes in the past 24 hours for the nightly backup, whereas the weekly backup will look back and capture changes over the past seven days. Thus if a failure occurred on Wednesday of the third week, a restore would involve the reference tapes from the first of the month, followed by the tape that brings things up to Sunday of the current week, and then the tapes from Monday and Tuesday night, in that order.

dump *and Incremental Backup Levels*

dump uses the term *increment level* to implement incremental backups. When you make a dump archive, you specify the increment level in the form of a number between zero and nine. Each time you do a dump, the date of the dump, the name of the file system dumped, and the dump level are recorded in the file */etc/dumpdates*. The next time the same file system is dumped, the increment level you specify at that time is compared to the increment level of the most recent dump for that file system as recorded in */etc/dumpdates*. The rule is that *dump* will archive all files that are new or were modified since the last dump of a lower level. A level zero dump by definition archives all files.

Consider the example of the calendar shown in Figure 7.1. The number shown in the middle of each day represents the dump level for a backup that runs that night at 1:00 A.M. The first Saturday of every month, a level zero dump runs, backing up the entire file system. Next a weekly cycle begins. Starting every Sunday, a daily incremental dump occurs, with the increment level increased by one each day. It is important to note that a separate tape would be used each day, for each increment level. Thus the level two dump of Sunday catches all of the changes between Saturday and Sunday. Likewise the level three dump Monday catches the changes since

S	M	T	W	T	F	S
			1	2	3	4 0
5 2	6 3	7 4	8 5	9 6	10 7	11 1
12 2	13 3	14 4	15 5	16 6	17 7	18 1
19 2	20 3	21 4	22 5	23 6	24 7	25 1
26 2	27 3	28 4	29 5	30 6	31 7	1 0

Figure 7.1 This calendar illustrates levels for a simple incremental tape rotation.

the level two dump Sunday, and so on. There are only nine increment levels supported, so we have to stop somewhere, and as a weekly cycle is easy to work with, the last increment runs at level seven on Friday. Finally on Saturday the 11th a level one increment runs, catching all of the changes for the previous week. Now the cycle can start all over again.

The old saying that what you may gain on the peaches will be lost on the bananas applies to incremental backups too. This becomes evident when you examine what happens if you need to do a restore in the sense that the incremental backup sped up the backup process, possibly a great deal. The balance comes in the fact that the restore process may take longer than it would with a nonincremental backup scheme.

Consider what happens if you lose a file system on Thursday the 23rd. The most recent backup was the level five increment of the 22nd. To rebuild the entire file system, it will be necessary to restore several tapes. The tape of the 22nd has only the changes that occurred on the 22nd. You will also need the tape that has the changes that occurred on the 21st, and the 20th, and so on. In fact, the sequence to restore would be as follows. First you restore the level zero tape made on the 4th, which brings you up to date as of the 4th. Then you would restore the level one tape of the 18th, followed by the level two of the 19th, the level three of the 20th, the level four of the 21st, and finally the level five of the 22nd. That is six tapes in total, and during these restores you may have restored different versions of some files as many as six times; hence the time you saved on the backup can get lost on the restore.

Different tape rotations can somewhat reduce the complexity of the restore. Consider the calendar shown in Figure 7.2. Derived from the famous Towers of Hanoi problem (see the accompanying "The Towers of Hanoi" sidebar), this scheme alternates odd and even numbered backup levels. You still start with a level zero reference on the first Saturday of the month, in this case the 4th. Then the rotation begins. On Sunday the 5th, a level three backup captures changes since the level zero reference. On Monday a level two dump occurs. As the rule, the last *lower* dump level determines how far back the dump looks. So, this backup also captures all changes since the level zero of the 4th. This will take longer than the previous rotation, as this tape has to capture two days worth of changes, but it simplifies the restore process, as we shall see. Next, on Tuesday a level five dump occurs, which records changes since the last lower level, the level three of Sunday. And so the rotation continues, each day leapfrogging the next until Saturday, when a level one dump saves the entire week's changes and the rotation begins again.

S	M	T	W	T	F	S
			1	2	3	4 0
5 3	6 2	7 5	8 4	9 7	10 6	11 1
12 3	13 2	14 5	15 4	16 7	17 6	18 1
19 3	20 2	21 5	22 4	23 7	24 6	25 1
26 3	27 2	28 5	29 4	30 7	31 6	1 0

Figure 7.2 The Hanoi incremental tape rotation looks like this.

How does this rotation help simplify the restore? Let's again look at the case of a crash on Thursday the 23rd. You will see that in this rotation, you need to restore only four tapes, starting with the level zero of the 4th, then the level 1 of the 18th, the level 2 of the 20th, and finally the level 4 of the 22nd. In the previous case, by contrast, six tapes were required.

Incremental Backups with dump

Here is an example of the dump syntax to implement the Hanoi tape rotation. If, for example, you were backing up the */home* file system to */dev/st0*, the default output device, the level zero backup command on the first Saturday of the month would be

```
# dump -0u /home
```

The *-0* option indicates the dump increment level and the *-u* option tells *dump* to update the */etc/dumpdates* file with the date of this level zero dump. In the Hanoi rotation, the next dump is a level three, which would require this command:

```
# dump -3u /home
```

THE TOWERS OF HANOI

It is said that in the Temple of Brahma in Benares there is a dome that marks the center of the world. Under the dome there is set a brass plate upon which there are three diamond needlepoints, a cubit high and as thick as the body of a bee. God placed 64 gold disks on one needle at the time of creation. It is the task of the priests of the temple to move these disks from the pin upon which God placed them to another, one disk at a time, never placing a larger disk on a smaller one. When they complete their task, the universe will come to an end.

The incremental dump tape rotation introduced in the main text is based on this famous problem in mathematics, which was first published by the French mathematician Edouard Lucas in 1883. The pattern of leapfrogging the increment levels every other day is similar to the sequence of moving disks from one pin to another necessary to solve the problem. The problem actually has several solutions and has been used as a programming challenge in colleges for many years. If you are concerned that the priests may be nearing the end of their task, consider that with 64 disks it requires at least $2^{64} - 1$ moves to complete the task. Assuming the priests move one disk each second and make no mistakes, it would take around 585,000,000,000 years to finish.

You continue through the rotation, changing the dump increment level accordingly each day. After several months or so, the daily and weekly tapes should get rotated out of the dump cycle and fresh tapes brought in.

It should be clear that keeping track of which tape is which is critical to the success of an incremental backup scheme. If you get the tapes mixed up, there is no way you can hope to do a successful restore operation. Thus some reliable means of labeling the tapes is an absolute necessity. For a smaller site using a single tape drive unit and handling tapes manually, simply physically labeling the tapes should be sufficient. It is also possible to include a data label in the header of the dump archive on the tape itself, and I strongly recommend that you do this as a backup for and a corroboration of the physical tape label. Inserting a label in the dump is done using the -L option to *dump*. Thus a better version of the earlier level zero *dump* command would be

```
# dump -0u -L"deut tape d22" /home
```

This command assumes that the host name of the server being backed up is *deut* and you have a labeling convention that has you using a tape physically labeled d22 for this dump. It is not necessary to include the dump level or the date in the label, as *dump* will add this information to the archive file header anyway. It is useful to add the host name, as *dump* does not include that in the header.

Useful dump *Options*

You should be aware of a few other options to *dump*. *dump* tries to estimate the size of the data being dumped and compare it to the tape storage capacity. If the size of the dump will exceed the tape storage, *dump* will break the archive into volumes sized to fit the tape. As most current tape drives support compression, this does not work well as the capacity of the tape will vary depending on how efficient the compression is. Consequently, it is better to let *dump* write until it reaches the end of the tape, and then start a second volume if necessary. You need to use the *-a* option to tell dump to behave in this fashion.

When building an automated backup system around *dump*, the *-F* option may be handy. This option causes *dump* to run a script at the end of each tape. The device name and the current volume number are passed to the script on the command line. The script must return 0 if *dump* should continue without asking the user to change the tape and 1 if *dump* should continue but ask the user to change the tape. Any other exit code will cause *dump* to abort. This would be useful as a means of sending an email or a page to an operator when a tape needs changing. The *-n* option may be useful in this case also. With this option specified, all users in the group *operator* are notified by means similar to the *wall* command whenever *dump* requires operator attention.

You should note that *dump* requires operator intervention at end of tape and end of dump, and on a tape write error, tape open error, or disk read error. *dump* interacts with the operator on its control terminal in situations when *dump* can no longer proceed or if something is grossly wrong. All questions *dump* poses *must* be answered, which means that the absence of an operator to say yes or no at the terminal will hold up the dump indefinitely. *dump* checkpoints itself at the start of each tape volume. Should writing that volume fail for any reason, *dump* will, with operator permission, restart itself from the checkpoint after the old tape has been rewound and removed, and a new tape has been mounted. *dump* tells the operator what is going on at periodic intervals, including (usually low) estimates of the number of blocks left to write, the number of tapes it will take, the time to completion, and the time to the next tape change. The output is verbose so that others know that the terminal controlling *dump* will be busy for some time.

restore: **The File System Recovery Tool**

restore is the other half of *dump*, so to speak, and is used to restore files or file systems from a *dump* archive. The simplest form of a *restore* command is

```
# restore -r
```

This command restores an entire physical file system from a dump archive located on a default storage device defined by the shell environment variable *TAPE*. The files will be restored into the current working directory of the *restore* command. Note that as the design intent of *restore* is to rebuild the entire file system metadata structure as well as restore the data files themselves, a restore will normally be run from the root directory of what is termed a pristine file system, meaning a brand new, completely empty one. For example:

```
# mke2fs /dev/sda1
# mount /dev/sda1 /home
# cd /home
# restore -r
```

Like *dump*, the -*f* option can be used to specify the archive location on the command line, and like *tar*, the -*v* option tells *restore* to echo file names to *stdout* as they are restored. For example:

```
# restore -rvf /dev/st0
```

If you are restoring an incremental archive, you repeat this same command once for each successive incremental archive tape in the sequence.

You may only want to extract a single file or a limited number of files from a *dump* archive. This can be done using the -*x* option. Consider an archive created with dump like this:

```
# dump /home
```

In this case, I could extract a single file from that archive like this:

```
# restore -xvf /dev/st0 ./iain/data
```

If */home/iain/data* is a directory, it will be recursed so the entire directory subtree will be restored. Note too that in the archive the directory paths for the files are specified relative to the mount point of the file system that was dumped.

Another really interesting thing you can do with *restore* is an interactive extraction. Remember that *dump* stores the inode table for the file system along with the files themselves. This means that the structure of the directory tree for the file system in the archive is available from the archive. The presence of this metadata allows *restore* to navigate through the archive as if it were a file system rather than a flat file, which it in fact is. This functionality is accessed using the *-i* option to restore, as in this example:

```
# restore -if /dev/st0
```

This *restore* command opens a shell-like command line interface in which you can use commands like *cd* and *ls* to navigate the directory tree stored in the archive and locate the file or files you want to restore as if you were navigating a live file system. As you find files you want to restore, you use the *add* command to mark them for extraction. When you have added all the files you want, issue the command *extract* to start the extraction. When all the files you selected have been restored, the *restore* command returns. For example, if the tape in */dev/st0* contained a dump of the root file system and you needed to extract */etc/fstab*, */etc/hosts*, and */etc/lilo.conf* from it and write them to */tmp* on the local system, this is what the interactive *restore* session would look like

```
# cd /tmp
# restore -if /dev/st0
restore > h
Available commands are:
        ls [arg] - list directory
        cd arg - change directory
        pwd - print current directory
        add [arg] - add 'arg' to list of files to be extracted
        delete [arg] - delete 'arg' from list of files to be extracted
        extract - extract requested files
        setmodes - set modes of requested directories
        quit - immediately exit program
        what - list dump header information
        verbose - toggle verbose flag (useful with "ls")
        prompt - toggle the prompt display
        help or '?' - print this list
If no 'arg' is supplied, the current directory is used

restore > verbose
verbose mode on
restore > what
Dump   date: Sat Jun 16 23:48:58 2001
Dumped from: the epoch
Level 0 dump of / on sandbox:/dev/hda1
Label: /
restore > pwd
/
```

```
restore > cd /etc
restore > ls fstab hosts lilo.conf
32967 fstab
32971 hosts
32959 lilo.conf
restore > add fstab hosts lilo.conf
Make node ./etc
restore > extract
Extract requested files
You have not read any tapes yet.
Unless you know which volume your file(s) are on you should start
with the last volume and work towards the first.
Specify next volume #: 1
extract file ./etc/lilo.conf
extract file ./etc/fstab
extract file ./etc/hosts
Add links
Set directory mode, owner, and times.
set owner/mode for '.'? [yn] n
restore > q
# ls -lR etc
etc:
total 3
-rw-r--r--    1 root     root          614 May 22 15:24 fstab
-rw-r--r--    1 root     root          283 May 22 17:13 hosts
-rw-r--r--    1 root     root          179 May 22 11:18 lilo.conf
```

Building Your Own Backup System

Now that we have an understanding of some basic archiving tools, we return to the backup system to-do list I developed earlier and see how many points we can check off that list with a backup system based on *tar*, *dump*, and *restore*. To meet the first requirement on the list, the backup system needs a companion database of some sort that keeps track of what was backed up in which archive, on which tape, and when. That database needs to be accessible enough to point you quickly to a specific tape. A large backup may not fit on only one tape, thus creating multi-volume tape sets that need to be kept together. Incremental backups also result in multi-volume sets, as all of the increment levels together are necessary for a full recovery. Your system thus needs some consistent means of cataloging and identifying these tapes.

Obtaining a list of the files backed up by *tar* or *dump* is easy. If you use *tar*, make sure to include the *-v* option and save the output to a file. If using *dump*, you can get a list of the files in the archive after it has completed with the command:

```
# restore -t
```

Now add to these listings the date of the backup and the tape they are stored on, and you have your database. For quick access to this simple database at restore time, keep multiple copies of it on different physical disks on the server as well as an off line copy on tape or diskette. You may even want a printed copy if you cannot be certain of having access to a device to read the tape or diskette in a restore situation. This is a simple system and will soon become difficult to manage should your server grow larger, but it is quite adequate for a server that can be completely backed up onto one or two tapes. When your system gets too large to manage this way, start evaluating some of the backup management software packages reviewed at the end of this chapter.

Managing File System Backups

The second requirement on the list, that of dealing with file systems as data entities, is easy to do using *tar*, as long as you always remember to start the recursion at the mount point of a file system and use the *-l* option as shown earlier to prevent the recursion crossing file system boundaries. *dump* is, of course, an even better tool for backing up file systems, as that is precisely what it is designed to do.

Metadata is also important as you need to know which file systems were located on which disks so you know what file systems need to be restored in the event of a disk failure. Also, once a disk has failed, you cannot rely on being able to run a command like *df* or *du* to determine how much data there was in the lost file system or file systems that resided on the failed disk. If you can be sure of getting a replacement drive that is larger then the failed drive, then you won't have a problem. But, what if you can't quickly get a larger drive and you have a spare smaller drive immediately available? You need a means of knowing whether it is large enough to hold all your data. Clearly this information needs to be stored as a part of the backup itself, so as to be available independent of any disk hardware. For a small site, this can most easily be done on good old-fashioned paper in the form of a printed copy of */etc/fstab* and a copy of the output of *df* so that the sizes of the partitions and how full they were are also noted. In a larger site the volume of metadata information will grow and you may want to consider an automated system for collecting and storing this information in electronic form. If you do, the media you use should be quickly accessible. A diskette or a removable drive can be accessed more quickly, easily, and on a wider variety of client server than a tape, generally speaking. Once you get to doing things on this scale, you should consider a backup package. I review several at the end of this chapter.

The Consistency Problem

The third requirement in the to-do list raises what I call the consistency problem. Let us say that you have a 2-GB file system in production that you need to back up. If you are using a SCSI tape device of some sort, that backup will take several minutes, depending on the speed of the tape drive, how busy the bus is, how fast the data can be read from disk, and the overhead of any compression that may be used. As this data is in production, it will change during the backup process. If the backup starts at 1 A.M., and completes at 1:20 A.M., and somewhere during that time interval only one file in the file system being backed up changes, how can you be sure that the newer version of the file made it to the tape? The answer is, you can't be sure because the file may have changed after it had been written to tape. The only way to guarantee that all of the data in a live file system gets backed up is to take the data out of production, freeze it, so to speak, while you do the backup, and then return it to production. This is clearly a challenge as that means application downtime. What can be done?

If you have used the Titanic principle (explained in Chapter 4, "Installing and Configuring for Reliability") in laying out your disk partitions and file systems, this helps since each physical file system will contain a distinct body of data associated with either an operating system function or an application function. This helps with the consistency issue, as data logically sorts itself out by file system into configuration and binary files that do not change dynamically and are not subject to the consistency problem, and data and logs that are dynamic and are subject to the consistency problem. If you have made this separation, then all of the dynamic files are concentrated in different file systems from the static files and you can apply a different backup method to each accordingly. This is one place where incremental backups may be helpful, as they speed up the backup process. You will still need to take the data out of production (normally by either unmounting the file system or stopping the application); but as the backup is quick, the downtime may be acceptable.

If incremental backups are still taking too long, see if the data can be restructured to make it faster to back up. In some cases an application has its own data backup and recovery procedures. In a UNIX environment, these procedures may use tools like *tar* or *dump*, but also include internal application functionality that allows successful backups of live data. This kind of functionality is a great asset in an application. It also means, however, that there will almost certainly be an application specific recovery procedure that you will need to take into account when planning recovery procedures. It may be necessary to have someone with application specific knowledge on site in a recovery situation. It may also be necessary to have access to passwords or other data security keys in order to successfully get the application data back into production shape.

Finally, if you are considering using Logical Volume Management (LVM), described in Chapter 8, you may be able to make use of the snapshot capability of the LVM code. This allows a temporary copy, or snapshot, of a data entity such as a file system to be made with minimal downtime. The snapshot image can then be backed up offline as the data remains in production.

Automatic Backups

Point four on our to-do list requires an automatic backup system. Clearly you do not want to rely on someone remembering what command to run and when, and with which tape. You need a scripted, automatic system that will run backups by the clock. As it is rare to be necessary to do backups more than once in a day, the */etc/cron.daily* directory should be all you need. The accompanying sample script run each day should get you started:

```ksh
#!/bin/ksh

# this script implements the Hanoi sequence of incremental
#     backups using the dump command

# what day of the week/month is it?
day_of_week=$(date +"%w")
day_of_month=$(date +"%d")

case "$day_of_week" in

0) print "Sunday 13 dump"
   dump -3u -f /dev/st0 /home
   restore -tf /dev/st0 > /var/log/dump.log.$(date -I) ;;
1) print "Monday 12 dump"
```

Listing 7.1 Sample daily script

```
     dump -2u -f /dev/st0 /home
     restore -tf /dev/st0 > /var/log/dump.log.$(date -I) ;;
 2) print "Tuesday 15 dump"
     dump -5u -f /dev/st0 /home
     restore -tf /dev/st0 > /var/log/dump.log.$(date -I) ;;
 3) print "Wednesday 14 dump"
     dump -4u -f /dev/st0 /home
     restore -tf /dev/st0 > /var/log/dump.log.$(date -I) ;;
 4) print "Thursday 17 dump"
     dump -7u -f /dev/st0 /home
     restore -tf /dev/st0 > /var/log/dump.log.$(date -I) ;;
 5) print "Friday 16 dump"
     dump -6u -f /dev/st0 /home
     restore -tf /dev/st0 > /var/log/dump.log.$(date -I) ;;
 6) if (( day_of_month <= 7 ))
    then
print "First Saturday 10 dump"
        dump -0u -f /dev/st0 /home
        restore -tf /dev/st0 > /var/log/dump.log.$(date -I)
    else
print "Not first Saturday 11 dump"
        dump -1u -f /dev/st0 /home
        restore -tf /dev/st0 > /var/log/dump.log.$(date -I)
    fi ;;

esac
```

Listing 7.1   Sample daily script (continued)

In conjunction with this daily *dump*, it is critical that operations staff remember to change the tapes and label them as necessary. You may also want to store the *dump* logs on other media, such as a floppy disk, or print them out. This example assumes that an incremental backup will satisfy the consistency problem. It may be necessary to stop applications and unmount file systems before backing them up, then remounting them and start the application after the backup completes. In that case you would have to alter the script accordingly.

This is admittedly a simple backup system, but it has all of the basic elements needed. As data volumes grow larger and the number of servers to be backed up increases, processes get more complicated and your investment in building your own system will either have to grow or you may want to consider one of the backup management packages discussed at the end of this chapter. Either way, however, the basic elements in this simple system will still form the foundation of any more complex one.

Operating System Recovery

Progressing down our backup system to-do list, we come to point five, which requires a plan for recovering an operating system disk. While recovering the disk that Linux was installed on is fundamentally no different than recovering any other failed disk, there are two complications when it is an operating system recovery.

The first is a Catch-22 problem. If you have a *dump* archive tape of the operating system installation, all you need is to run *restore*, right? The only problem is, how do run *restore* when you have no operating system? To recover the operating system, you need a way of running some sort of restore utility that can read from your backup tape and has a device driver for your new disk in order to extract the data from your backup tape and write it to that disk.

The second problem is making the recovered disk able to boot the restored operating system. This operating system recovery process is known as a *bare metal recovery,* and your backup system must have a plan to deal with it. Let's examine how it is done.

Tom to the Rescue!

What you would start with is what is known as a rescue disk. This is a bootable diskette containing a small Linux kernel, a variety of device drivers, and a selection of basic storage management commands. You could make one of these yourself. If you want to try, I recommend the Linux Bootdisk HOWTO, which leads you through the steps to produce a bootable diskette or CD-ROM. You will find, however, that it is a nontrivial proposition.

I much prefer to use one of the existing rescue disks available on the Internet. One of the better known ones is Tom Oehser's root boot disk, or tomsrtbt as he calls it, which I mentioned in Chapter 4. You can find it at www.toms.net/rb. This site has instructions on how to download the package and create the actual bootable rescue diskette. You will be able to boot a Linux kernel from this diskette and find on it device drivers for a wide range of common hardware devices, as well as commands such as *fdisk* and *mke2fs* to allow you to partition and create file systems on your replacement disk. It is important that you make sure that you have any necessary drivers to support your hardware on your version of rescue diskette. Tom has included an excellent selection of drivers, but it is not exhaustive. Check this out before you have to use it. If you need to add a driver, Tom has included instructions and scripts to do it. Tom has, in fact, done an excellent job.

Also included on the rescue diskette are *tar* and *cpio* to enable you to restore files from an archive. Note that *restore* is *not* included. That means that your operating system backup must be made with *tar* or *cpio*. In fact, although it appears that *tar* and *cpio* are included, you will find that they are actually links to *pax*, a utility intended by POSIX to be a generic low-level archive utility. In practice, few use it, but is has the advantage in this context of being able to read both *tar* and *cpio* format archives, so Tom chose it to get the equivalent of two commands in one, which is important when you are trying to squeeze as much as you can onto one diskette. (The tomsrtbt motto is: "The most GNU/Linux on one floppy disk.") Be aware that while *pax* will behave like *tar*, it does not behave like GNU *tar*, which has extensions over and above the generic version of *tar* that *pax* is intended to support. One significant difference is that generic *tar* does not support inline compression as an option, as does GNU *tar*. Using GNU *tar*, had you created an archive with the -z option, you would extract it with the command:

```
# tar -xzvf /dev/st0
```

Using the commands available on tomsrtbt, you would have to uncompress the tarball as a separate operation in a pipe, like this:

```
# gzip -d < /dev/st0 | tar -xvf -
```

Now let's look at an example of using tomsrtbt to recover an operating system.

Preparing for Bare Metal Recovery

Before you can do a recovery, you need a backup, so your procedure must start there. Using tomsrtbt, we are restricted to using either *tar* or *cpio* on the restore; I choose to use *tar*. According to the Titanic principle mentioned in the section *The Consistency Problem* earlier in this chapter, the operating system on a production server should be divided among several file systems, at the least the root file system and possibly */boot*, */var*, */home*, */tmp*, and others.

Consider an example with three file systems: */*, */home*, and */tmp*. You can add further archive commands for any additional file systems your server may have. These *tar* commands run on my server when it is healthy will back up my current operating system:

```
# tar -clvf /dev/nst0 /
# tar -clvf /dev/nst0 /home
```

```
# tar -clvf /dev/nst0 /tmp
# mt -f /dev/st0 rewind
# mt -f /dev/st0 offline
```

Note that the */dev/nst0* device is used rather than */dev/st0*. The *n* in the device name means no rewind. This writes each of the three tarballs to the same tape one after the other, (assuming the tape is large enough) so it is not necessary to keep track of multiple tapes. The first *mt* command rewinds the tape, and the second one ejects the tape from the drive.

Next comes an important issue. During the operating system restore, it will be necessary to create partitions and file systems on the new drive to hold the restored data. The backup must store the information necessary to create those partitions and file systems in a form accessible during the restore operation. (For my money, paper is the most reliable method.) These commands should dump the partition table and the file system table to the system default printer:

```
# fdisk -l /dev/hda > lpr
# cat /etc/fstab > lpr
# mount > lpr
# df -kl > lpr
```

I include the output of the *mount* command as well as a copy of */etc/fstab*, as the partition name (for example, */dev/hda5*) does not necessarily appear in */etc/fstab*. You will need to know that name when you need to create the new partitions. I also include the output of the *df* command so that I know how full the original file systems were. If I cannot find a replacement disk as large as the original, this will at least tell me the minimum size I can make do with. If you store these printouts along with the rescue diskette and the backup tape, you have a bare metal recovery kit.

Bare Metal Recovery Procedure

Let us assume the worst, that the operating system disk fails. How do we put the rescue kit discussed in the preceding section into action? First you source and install a replacement disk of sufficient size to replace the failed one. You have the printed version of the disk partition table so you can make sure that your replacement disk will do the job. If the replacement is not identical to the failed disk, that is okay as long as there is enough space on it for all of the files you will restore. You could even use two disks, if necessary, although you would have to alter the partition layout as you do the restore. All this is possible, but it is critical that you have the original partition table layout so you know what you need to replace. It is also critical that you test this procedure before you have to use it. What is presented here is applicable to a generic Linux installation. Your hardware selection and partition layout will differ to some extent, so you need to develop a set of instructions specific to your case.

The next thing is to boot the server from the rescue floppy. You will see the tomsrtbt logo and this boot prompt:

```
boot:
```

Just press Enter and the boot will proceed. Next you have a choice of video modes, after which the kernel initializes. Then you have the option of choosing your keyboard (the default should be fine) and finally a login prompt. Login as root (the default password is *xxxx*, as it says in the prompt). You can visit www.dailyglobe.com/discord.html to understand what you see next, which will be something like this:

```
Today is Boomtime, the 21st day of Confusion in the YOLD 3167
```

You have by this point booted a Linux kernel and configured all of your devices, and you should be at a shell prompt. Issue the *mount* command and you will see

```
# mount
/dev/ram0 on / type minix (rw)
none on /proc type proc (rw)
/dev/ram1 on /usr type minix (rw)
/dev/ram3 on /tmp type minix (rw)
```

This tells you that the kernel has used no disk other than the boot diskette. It has made three RAM disks in memory, created file systems in those RAM disks, mounted them at /, /usr, and /tmp respectively, and restored all of the files stored on the boot diskette that are intended to populate these file systems.

Now you are ready to partition your new operating system disk. Issue *fdisk*, passing the operating system disk device as an argument, as follows:

```
# fdisk /dev/hda
```

Follow the *fdisk* dialog to rebuild the partition table from the information that you printed as discussed in the preceding section. This is exactly the same procedure you would have used during your original Linux installation. Once your partitions are created and the partition table is written to disk, make fresh file systems in the new partitions, like this:

```
# mke2fs /dev/hda1
# mke2fs /dev/hda5
# mke2fs /dev/hda7
```

Now, format the swap space:

```
# mkswap /dev/hda6
```

Before you can restore the files from your tape, you need to mount the file systems you just made. Notice something very important. *You cannot mount your new root file system at /.* If you did, you would mount over the ramdisk root file system and crash the running kernel. Use */mnt* instead, like this:

```
# mount /dev/hda1 /mnt
# mount /dev/hda5 /mnt/home
# mount /dev/hda7 /mnt/tmp
```

Now you can restore from your tape, like this:

```
# cd /mnt
# tar -xvf /dev/nst0
# cd /mnt/home
# tar -xvf /dev/nst0
# cd /mnt/tmp
# tar -xvf /dev/nst0
```

If you stacked all of your tarballs serially on one tape, it is important that you know the order in which they reside. In my example, I backed up the root file system first; the second tarball was */home* and the third was */tmp*. You will need to note the order in which you backed up yours to know the proper order for the restore. (If you lose that information, you can use a *tar -t* command to examine the contents of each archive, but that will be time consuming and delay the recovery procedure.)

Making the New Disk Bootable

The last thing to do is to make sure that you will be able to boot from your newly restored disk. This involves running the *lilo* boot loader (which, helpfully, is included on tomsrtbt) as you would do on a normal running system. There is a catch, however, because the root file system of your system at this point is a RAM disk rather than the actual disk root file system. To make the boot loader install work, you need to use the *chroot* command to fool *lilo*. Recalling that earlier I mounted */dev/hda1*, the disk root file system, at */mnt*, you would issue this command:

```
# chroot /mnt /usr/bin/lilo
```

This makes */mnt* appear to be */* to *lilo*, and the boot loader should install properly. Now take the rescue diskette out of the drive and issue the *reboot* command. Your restored operating system will come to life.

A final note: If you prefer to look for a commercial packaged solution for bare metal recovery, there are several choices on the market. Examples include QuickStart (www.estinc.com), BackupEDGE (www.microlite.com), and RescueRanger (www.lone-tar.com).

Reducing Risk Due to Operating System Failure

While it is absolutely necessary to have in place an operating system recovery plan as I have just laid out, there are some other tactics you should consider to reduce your liability in the case of the loss of the operating system disk. These tactics address point six in our backup system to-do list. I would point out that if you are willing to accept a higher level of risk, you might feel that using redundant servers is more than you need. If your operating system disk fails, you may be willing to accept as inevitable several hours of downtime while you go through the bare metal recovery detailed in the preceding sections. On the other hand, you may want some further options.

In the short term, one option is to move an application to a different machine while you repair the damaged operating system. To allow this option, I generally prefer to see application disks implemented in a separate external enclosure from the server. That way, if the operating system dies, you can unplug the external case containing the entire application—binary code as well as data—move it to a functional machine, plug it in, and turn it on. You may need to resolve differences in device identifiers or address conflicts with existing devices on the new server, but that shouldn't take long. This data portability is one of the basic concepts underlying the high availability clusters discussed in Chapter 10, "Server Clustering." In that case, the spare server is already attached to the data drives, and the fail-over from one operating system and server to the other happens as automatically as possible.

Another option you may want to consider is to have a spare operating system disk. Simply install Linux onto a single disk and then store the disk against the possibility of needing it. If a server fails, install the spare operating system disk and boot. If you are careful to ensure that your partition names and file system layouts are the same for your spare operating system as for the production system, you should be back up right away. You will need to be careful to track any changes made to the production system since they will need to be reproduced in the spare to avoid problems if you need to use the spare. You can then replace the faulty drive and create a new spare at your leisure. This does mean you have to dedicate a drive as a spare, which you may not have in your budget, although drives, especially ATA drives, are so cheap these days that you could consider this pretty cost effective insurance.

Managing Site Recovery

We have now reached the seventh and last item on our to-do list, the issue of site recovery. The central element in a site recovery plan is maintaining the data needed to recover your site in a safe off-site location. When choosing the off-site data storage location, consider the following:

If a natural disaster is what you are protecting against, ensure that the off-site storage location is not subject to the same risk. For example, if hurricanes are a factor in your area, the off-site storage needs to be removed a significant distance from the production site as a hurricane can affect a large contiguous area. If a tornado is your concern, a few miles distant may be sufficient as tornadoes affect a much smaller area.

The off-site data storage site should be as close as possible to the site where the replacement server will be set up, if you have an alternate server site. That minimizes time spent getting the backup to the replacement server. Ideally the off-site tape is stored on site with the backup server.

Consider security. Many smaller businesses have an employee take the off-site backup home. While at first sight this seems a simple and effective plan, it leaves out the consideration that all of the company's production data is stored in a private residence. This can place both the employee holding the data and the data itself at risk if that data has significant monetary value to your company or to a competitor. It also places your entire company's operation in the hands of a single employee.

Another issue in the case of a site loss is metadata. A critical element of the off-site backup must be metadata describing the hardware and software configuration of the original server since this will be necessary to build a replacement server. If you can justify purchasing a complete spare unit to sit idle in a backup location against the possibility of the production site going down, this is the ideal situation. That may be not be practical if your production server is an expensive machine or the primary production site is home to a number of servers. In this case, existing machines at your backup site may have to be pressed into service in an emergency. That hardware and software configuration metadata is essential in this case as you will have to determine which backup servers may or may not be suitable replacements for the lost units.

You may also need to source new hardware for the backup site, in which case you need to know what to buy. You do not want to find yourself experimenting to get things back online in this situation. The hardware information you compile and store should include manufacturer, model, and serial number information. The manufacturer and model numbers ensure that you can get the proper software drivers and source equivalent hardware as necessary. The serial numbers are important after you get things back online at the recovery site as there will be insurance claims to make regarding the equipment lost at the production site. If you can provide, from the backup site, a detailed inventory of the lost equipment, that will make any insurance claim a great deal easier.

I know it sounds low tech, and I have made the point before, but I prefer to see this information printed on good old-fashioned paper, as well as stored in electronic form. A full site recovery is a crisis situation. You cannot depend on knowing who may or may not be available at the recovery site during the recovery period. If the information is stored only on tape, you will need a drive to read the tape and someone who knows how to use the drive as well as knowing what files to extract from what tape. If the information is also there in print, it is available in the most generically accessible data format there is. It doesn't matter who you are dealing with. Anyone will be able to open and read or fax that information as necessary.

Long Distance Backups

The increasing availability of high bandwidth long distance data connections is making backups to remote sites a practical possibility. While it has been possible for a long time to do backups across a network using LAN technology, this was typically limited to the scope of the local network, usually measured in terms of a few hundred feet or so. A sufficiently fast modern data connection allows backups to run directly from the satellite site to a tape located at a central location—possibly hundreds or even thousands of miles distant. With appropriate software support and ruling out the possibility of a loss of the entire satellite site, the restoration of any file, file system, or drive should be manageable from the central facility. This has the advantage of allowing fully centralized collection and management of all backups, reducing the need for backup expertise and hardware at the distant sites. It is also possible for the backups to be run to a business recovery (BR) provider site. In this case, the BR provider may provide not only the recovery service, but the backup service too.

The Importance of Fire Drills

Recovering from a site loss involves coordination among different people in different places in a time of crisis. To be confident that all know their part recovery drills are an important part of ensuring the success of recovery operations. The procedures for preparing the backup site equipment, getting the backup data to the recovery site if it isn't already there, and getting the necessary staff to the recovery site should be planned and clearly laid out in written procedures.

When you write these procedures, make no assumptions about who will be carrying them out. A good rule is to write them with the idea that the entire operation will be carried out by total strangers who have never seen your operation before. Many companies require a full simulation of a site loss, including shipping the staff and data to the backup site, doing the recovery, and bringing the backup site online to ensure that all will go smoothly when the worst happens. Like fire drills, recovery drills should be done regularly, because configurations and staff change frequently and a drill done at the beginning of last year may no longer really reflect the current situation. I suggest a drill every 12 to 24 months.

Using Business Recovery Services

If you do not have access to a viable recovery site, you may choose to use the services of a BR service provider. For a fee, BR providers supply a backup site, hardware, and technical expertise to provide a temporary home for your operations in time of disaster. This is an increasingly popular option, one that may be more cost effective for you than investing in your own duplicate facility and redundant hardware. When using a BR provider, a fire drill is critical since BR providers do not normally guarantee that they will be able to exactly reproduce your hardware and operating system setup. You need to carefully examine the infrastructure they will provide and ensure you have procedures in place that will get *your* application restored from *your* backups to *their* servers using *their* tape drives and operating on *their* communications networks, and possibly also using *their* staff to get it and keep it running. Make sure that your agreement ensures that whatever resources were available to you at the time of the test will not change without notice. The BR provider should also be able to offer you the option of a secure storage location for your off site backup as part of the deal, which is ideal as the BR provider's site is the logical place for the tapes to be held.

If you choose to go this route, realize that you will also need to consider getting your own site either repaired or replaced as soon as possible as the cost and inconvenience of running your business from the BR provider's site may soon become a problem. Also consider that the BR site may be a long distance from your own office, which can involve ongoing travel expenses while your business is running from their site.

Available Backup Packages

Having reached the end of the to-do list, you should now have a clear idea of what is involved in producing a fully featured backup and recovery system. I have also presented some basic tools and scripts to get you started. You may decide, however, that you prefer to consider prebuilt backup packages that may suit your purposes.

If you have only a small number of servers to manage, using these packages is probably overkill; you may spend more time learning how to set them up and use them than you would spend building your own system. On the other hand, for a larger number of servers these packages come into their own as they are structured to handle the issues involved with backing up multiple networked servers. But if you decide to use one of these packages, don't discard the preceding material in this chapter. You will discover that at the heart of these packages lie basic tools like *tar* and *dump*, and all of the issues I have dealt with so far are still relevant whether you build your own system or use a prebuilt one.

I first present some open source offerings, followed by a selection of commercial products:

AMANDA. The Advanced Maryland Automatic Network Disk Archiver (AMANDA) is written and maintained by volunteers at the University of Maryland and is distributed under the Berkeley Standard Distribution (BSD) license. It is a backup system that allows the administrator of a LAN to set up a master backup server to back up multiple hosts to a single, large capacity tape drive. AMANDA uses native *dump* or GNU *tar* facilities and can back up a large number of workstations running multiple versions of UNIX. Recent versions can also use SAMBA to back up Microsoft Windows 95/NT hosts. AMANDA is supported by several mailing lists that you can find at AMANDA's Web home, located at www.amanda.org, or at the SourceForge home, sourceforge.net/projects/amanda.

afbackup. Written by Albert Flugel, *afbackup* is a client-server backup system allowing many workstations to backup to a central server, simultaneously or serially. Backups can be started remotely from the server or via *cron* jobs on the clients. Any streaming device, including a drive partition acting as a virtual tape changer, can store the data. Autochangers can be used if an appropriate auxiliary program, such as *mtx* or *stctl*, is available. The author states that *afbackup* has been tested on Linux, AIX, IRIX, FreeBSD, Digital UNIX (OSF1), Solaris, and HP-UX. The client side has also been tested on SunOS and OpenBSD. However, the author discourages using Solaris prior to version 2.6. Distributed under the GNU GPL, you can find *afbackup* at www.afbackup.org.

taper. Written by Yusuf Nagree, *taper* is a user-friendly archive program especially designed for backing up to tape drives. *taper* produces indexed databases files listing the files stored in each archive to speed the process of locating files for restoration. It also provides the ability to append files to an existing archive. On the down side, it has had little recent development and isn't designed for backing up more than about 30,000 files unless you have a large amount of physical memory. You can find *taper* at taper.e-survey.net.au.

Burt. The Backup and Recovery Tool was written at the University of Wisconsin by Eric Melski. He describes Burt as an extension for Tcl/Tk 8.0, designed to perform backup to and recovery from tapes. A Burt installation consists of the Burt extension module and a set of Tcl/Tk 8.0 scripts to make use of that module to perform backups. Burt should be able to backup most systems because of its integration with Tcl/Tk. The University of Wisconsin-Madison uses Burt to backup about 350 workstations and a substantial AFS filespace, for a total of roughly 750 GB of data. It allows for the parallel backup of multiple streams of data directly to tape, which allows for speedy backups. Burt checksums every packet of data that is written to the tape; those checksums are then stored on the tape and can be read off the tape and verified against the actual data read from the tape to ensure the integrity of the data. To fully realize the potential of Burt, you should know something about Tcl scripting. You can meet Burt at www.cs.wisc.edu/~jmelski/burt. The definitive Tcl reference would be *Tcl and the Tk Toolkit,* by John Ousterhout (Addison-Wesley, 1994).

Here are some of the commercial offerings:

Arkeia. This product is from Knox Software, which claims to simplify data protection by providing automated backup and recovery. It supports a variety of computers, operating systems, and storage devices. Arkeia is easy to install and configure, and scales from a simple network to a complex enterprise. Arkeia accommodates full and incremental backups, scheduled or on demand, and preserves directory structure, registry, symbolic links and special attributes. The system manages file system data and, with extension modules, provides online backup for databases. By using a multi-flow technology and client-side compression, the software's publisher claims that Arkeia is capable of backup speeds that can exceed the network's rated speed. (The strength of this claim requires testing, as compression efficiency varies widely with the type of data being handled; compression also carries a client-side CPU overhead.) The transaction engine allows reliable multiple, simultaneous backups and restores. In the case of network and system errors, Arkeia is designed to restart, recover, and survive. Arkeia's centralized catalog keeps a full record of all data and metadata managed by the system, appending the relevant part of the catalog onto each tape. In the event of complete backup server failure, a restore utility is supplied to allow the catalog to be rebuilt and the data recovered. A free version of Arkeia is available with the limitation of supporting one Linux server and two client machines running Linux, Windows 95/98, or Windows NT for Workstations. Arkeia can be found on the Web at www.arkeia.com.

BRU. Backup and Recovery Utility is a product of Enhanced Software Technologies (EST), who are the originators and operators of the Linux Tape Device Certification program (www.linuxtapecert.org). The current product, BRU Pro, is based on the popular BRU package, which has a 16-year product history in the UNIX backup market. BRU Pro is a fully featured product that focuses on using a UNIX server as a centralized backup platform for a wide variety of client operating systems. BRU Pro claims native support for a wide variety of tape drives, including many tape libraries. BRU-Pro is targeted to meet the needs of a small- to medium-sized enterprise by combining the reliability of the well-established BRU product with a comprehensive indexing and archive management capability. Easy to install and use, remotely or locally, BRU-Pro promises reduced overhead by automating setup and configuration and by supporting unattended backup. Further information and trial downloads are available from www.estinc.com.

NetWorker. A product of Legato and one of the best-known storage management packages, Legato claims its product delivers superior results in manageability, performance, and scalability. It promises fast, reliable, and complete data backup and recovery for databases and enterprise servers running critical applications. NetWorker 6 supports functions useful in heterogeneous operations, such as serverless backup and library sharing for LANs or SANs. NetWorker 6 includes an indexing architecture designed to improve performance and scalability in backup and recovery operations. This can be a benefit in large operations, as the backup system database grows to supporting hundreds of tapes and thousands of files. Without indexing, it can take a long time for the system to determine which tape a particular file is stored on. NetWorker 6 features NDMP support, Open File Connection, support for Linux (client, server, and storage node), and support for Windows 2000. It provides cluster support for Legato Cluster, Sun Clusters, Hewlett Packard MCSG, Compaq Tru-Cluster, and Microsoft Cluster Services. More about NetWorker may be found at www.legato.com.

ARCserve for Linux. This is a Linux version of Network Associates' flagship storage management product. ARCserve for Linux is an enterprise-scale product offering a wide range of capability. Based on a distributed storage model, backups can be managed on multiple backup units remotely using a password protected web browser interface. The usual functions found on large-scale systems, such as unattended scheduled backups, incremental backup, a scalable, recoverable database, support for multiple data streams, use of data compression, and support for a wide variety of clients systems and tape devices, are there in ARCserve for Linux. In addition, some interesting features include support for native Linux archive formats, such as *tar* and *cpio* (a format similar to *tar*, but less common), integrated virus scanning, and bare metal recovery. Another extra claimed for ARCserve is the ability for hot backups of Oracle databases, which are a significant advantage if you are running Oracle.

More about ARCserve can be found at www.ca.com/arcserve/arc-serve_linux.htm.

What You Can Do Now

1. If you have a backup and recovery system currently in place, assess what it is doing for you now. Are you confident that it can handle each of the four causes of data loss enumerated in the "Causes of Data Loss" section near the beginning of this chapter?

2. If your backup system falls short, identify the weak areas and make plans to fill them in.

3. If you don't have a backup plan now, use the seven-step to-do list in the "Backup System Requirements" section earlier in this chapter to build your own. If you would rather use a prewritten package, evaluate it against the four causes of data loss and the seven-step to-do list to ensure that it is a comprehensive solution.

4. When you have your system in place and working, test it. Simulate a data loss situation and go through the entire process of restoring the data. Make sure you can read the actual data back from the actual tape; don't assume that if you get as far as successfully locating the correct backup tape that the rest of the process will work too.

5. Write on your calendar at least two random dates in the next 12 months when you will perform another test of your backup system. Make this sort of random testing a habit.

6. At least once in the next 12 months, test your ability to do a bare metal recovery of one of your main production servers.

7. At least once in the next 12 months, do a fire drill of a site loss recovery.

PART

Three

Linux Reliability
Enhancements

## CHAPTER 8

Logical Volume Management

"Contrariwise," continued Tweedledee, "If it was so, it might be; and if it were so, it would be; but as it isn't, it ain't. That's logic."

—Lewis Carroll in Through The Looking Glass

This and the remaining two chapters introduce several new Linux kernel features that have great promise in terms of building larger and more reliable servers. The subject of this chapter is Logical Volume Management (LVM), a way to flexibly manage physical data storage at the server level. LVM introduces a software abstraction layer between the user of a storage device and the device itself, enabling a new level of configuration flexibility that eases storage management and has spin-off reliability benefits in terms of reliable backup management and data portability.

The portability features of LVM also lay necessary groundwork for the construction of shared data server clusters discussed in Chapter 10, "Server Clustering." I will give some brief implementation examples in these chapters, but as much of the functionality described is in the development stages, you will find that the code levels available to you by the time you read this have changed. Please keep this in mind and be sure to read the documentation for your kernel release and distribution. My primary goal in the final chapters is to give you a view of the forest without getting lost in the trees.

LVM Theory

In the traditional UNIX data storage model, data is stored in the form of data files. To store these files on disk, the files are broken into small blocks (anywhere from 512 bytes to 8 KB, depending on the UNIX flavor), sufficient blocks being allocated to store all of the file data. These blocks are allocated from a pool of empty blocks available from a physical file system. Each file system has an index that keeps track of which blocks make up which files. This index is called the i-node table, which has storage space allocated to it in the physical file system. The file system, including full and empty data blocks and an i-node table, is created in a single contiguous disk partition. The size of the partition determines the size of the file system, hence the number of data blocks that will be available in the file system, and so also the amount of file data that can be stored in this file system before it is full. This storage model is illustrated in Figure 8.1.

This simple model has significant limitations. As a file system has a discrete size, it needs to be manually extended if it becomes full. That in itself can be done; the problem lies in the requirement that the entire file system lie in a contiguous disk partition. If a disk contains two or more partitions and one fills, that full partition cannot be extended without making another partition smaller, thus initiating a domino effect that can be problematic to manage.

If the full partition spans an entire disk, there is no remedy except moving the entire file system onto a larger disk. This means downtime, more management overhead, risk to data in the transition, and upper limits on the file system size based on the largest disk available. From a reliability standpoint, it also forces file systems to reside on a single device, which then becomes a single point of failure. A RAID can be brought in to solve this latter problem, but a RAID (discussed in Chapter 5, "Building Reliable Disk Storage") cannot address all of the mentioned shortcomings. A new storage model is required.

The Logical Storage Model

The intent of the logical storage model is to divorce the file system structure from its tight connection to a physical disk partition. This separation is achieved by introducing a logical device layer between the file system and the disk partition. Thus, an LVM system still uses the traditional file system structure, which is good, as this is what the user space application knows how to deal with and we don't want to have to modify the application to work with a new storage model.

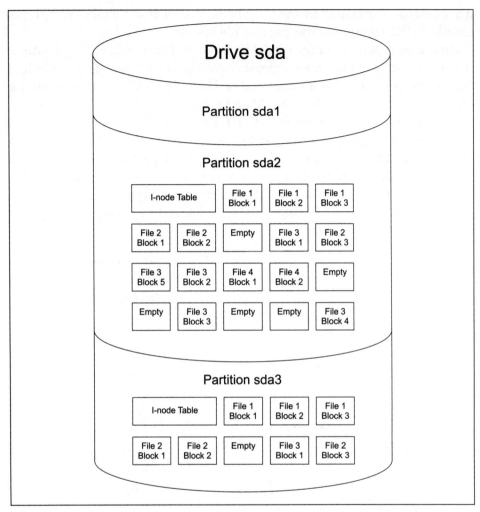

Figure 8.1 The traditional UNIX data storage model stores data as files in discrete blocks.

But instead of providing the file system code with a physical partition to write to, the LVM provides a virtual partition called a Logical Volume (LV). An LV has a device driver that a file system can read and write to, and that looks to the file system in all respects the same as a real physical partition device. Underneath the virtual LV device, the LVM is still using fixed-size contiguous disk partitions to provide the storage available through the LV device. The trick is that a single LV can be made up of more than one physical disk partition. Further, these partitions need not reside on the same physical drive. Thus, several disk partitions that are spread over several drives can be aggregated by the LVM layer to appear as a single contiguous chunk of disk storage for the use of a file system.

An example of this storage model is shown in Figure 8.2. The figure illustrates two file systems. One resides completely in partition */dev/sda1*, while the second resides in the logical volume *LV01*. This LV is composed of the partitions */dev/sda2* and */dev/sdb1*. At one time, this file system likely resided only in */dev/sda2*, but that partition filled. Using LVM, the second drive was added and the logical volume created, allowing the file system to expand into the second drive. As there is still an unused partition on the second drive, a second LV could be created made up of */dev/sda1* and */dev/sdb2*. That allows more space for the file system currently in */dev/sda1*, which appears to be almost out of empty data blocks. You might argue that this is

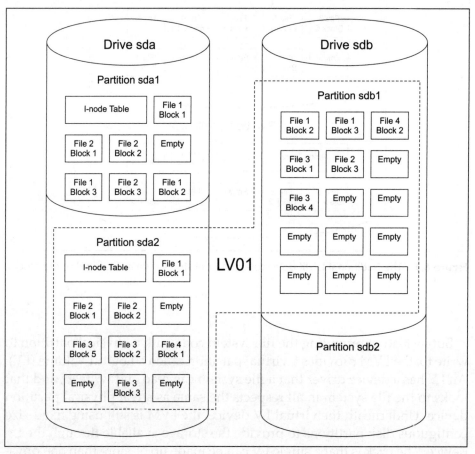

Figure 8.2 This LVM storage model illustrates two file systems mapped across two physical drives.

really the same as what can be done using a Linear RAID as discussed in Chapter 5, and you would be quite correct. The RAID driver can in fact also be called a Volume Manager of sorts, as the kind of partition concatenation illustrated in Figure 8.2 can be done with any of the RAID levels.

Linux LVM Details

What, then, does the Linux LVM implementation have that goes beyond the volume management abilities of RAID drivers? To explain the way that LVM works in the 2.4 kernel, I need to define a series of terms. These definitions lay out the structure and function of the Linux LVM implementation.

Referring to Figure 8.3, the first term is the Physical Volume (PV). A PV is a disk partition that has a small data entity written into it by the LVM code that identifies it as a PV. The underlying partition also should be flagged as type 0x8e in the disk partition table, which is the partition type set aside to designate a Linux PV. The disk space inside a PV is further divided into allocation units called Physical Extents (PE). A PE is most often a few MB in size, although the size can range to a maximum of 512 MB. One or more PVs are then grouped together into a Volume Group (VG). A VG thus aggregates all of the PEs of its PVs into a single large pool of available PEs. PEs can now be drawn from this pool and put together to form Logical Volumes (LV), which are the final product, so to speak, that the LVM provides as a virtual partition to the file system or application.

You can see this in operation if you examine the illustration in Figure 8.3. Partitions *sda1* and *sdb1* are PVs one and two, respectively, of *VG01*. *VG02* is larger, having four PVs, namely partitions *sda2* (*PV01*), *sdb2* (*PV02*), *sdc1* (*PV03*), and *sdd1* (*PV04*).

Note that partition *sdd2* has not been made into a PV, so it cannot participate in the LVM structure. This also shows, however, that it is not a requirement for an entire disk to be managed by the LVM. Examining *VG01*, you can see that two LVs are defined, *LV01* and *LV02*. *LV01* has the lightest shading in the illustration, having five LEs, three on *PV01* (*PE01*, *PE02*, and *PE03*) and two on *PV02* (*PE01* and *PE02*). The second LV in *VG02* has the medium shading and is smaller, having only two LEs, *PE05* on *PV01* and *PE04* on *PV02*. *VG02* is much larger, but has only one LV defined in it, shaded in the darkest tone. This LV, however, has 18 LEs, some of which are on each of the four PVs of the VG, including all of *PV03*, which is all of disk *sdc*. Each of the three LVs illustrated provides a device driver that will make the LV appear to be a single contiguous piece of disk storage, even though the actual storage is not contiguous, and not even confined to one disk.

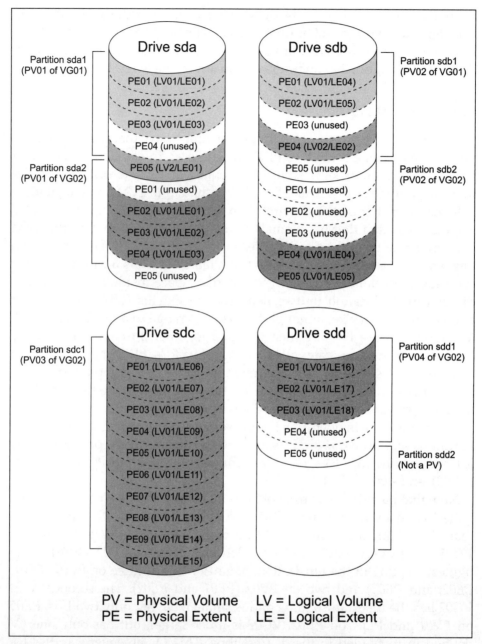

Figure 8.3 This figure illustrates all of the components in the Linux LVM model.

The scale of the data structures have upper limits, but they are generous. A single system may support a total of 99 VGs and a maximum of 256 LVs across all VGs. These are not limitations of the LVM as such; rather, they stem from the 8-bit major device number size in current kernels. Likewise, it is theoretically possible to support an LV as large as one petabyte (a quadrillion bytes). Currently, some 32-bit code in the kernel restricts the maximum LV size to two terabytes; however, work is underway to convert all of the remaining code to support the new Intel 64-bit architecture. Check the documentation for your kernel version. There is also a limit of 65,534 LEs in an LV, and PVs are also limited to 65,534 PEs. As the LVM driver matures with the underlying kernel support to fully embrace the 64-bit address space of the new Itanium processor, these limits can be expected to grow accordingly.

LVM Management Tools

It is necessary to include in any LVM implementation a set of tools to create and manage the different elements of this structure. A good set of tools brings out the real utility of the concept, and the Linux LVM implementation is well equipped in this respect. Tools are available to create, list, modify, and delete PVs, VGs, and LVs. These requirements are basic to any LVM implementation. Your distribution may include these tools. If it doesn't, you will need to download the source code from www.sistina.com/lvm and build them yourself.

In addition, these tools support dynamic modification of all these entities. By dynamic I mean that many significant attributes of the LVM data entities can be modified while the server is in production, with minimal data downtime. Logical volumes, for example, can be expanded or reduced in size while the data they contain is in production. This is significant as it allows a high degree of flexibility in altering the disk storage element of a server with minimal downtime. It also gives the system administrator more tools to deal with unexpected situations, like data that grows more quickly than anticipated or an application that turns out to require a faster disk or a different data layout than was originally planned.

Without LVM, administrators faced with these situations are forced to improvise. File systems are extended by resorting to using symbolic links to point to further disk partitions. Significant disk restructuring can involve all-night backup and restore sessions, which in turn involves server downtime, expense, and servers built in time-constrained situations that yield a solution that is the best compromise between good design and expedience.

LVM and Reliability

There are several significant ways in which using the LVM can improve the reliability of a production server, including:

Using LVM allows you to tailor the amount of space allotted to a file system or other data object so that the space allotted closely follows the actual space needed. This leads to a fundamentally different way of budgeting disk space. Because the LVM can dynamically assign storage, it is not necessary to attempt to predict how much storage will be needed in the future. Instead, you can allocate enough storage to a file system to meet its current needs and then add to that dynamically as the file system requires. You will tend to keep aside any space not really needed in the pool of unallocated space so that you can direct it where and when it is required. If you run low on unallocated space, further storage can be added to the pool dynamically also. Thus, there is little likelihood that you will run into the case in which you fill a file system and need to schedule downtime for the time-consuming and risky job of disk repartitioning and data juggling common to fixed-space allocation systems.

Using LVM removes the temptation for administrators to resort to quick-fix solutions such as using symbolic links pointing from one file system to another. Using links to point from one file system to another is a simple but crude way to effectively extend the storage available for a directory structure. It removes the overhead involved in restructuring fixed-space allocation disk systems, which makes it attractive. It also leads to convoluted data structures, and is still limited by the restrictions implied by contiguous partitions, however. All this leads to extra administrative complexity, which does not improve reliability.

The data structures used by the LVM make PVs and VGs self-contained data entities, carrying all of the necessary metadata for the proper operation of the VG in the VG itself. This makes a VG a completely portable data entity that does not rely on any data stored on the operating system of its host server to be functional. This means that whole applications and their data can be easily moved from one server to another. This can be a distinct advantage if a server fails and sets the necessary groundwork to allow disks to be shared between primary and backup servers in the high availability server clusters discussed in Chapter 10.

The Linux LVM offers a very useful feature called LV snapshots. A snapshot allows the data in an LV to be frozen at a moment in time and made available in a read-only mode for backups, while the production LV remains available for read-write production activity. You will see how this works later in this chapter.

The Linux LVM code is fully compatible with the software RAID driver. It is quite possible—even highly desirable—to create a RAID device such as */dev/md0* and then use that as a PV in an LVM VG. Thus, the flexible storage management advantages of the LVM can be combined with the reliability of RAID to produce a reliable, flexible, manageable, and scalable storage management system.

The dramatically improved flexibility in disk management that LVM gives the administrator makes it easier to do a good job of storage management, which inevitably pays a dividend in server stability and reliability. I have had the pleasure of working in a commercial UNIX environment that has always offered LVM functionality and, until the introduction of LVM to Linux, have always felt that its absence was one of the major obstacles to Linux becoming a practical and useful production system. Once you have worked in an LVM environment, it's hard to go back!

Working with Linux LVM

The next several pages provide some practical examples of LVM commands and functionality. Please note that these examples were worked using v0.9.1 beta 2, a preproduction release of the Linux LVM. Your version may be newer and different, thus some of the commands may look or behave differently from these examples. Be sure to check the information supplied with your distribution and the appropriate *man* pages for the LVM commands on your server for accurate information. Note too that your kernel needs to have LVM support compiled in. Test your kernel by looking for the existence of the directory */proc/lvm*. If that directory exists, then you have basic kernel LVM support. You can determine the LVM code version and the current state of any LVM objects by examining the file */proc/lvm/global*. You will also need the user tools and library to be able to use the LVM kernel code. Note that the stock kernel in the Red Hat 7.1 distribution does *not* include LVM support; nor does this distribution contain the necessary user utilities. You will need to build a kernel with LVM support and get the tools and user library from the developers at www.sistina.com/lvm.

Building a Logical Volume Structure

The following section works through the commands that are necessary to build the structure shown in the example in Figure 8.3. Remembering from the theory that creating an LV itself is the last stage in the process, the first thing we must do is to create some PVs.

Creating Physical Volumes

The *pvcreate* command creates a PV from a disk partition. Referring to Figure 8.3, the command to create the necessary PVs is:

```
# pvcreate /dev/sda1 /dev/sda2 /dev/sdb1 /dev/sdb2 \
           /dev/sdc1 /dev/sdd1
pvcreate -- physical volume "/dev/sda1" successfully created
pvcreate -- physical volume "/dev/sda2" successfully created
pvcreate -- physical volume "/dev/sdb1" successfully created
pvcreate -- physical volume "/dev/sdb2" successfully created
pvcreate -- physical volume "/dev/sdc1" successfully created
pvcreate -- physical volume "/dev/sdd1" successfully created
```

This command has created a data structure written at the beginning of the PV called the Volume Group Descriptor Area (VGDA). This is a core LVM data entity. There is a redundant copy of the VGDA held on each PV of a VG. The VGDA completely describes the entire VG structure. The VGDA can be read from the PV using the *pvdata* command:

```
# pvdata -a /dev/sda1
--- NEW Physical volume ---
PV Name                 /dev/sda1
VG Name
PV Size                 1004.03 MB
PV#                     0
PV Status               NOT available
Allocatable             NO
Cur LV                  0
PE Size (KByte)         0
Total PE                0
Free PE                 0
Allocated PE            0
PV UUID                 iUtVqG-nkgS-YW3F-vvTq-QC0H-DBS1-dI0O3M

--- Volume group ---
VG Name
VG Access               read
VG Status               NOT available/NOT resizable
VG #                    0
```

```
MAX LV                  0
Cur LV                  0
Open LV                 0
MAX LV Size             0
Max PV                  0
Cur PV                  0
Act PV                  0
VG Size                 0
PE Size                 0
Total PE                0
Alloc PE / Size         0 / 0
Free  PE / Size         0 / 0
VG UUID                 HM
```

--- List of logical volumes ---

--- List of physical extents ---

--- List of physical volume UUIDs ---

Notice that although this VGDA copy has been read from only one PV, it contains information about not only the PV itself (in the first section of the output), but also information about the entire VG this PV is a member of. The same will be true of each PV in a VG. This is good for reliability as it means that there is redundancy in the VGDA. So if one PV is lost in a VG, the LVM still has a source for the information it needs to use the VG (or at least as much of the VG as survived the loss of the PV that failed). It also means that a PV carries on itself all of the data necessary to use the entire VG. This makes a VG a portable data structure. This is good in terms of the Titanic principle (as described in Chapter 4, "Installing and Configuring for Reliability") as it means that you could remove an entire VG from a failed server and plug into a backup machine, read the VGDA information from any of the PVs in the VG, and be able to use the entire VG in its new home. Notice that each PV is allocated a Uniform Unique IDentifier (UUID); you can see it in the previous VGDA output. This is a number created by an algorithm designed never to duplicate an identifier and is used to distinguish this PV from any other PV in creation. This is necessary if VGs are to be portable from server to server, as a disk that is /dev/sdb on one server may turn out to be /dev/sdg on another, dependent upon what SCSI address and controller the disk is configured at on the second server. Thus, identifiers like /dev/sda1 are not reliable when transporting VGs from machine to machine, but the UUID is. This data portability can become a key component in a high availability server cluster.

Because the VGDA is a critical data structure for the LVM, backups of the VGDA are automatically made by any of the commands that manipulate the VGDA data to data files in the directory */etc/lvmconf*. Any of these VGDA backups can be restored to a damaged disk using the command *vgcfgrestore*. Be sure to include these VGDA backups in your backup rotation.

Creating Volume Groups

Now that we have some PVs, the next thing to do is to bring them together into VGs. Remember that you cannot define an LV unless you first have defined the VG in which it will reside. We need to create two VGs for our example using the *vgcreate* command:

```
# vgcreate VG01 /dev/sda1 /dev/sdb1
vgcreate -- INFO: using default physical extent size 4 MB
vgcreate -- INFO: maximum logical volume size is 255.99 Gigabyte
vgcreate -- doing automatic backup of volume group "VG01"
vgcreate -- volume group "VG01" successfully created and activated
# vgcreate VG02 /dev/sda2 /dev/sdb2 /dev/sdc1
vgcreate -- INFO: using default physical extent size 4 MB
vgcreate -- INFO: maximum logical volume size is 255.99 Gigabyte
vgcreate -- doing automatic backup of volume group "VG02"
vgcreate -- volume group "VG02" successfully created and activated
```

Now that we have VGs, we can use the *vgdisplay* command to examine them:

```
# vgdisplay VG01
--- Volume group ---
VG Name               VG01
VG Access             read/write
VG Status             available/resizable
VG #                  1
MAX LV                256
Cur LV                0
Open LV               0
MAX LV Size           255.99 GB
Max PV                256
Cur PV                2
Act PV                2
VG Size               1.46 GB
PE Size               4 MB
Total PE              375
Alloc PE / Size       0 / 0
Free  PE / Size       375 / 1.46 GB
VG UUID               FzEKW3-v61m-PPrO-gY8c-Lk37-b9Aj-zUKcG6
```

Notice that the new VG has been assigned a UUID, so that not only can PVs be uniquely identified, but so can VGs. Notice too that the *vgcreate* command used a PE size of 4 MB when creating this VG, as that is the default. Note that the PE size is an attribute of the VG, not the PV. This means that all PVs in a VG must use the same PE size and that once the PE size is determined at the creation of the VG, it cannot subsequently be changed. As there is an upper limit of 65,534 PEs on a PV, the PE size will effectively limit both the maximum size allowable for a PV and place limits on the maximum VG size. If you anticipate large VGs, it may be prudent to increase the PE size (use the *-s* flag to the *vgcreate* command).

Creating Logical Volumes

The final step is to make LVs, which we can do using the *lvcreate* command:

```
# lvcreate -l 5 -n LV01 VG01
lvcreate -- doing automatic backup of "VG01"
lvcreate -- logical volume "/dev/VG01/LV01" successfully created
# lvcreate -l 2 -n LV02 VG01
lvcreate -- doing automatic backup of "VG01"
lvcreate -- logical volume "/dev/VG01/LV02" successfully created
# lvcreate -l 18 -n LV01 VG02
lvcreate -- doing automatic backup of "VG01"
lvcreate -- logical volume "/dev/VG02/LV01" successfully created
```

The size of *LV01* was determined by the *-l* flag, the *5* representing five LEs. As the PE size for *VG01* is 4 MB, that makes *LV01* a 20 MB LV. The *-n* flag allows you to explicitly name the LV; otherwise, *lvcreate* manufactures a name of the form *lvoln*, where *n* increments with each LV created and will be unique within a VG. The *vgdisplay* command should now show the new LVs:

```
# vgdisplay VG01
--- Volume group ---
VG Name                VG01
VG Access              read/write
VG Status              available/resizable
VG #                   1
MAX LV                 256
Cur LV                 2
Open LV                0
MAX LV Size            255.99 GB
Max PV                 256
Cur PV                 2
Act PV                 2
VG Size                1.46 GB
PE Size                4 MB
Total PE               375
Alloc PE / Size        7 / 28 MB
```

```
Free  PE / Size        368 / 1.44 GB
VG UUID                FzEKW3-v61m-PPrO-gY8c-Lk37-b9Aj-zUKcG6
```

Notice the *Cur LV* line shows two LVs in the VG. Also, at the end of the output an accounting of the PEs in the VG is given, showing that, of the total of 375 PEs in the VG, seven PEs are allocated to LVs for a total of 28 MB of space, leaving 368 PEs free for allocation representing 1.44 GB of space. Make note of one very important point. All of the allocations for any LV must come entirely from *one* VG. In other words, *LVs cannot span VGs.*

One question that arises is, where on the PVs of a VG are LVs physically mapped? The *pvdata* command will list all of the physical allocations from a PV, if passed the -*E* flag:

```
# pvdata -E /dev/sda1

--- List of physical extents ---

PE: 00000  LV: 001  LE: 00000
PE: 00001  LV: 001  LE: 00001
PE: 00002  LV: 001  LE: 00002
PE: 00003  LV: 001  LE: 00003
PE: 00004  LV: 001  LE: 00004
PE: 00005  LV: 002  LE: 00000
PE: 00006  LV: 002  LE: 00001
PE: 00007  LV: ---  LE: -----
PE: 00008  LV: ---  LE: -----
<output edited>
PE: 00247  LV: ---  LE: -----
PE: 00248  LV: ---  LE: -----
PE: 00249  LV: ---  LE: -----
```

You can see that the first five PEs of this PV have been allocated in sequence to the first LV in the VG, which is *LV01*. Then *PE00006* and *PE00007* are allocated to the second LV, which is *LV02*. (Note that the actual allocation in this example will not exactly match my illustration in Figure 8.3 as there isn't enough space on a page to show the hundreds of PEs that typically exist in a real VG.)

We have seen that in theory the idea of the VG is to create a storage pool of PEs that can be assembled flexibly into LVs at will, independent of which PV the PEs actually reside on. Keeping the future in view, however, it may be that you would prefer to keep some LVs together on one or two disks of a VG rather than allow them over time to become spread out over multiple PVs. There are several reliability advantages to this:

The risk of data loss due to hardware failure rises as the allocation of an LV spreads across multiple PVs, as the loss of any of the PVs holding allocations for the LV will cause some data loss in the LV. If an LV were spread across four PVs, the loss of any of the four would cause the loss of fully one quarter of the PEs of the LV. Because the LV is presented to the application or file system using it as a single storage entity, the application has no way of determining which quarter of its storage has been lost, so cannot recover from such a loss. It would appear to the application as if one quarter of its disk storage blocks had suddenly gone bad. Thus, there is a 100 percent probability that any failure in the four PVs will render the distributed allocation LV useless. On the other hand, if the LV is concentrated onto only one of the four PVs in the VG, then there is only a 25 percent chance that a PV failure in the VG will affect that LV.

Concentrating the allocations of an LV onto a minimum number of PVs means that the LV can be moved from one server to another more easily. If all of the LVs in a VG are mixed together across all of the PVs in the VG, then it would be difficult to separate one particular LV from the rest in case it needs to be moved to a backup server. In all likelihood you would need to move the entire VG.

If you want to split a VG into two VGs in the future, keeping LV allocations together as much as possible on one or two PVs will reduce the amount of data shuffling necessary when you want to do the split. (The next section of this chapter covers splitting and joining VGs.) That translates into a faster and easier restructuring process, meaning less source of error and less reconfiguration downtime.

Allocation of PEs for an LV to a particular PV can be requested using this form of *lvcreate*:

```
# lvcreate -l 3 -n LV03 VG01 /dev/sdb1
lvcreate -- doing automatic backup of "VG01"
lvcreate -- logical volume "/dev/VG01/LV03" successfully created
```

Using the *lvdisplay* command, we can show that the PEs were indeed allocated to the second PV of the VG:

```
# lvdisplay -v /dev/VG01/LV03
--- Logical volume ---
LV Name                /dev/VG01/LV03
```

```
VG Name                    VG01
LV Write Access            read/write
LV Status                  available
LV #                       3
# open                     0
LV Size                    12 MB
Current LE                 3
Allocated LE               3
Allocation                 next free
Read ahead sectors         120
Block device               58:2

    --- Distribution of logical volume on 1 physical volume  ---
    PV Name                     PE on PV      reads         writes
    /dev/sdb1                   3             0             2

    --- logical volume i/o statistic ---
    0 reads   2 writes

    --- Logical extents ---
    LE      PV                      PE       reads         writes
    00000  /dev/sdb1                00000   0             2
    00001  /dev/sdb1                00001   0             0
    00002  /dev/sdb1                00002   0             0
```

As a performance-related aside, it is also possible to create a striped logical volume. This involves spreading the LV over two or more drives and specifying a stripe size in the order of several kilobytes. For a striped LV having three stripes and a stripe size of 32 KB, data will be allocated in a sequential fashion 32 KB at a time to each of the three partitions, or stripes, in the LV. This is functionally the same as a RAID0 array described in Chapter 5 and gives the same performance-related advantages as the RAID0. (It also illustrates why a RAID can be termed a volume manager.)

The *-i* flag is used to specify the number of stripes (which is the number of drives the LV is striped across), and the *-I* flag determines the width of each stripe. Thus, a command to create an LV named *stripedlv* having 30 LEs striped across three drives in 32 KB chunks in a VG named *VG08* is:

```
# lvcreate -l 30 -i 3 -I 32 -n stripedlv VG08
```

Using Logical Volumes

Notice the structure of the path to the LV device file. It is always of the form */dev/<VG name>/<LV name>*. This is the device that you would use if you want to, for example, create a file system in the LV, like this:

```
# mke2fs /dev/VG01/LV01
mke2fs 1.19, 13-Jul-2000 for EXT2 FS 0.5b, 95/08/09
Filesystem label=
OS type: Linux
Block size=1024 (log=0)
Fragment size=1024 (log=0)
5136 inodes, 20480 blocks
1024 blocks (5.00%) reserved for the super user
First data block=1
3 block groups
8192 blocks per group, 8192 fragments per group
1712 inodes per group
Superblock backups stored on blocks:
        8193


Writing inode tables: done
Writing superblocks and filesystem accounting information: done
```

The new file system can then be mounted in the normal way:

```
# mount /dev/VG01/LV01 /opt
```

LVM Startup and Shutdown

One final topic that needs to be addressed to get an LVM system up and running is the addition of a few LVM commands to the procedure for shutting down VGs cleanly when shutting down the operating system and for getting VGs recognized and activated at boot time. VGs should be moved to an inactive state before bringing the system down, using the following command:

```
# vgchange -a n
```

The -*a* flag followed by the *n* argument indicates a request to deactivate. With no specific VG named, the command will attempt to deactivate all active VGs. To deactivate a specific VG, for example the VG named *VG02*, the command would be as follows:

```
# vgchange -a n VG02
```

Any LVs that contain file systems need to be unmounted and inactive before this will work, however, so the command needs to be inserted toward the end of the system shutdown process. For a Red Hat 7.1 system, that would be the script */etc/rc.d/init.d/halt*. Add the lines shown in bold towards the end of the supplied script, like this:

```
# Remount read only anything that's left mounted.
#echo $"Remounting remaining filesystems (if any) readonly"
```

```
mount | awk '/ext2/ { print $3 }' | while read line; do
    mount -n -o ro,remount $line
done

# lvm shutdown

echo $"Deactivating Volume Groups"
/usr/sbin/vgchange -a n

runcmd $"Unmounting proc file system: " umount /proc
```

Recall that when you partitioned your disk to prepare for creating PVs, you ensured that the partition type was set to *0x8e*. This allows automatic recognition of VGs at boot time. To enable this, the *vgscan* command must be run as part of the boot process. For a Red Hat system and assuming your LVM tools are installed in */usr/sbin* (the default install location), add the lines shown in bold to */etc/rc.d/rc.sysinit*:

```
# Mount all other filesystems (except for NFS and /proc, which is already
# mounted). Contrary to standard usage,
# filesystems are NOT unmounted in single user mode.
action $"Mounting local filesystems: " mount -a -t nonfs,smbfs,ncpfs

# lvm startup

action $"Scanning  Volume Groups: " /usr/sbin/vgscan
action $"Activating Volume Groups: " /usr/sbin/vgchange -a y

if [ X"$_RUN_QUOTACHECK" = X1 -a -x /sbin/quotacheck ]; then
```

The *vgscan* will detect VGs and the *vgchange* will activate all discovered VGs. Note that in this case the *y* argument following the *-a* flag indicates a request to activate VGs. You can test to see that this is working by rebooting and examining */proc/lvm/global*. The output you get should show all of your VGs and LVs:

```
# cat /proc/lvm/global
LVM driver version 0.9.1_beta2 (18/01/2001)

Total:  2 VGs  6 PVs  4 LVs (0 LVs open)
Global: 10997 bytes malloced   IOP version: 10   4:07:32 active

VG:  VG01  [2 PV, 3 LV/0 open]  PE Size: 4096 KB
  Usage [KB/PE]: 1536000 /375 total  40960 /10 used  1495040 /365 free
    PVs: [AA] sda1           1024000 /250       28672 /7       995328 /243
         [AA] sdb1            512000 /125       12288 /3       499712 /122
      LVs: [AWDL ] LV01                         20480 /5       close
```

```
        [AWDL ] LV02                          8192 /2    close
        [AWDL ] LV03                         12288 /3    close

VG:  VG02  [4 PV, 1 LV/0 open]   PE Size: 4096 KB
  Usage [KB/PE]: 2822144 /689 total  73728 /18 used  2748416 /671 free
  PVs: [AA] sda2             1024000 /250       73728 /18      950272 /232
       [AA] sdb2              536576 /131           0 /0       536576 /131
       [AA] sdc1             1056768 /258           0 /0      1056768 /258
       [AA] sdd1              204800 /50            0 /0       204800 /50
   LV:  [AWDL ] LV01                           73728 /18      close
```

These changes apply to a Red Hat distribution; other distributions have different startup and shutdown procedures. The LVM HOWTO available from sistina.com/lvm has information on procedures for several other distributions. If in doubt, consult the references for your distribution.

Managing a Logical Volume Structure

So far we have seen how to create a Logical Volume structure. Once in service, you will want to be able to make changes to the structure to take full advantage of the flexibility afforded by the logical storage model. The first one we'll look at is extending and shrinking the size of VGs.

Extending and Shrinking Volume Groups

At some point in time, all of the PEs available in a VG may be allocated to LVs, with no room left for extending existing LVs or creating new ones. At this point, you will want to add a new PV to the existing VG.

In Figure 8.3 the disk partition /dev/sdd2 is not a PV. Let's see how we could make it a PV and add it to VG02. First, examine the partition table to ensure that the partition has the proper LVM flag set, as shown under the System column:

```
# fdisk -1 /dev/sdd

Disk /dev/sdd: 64 heads, 32 sectors, 515 cylinders
Units = cylinders of 2048 * 512 bytes

    Device Boot    Start      End     Blocks   Id  System
/dev/sdd1              1      201     205808   8e  Linux LVM
/dev/sdd2            202      515     321536   8e  Linux LVM
```

Next, make the disk partition into a PV:

```
# pvcreate /dev/sdd2
pvcreate -- physical volume "/dev/sdd2" successfully created
```

Finally, use *vgextend* to add the new PV to *VG02*:

```
# vgextend VG02 /dev/sdd2
vgextend -- INFO: maximum logical volume size is 255.99 Gigabyte
vgextend -- doing automatic backup of volume group "VG02"
vgextend -- volume group "VG02" successfully extended
```

It's that easy. A *vgdisplay* confirms the makeup of the extended VG:

```
# vgdisplay VG02
--- Volume group ---
VG Name               VG02
VG Access             read/write
VG Status             available/resizable
VG #                  1
MAX LV                256
Cur LV                1
Open LV               0
MAX LV Size           255.99 GB
Max PV                256
Cur PV                5
Act PV                5
VG Size               3 GB
PE Size               4 MB
Total PE              767
Alloc PE / Size       18 / 72 MB
Free  PE / Size       749 / 2.93 GB
VG UUID               Beplwe-mfwO-ImNq-JVkR-2WaW-Jiqx-dG4XEu
```

It is just as easy to remove a PV from a VG:

```
# vgreduce VG02 /dev/sdd2
vgreduce -- doing automatic backup of volume group "VG02"
vgreduce -- volume group "VG02" successfully reduced by physical volume:
vgreduce -- /dev/sdd2
```

Note that for this to work no PEs from the PV to be removed may be allocated to any LV. Clearing allocations would involve moving data from one PV to another, which can be done with the *pvmove* command. For example, look at the current allocations per PV in *VG01*:

```
# vgdisplay -v VG01

<output edited>

--- Physical volumes ---
PV Name (#)           /dev/sda1 (1)
```

```
PV Status              available / allocatable
Total PE / Free PE     250 / 243

PV Name (#)            /dev/sdb1 (2)
PV Status              available / allocatable
Total PE / Free PE     125 / 122
```

We can see that the total PE and free PE figures are not equal on both PVs, indicating that there are PEs allocated from both PVs. Subtracting the free PEs from the total, */dev/sda1* has seven PEs allocated to LVs and */dev/sdb1* has three, for a total of 10 PEs allocated from the entire VG. Clearly there is plenty of space on */dev/sda1* alone for these allocations. If the allocations currently on */dev/sdb1* could be moved to */dev/sda1*, then */dev/sdb1* could be removed from *VG01* and its capacity used elsewhere. We will move the allocations like this:

```
# pvmove /dev/sdb1 /dev/sda1
pvmove -- moving physical extents in active volume group "VG01"
pvmove -- WARNING: moving of active logical volumes may cause data loss!
pvmove -- do you want to continue? [y/n] y
pvmove -- doing automatic backup of volume group "VG01"
pvmove -- 3 extents of physical volume "/dev/sdb1" successfully moved
```

This will move all allocations from */dev/sdb1* to */dev/sda1*, space permitting, which can be seen from a fresh *vgdisplay* command:

```
# vgdisplay -v VG01

<output edited>

--- Physical volumes ---
PV Name (#)            /dev/sda1 (1)
PV Status              available / allocatable
Total PE / Free PE     250 / 240

PV Name (#)            /dev/sdb1 (2)
PV Status              available / allocatable
Total PE / Free PE     125 / 125
```

Should there be insufficient space in */dev/sda1*, specific PE allocations can be moved to available PVs using extra arguments to *pvmove*; refer to the *man* page for details. Note also that this operation can be performed on an active production VG, with the caveat of course that a backup before the move would be a good idea. That is always wise when performing such substantial data transfers and restructuring as this represents.

Merging and Splitting Volume Groups

It is also possible to merge two VGs into one using *vgmerge*. Both VGs must be inactive and must share the same PE size for this to work. Here is the command sequence that would merge *VG02* into *VG01*:

```
# vgchange -a n VG02
vgchange -- volume group "VG02" successfully deactivated
# vgchange -a n VG01
vgchange -- volume group "VG01" successfully deactivated
# vgmerge VG01 VG02
vgmerge -- doing automatic backup of volume group "VG01"
vgmerge -- volume group "VG02" successfully merged into "VG01"
# vgchange -a y VG01
vgchange -- volume group "VG01" successfully activated
```

Note that both of the original VGs contained an LV named *LV01*. An examination of the structure of the merged VG shows how this was handled:

```
# cat /proc/lvm/global
LVM driver version 0.9.1_beta2 (18/01/2001)

Total:  1 VG  6 PVs  4 LVs (0 LVs open)
Global: 8582 bytes malloced   IOP version: 10   4:16:24 active

VG:  VG01  [6 PV, 4 LV/0 open]  PE Size: 4096 KB
   Usage [KB/PE]: 4358144 /1064 total  114688 /28 used  4243456 /1036 free
   PVs: [AA] sda1         1024000 /250        40960 /10        983040 /240
        [AA] sdb1          512000 /125            0 /0         512000 /125
        [AA] sda2         1024000 /250        73728 /18        950272 /232
        [AA] sdb2          536576 /131            0 /0         536576 /131
        [AA] sdc1         1056768 /258            0 /0        1056768 /258
        [AA] sdd1          204800 /50             0 /0         204800 /50
   LVs: [AWDL ] LV01                           20480 /5         close
        [AWDL ] LV02                            8192 /2         close
        [AWDL ] LV03                           12288 /3         close
        [AWDL ] lvol4                          73728 /18        close
```

Because *VG02* was merged into *VG01*, all of the LVs in *VG01* survive untouched. What was *LV01* in *VG02* has been renamed using the standardized naming scheme to *lvol4*, as shown in bold in the last line of the output.

It is also possible to split an existing VG, with the restriction that no LV can exist in the original VG such that it would be divided in two by the VG split. The command is *vgsplit*. This example would reverse the earlier merge:

```
# vgsplit VG01 VG02 /dev/sda2 /dev/sdb2 /dev/sdc1 /dev/sdd1
vgsplit -- doing automatic backup of volume group "VG01"
vgsplit -- doing automatic backup of volume group "VG02"
vgsplit -- volume group "VG01" successfully split into "VG01" and "VG02"
```

Upon examination we can see that the new name for the sole LV in *VG02* has survived the split, as shown in bold at the end of this output:

```
# cat /proc/lvm/global
LVM driver version 0.9.1_beta2 (18/01/2001)


Total:  2 VGs  6 PVs  4 LVs (0 LVs open)
Global: 10997 bytes malloced   IOP version: 10   4:31:42 active

VG:  VG01  [2 PV, 3 LV/0 open]  PE Size: 4096 KB
   Usage [KB/PE]: 1536000 /375 total  40960 /10 used  1495040 /365 free
   PVs: [AA] sda1         1024000 /250       40960 /10       983040 /240
        [AA] sdb1          512000 /125           0 /0        512000 /125
     LVs: [AWDL ] LV01                       20480 /5        close
          [AWDL ] LV02                        8192 /2        close
          [AWDL ] LV03                       12288 /3        close

VG:  VG02  [4 PV, 1 LV/0 open]  PE Size: 4096 KB
   Usage [KB/PE]: 2822144 /689 total  73728 /18 used  2748416 /671 free
   PVs: [AA] sda2         1024000 /250       73728 /18       950272 /232
        [AA] sdb2          536576 /131           0 /0        536576 /131
        [AA] sdc1         1056768 /258           0 /0       1056768 /258
        [AA] sdd1          204800 /50            0 /0        204800 /50
     LV: [AWDL ] lvol4                        73728 /18       close
```

Exporting and Importing Volume Groups

The ability to export and import VGs is central to the reliability aspect of the LVM. It is this that allows an entire VG to be moved from one server to another quickly and easily. To remove a VG from one server, use the *vgexport* command, first ensuring that the VG is inactive:

```
# vgchange -a n VG02
vgchange -- volume group "VG02" successfully deactivated
# vgexport VG02
vgexport -- volume group "VG02" sucessfully exported
```

The disks can then be moved to a second machine and imported with this command sequence:

```
# pvscan
pvscan reading all physical volumes (this may take a while...)
pvscan ACTIVE  PV /dev/sda1 of VG VG01      [1000 MB / 960 MB free]
pvscan inactive PV /dev/sda2 is in EXPORTED VG VG02 [1000 MB / 928 MB free]
```

```
pvscan ACTIVE   PV /dev/sdb1 of VG VG01      [500 MB / 500 MB free]
pvscan inactive PV /dev/sdb2 is in EXPORTED VG VG02 [524 MB/524 MB free]
pvscan inactive PV /dev/sdc1 is in EXPORTED VG VG02 [1.01 GB/1.01 GB free]
pvscan inactive PV /dev/sdd1 is in EXPORTED VG VG02 [200 MB/200 MB free]
pvscan inactive PV "/dev/sdd2" is in no VG  [314 MB]
pvscan total: 7 [4.48 GB] / in use: 6 [4.17 GB] / in no VG: 1 [314 MB]
# vgimport VG02 /dev/sda2 /dev/sdb2 /dev/sdc1 /dev/sdd1
vgimport -- doing automatic backup of volume group "VG02"
vgimport -- volume group "VG02" successfully imported and activated
```

In a cluster, the disks would be implemented on a physically shared interconnect, so that the production server and its backup would be simultaneously connected. In this case both servers import the shared VG, but only one activates it.

Extending, Shrinking, and Removing Logical Volumes

The same flexibility applies to managing LVs as VGs. An LV can be extended using *lvextend* and made smaller with *lvreduce*. For example, *LV01* of *VG02* could be extended by 20 PEs using this command:

```
# lvextend -l +20 /dev/VG02/LV01
lvextend -- extending logical volume "/dev/VG02/LV01" to 152 MB
lvextend -- doing automatic backup of volume group "VG02"
lvextend -- logical volume "/dev/VG02/LV01" successfully extended
```

The new size could also be specified in terms of the absolute size rather than number of PEs, using this command:

```
# lvextend -L 165M /dev/VG02/LV01
lvextend -- rounding size to physical extent boundary
lvextend -- extending logical volume "/dev/VG02/LV01" to 168 MB
lvextend -- doing automatic backup of volume group "VG02"
lvextend -- logical volume "/dev/VG02/LV01" successfully extended
```

Notice in this example that the size of the LV must be an even multiple of the PE size. This is always true, whether enlarging an existing LV or creating a new one. If the size specified in the command is not an even multiple of the PE size, it will be rounded up to the next even multiple, as you can see from the command output.

In any case in which an LV is to be made larger, sufficient unallocated PEs must be available in the VG to accommodate the request. Remember, too, that LVs cannot be extended outside their VG, as this command shows:

```
# lvextend -l +2 /dev/VG02/LV01 /dev/sda1
lvextend -- physical volume /dev/sda1 doesn't belong to volume group VG02
```

As easily as the LV can be made bigger, it can also be made smaller:

```
# lvreduce -l -5 /dev/VG02/LV01
lvreduce -- WARNING: reducing active logical volume to 148 MB
lvreduce -- THIS MAY DESTROY YOUR DATA (filesystem etc.)
lvreduce -- do you really want to reduce "/dev/VG02/LV01"? [y/n]: y
lvreduce -- doing automatic backup of volume group "VG02"
lvreduce -- logical volume "/dev/VG02/LV01" successfully reduced
```

Please note the warning. Finally, an LV can be removed altogether using *lvremove*:

```
# lvremove /dev/VG01/LV03
lvremove -- do you really want to remove "/dev/VG01/LV03"? [y/n]: y
lvremove -- doing automatic backup of volume group "VG01"
lvremove -- logical volume "/dev/VG01/fred" successfully removed
```

The same warning concerning data loss when reducing an LV applies equally when deleting an LV, which explains why you will be prompted to confirm the removal.

Changing Volume Group, Physical Volume, or Logical Volume Attributes

There are a few VG attributes that can be changed after the VG is created using the *vgchange* command:

autobackup. This attribute controls whether Volume Group Descriptor Area (VGDA) backups are created in *etc/lvmconf* and *etc/lvmtab.d* whenever the VGDA changes. The default is yes and there is little reason to change it.

available. This attribute makes a VG known to the kernel and thus able to be used, or not. The primary use for this would be making the VG unavailable prior to shutdown or, in the case of a VG shared between two servers in a cluster (in which case only the primary server would need to know about the VG), until a fail-over, when the backup server would make the VG available as part of the takeover procedure.

logicalvolume. This attribute sets the maximum number of LVs allowed in this VG.

allocation. This attribute controls whether or not the VG may be extended or reduced.

Before any changes can be processed, the VG must be inactive. For example, this series of commands would set the maximum number of LVs in *VG01* to five and prevent extension or reduction of the VG:

```
# vgchange --available n VG01
vgchange -- volume group "VG01" successfully deactivated

# vgchange --logicalvolume 5 VG01
vgchange -- doing automatic backup of volume group "VG01"

# vgchange --allocation n VG01
vgchange -- doing automatic backup of volume group "VG01"
vgchange -- volume group "VG01" successfully changed

# vgchange --available y VG01
vgchange -- volume group "VG01" successfully activated
```

When dealing with PVs with *pvchange*, these are the changeable attributes:

autobackup. In the same fashion as for *vgchange*, this attribute controls whether VGDA backups are created in */etc/lvmconf* and */etc/lvmtab.d* whenever the VGDA changes. The default is yes and there is little reason to change it.

allocation. This attribute governs whether allocation of PEs from this PV will be allowed.

For example, to prevent allocations from */dev/sda1*:

```
# pvchange --allocation n /dev/sda1
pvchange -- physical volume "/dev/sda1" changed
pvchange -- doing automatic backup of volume group "VG01"
pvchange -- 1 physical volume changed / 0 physical volumes already o.k.
```

Lastly, the following LV attributes can be altered using *lvchange*:

autobackup. This attribute is the same as for *vgchange* and *pvchange*.

available. This attribute makes an LV available for use. One LV attribute that cannot be changed using *lvchange* is its name. A name change requires the *lvrename* command, and it is necessary to deactivate the LV before changing the name.

contiguous. If set to yes, this attribute ensures that all of the PE allocations to this LV will be contiguous on the PV. This may improve performance and helps to ensure that the LV does not spread over multiple PVs. If an existing LV was created with *contiguous* set to *no* (the default), all of its current allocations must be contiguous for this attribute to be changed to *yes*.

permission. This attribute allows the LV to be writeable or read only. Set to read only, this can be useful to prevent a user or application accidentally trying to write to an LV that they shouldn't be writing to.

readahead. Primarily a performance issue, this attribute sets the number of sectors per LE the LVM code will read ahead.

The following command, for example, would make *LV01* of *VG01* a read-only LV:

```
# lvchange --permission r /dev/VG01/LV01
lvchange -- logical volume "/dev/VG01/LV01" changed
lvchange -- doing automatic backup of volume group "VG01"
```

Migrating an Existing Server to LVM

It is important to realize that you cannot easily migrate an existing production server to use the LVM. If you have existing partitions with production data, those partitions cannot be converted into PVs and placed in VGs without damaging the data stored on them. It is necessary to set up separate storage using the LVM and copy your production data from non-LVM storage into your LVM storage. If there is enough excess capacity on your existing disks, you can migrate using this procedure:

1. Back up all of your production data before you start. This procedure involves a major restructuring of all your storage, so if something fails or crashes part way through, there is an excellent chance you will need these backups.

2. Create new partitions for use by the LVM in the excess disk space. If you have allocated all of your disk to partitions already but they are less than full, use the *parted* command (Red Hat 7.1 includes *parted*; if your distribution does not, you can get it from www.gnu.org) to shrink the partitions, then use the space freed to make new partitions. Make sure you mark the new partitions as type 0x8e so the LVM will recognize them.

3. Convert the new partitions into PVs (using *pvcreate*), collect the new PVs into VGs (using *vgcreate*), and create LVs (using *lvcreate*) to hold your existing data.

4. Create file systems in your new LVs and mount them at temporary mount points.

5. Copy all of your production data from the existing file systems into your new LV-based file systems.

6. Edit */etc/fstab* so that your LV-based file systems will be mounted at the proper production mount points, then reboot.

7. The server should come up using the LV-based file systems. Test it thoroughly to ensure that your applications are working properly.

8. Finally, convert the old data partitions into PVs and add the PVs into your new VGs so you can use that space as your data needs grow.

If you do not have sufficient extra storage to follow this procedure, you will have to add enough new storage to accommodate your existing data. If you have several production file systems, they could be processed one at a time. In that case you would only need enough extra space for each one at the time you process it. Alternatively, you can back up your data to tape, restructure your storage into an LVM-based system, and restore from tape. In any case, the server will need to be brought out of production for the procedure, so you will have to plan on some downtime.

Backup and Restore Using Logical Volume Snapshots

One very useful functionality of the LVM driver is the ability to create snapshot LVs. (See the sidebar "How Snapshots Work" for more information.) They are designed as a solution to the backup consistency problem discussed in Chapter 7, "Backup and Recovery Strategies." Recall that backing up a live file system creates potential problems in that the data in the file system may change over the time taken by the backup, hence it is impossible to get a consistent picture of the entire file system as it existed at one moment in time. There is thus no guarantee that data that changed some time between the beginning and the end of the backup made it into the backup. The only clear solution to this problem is to take the data out of production during the backup. This, however, means downtime, and in the case of large data structures that take hours to back up, significant downtime.

Is there a solution? The Linux LVM offers the ability to make a snapshot of a production LV. The snapshot appears to the backup application as a separate LV in the same VG as the production LV, except that all of the data in the snapshot LV is frozen in time at the state the data was in the moment the snapshot was created. After the backup is complete, the snapshot LV can be safely deleted. During the entire backup cycle the production LV remains in production and is in no way affected by the creation or destruction of the snapshot.

HOW SNAPSHOTS WORK

When a snapshot LV is created, PEs are allocated to the LV in the same way as any other LV; however, no production data is actually copied into the snapshot LV. Nevertheless, immediately after its creation, the snapshot LV can be accessed in read-only mode and all of the data from the production LV can be read from the snapshot LV.

But if no data is copied into the snapshot LV, how can this be? In fact, any data read request from the snapshot LV is simply diverted to the production LV and it is the production data that is read. This continues until a write occurs to the production LV. At that point, a copy-on-write operation is invoked. This means that a copy of the old version of the data in the production LV is written into the snapshot LV while the production LV data is changed to its new values. Any subsequent read request from the snapshot LV for this specific data address will now be satisfied from the older version of the data that was copied into the snapshot LV and not from the current production LV version. If this data address were to be requested from the production LV, the current version of the data would be returned.

To make this work, the snapshot LV has to keep track of which data addresses have changed since the snapshot was taken, as this list determines whether the snapshot LV will return data from its copies for data that has changed since the snapshot was taken, or from the production LV if the data has not changed since the snapshot was made. This metadata is persistent, thus snapshot LVs will continue to function properly across a reboot. When creating a snapshot LV, you only need to allocate enough space to accommodate the amount of data that will change in the production LV during the lifetime of the snapshot. You can monitor how much of the space in the snapshot LV has been used with the *lvdisplay* command. Look for the line labeled "Allocated to snapshot," as shown in the example in the *Using the Snapshot* section in this chapter.

It is important that the snapshot LV does not become full; otherwise it must be disabled. If it is hard to estimate how much of the production data might change, as it well may be, you can always make the snapshot LV the same size as the production LV, provided that you have enough unallocated space in the VG.

Taking an LV Snapshot

The snapshot LV is created using *lvcreate*. A snapshot could be taken of *LV01* in *VG02* with this command:

```
# lvcreate -l 40 -s -n snaplv /dev/VG02/LV01
lvcreate -- WARNING: the snapshot must be disabled if it gets full
lvcreate -- INFO: using default snapshot chunk size of 64 KB for
"/dev/VG02/snaplv"
lvcreate -- doing automatic backup of "VG02"
lvcreate -- logical volume "/dev/VG02/snaplv" successfully created
```

Using the Snapshot

The snapshot LV can now be mounted and backed up:

```
# mount /dev/VG02/snaplv /mnt
# dump /mnt
```

While the snapshot is in use, you should monitor it to ensure that it does not get dangerously full. Use the *lvdisplay* command:

```
# lvdisplay /dev/VG02/snaplv
--- Logical volume ---
LV Name                /dev/VG02/snaplv
VG Name                VG02
LV Write Access        read only
LV snapshot status     active destination for /dev/VG02/LV01
LV Status              available
LV #                   2
# open                 1
LV Size                236 MB
Current LE             59
Allocated LE           59
snapshot chunk size    64 KB
Allocated to snapshot  8.89% [14 MB/157.5 MB]
Allocated to COW-table 2.5 MB
Allocation             next free
Read ahead sectors     120
Block device           58:3
```

The key number to monitor is the line shown in bold. This represents the amount of the storage allocated to the snapshot it has used for copy-on-write operations to maintain the snapshot. If this approaches 100 percent, you *must* increase the size of the snapshot LV. Note too that in this output the "Allocated LE" figure of 59 LEs represents the size of the production LV, not the snapshot LV. The figure of 157.5 MB shown in the "Allocated to snapshot" line represents the true size of the snapshot LV (40 LEs or 160

MB; check the *lvcreate* command used earlier to define the snapshot) minus the 2.5 MB shown as "Allocated to COW [copy-on-write] table."

When the backup completes, you can unmount the snapshot and delete it:

```
# umount /mnt
# lvremove /dev/VG02/snaplv
lvremove -- do you really want to remove "/dev/VG02/snaplv"? [y/n]: y
lvremove -- doing automatic backup of volume group "VG02"
lvremove -- logical volume "/dev/VG02/snaplv" successfully removed
```

Consistency Limitations of Snapshots

While the idea of snapshots is to remove the problem of data consistency when backing up live data, there are still challenges to be overcome. If, for instance, a snapshot is made of an LV that contains an active file system, when the snapshot is mounted the file system will appear to have inconsistent metadata as it is likely that some metadata transactions were in progress at the moment the snapshot was made. (The metadata in fact looks exactly as it would have had the system crashed at the moment the snapshot was taken.)

The file system will want to either do a full metadata check or, if it is a journalling file system, a journal log replay. As either of these scenarios requires read-write access to metadata to correct inconsistencies, and as by definition a snapshot can only be accessed as read only, the mount will fail. You could back up directly from the device file without mounting the LV, but you would still be backing up an inconsistent file system structure. The only cure for this is to quiesce the file system, which means stopping all file system requests for a moment. This allows any pending metadata transactions to complete. The snapshot is then taken, after which production can resume. Unmounting the file system will do this, but that means downtime.

Ideally, the process that creates the snapshot should be able to request the file system to quiesce itself. Currently, work is proceeding on necessary modifications to the file system layer in the kernel to allow this. Monitor future kernel releases to track the progress of this work.

Though the file system consistency problem can be solved, the problem of application data consistency remains. Even if the file system data were consistent, it is still possible that the application data is in an inconsistent state. If the application needs to do a series of writes to complete a transaction, for example, and the snapshot is taken part way through those writes, the application may not be able to properly deal with the partially completed transaction as it would appear in the snapshot. It will be necessary to ensure that the application is directed to bring itself to a consistent state while the snapshot is taken. Transaction-oriented applications typically include commands to achieve this; however, as there is no standard programming interface between the application and the LVM, these operations need to be done manually at the application level before the snapshot can be safely taken.

Matrix of LVM Commands

At this point you probably feel like you are drowning in LVM commands. I've put together a matrix in Table 8.1 that should help you navigate the maze. The operations that can be performed, such as creation or deletion, are listed across the top of the matrix, while the objects of the operations, such as LVs or VGs, are listed down the left-hand side. If you want to create a PV, for example, follow the create row across to the PV column; the intersection yields the command you need, in this case *pvcreate*.

Table 8.1   Matrix of LVM Commands

	VOLUME GROUP (VG)	PHYSICAL VOLUME (PV)	LOGICAL VOLUME (LV)
Create	*vgcreate*	*pvcreate*	*lvcreate*
Delete	*vgremove*	N/A	*lvremove*
Change	*vgchange* *vgrename* *vgsplit* *vgmerge*	*pvchange* *pvmove*	*lvchange* *lvrename*
Expand	*vgextend*	N/A	*lvextend*
Shrink	*vgreduce*	N/A	*lvreduce*
Query	*vgdisplay*	*pvdisplay* *pvdata*	*lvdisplay*
Scan	*vgscan*	*pvscan*	*lvscan*

What You Can Do Now

Using the information from this chapter, you are now equipped to take advantage of the logical storage management capabilities of the current Linux kernel. Here's what to do:

1. Examine */proc/lvm* to determine if your kernel has LVM support. If it doesn't, build a kernel that does. If you have never built a kernel before, refer to the Kernel HOWTO or your favorite Linux Systems Administration reference.

2. List your current and projected storage requirements, and plan a structure of VGs and LVs that support what you need now, and leave maximum flexibility for the future. Keeping in mind the Titanic principle, divide different applications and their data into separate VGs and LVs accordingly.

3. Consider which of your current servers you want to convert to the LVM and use the procedure in the *Migrating an Existing Server to LVM* section of this chapter to do the conversion.

4. Keep the flexibility of LVM in mind as you plan storage expansion to existing servers and storage architecture for future servers.

Alternative File Systems

*"Thus times do shift, each thing his turn does hold;
New things succeed as former things grow old."*
—Robert Herrick

Having earlier presented a discussion of disk storage hardware and then progressing through the RAID and LVM storage layers, we have finally reached the top of the storage hill, so to speak, at the file system level. File systems can be broadly divided into two categories: local file systems that support disk storage directly attached to a server, and network file systems that allow data to be stored on a remote device and to be made accessible to the server using a communications network.

This chapter examines both categories of file systems. The state of the art in local file systems is considered first, and four new file system designs currently competing for your attention are reviewed and compared. In the second part of the chapter, three different approaches to the concept of the network file system are examined, each approach being represented by two implementations.

Local Disk File Systems

So far I have been using the *ext2* (to give it its full name, the *Second Extended File System*) file system in all my examples. This has been the standard Linux local file system for years, and it is a solid, well-tested implementation of the classic UNIX file system model as it was originally proposed over 30 years ago. This file system model, however, has always been vulnerable to damage in the case of a disk or system crash, in which case the file system's metadata may suffer loss or corruption. The *ext2* file system has no mechanism to recover from such loss, which places production data at risk. In recent years much work has been done to address this issue, and this has resulted in several new file system implementations becoming available to the Linux world. Some of these are ports of older and well-tested, fault tolerant file systems whose origins lay in commercial UNIX variants, while one is a completely open source effort. To begin, let's take a moment to review the *ext2* file system so you can see the weaknesses inherent in it, then we will see can be done to improve reliability. After that, we'll look at ReiserFS, XFS, JFS, and ext3—all of which are alternative file systems to *ext2*.

The *ext2* File System

Chapter 4, "Installing and Configuring for Reliability," touched on some of the commands that work on the structure of an *ext2* file system. In this section I want to present a bit more of the theory underlying those commands. Any file system is really only a mechanism for storing data objects in some fashion that allows the end user, person, or application a means of giving a name to the file and storing it in a known location from whence it can later be retrieved for further reading or writing. Given that the files can contain a variety of different data ranging from binary code to ASCII text to a database file, it is important that the file system not need to know anything about the data objects it deals with. Accordingly, the *ext2* file system allocates blocks of disk storage to files as necessary to store the data in the file, irrespective and unknowing of the file's data content. To make these data blocks available to the user as a complete and contiguous file, the file system must maintain ordered lists of data blocks and the files they contain. In addition, the file system must supply an access control mechanism, so each file must also carry data concerning ownership, permissions, and date stamps. None of this data is part of the actual file data, yet it is necessary to allow the file to be accessed. Data of this sort is termed *metadata*, and, as we shall see, maintaining the integrity of this metadata becomes the primary focus of a reliable, fault tolerant file system.

Consider the illustration shown in Figure 9.1. With its roots in the original UNIX file system devised by Ken Thompson, Dennis Ritchie, and Rudd Canaday as long ago as the spring of 1969, *ext2* retains the concept of the i-node (or *information node*) as the central building block of the metadata

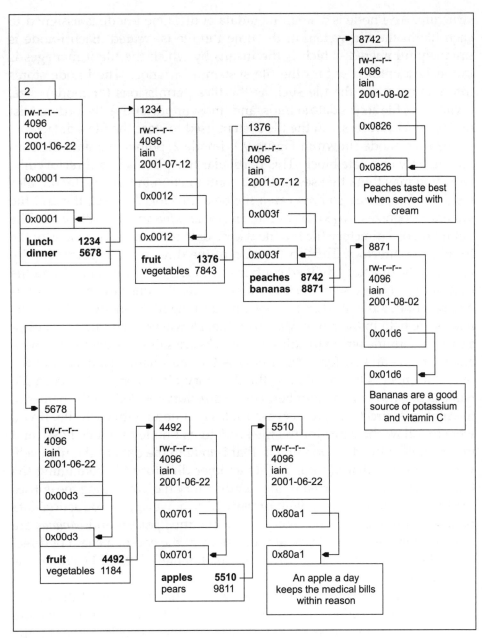

Figure 9.1 The ext2 file system metadata structure uses the traditional UNIX i-node concept.

structure. An i-node is a small metadata entity. One i-node is assigned to each file in the file system at the time the file is created. Each i-node is uniquely numbered, which is the means by which the file it manages is uniquely identified within the file system as a whole. The i-node stores information about the file such as the files permissions (or mode), size, ownership, file access date stamps, and (most importantly), the ordered list of data block addresses in the file system used to store the file's data.

The first i-node shown in Figure 9.1, i-node 2, points to a data file containing only one data block. This particular file is actually a directory file. Now you may think that seems like a contradiction in terms; after all, files reside in directories, so how can a file be a directory? In fact, the *ext2* file system recognizes two kinds of file, an *ordinary file* and a *directory file*. The definition of a directory file is a file whose data represents the names of the files in the directory. Thus in the case of the directory file pointed to by i-node 2, the directory defined contains two files, one named *lunch* and the other *dinner*. Notice something of interest here. The one key piece of information about a file, its name, is *not* stored in the file's i-node. Instead, file names are held in the parent directory file. However, if an i-node is necessary to determine where the files data blocks are stored, as well as it s ownership, mode and so forth, then how is the file's name connected to the i-node number? Observe that in the directory file, listed next to each file name is that file's i-node number. Thus a directory file defines the names of the files in a directory, and also associates an i-node with each file. If you were to follow the entry for the file *lunch* to its i-node (number 1234), and in turn follow the data pointers in that i-node to the data of the file itself, you would find that *lunch* is in fact another directory file containing the files *fruit* and *vegetables*. *fruit* is another directory file, containing the entries *peaches* and *bananas*. The content of these files, however, is production data rather than file names and i-node numbers, thus *peaches* and *bananas* are ordinary files, and must by definition reside at the end of a chain of directory files. Thus we could write the pathname of the file *peaches* as *lunch/fruit/peaches*.

This is a relative directory path, however. What is its parent directory? Or, to ask the question in terms of i-nodes, if the directory file having i-node 1234 is identified as the directory *lunch*, what is the identifier for the i-node numbered 2? This particular i-node number is special, as by definition i-node 2 is always the starting point of any descent through the directory tree specified in an *ext2* file system. Thus i-node 2 is always the root directory file for any file system. The name associated with that root directory will be given by the operating system *mount* command when this file system is added to the single logical file system tree the user or application sees. Thus if the file system structure illustrated here existed in the partition */dev/sda1*, for example, and if this command

```
# mount /dev/sda1 /home/iain/meals
```

were used to mount it, then the fully qualified path name of the file *peaches* would be */home/iain/meals/lunch/fruit/peaches*.

In similar fashion, the file *apples* would have a fully qualified path name */home/iain/meals/dinner/fruit/apples*. Notice that there are two directories both named *fruit*, however they cannot be confused as they have different i-node numbers. You will recall that i-node numbering is by definition unique within a single file system. If you want to investigate this on your system, use the *-i* flag to the *ls* command to examine i-node numbers. For any regular file, the output will look similar to

```
$ ls -i sample1.eps
  503939 sample1.eps
```

This indicates that *sample1.eps* is defined by i-node 503939, and for a directory that is a mount point, the i-node number should always be 2, like this:

```
$ mount
/dev/hda5 on / type ext2 (rw)
/dev/hda1 on /RH71 type ext2 (rw,usrquota)
$ ls -id /
  2 /
$ ls -id /RH71
  2 /RH71
```

Reliability Issues with ext2

While the design of the *ext2* file system is sound and the implementation has proved itself stable over many years of service, there is an inherent problem that arises in the case of a disk or system crash, in that there is no fault tolerance built in to the file system design. In Figure 9.1, each of the ordinary files was shown to have only one data block each. In practice this is unusual. As the default data block size is 4 KB, most files will normally have many data blocks. To keep track of these blocks for allocation purposes, the file system sets aside special data blocks called super blocks. One of the key pieces of data stored in these super blocks is the free list, a list of data blocks in the file system not yet assigned to a file. When a new file is created or an existing file is extended, the file system code chooses blocks from the free list and adds their addresses to i-nodes as necessary to fulfill the space requirements of the new or larger file.

Consider what might happen if the server crashes part way through the operation of creating or extending a file. It is possible that the *ext2* code got as far as crossing a data block off the free list, but had not yet added the data block address to the proper i-node when the system crashed. When the system reboots, the file system will have a dilemma. Because a transaction was in process at the time of the crash, the super block will be marked as "dirty." This triggers the file system checker, *e2fsck*, to automatically check the consistency of the file system before it is mounted. The check will examine the free list as well as all of the i-nodes, which for a large file system can be time consuming. The nature of the problem means that the time to check a file system will increase with the number of data blocks in the file system, and a complete check on a file system ranging into gigabytes in size can take hours. Much worse than the delay, however, is the fact that in this case the check will turn up a data block that does not reside on the free list, yet also has no home in any i-node. The file system has no way of determining what that block may contain. It may contain data that belongs to a file; but if it does, the surviving metadata offers no clue as to which file, or where in the file that block belongs. It may also be that a file was being reduced in size at the time of the crash, and the data stored in the block is in fact not needed by any file. Not only does the file system have no way of knowing what file this block belongs to, if any, it also has no way of knowing whether the data in the block is current or not. After all, the crash may have occurred between the addition of the block to the i-node and the writing of data into the block. In short, the file system has indeterminate and irreparable data inconsistencies and cannot be trusted. The original UNIX file system implementations operated primarily in research and academic settings, accepted this as a fact of life, and relied upon backups to recover from such problems. Something better is clearly needed in a commercial environment.

Scalability Issues with ext2

Another issue arises when you consider that *ext2* has an inherent size limitation in that it is a 32-bit file system, resulting in a maximum file system size of 4 TB and a maximum file size of 2 GB. *ext2* also allocates space to files in blocks that are relatively small in size (block sizes range from 512 bytes to 4 KB). This means that as files become very large, correspondingly large numbers of blocks must be allocated and managed. *ext2* has no means of dealing with the large volumes of metadata this will produce in any particularly efficient manner, which becomes a performance limitation in the case of either very large files or very large numbers of small files. *ext2* does uses a technique of preallocating groups of data blocks to files in order to reduce fragmentation, and like the classic UNIX FFS (the Berkeley Fast File System) implementation, it distributes i-nodes throughout the file system to keep data and metadata as close to each other as possible. The goal is to reduce disk seeks. These techniques of data block grouping and keeping i-nodes close to data combine to give a practical middle ground performance that is quite acceptable up to the limited upper size of an *ext2* file system. But with support for larger commercial data structures now climbing into terabytes in size is required, something more scalable than *ext2* is necessary.

Improving on *ext2*

At its introduction in 1993, *ext2* was a welcome improvement over its pre-decessors (*minix* and *ext*) and soon came to be the de facto standard Linux file system. For a number of years it has served well, but as Linux moves more and more into the commercial world and into larger and larger scale computing, it has become clear that something beyond *ext2* is required. In this section I present several technologies to address the reliability and scalability issues of *ext2*, and, following that, I examine several new file system designs that incorporate these technologies.

Metadata Journaling

Recall that one of the major reliability shortcomings of *ext2* lies in its weak fault tolerance. If an active *ext2* file system crashes, there is every likelihood that upon reboot its metadata may be in an inconsistent state. To solve this problem, file system architects turned to the concept of transaction journaling, a technique perfected by the authors of transaction processing databases.

Applied to a file system, the concept of a transaction journal works like this. At the start of the process of extending a file, an entry is made in a journal log, typically a data area set aside either within the same file system or in a central location to serve multiple file systems. This entry notes the details of the transaction step by step. If, say, seven separate operations are involved in extending a file, such as locating a free block and marking it taken, then noting the block number in the i-node, and so on, each step is noted in turn in the log. When the final step is complete the file has been successfully extended, the file system metadata structure is in a consistent state and would not be harmed by a crash, so the transaction is marked in the log as complete. On the other hand, if the system were to crash between steps three and four, then upon a reboot the file system journaling code sees a partially completed transaction in the journal log when it first attempts to mount the damaged file system. The journaling code can then complete the transaction, if possible. (However, because the data to be written to the file in the case of extending a file would usually have been sitting in a memory buffer at the time of the crash, more often than not this is not possible.) If the transaction cannot be completed, the journal code will reverse the steps that were complete, returning the file system metadata to the consistent state it was in before the transaction started. No blocks will be left unaccounted for, the file system i-node data structure will be consistent, and the file system can be mounted and placed into production.

A very important point: *Journaling as described here ensures only the integrity of the file system metadata, not the file system production data.* In the example of extending a file, the file system journal will repair the damage done to the file system metadata structure by the crash, but the data that was to be written to the extended file has in all likelihood been lost. Like RAID, *metadata journaling is never a substitute for reliable backups.*

If journaling cannot guarantee the integrity of file data, then why bother with it? The primary motivation behind journaling is often an issue of balancing the requirements of performance and reliability. If you are willing to accept that data will be lost in a crash, then on the face of it the *ext2* file system, with no journaling, would suit your purposes. It is true that with no metadata journaling, a crash may force the file system checker to comb through the file system for metadata inconsistencies; but in most cases those inconsistencies can be resolved, if only by resorting to arbitrary decisions regarding inconsistent situations.

The problem with it is that this sort of "scavenger" metadata checking simply takes too long. As file system sizes move into the terabytes, these exhaustive checks can take many minutes or hours, even on reasonably fast servers. A file system that journals transactions, however, need only resolve problems outstanding with those transactions that were in process at the time of the crash. Normally this is such a small number that the journal log processing at reboot may take only a few minutes, in some cases only seconds. The difference in boot time between a nonjournaling file system like *ext2* and a journaled one can be dramatic. This reduces down time waiting for journal checks to occur.

Journaling techniques can also be used to speed operations on very busy file systems. In this case, multiple operations on a single file can be collected in the journal and consolidated into larger, more efficient operations. For example, if it were desired to add a large number of files to a directory, a non-journaled file system might create the directory entries one by one. This would require a separate write operation to the parent directory file inode for each file to be created. This would involve separate disk write operations for each file created an inefficient pattern of disk access. A file system journal could be used to accumulate multiple file creation requests into a single large write request for the directory file that could be satisfied with a single disk seek and write operation. It is these two issues, reducing file system check time at boot and improving the efficiency of disk meta-data management that are the primary factors driving the use of journaling in Linux servers today.

Full Data Journaling

If journaling is useful in protecting against metadata damage in a crash, could the concept be extended to the file data being written and journal that too? That way file data *would* be protected in the case of a server crash. Unfortunately, it is not as simple as that. Recall that the real issue with metadata changes is that they occur in several atomic steps. The danger is that a crash interrupts the sequence, leaving some steps in the process incomplete. The task of the journal log is keep track of the steps and ensure that if the process is interrupted it can be re played after a reboot. To apply the same concept to data would involve copying the data from the application write buffer to a journal area, then copying it again to disk. This is really only a form of mirroring. If the crash occurs while the data is being written from the journal to disk, certainly you can recover the data after the reboot from the journal. But what if the crash happens as the data is being written from the buffer to the journal? At some point in time the data is vulnerable; no level of data journaling can avoid it entirely. (Data journaling does have a performance-related application, however; see the "Data Journaling and SMTP Performance" sidebar for an example.)

One proposed solution to make data journaling a viable reliability enhancement is to implement the full data journal on a separate disk than the destination file system. This would protect data in the case of a disk crash (although the same protection could be had from a RAID). Another possibility would be to store the data journal on a fast, persistent storage device, such as non-volatile memory (NVRAM). It is conceivable that an NVRAM hardware device could be designed in such a way as to allow any pending writes to be safely transferred to the NVRAM unit, even in a complete server failure situation, as the persistent storage device would have its own power supply (likely a small on board battery). Such devices are in the developmental stages and should be viable in the future.

DATA JOURNALING AND SMTP PERFORMANCE

Data journaling offers a real advantage for certain applications, but for performance rather than reliability reasons. One is the case of Simple Mail Transfer Protocol (SMTP) mail forwarding servers. SMTP servers handling large volumes of mail have an inherent problem due to a reliability requirement of the SMTP protocol. If one SMTP server receives a mail message forwarded from another, the receiving machine is not supposed to acknowledge to the sender the receipt of the message until it has been safely written to disk on the receiving machine. This ensures reliable passing of mail between the servers, as there is no way the mail message could get lost if the receiving machine crashes at any time in the message handling process. The problem this poses for the receiving machine, however, is that it must take the time to write each individual incoming mail to disk before it can acknowledge it, which makes the server's performance heavily disk bound. For large servers, this can be a source of significant performance troubles. The receiving server could solve the problem by receiving messages into a fast cache. As soon as the message is in the cache, it could be acknowledged and then the message could be scheduled to be written out to disk asynchronously, in the normal way that a buffer cache works. The problem with this, however, is that in a crash this cache would be lost, and with it all the mail messages held in it, violating the requirements of the SMTP protocol.

A data journal solves this problem by writing the mail message into the journal log first. As soon as this write is complete, the acknowledgment can be returned. The receiving machine can then write the data back to the file system at its leisure. If the journaling system is written efficiently, it will accumulate batches of writes that it periodically flushes to disk. This type of writing generally makes more efficient use of the disk than writing each file individually, thus the overall effect is to improve mail handling throughput. The data journaling option available in the *ext3* file system discussed later in this chapter offers some promising possibilities for this application.

This is an interesting case, as the issue is really one of performance, not reliability. However, if your mail server is too slow to keep up with incoming traffic, clients may time out and return errors to end-users. As far as they are concerned, the mail server is down. It isn't really, but if periods of heavy load make it temporarily unable to serve all your clients, then for those clients that has become an unreliable server. It can be dangerous to consider performance and reliability as separate issues; one often intrudes upon the other.

Application Journaling

As a final note on journaling, it is important to remember that the idea of journaling originated not at the operating system level, but at the application level, specifically, with database applications. Applying the idea to the underlying file system structure was intended as a means of extending the data protection offered by journaling to applications that did not, would not, or could not do the journaling themselves, by means of journaling at the file system level. The most obvious application benefiting from this is the operating system itself. It may very well be, however, that the nature of an application makes it necessary for it to perform the journaling. For example, your database may not use an operating system file system at all, but it may use a raw disk partition in which it stores its own data structures. In this case the application will commonly have journal logs stored somewhere in this raw partition. Along with these logs there would be commands internal to the application for managing journaling, the most important being commands for performing journal replays after a crash. It may also be that there is internal state information is necessary for the operation of the application that may not be stored in a file system as such, and that may require application-specific recovery procedures after a crash. A complete data availability solution will take into consideration what can and cannot be done at both the operating system and application levels. It is not sufficient to apply an operating system journaling solution as a silver-bullet solution to guarantee data security across all of your applications.

Scalability, Extents, and B-trees

To support very large files and file system sizes into the terabytes, newer file systems use *extent allocation* to reduce the overhead of managing large lists of data blocks. An extent-based file system still uses a relatively small basic unit of storage space (often the 512-byte disk block); however, it groups large contiguous chunks of these small blocks into extents, which can be identified by only a starting address and the size of the extent. Thus thousands of blocks can be assigned to a file using a small amount of metadata. In this case the i-node contains extent descriptors rather than lists of data blocks. This scheme allows managing of large files to be managed with dramatically reduced metadata volumes.

The second scalability issue arises in the case of large numbers of files. In this case managing the sheer number of i-nodes required to define thousands of files becomes a problem. To solve the problem, data indexing techniques (the best suited indexing algorithm for metadata is known as B-tree indexing) can be used to efficiently manage these large volumes of metadata. Thus you will hear the terms *extent allocation* and *B-tree* used heavily in discussions of alternative file systems. It is important to realize that *neither of these techniques has a significant effect on the reliability of the file system*. They are primarily terms related to scalability and performance. It is important to realize, however, that as file systems grow in size, performance must keep pace with reliability. An exceedingly fault-tolerant file system may give good reliability; but if it comes at such a performance cost as to make it impracticable, then it is useless. Happily, as we shall see, this is one area in which these techniques introduced to improve the performance and scalability of large file systems actually pay reliability dividends, too.

Alternative Local File Systems

We have pointed out the shortcomings of the *ext2* file system and introduced journaling and metadata indexing as techniques to improve upon *ext2*. Recently, several new file systems have become available to the Linux world that implement these technologies, and each is vying to be the replacement for the old faithful *ext2*. All of the contenders claim to have better reliability and fault tolerance; some also claim performance and scalability benefits. I'll review four of them and assess their capabilities in a reliability context. Hans Reiser's ReiserFS is a completely new, clean sheet design, while two are well-established commercial UNIX file systems recently ported to Linux, XFS coming from Silicon Graphics (SGI) IRIX, and Journalled File System (JFS) from IBM's AIX and OS/2 Warp. Last, although certainly not least, is *ext3*, Stephen Tweedie's journaling extension to *ext2*.

It should be noted that of these four, three (XFS, JFS and ext3) are, as of Red Hat 7.1, either brand new version 1.0 releases or in beta test stages. Only ReiserFS has a significant Linux production history. Though Red Hat does not yet include ReiserFS in its stock v7.1 kernel, the SuSe distribution (the most popular European distribution) does include ReiserFS, and it has been included in the standard Linux kernel source tree from kernel version 2.4.1 on. Also, Red Hat has indicated to me that beyond v7.1 of the Red Hat distribution they intend to support only *ext3*, although the others may be included in the distribution. This means that Red Hat users may need to build a custom kernel to support file systems other than *ext3*, as well as building the management tool sets that will come along with each file system.

The ReiserFS

First in line for consideration is a completely new file system design. Designed by Berkeley alumnus Hans Reiser, ReiserFS was born not so much as a file system, as an initial step towards the much larger goal of unifying name spaces in the overall operating system environment. (This is an interesting idea, though beyond the scope of this book. Dr. Reiser has an interesting paper on the topic that can be found at www.namesys.com.)

From a file system point of view, what comes from this project is a metadata journaling file system making extensive use of B*-tree indexing. It is particularly good at dealing with very large files, and large numbers of very small files (small being in the order of 100- 1,000 bytes). It is also makes efficient use of disk space when storing small files, traditionally a weakness in file systems using disk block allocations. Work started on this project in 1993, and today ReiserFS is in its third production release cycle. Of the competitors to *ext2*, this gives ReiserFS an edge in the area of Linux stability. The primary strong points of ReiserFS are:

- It offers a maximum file and file system size of 17 TB. (The file system code can support larger sizes than this, but as of kernel 2.4.5 is limited by 32-bit kernel code limitations.)

- ReiserFS does metadata journaling and has proved in testing to be one of the faster journaling file systems, particularly where large numbers of small files are involved; it is as fast or faster than *ext2*, which does no journaling.

- ReiserFS supports all Linux software RAID levels using the 2.4 kernel. (At 2.2 kernels, only RAID0 is supported, which does nothing for reliability.)

- ReiserFS supports kernel LVM, allowing file system snapshots.

- ReiserFS supports quotas.

- ReiserFS can be used as a root file system, and it supports the *lilo* boot loader.

- ReiserFS ships with its own utilities, including a file system resizer able to both expand or shrink the ReiserFS.

- ReiserFS has been a part of the core kernel code since kernel 2.4.1 and has gone through several production generations. It is a standard file system in the SuSe distribution, and is widely used in the European Linux community.

Because of its ability to perform well in dealing with large numbers of small files, ReiserFS works particularly well with applications such as mail and news spools, and HTTP caches, and proxy servers. It is also competitive in general purpose usage, equaling or bettering the performance of *ext2* in most categories. This is attractive considering that journaling file systems normally come with a measurable performance cost. ReiserFS is not tied to architectural designs that are now several years old, and it is an innovative use of the most current data indexing algorithms that allows it to offer metadata journaling with minimal performance cost.

Remember, though, that metadata journaling is not a guarantee of data integrity. On the other hand, an application like a news spool or an HTTP proxy would not be hurt by the loss of some data in a crash. As long as the file system metadata survives, any data lost from the cache as a result of the crash would only mean one less cache hit afterwards, or one news article that needs to be requested again from the upstream news server.

The current version of ReiserFS (version 3.6) does not support ACLs (Access Control Lists). ACL support is scheduled for inclusion in the version 4 release of the product by the use of external plug-in modules. These modules are a significant part of the evolution of the ReiserFS. They will allow a third party to effectively extend the functionality of the file system to suit their own purposes. This is intended to increase the developer community for ReiserFS to include anyone able to write a plug-in, so future functional improvement will not be restricted by the limited time the core ReiserFS developers have available. The first plug-ins to be written will be security related, as The Defense Advanced Research Projects Agency (DARPA) is the primary sponsor of this work and its focus is on improving the security mechanisms available in a Linux file system. Reiser v4 is scheduled for release later in 2002. You can follow its progress and track other ReiserFS issues at www.namesys.com. There is also a mailing list available for subscription on this Web site that will keep you up-to-date on day-to-day ReiserFS issues.

The XFS

XFS was introduced by SGI as a new file system design into IRIX in 1994, and has been the standard IRIX file system since 1996. As part of SGI's commitment to Linux, in 1999 a Linux port of XFS was started and version 1.0 was released under the terms of the GPL in May 2001. XFS is a mature, stable file system design especially oriented towards very large file systems, both in terms of the aggregate size of the file system as well as the size and number of files in the file system. As the stability of the Linux port is proven, the strengths of XFS as they are apparent on IRIX should become available to the Linux world too. Here is a list of the strong points of XFS:

- XFS is a 64-bit file system implementation that makes use of B-tree indexing, variable data block sizes, and space assignment by extents to scale to large data storage needs while retaining good performance. (XFS has demonstrated single file throughputs under IRIX as high as 7 GB/s.)

- XFS's use of the full 64-bit address space supports a maximum file system size of 18 million terabytes, and a maximum file size of 9 million terabytes (although, as for ReiserFS, the current Linux kernel limits this to 2 TB).

- XFS metadata journaling allows for file system restarts following a crash in seconds; and XFS supports journal logs being kept on a separate physical device than the file system data, which is a reliability plus.

- XFS supports sparse files and Linux software RAID.

- XFS supports quotas, and quota transactions are journaled.

- ACLs are supported using XFS in conjunction with samba. (Integration of XFS and Linux ACLs is a work in progress.)

- XFS supports the current 32-bit LVM implementation, including the ability to do file system snapshots, and has indicated a commitment to retain compatibility with the kernel LVM implementation as it makes the transition to a full 64-bit system.

- The Linux XFS port supplies a complete toolkit, including commands to dump, restore, extend, and repair the XFS.

- XFS can be used as a root file system and supports the *lilo* boot loader.

- XFS has a long and stable history as a production file system in a major commercial UNIX. In addition the Linux XFS port was done directly by SGI and appears to have their full and ongoing support.

You will note that most of the features claimed for XFS are in the size, scalability, and performance areas. What about reliability? The fact that XFS is a stable file system design with a history in large commercial use is a definite plus, as is the fact that it is actively supported in the Linux world by SGI. On the other hand, the port to Linux is new, and will no doubt need to go through a debugging period. All in all, XFS is a strong contender in the Linux file system race and it seems likely that distributors will begin to include XFS in the future as an alternative file system. More information about the XFS for Linux project can be found at oss.sgi.com/projects/xfs, or you can subscribe to the XFS mailing list by sending a message to major-domo@oss.sgi.com with body text **subscribe linux-xfs** *your@email-address*.

The JFS

The JFS is to IBM's AIX and OS/2 as XFS is to IRIX; that is, JFS has been the standard file system in AIX for many years and in OS/2 Warp since 1999. The task of porting JFS to Linux was started by IBM's open source software initiative early in 2000, and v1.0 of the file system was released in June 2001. What can be said about the JFS Linux port is similar to the XFS port, specifically:

- JFS is a 64-bit file system implementation, and makes use of B-tree indexing, variable data block sizes, and space assignment by extents to scale to large data storage needs while retaining good performance.

- JFS metadata journaling allows for file system restarts following a crash in seconds.

- JFS supports sparse files.

- JFS supports Linux LVM, including use of the LVM snapshot facility.

- JFS has a long and stable history as a production file system in two of IBM's major commercial operating systems. In addition the Linux JFS port was done directly by IBM and appears to have their full and ongoing support.

JFS is not as aggressively oriented toward very large file systems and high performance as is XFS, but has a long history with a large installed base in the AIX and OS/2 worlds. At the time of this writing, there appears to be no intent to port the AIX LVM to Linux; rather, the JFS port team has expressed their intention to ensure that Linux JFS will use the LVM support currently available in the 2.4 kernel. There is no support in the current JFS release (v1.0) for ACLs, quotas, or journaling on a separate drive; however, all these features are on the developers' to-do list for future releases. You can keep track of the JFS for Linux project at oss.software.ibm.com/devel-operworks/opensource/jfs. There is also a mailing list available at this site if you want to follow current events in the JFS world.

The ext3 *File System*

The *ext3* file system is designed as an attempt to build upon the stability and speed of the well-accepted *ext2* standard by adding journaling capabilities to the existing *ext2* file system. *ext3* is thus a journaling extension to *ext2*; an existing *ext2* file system can be converted into an *ext3* file system by the addition of a journal log, and an *ext3* file system can be mounted as either *ext2* or *ext3* using a flag to the *mount* command to control whether the journal log is used or not.

The journaling function of *ext3* was written primarily by Stephen Tweedie, one of the original authors of *ext2*. One significant thing about *ext3* journaling is that it supports both full data journaling as well as metadata journaling. Once support for journal logs on separate devices is added (which is currently in development), this could have a reliability benefit should the log be implemented on an NVRAM device, as discussed previously. There is also a branch of the *ext3* project being directed towards developing a log structured file system, which is another means of doing data journaling designed to offer improved data reliability. Combining the basic functionality of *ext2* and the *ext3* extensions, the feature list reads like this:

- It offers a 32-bit data structure supporting a 4 TB file system size and a 2-GB file size.

- *ext3* can be used as the root file system and supports the *lilo* boot loader.

- *ext3* works with Linux LVM, including snapshot capabilities.

- *ext3* will support quotas and ACLs.

In addition, in a post to the *ext3* mailing list in June 2001, Stephen Tweedie, the chief architect of *ext3*, notes that there are a number of advanced performance features available as patches to *ext2*, including indexed directories for fast operation on large directories and tail-packing for high efficiency on small files. There are also ACL patches available for *ext2*, which are hoped to be officially merged into *ext3* at some point. The *ext3* developers also have prototypes working for additional *ext3* specific functionality, such as using a separate disk for the journal. Add this functionality to the above list and *ext3* adds up to a file system that can certainly compete. You should *not* rule *ext3* out as a retread or a case of extending a current technology beyond its real structural capabilities.

As of this writing, *ext3* is in the beta testing stage, however Red Hat has indicated to me that it intends to support *ext3* as its next generation standard file system. There is no Web site at the moment devoted to *ext3*, but you can keep track of developments by subscribing to the *ext3* mailing list available at http://listman.redhat.com/mailman/listinfo/ext3-users.

Local File System Summary Comparison

Each of the four presented file system designs offers reliability as well as performance and scalability gains over the *ext2* file system. It is up to you to assess the relative strengths of each as you make your decision. To help you compare point for point, Table 9.1 summarizes the major areas of comparison for *ext2* and the four competitors.

Red Hat users should note the last line in the table. The entries here refer to my comment earlier regarding Red Hat's intent concerning file system support in future Red Hat releases. While a *no* in this category means that Red Hat will not be supporting this file system, it does not mean that you cannot use it in a Red Hat distribution. It does mean that you will probably need to download source code from the file system developer and compile the file system management tools and either a new kernel or kernel module to support it.

Table 9.1   File System Comparison Chart

FEATURE	EXT2	XFS V1.0	JFS V1.0.1	REISERFS V3.6	EXT3 V 0.0.7
Maximum FS size	4 TB	18,000 PB	32 PB	17 TB	4 TB
Maximum File size	2 GB	7,000 PB	4 PB	17 TB	2 GB
Metadata journaling	no	yes	yes	yes	yes
Data journaling	no	no	no	no	yes
Metadata indexing	no	yes	yes	yes	future
Quota	yes	yes	no	yes	yes
ACL	no	yes	no	no	no
LVM	yes	yes	yes	yes	yes
Software RAID	yes	yes	yes	yes	yes
Snapshots	LVM	LVM	LVM	LVM	LVM
root/boot support	yes	yes	yes	yes	yes
Red Hat support	yes	no	no	no	yes

Network File Systems

The second part of this chapter is devoted to three different ways in which data communication network may be used to implement reliable data storage. Each of the three different techniques has its pros and cons, and you will need to evaluate each of them against your own requirements and your risk analysis.

Each of these data reliability techniques relies on using a network to allow data to be stored at a distance from the server that is reading or writing it. Further, each allows a duplicate copy of the data to be kept at the remote site. This backup may be used by a backup server at the remote site to take over in case of a primary site failure, or simply as a form of online offsite backup. First to be considered is the concept of the network block device.

Network Block Devices

The idea of a network block device extends the basic block device over a network. The concept of the block device is common to most versions of UNIX. The operating system provides two types of software device driver to access a disk storage device, the raw device and the block device. The raw device accepts a stream of bytes that it writes to a physical location on the disk specified by the function call that supplied the data to be written. No restrictions are placed on the size or structure of the data, and data is written directly to the physical device with no buffering. Some applications that want to store information in their own data structures directly on a disk partition with minimal intervention by the operating system will choose to use these raw device drivers. A block device, on the other hand, accepts data to be written in fixed-size blocks. It will cache this data in memory until such time as it is most efficient to write it out to disk. The block device may also rearrange the order in which the data gets written to disk, if doing so makes more sense from a performance point of view to do so. Block devices are those normally used by file systems to write their data to disk. An example of a block device would be an entry in */dev*, such as */dev/sda1*, representing a disk partition in which any of the file systems discussed earlier in this chapter could be built. The data flow from an application to a local disk file system via a block device is illustrated in Figure 9.2.

The network block device extends this concept across a network. As shown in Figure 9.3, an application on server A writes to a network block device. Rather than being tied to a local disk, this network device routes the request through TCP/IP via a network to a disk physically local to

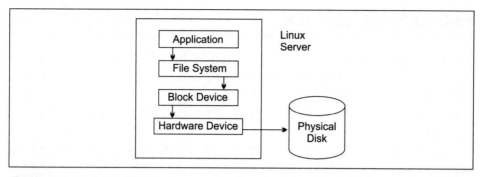

Figure 9.2 The data flow from an application through a block device to a local disk is illustrated here.

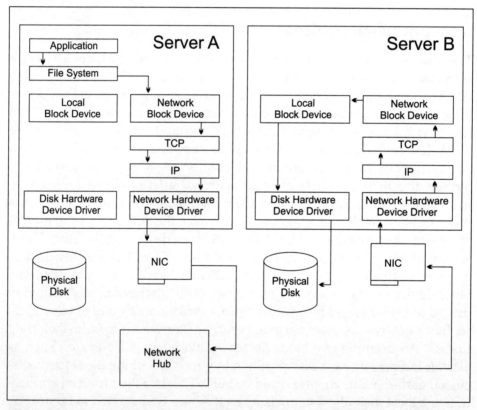

Figure 9.3 The data flow from an application to a remote disk using a network block device looks like this.

remote server B. Remote server B then uses a local block device to write the data to its local disk.

The network block device looks to the file system on server A to be no different than if the disk were local, hence the application has no idea, and does not need to have any idea, that its data is actually being written to a remote machine. From a reliability point of view this gets interesting if we consider the possibility of having both local and network devices in operation simultaneously.

Consider Figure 9.4, for example. In this case the application file system has been implemented on a software RAID1 array on server A. One half of the data mirror is on a block device pointing to a local disk (/dev/sda1), while the other half of the mirror references a network block device

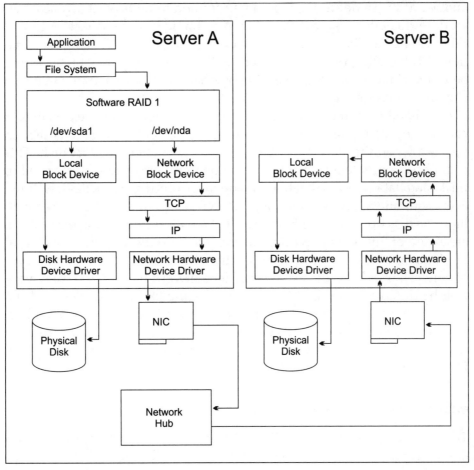

Figure 9.4 Here, a network block device is used together with a software RAID to maintain a remote data mirror.

(*/dev/nbd*) pointed to a disk on the remote server B. If server A fails, there should be a complete and timely data copy available immediately to server B. This kind of network disk sharing is a core functionality required of the highly available processing clusters discussed in Chapter 10, "Server Clustering." If sufficient network bandwidth is available between the two servers, there is no reason that they could not be separated by a significant distance, effectively allowing a warm standby backup server to be in place many miles from the primary server location.

There are challenges to be overcome, however. The primary one is network bandwidth. Few LAN technologies can match the bandwidth of a local bus technology such as ATA or SCSI, and the network traffic bottleneck in a network block device setup needs to be carefully evaluated. In local clusters (those in which both servers are located adjacent to one another at the same site), it would be common to dedicate a physical network to this inter server disk traffic. A technology such as fast or gigabit Ethernet, FDDI (Fiber Distributed Data Interface, a 100 MB/s implementation of Token Ring running on fiber media), or Fibre Channel (FC) would be viable choices. There is also CPU overhead to network traffic that also should be considered.

As reliability is the focus of this setup, it would seem reasonable to choose a journaling file system to ensure that metadata will be consistent in the case when the standby server needs to take over the data disk. This could pose a problem in that by definition journaling file systems need to track metadata changes that have a sequence ordering. Block devices, however, commonly reserve the right to reorder requests they receive to improve disk operational efficiency. All of the Linux journaling file systems are aware of this and are written to take into account the behavior of local block devices and cooperate successfully with them. With the added layer of network transport, the behavior of the network block device may very well be different than the behavior of a local disk block device, and the interaction between the journaling file system and the network block device will have to be carefully examined. Two network block devices currently are available in the Linux environment, *enbd* (the Enhanced Network Block Device) and *drbd*. We'll look at them next.

enbd: *The Enhanced Network Block Device*

The *enbd*, now maintained by Peter Breuer, is the current implementation of the original *nbd* first written in 1997 by Pavel Machek. Much development effort has been put into the project since its inception, and today *enbd* offers the following features:

- *enbd* can use either a disk partition as its local storage or an empty disk file as its local storage, giving it good configuration flexibility.

- *enbd* can be used in conjunction with software RAID to implement a remote mirror, as illustrated in Figure 9.4.

- *enbd* will generally exceed the performance you would expect of a read-write mounted NFS; at modest CPU utilization, throughputs in the order of 6 MB/s have been observed using a 100 MB/s switched Ethernet fabric; Gigabit Ethernet should scale proportionally, as long as CPU capacity allows.

- *enbd* supports the use of multiple physical network interfaces to increase available client-to-server bandwidth, which would further improves the throughputs mentioned in the previous point.

- *enbd* client server network connections are continually checked and, in the event of a network interruption, will be renegotiated and recovered automatically with no disruption apparent to the user of the device so long as at least one network connection remains functional. This is a reliability plus.

- *enbd* optionally supports the use of Secure Sockets Layer (SSL) authentication and encryption to ensure data security across IP networks, although at a performance cost of a 50 to 80 percent reduction in throughput, dependent on the strength of the encryption chosen.

enbd is in use in production sites today, however, Red Hat has indicated to me that they have no plans to support it in future Red Hat distributions. The older *nbd* device is included in the current v7.1 distribution, however, as it has been in the core kernel for some time now. Be sure not to confuse *nbd* and *enbd*! *enbd* is newer and has considerably improved functionality. If you compile a Red Hat kernel and ask for network block device support, you will be getting the older *nbd* code. To get *enbd* you will have to get and compile the source from the maintainer at www.it.uc3m.es/~ptb/nbd/. *enbd* compiles as a kernel module, so it is unlikely that an entire kernel build will be necessary. Further information on both *nbd* and *enbd* can be found in an excellent and comprehensive article in the Linux Journal, volume #73, available at www.linuxjournal.com/lj-issues/issue73/.

The final note on *enbd*, however, is a mild warning. When used in conjunction with a journaling file system, *enbd* does *not* guarantee to preserve the order of disk writes to the remote mirror, consequently the safe recovery of incomplete metadata transactions following a server failure can not be guaranteed using an *enbd* mirror. In most cases, a journal replay would occur when the backup server mounted the file system and those transactions in process at the time of the failure would be lost, in the worst case, a complete file system check may be necessary to recover, if the out of order data sufficiently confuses the journal replay mechanism. An alternative to *enbd* that was JFS-aware would be nice, which is why we shall look at *drbd* next.

drbd

An alternative to *enbd*, Philipp Reisner's *drbd* rolls the network block device idea together with internal RAID1 functionality and adds write-order preservation to keep journaling file systems happy. A *drbd* server pair is illustrated in Figure 9.5.

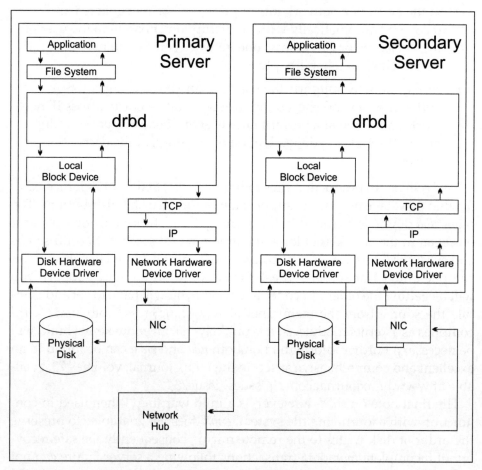

Figure 9.5   Here, the structure of a drbd server pair can be seen.

As can be seen, the basic idea is very similar to the pair of servers running *enbd* configured using software RAID1 shown in Figure 9.4. Note however that when using *drbd* the mirroring is done by *drbd* itself; the software RAID is not necessary. Also note that the two servers have explicit identities, one being designated as the primary and the other the secondary. The data is writeable on the primary only, but is read-only on the secondary. In most *drbd* installations a heartbeat mechanism would be put into place to determine if the primary server has failed, in which case a script is initiated on the secondary causing it to switch to acting as the primary server. This would involve mounting the data as read-write, in process of which any journal replay necessary would be done.

Journaling is supported in a *drbd* environment as the driver maintains the same ability to control write ordering that a standard local block device provides. There is a performance cost to this, however, as by definition any write ordering scheme must delay writing the next sequential data item until it has confirmation that the current data item has been safely written to disk. When dealing with as local hardware driver, these confirmations come back quickly; however, when a network is placed between the *drbd* driver and the disk on the secondary server, the confirmations are subject to the network latency, which will be noticed in the file system throughput. As we have consistently seen, however, increased reliability rarely comes without a cost of some sort, in this case performance.

drbd supports three different acknowledgment protocols you can choose from to govern the disk write acknowledgment mechanism and balance acceptable performance against the level of reliability in case of failure:

- The fastest operation is achieved using Protocol A, which reports a write to be complete after it has gone to disk on the primary server and been sent over the network to the secondary server. The reliability risk is highest here in the case, for example, of a transaction-processing engine, as a transaction may have been reported complete by the primary node before the transaction data has safely made it across the network to the secondary. Should the primary node fail after acknowledging to its client that the transaction was complete but before the data made it to the secondary, then when the secondary server comes up to serve the database, the completed transaction will not exist in the backup database.

- The second option, Protocol B, is stronger, delaying acknowledgment of the write to the application on the primary server until the data has been safely received by the secondary server. There is still a risk that the secondary server may fail between receiving the data and writing it to disk, of course, but in this case the primary server would still have the data safely stored. There is a small risk if the primary server fails before the secondary server can be recovered. In this case the secondary server would come up as the primary, and its disk would be missing the transaction data. The chances of both servers failing in the same time frame are low, however.

- The final and strongest acknowledgment mechanism, Protocol C, does not signal the write to be complete on the primary until it has been acknowledged that the write is complete all the way to disk at the secondary server. This covers all the bases, but clearly is the slowest option. This may be workable for a fast and short network connection between two servers in a local cluster, but it is unlikely to be practical if the secondary server is many miles distant.

One further issue that needs to be addressed is synchronization. If the secondary server goes down and, for example, after the repair comes back up several hours later, it will be necessary for that server to catch up with the changes that have happened on the primary server during the down time period. *drbd* uses a form of journaling to reduce the amount of data transfer needed on recovery. If the secondary server goes down, the primary server uses a bitmap stored in memory to note which disk blocks were touched while the secondary server was down, and only copies these changed blocks to the secondary servers' mirror when it comes back. The amount of network bandwidth allotted to the synchronization is also limited in order not to adversely affect the production traffic. *drbd* refers to this as *quick synchronization*.

Unfortunately, quick synchronization is not possible following a primary server failure, as the changed blocks bitmap is held in memory on the primary server. If the primary server does a write to disk that does not make it across the network to the secondary server and then fails, the secondary server will take over the application but will be missing the data that was written safely to the primary servers' disk just before the failure. When the primary server returns (acting now as the secondary) there will be inconsistency between the data on the two servers; and no way other than a full synchronization of the two mirrors can correct it. In this case it is critical to determine which of the two versions of the data should be consider to be correct, so *drbd* has a mechanism to determine which of the two copies should be considered up to date and definitive, and will do a full data synchronization accordingly.

Red Hat users need to take note that, like *enbd*, *drbd* is not destined to be supported in future Red Hat distributions. You will need to get the source and compile it yourself. The code as well as documentation and status information on the *drbd* project is available from www.complang.tuwien. ac.at/reisner/drbd.

The discussion of *drbd* has introduced us to the cluster model of assuring highly available data, so the next logical topic to examine is file systems specifically oriented towards cluster operations. As these cluster-oriented file systems largely rely on the concept of the Storage Area Network, however, I need to talk about that first, so that you can place the cluster file systems in proper perspective.

Storage Area Networks

The Storage Area Network (SAN) concept is a fairly new one, born of recent technology advancements in disk peripheral interconnects. The idea of the SAN is to divorce a disk from dependence on a local server for support, instead making the disk simultaneously available via a generic network to multiple servers simultaneously. To understand this concept, consider Figure 9.6.

This figure shows what I will call the traditional means of making disk storage available to a network of servers. As you can see, the physical disk device is connected to a single server using a local bus technology. (The figure uses SCSI, as it is the most commonly used in production server

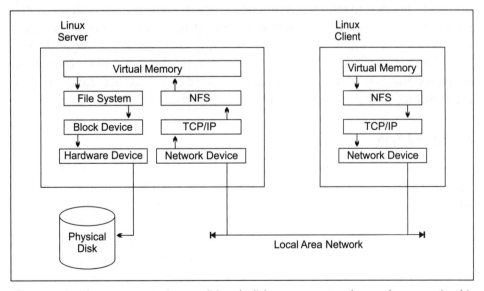

Figure 9.6 The structure of a traditional disk server network can be seen in this illustration.

environments.). The servers themselves are then connected using a LAN technology such as Ethernet. A communications protocol such as TCP/IP operates on the LAN, in conjunction with a data sharing application such as NFS to make data local to any one server available to another. While this approach is stable, well understood and well supported, from a true distributed data standpoint it has several drawbacks, namely:

- The server hosting any disk is a single point of failure for the data stored on that disk.
- There is no way for one server to take over a disk from a failed server without physically moving the disk to the backup server.
- There is no mechanism for duplicating data across multiple disks without additional code such as *enbd* or *drbd*, discussed in earlier sections of this chapter.
- The data transfer speed between disks is limited by the LAN speed and the multiple software layers involved.
- There is no way for more than one server to have direct simultaneous access to the same disk.

These shortcomings are addressed in the SAN model. Consider Figure 9.7.

In this structure, disks are attached simultaneously to several servers using a physical interconnect that provides the speed of a local bus, but the physical connection characteristics of a LAN. By connection characteristics I mean distance between servers and a communications protocol that gives any of the servers the ability to address any disk on the network. In this case, disks become stand alone network storage devices. This interconnect is clearly the key element to a successful SAN. There are currently two technologies in this area: FC-based SAN and iSCSI.

FC-Based SAN

The most common current SAN communications technology is FC. Being light based, FC offers network distances typical of fiber optic systems, allowing distances between devices on an FC network to stretch several miles. Also common to light-based transports, the bandwidth offered is relatively high, in the order of 1 Gb/s. As applied to a SAN, FC is used only as a transport for the tried and true SCSI protocol. This means that each disk on an FC SAN is actually a standard SCSI disk, with the additional FC hardware to allow it to pass SCSI commands across the fiber optic network

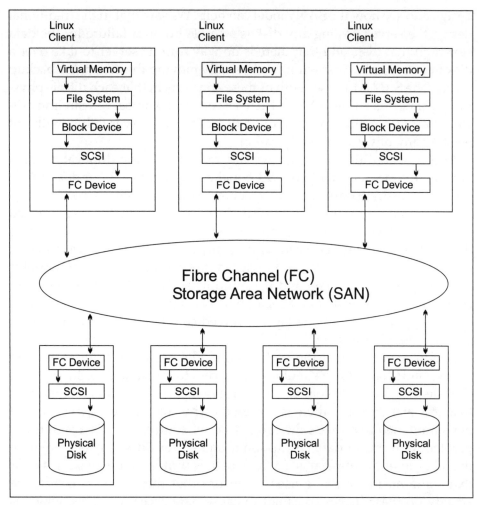

Figure 9.7 Contrast this Storage Area Network structure with the traditional structure of the previous figure.

connection. At the server, each disk device on the SAN appears to the operating system as a locally attached SCSI disk. The operating system treats disk operations exactly as it would for a local SCSI disk, with the commands translated into the appropriate FC commands only at the level of the FC driver. As each drive on the SAN is physically attached via the FC network to several servers, any one drive on the SAN can appear to be local to each server. This is what I have shown in Figure 9.7.

How does this concept address the shortcomings of the traditional file server model listed earlier? Let's revisit the drawbacks of the traditional design and see how the SAN model can help. We saw that in the traditional design the server hosting any disk is a single point of failure for the data stored on that disk, and that there is no way for one server to take over a disk from a failed server without physically moving the disk to the backup server. The SAN addresses both of these concerns in that each disk is physically connected in the SAN to each server; a backup server can immediately start addressing any disk upon detection of a server failure with out needing any physical reconfiguration.

Also, the traditional design has no mechanism for duplicating data across multiple disks without additional code such as *enbd* or *drbd*. In the SAN, each disk appears local to any server, so any combination of disks can be configured into a software RAID in the normal way that locally attached disks would be used. No additional network-based support is required, as the SAN enables any server to address any SAN disk as if it were a local device. The data transfer speed between disks in the traditional model is limited by the LAN speed and the multiple software layers involved. By comparison, the speed of an FC-based SAN is relatively high (1 Gb/s) and the only additional software layer involved compared to a local SCSI disk access is the FC transport.

Finally, we noted that the traditional model has no way for more than one server to have direct simultaneous access to the same disk. In the SAN, all disks are physically connected to all servers, so it is trivial for any server to access any disk and there is no reason why two or more servers could not simultaneously access the same disk. Of course, there is a significant problem in terms of data corruption if one server doesn't cooperate with the other in terms of what and where data is written to the disk. It is clear that some means must be used to ensure that these servers coordinate activity on these drives so as not to cause data access conflicts, which is where cluster file systems come in. We will look at that issue in the *Cluster File Systems* section that follows. Before we leave the topic of the SAN, however, I introduce iSCSI.

iSCSI: The Internet SCSI Protocol

Intended to be competition for FC, iSCSI is an emerging specification that defines a means of transporting SCSI commands over a generic IP-addressed network. It is designed to enable the use of technologies such as gigabit Ethernet to be the transport for a SAN. Development of the iSCSI specification is proceeding under the authority of the IP Storage working group of the Internet Engineering Task Force (IETF). A draft standard was produced in April 2001, and a finished standard was presented for adoption by the Internet Engineering Steering Group (IESG) in the Fall of 2001. As this is a standard currently being formed it will be some time after this writing that iSCSI hardware becomes widely available. However, there are already iSCSI implementations based on the draft specification and a Linux driver is also being developed. As iSCSI becomes more widely supported, it will be presented as a cost effective alternative to FC-based SAN. You should consider it if you intend to build a SAN.

You can monitor the progress of the iSCSI standard at www.ietf.org/html.charters/ips-charter.html and also at www.ece.cmu.edu/~ips. The Linux iSCSI project can be found at sourceforge.net/projects/linux-iscsi.

Cluster File Systems

So far, our discussion of network file systems has only considered the case of a pair of servers that maintain a data mirror. Although this could be considered a simple cluster, it is limited in that only one of the servers is really in production, the other functioning as a life support system for the mirror disk. A more complicated cluster arrangement will scale to more than just two servers, and can see each server in the cluster actively running applications. It also is, as well as being available to stand in on a temporary basis for a failed cluster member. Such a cluster would need a more sophisticated approach to sharing file systems between cluster nodes (as the servers in clusters are typically called) than the network file systems we have seen so far. Certainly to implement a SAN approach to storage, multiple nodes will be connected to multiple network storage devices. In this section I'll present two SAN-aware file systems: the Global File System (GFS) and Inter-Mezzo.

GFS: The Global File System

Begun in 1995 at the University of Minnesota with support from NASA and the U.S. Navy, GFS is now in its fourth generation of development. GFS was originally developed to support multiple cluster node access to large data objects. The first version of GFS was developed on an SGI IRIX platform, and used the new (at the time) FC–based SAN concept. The earliest version of GFS allowed nodes to share disk devices on the SAN using a locking mechanism based on the ability to issue a SCSI command that temporarily reserves a drive for the exclusive use of one node, and then releases it when it is done.

While this allowed disks to be shared, clearly it was an awkward arrangement, as it involved locking the entire disk while one node worked with it. A locking mechanism with better granularity was needed, one that would allow locking at a file-by-file level rather than disk-by-disk. The second generation of GFS added such a fine-grained lock mechanism. At version three, GFS was ported to Linux, as the closed source nature of the IRIX kernel precluded the kernel modifications necessary to move GFS this next step, which incorporated the ability of the Linux nodes on the SAN to cache file data, file system metadata, and file locking data. This caching ability enhanced performance and made the design practicably scaleable to large SAN environments. Finally, the current generation, version four, added a distributed file system journaling mechanism to enhance the reliability of the file system.

GFS has been adopted by Sistina Software to be a core component of their highly available cluster product, which is discussed in Chapter 10. The current version being supported by Sistina as I write is GFS 4.1.1, designed to support kernel 2.4.5. While GFS is a sophisticated and mature distributed file system, there are a few things it doesn't do. Support for using a GFS as a root file system is currently in the alpha stage, and work is underway to remedy shortcomings in GFS support for memory mapped files. (This support is necessary for GFS to be used as a backing store for a Samba server, for example.) The 32-bit kernel limitations that we saw earlier regarding the theoretical upper size of local file systems apply also to GFS, although that should change as the kernel moves to a full 64-bit implementation.

A greater challenge for a distributed file system is the problem of commands like *df* and *du*, as well as implementing disk quotas. Each of these functions requires the ability to scan the entire file system to get summary file system usage statistics. In any distributed file system this is a challenge as any node accessing the file system can write or delete data that would affect the totals, and these servers are simultaneously, and quite likely continuously accessing the storage pool. Thus obtaining an accurate snapshot of true overall usage becomes a challenge. The GFS developers are currently investigating what they term "fuzzy" solutions that give an estimate of true file system usage within a few percent of truth.

GFS currently lacks a scavenging file system checker such as *e2fsck*. On the other hand, the likelihood of needing one is slight. The manner in which GFS servers manage the distributed metadata is such that so long as only one server remains, any pending metadata changes can be resolved using the journaling procedures discussed earlier in this chapter. It would require all of the nodes in a cluster to fail more or less at the same time for the entire file system metadata structure to become irretrievably damaged.

GFS is also not known for its stellar performance; however, the reason for this is a comforting one from the reliability standpoint. The v 4.1.1 release notes observe that, to date, the authors have concentrated on reliability to the exclusion of other aspects. Future work on GFS will be split between bringing in new features and implementing performance enhancements. You can keep track of that work at the GFS home page, www.sistina. com/gfs.

InterMezzo

The last file system to examine is InterMezzo. InterMezzo builds on the Coda distributed file system (www.coda.cs.cmu.edu) developed earlier by Peter Braam at Carnegie Mellon University. InterMezzo is described by its author as a replicating file system. In a paper describing InterMezzo (www.inter-mezzo.org/docs/intermezzo-2001.pdf), Dr. Braam writes:

> Replicating and synchronizing file and directory data to multiple locations is a key problem in networked storage systems. The InterMezzo high availability file system is a powerful tool for attacking this problem. Companies with significant Internet-based operations cannot leave their systems vulnerable to a single point of failure. Web sites and corporate intranets have become of such strategic and operational importance that companies replicate these functions across multiple servers. This kind of clustering satisfies the need for high availability. Successfully deploying high availability clusters depends, however, on having a reliable strategy for replicating and synchronizing across servers. The InterMezzo file system has been designed to address synchronization problems in a scaleable, efficient, and secure manner.

Similar to the network mirrors illustrated in Figure 9.4 and Figure 9.5, InterMezzo maintains replicas of file system data across multiple server machines. If either server fails or the network connection is lost, InterMezzo records file system updates in operation logs. When the server or network problem is resolved, these logs are used to bring all servers up-to-date.

In effect, InterMezzo does a form of cluster-aware journaling. One of the advantages of InterMezzo is that it operates in conjunction with a standard Linux supported file system. The nodes holding the data store it in a local *ext3* or ReiserFS, for example, as they would for any other local storage. InterMezzo then acts as a wrapper around all data flow in and out of these local file systems, tracking data changes made by client nodes and ensuring that any server nodes that have been down will be updated at the next opportunity. The kernel module that implements this wrapper is called *Presto*. Presto intercepts updates made to file system data, writing log records detailing both what was done and which version of the directory or file affected by the update. On an InterMezzo client, the local native file system contains only cached copies of files currently or recently in use. This cache is handled by InterMezzo's *Lento* cache manager. On the server, the disk file system contains authoritative copies of all files in a folder collection.

An interesting side effect of this is that the client nodes can remain disconnected for extended periods of time. In fact, InterMezzo is also proposed as a solution to keeping data stored on laptops that only periodically connect to a central network synchronized with centralized data sources. Because InterMezzo allows simultaneous access to multiple data replicas, it also works well as a backing store for high performance clusters, where for performance reasons large data volumes are spread over multiple server nodes. In this application, Dr. Braam notes that, by using a load balancing mechanism such as round robin DNS or Linux Virtual Servers (discussed in Chapter 10), the outside world sees a single Web server, which is implemented as a clustered service. A clustered service offers both availability and load balancing.

There are limitations, however, and it is important to note that where cluster nodes need simultaneous write access to centrally stored data, InterMezzo may not be the best choice. Dr. Braam cautions:

> Clustered services require multiple instances of Web, e-mail, IMAP, POP, Samba, and other servers, which are running on different systems in the cluster, to have simultaneous access to the underlying file store. This poses challenges to the file system and, while InterMezzo will likely support clustered versions of these services above, it will probably not be capable of allowing concurrent access to a single file such as is needed by clustered databases and clustered NFS file service. For such applications cluster file systems, such as GFS, are likely more suitable.

InterMezzo is not yet at a production release. A beta version was released in November 2000. Work is proceeding, however, and you can track the progress at www.inter-mezzo.org and also at sourceforge.net/ projects/intermezzo.

Data Reliability Isn't Just File Systems

In closing, I want to emphasize that none of the file systems presented in this chapter should be considered a sure ticket to data reliability. While each has features that will clearly reduce your risk, a good file system alone is not a guarantee of data safety. We have seen that while journaling is a reliability improvement, for example, it cannot entirely prevent data loss if a system crashes.

You can choose to look at data reliability two ways. The first approach concentrates on mechanisms to recover from failure. This approach tends to downplay mechanisms that protect against server crashes, relying instead on the storage system's ability to recover from a crash. A focus on journaling and mirrors is characteristic of this approach.

The other approach is to take a more conservative view of the ability of the file system to recover, in fact to assume that it cannot. In this case a crash becomes an event to be avoided at all costs, and your efforts are directed along those lines. In this case many of the hardware reliability and system monitoring issues I detailed in Chapters 3 and 4 become your focus, along with a reliable backup system. The latter approach is the more conservative, but I find it tends to be overlooked in favor of new technologies presented as the final solution to data reliability. The best path is of course to combine both. Do your best to prevent the failure, but at the same time invest in the best disaster recovery technologies to help bring you back from disaster with the least pain. Note also that very reliable servers by and large do not make heavy use of new technologies. You may be accused of lacking faith in new technologies; but while the leading edge is often the fastest and most feature rich, it is not generally seen as the most reliable place to be. Follow new file system technologies by all means. If you do not encourage new technologies, you will not be able to benefit from them as they mature. Install and test the newest code, even participate in beta testing, but never trust your production data to it until you have the highest confidence in that new file system's rock solid stability.

What You Can Do Now

1. Consider whether a journaling file system would reduce your liability to data loss. Take into consideration whether your application already journals data as an internal function.

2. Subscribe to the discussion groups for file systems that interest you and follow the state of the projects, paying attention to features you need that may be lacking, or bugs in functionality critical to your needs. Ask questions specific to your needs; you may be surprised to find that there are others in similar situations to you who are willing to share their experiences.

3. Prepare a server that you can use as a test bed for new file systems, making it resemble your production environment as closely as possible. Use this as your means of building confidence in a new file system.

4. If a SAN or cluster file systems are of interest, read the following chapter and consider whether a highly available cluster would be a good solution for your needs.

Server Clustering

"Union gives strength."
—*Aesop*

Previous chapters examined technologies such as Logical Volume Management and network-oriented file systems. They represent some of the basic building blocks for implementing shared disk storage between multiple servers. The next logical step is to manage such servers as an integrated group, a concept generally called *server clustering*.

This chapter is an examination of this clustering idea. First we'll define what clustering is and list the benefits claimed for it. Then we will examine the structure of a cluster in the general case, defining the major features that make up a cluster. This should help you to judge the relative merits of clustering for your needs. If you like the idea, you will need to know what sort of cluster implementations you have to choose from, so the chapter ends with a review of several cluster implementations, including both open source and commercial offerings.

The Cluster Concept

If you have several servers together in the same room, each performing a separate function, you have a group of servers clustered together, but you would not have what is termed a server cluster. What is the difference between a cluster of servers and a server cluster? A server cluster involves a group of servers that will be managed as a group, so that what happens on one server node (servers within a cluster are commonly called *server nodes*, or simply *nodes*; I'll use this terminology from now on) is reflected in another. This can be for performance purposes, where a heavy load carried by one node may be spread out across others by the cluster management code. It can also be for reliability purposes, so that a failure in any node in the cluster can be covered by bringing in a backup node to fill the gap. These two areas, performance and reliability, are thus the major driving forces behind clusters.

Although there is no single definition of a cluster, you will find that most will have many, if not all of the following elements:

- All of the nodes in the cluster are connected via a LAN. This is not necessarily used for production purposes (although it can be and often is), but primarily provides a communications path to all of the nodes in the cluster for use by the cluster management software.

- Monitoring software running on all nodes in the cluster to report on the status of each node, and possibly also the status of specific applications running on each node.

- Some form of shared data storage is implemented within the cluster, allowing multiple cluster nodes a path to access data stored on any single storage device in the cluster.

- In a reliability-oriented cluster, all of the nodes are connected in some fashion to a hardware-specific control or monitoring mechanism, allowing the physical health of each to be monitored and allowing for remote control of physical functions such as powering a node on and off.

- In a reliability-oriented cluster there will also be a mechanism in place to enable one node to take over the function of another if any of the monitors detects a hardware or software failure within the cluster.

- In a reliability-oriented cluster sufficient hardware redundancy ensures that no piece of hardware constitutes a single point of failure.

- In a performance-oriented cluster, there will be a mechanism in place to monitor the load carried by each node, and a means to redistribute that load among nodes in the cluster in order to maintain optimum performance from the cluster as a whole.

Figure 10.1 illustrates a generic server cluster, including each of the elements in this list.

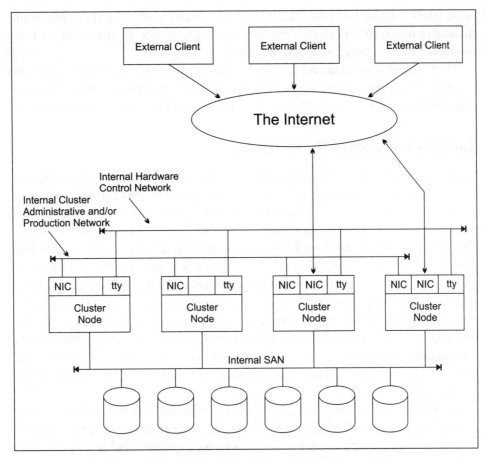

Figure 10.1 The basic components of a server cluster are illustrated here.

The nature of the hardware control network varies widely from cluster to cluster. In Figure 10.1 it is shown as a bus connection between multiple *tty* (that is, RS-232 serial protocol) ports. Some clusters use this type of connection for a *heartbeat*. This is a periodic signal sent from one node to another to ensure that the sending node is still working. A duplicate heartbeat is usually sent across the local cluster administrative network. The presence or absence of either or both of these signals can then be used to determine whether a node has failed completely or is experiencing network problems.

This distinction is important to make, as it affects the fail-over decision. If a node has failed completely, in which case neither heartbeat signal is present, then a complete fail-over to a backup node is indicated. If the network heartbeat is gone, but the serial heartbeat is still present, then a problem with the cluster administrative network is indicated. In this case the node itself may be just fine, and still quite properly serving its application through an external network connection to its clients. In this case no fail-over may be necessary, or even desirable.

What benefits are claimed for this model of collecting individual servers together into centrally managed clusters? As we observed earlier, the two primary benefits are availability and performance. Let's see how each works.

Server Availability Benefits

Clearly one of the advantages of clustering is the ability to designate a standby node for any production node in the cluster, and put into place an automated monitoring and fail-over mechanism. Thus a node failure can be recovered quickly and automatically. Used in conjunction with shared disk storage and journaling file systems (see Chapter 9, "Alternative File Systems") and applications, it is possible for a node fail-over to be completely transparent, in the ideal case, so that no data or transactions are affected. There are limitations to this, however, and realistically it is more common to find that a small amount of data or a few transactions may be affected by the fail-over. This is still far preferable, however, to the sort of production outage that would be the case for a manual monitoring and fail-over. In that case it could take minutes or hours for the failure to be detected and recovered.

Clusters also offer other reliability enhancements. The centralized nature of their management tends to make it easier to monitor multiple nodes effectively, encouraging centralized backups, logging, and software management, for example. It also encourages standardization. It is much easier to manage 10 cluster nodes if they are more or less identical. The greater the commonality of hardware and software, the easier it is to manage systems, as there are fewer variables to deal with, which encourages stability and reliability. Change tends to be managed more carefully, too, as a single change now has the potential to affect the entire cluster, rather than only one machine. This tends to enforce a conservative approach to cluster management.

There is of course a tension between this conservatism and market pressures urging you to implement the latest technologies. Being on the leading edge of technology rarely improves reliability, however, and every business needs to find that balance between the two that maintains a competitive edge in the market without creating a reputation for slow or unreliable service. Clusters can help the transition to new technologies as it may be possible to implement the new application on a node backed up by a node using the older, stable technology. This makes it possible to experiment with slipping the new technology into production either in parallel with the old, or as a replacement for the old. If problems arise with the new technology in the latter case, a fail-over to the old technology offers a plausible safety net.

Scalable Performance Benefits

The second basic reason for clustering is scalable performance. Note that I did not say just performance, but *scalable* performance. If better performance alone is what you want, you can buy a bigger, faster server. When you do, however, you will have to make a transition from your current server to the new one. It may be that this transition requires a different operating system or application environment to support the new server, so the transition from less to more power may not be seamless. In addition, the new server replaces the old one, leaving you with a used piece of hardware. It is well known that computer hardware depreciates in value faster than ice cream melts in the sun, so this is liable to cost you money. The advantage of a performance-oriented cluster lies in its ability to allow the incremental addition of computing capacity by adding more nodes to the cluster. Each node retains the same operating system and application environment as its peers in the cluster, and the old nodes continue to carry as much of the performance burden as they are capable of carrying, for as long as you choose to keep them in production. Furthermore, the addition of the extra capacity should involve little or no disruption in service.

I have made the point before that there is a connection between performance and reliability in that if your production environment can not keep up with demand, the perception this gives the end user can be one of unreliability as much as slow service, especially if the slow service causes client software to time out and give up on service requests. Also, overloaded servers will have a greater tendency to fail under excessive load, either from a software standpoint (buffers or queues that overflow and cause software failure) or a hardware standpoint (overloaded disks that fail prematurely due to continuously heavy use). Thus the ability of the cluster concept to flexibly scale capacity to meet demand with minimum restructuring overhead and downtime could also be considered a reliability advantage.

Cluster Architecture

Take another look at Figure 10.1, noting of the elements in the generic server cluster. In this section we will examine each of these elements separately.

Any cluster will incorporate some of these elements, although some cluster implementations that are oriented more towards performance than availability or vice versa may not include all of them. The final section of this chapter examines several specific cluster implementations, and you will see how each does or does not incorporate these elements.

Hardware Monitoring and Control

A cluster generally includes some means of monitoring, and in some clusters also controlling the state of its hardware. This can vary from simply determining if a node is functioning at all, to more sophisticated monitoring. Some clusters offer specialized hardware that incorporates monitoring sensors having similar functionality to the sensors we looked at in Chapter 3, "Choosing the Right Hardware." In some cases there may be a dedicated communications network set aside specifically for hardware-related sensor data. This is the most sophisticated approach, and is what I have illustrated in Figure 10.1, labeled as the Internal Hardware Control Network. In the figure the interface between nodes and this network is designated *tty*, implying an RS-232 serial connection, which is the most common form used in Linux clusters.

This hard-wired connection is used for what is termed *heartbeating* and in some clusters for hardware control. The heartbeat function of the hardware control connection is an important element in allowing the backup node to discern what the problem may be with a production node. If the application hosted by the production node disappears, it is possible that the node has failed, but that is not certain. It may be that there has been a network failure, or a problem in the disk storage system, for example. The hardware heartbeat connection is designed to enable the backup node to determine if the production has in fact failed, or whether it is still running, but experiencing some other problem that is making the application unavailable. The answers to these questions will affect how the backup server should behave. If the application were to disappear, yet the backup node is still getting a heartbeat from the production node, then the backup node may choose to delay a takeover in the hope that the production node may be able to recover itself. For example, consider the case in which a network failure is the cause of the outage. To guard against this failure mode, both nodes can be equipped with a second network connection to a parallel, redundant network. The production node would be able to fail-over to the backup network, and the backup node does not need to do anything. If, on the other hand, the backup node detects no heartbeat from the production node, then it will need to take over the application immediately.

This raises another issue: If the backup node decides to take over, but the real problem with the production node happened to be a transient one, there is a risk that the original production node could recover and try to return to service the application after the backup node has become active. This risks both nodes believing themselves to be in control of the application and attempting to access common data, a problem termed the *split-brain* scenario. The application making use of the data may not be written to cope with this possibility. The result is that neither node functions properly-or worse, both try to work and end up corrupting the production database. In the case of a takeover, then, it is useful for the backup node to be able to exercise hardware control over the production node, actually shutting the production node down as a part of the takeover process to ensure that there can be no conflict between the two. (In documentation you will usually see this function referenced by the acronym STONITH, which stands for Shoot the Other Node in the Head.) For this, the hardware network must allow commands to be issued between nodes as well as heartbeat messaging. This may involve specialized control hardware in addition to the hardware network itself.

Software Monitoring and Control

Clusters will usually include a means of monitoring the availability and/or performance of discrete software components. This involves code installed on cluster nodes designed to track specific applications. In some clusters, a separate network is set aside for the use of these monitors. In the same way that a loss of a heartbeat on the hardware monitor will initiate a takeover, the loss of an application detected by the software monitor can also initiate a takeover. The software monitor network can also operate in conjunction with the hardware monitor in a process of elimination to isolate the cause of a problem. For example, if the software monitor detects the loss of an application, yet the hardware monitor indicated that the node running the application is still functioning, then the next step may be to check for a network failure. If that turns out to be the source of the trouble, the fix may be to direct the production node to switch to the backup network, rather than a complete fail-over to a backup node. This suggests that, like the hardware network, the software monitor must also be able to exercise a degree of control over the nodes, issuing commands across the cluster administrative network as appropriate to manage recovery procedures.

In some clusters a separate node is set aside to perform this monitoring and control function, while in others the function is distributed collectively over all the nodes. In the case of a performance-oriented cluster, one node may be designated as a workload manager. This node would typically act as the entrance to the cluster as seen by external clients. It would monitor the production nodes to see how heavily loaded each is, and dynamically direct incoming queries to the least loaded node. In the case of the availability-oriented cluster, a single control node becomes a central point of control for the cluster. In this case the control node may host a database of cluster related information. This database is used to manage things like software distribution or individual node configuration, as well as being a central point for monitoring and controlling the cluster.

High-Speed Network Fabric

The last major element in a server cluster is usually a high speed data interconnect between the nodes, and possibly also to client networks outside the cluster. This network may be used to support shared storage, in which case it is performing the function of a Storage Area Network (SAN). It may be used for data transfer between nodes, commonly the case for performance-oriented clusters whose nodes are set to work in parallel to solve a large problem. In this case nodes may need to share data between themselves and can make good use of a fast interconnect. If there is a substantial flow of data in and out of the cluster as a whole, this interconnect is the highway to distribute that flow to all of the nodes. This high-speed network may also be used for internal maintenance functions such as software distribution and maintenance or node backup and restore.

Most clusters use generic technologies such as Ethernet or FC to implement this network, but some choose specialized proprietary technologies where very high performance is required. It is important to note that this high-speed network is not a requirement for every cluster. In the case of a cluster made up primarily of production and backup node pairs, for example, it may not be necessary to implement a cluster-wide fast network. If the storage to be shared is only shared between each of the node pairs, then each pair need only share a SCSI bus.

Cluster Implementations

Now that we have a picture of the generic cluster structure, we'll look at several cluster implementations currently available or in development. We will see how each approaches the task of implementing hardware monitoring and control, software monitoring and control, and the high-speed interconnect. Keep in mind as you review these choices that the open source principle of encouraging multiple parallel solutions to a challenge in order to let the best one win is evident here. It is likely that some of these projects will either die, be merged together, or simply be discarded as interesting but not as good as another. At this point in time, clustering is in its first generation and there will be a great deal of innovation and change in this area in the future.

The Linux High Availability (HA) Project

The Linux HA Project is a purely open source, community-based project aimed at producing a primarily reliability-oriented cluster structure. Linux HA had its genesis with Alan Robertson's *heartbeat* code, originally developed early in 1999. *heartbeat* supports monitoring of cluster nodes to determine their availability using either serial, TCP/IP, or PPP connections. It supports multiple IP addresses, but in its current version (v 0.4.9) scales to only a two-node primary-backup configuration. It is said to work well with applications such as DNS, Web, or proxy servers as these applications carry maintain minimal state and support built-in replication, and can easily use storage provided by a second back-end server. *heartbeat* is free, distributed under the GPL.

To date *heartbeat* is the only substantive piece of code the Linux HA project has produced, but the project has also served the purpose of drawing interest and focusing attention on the need for a good HA solution as Linux moves into the commercial server mainstream. The HA project Web site, linux-ha.org, is home to *heartbeat*, as well as being an excellent place to go for good reading on the subject, including several design proposals for future open source cluster development, and a wealth of links to a variety of interesting HA related sites and topics.

The Linux Virtual Server (LVS) Project

The LVS Project is another open source community project. The goal is to produce an infrastructure to allow a scaleable, reliable cluster that appears to the end user as a single machine. This is achieved using the cluster architecture shown in Figure 10.2.

The entire structure within the dashed rectangle in the figure is the LVS. There is only one entry point to the cluster, the single IP address entering at the top of the virtual server. To the outside world, this single address is all that is visible; hence, the entire cluster appears to be a single server. All requests entering the LVS pass through this external IP address to the

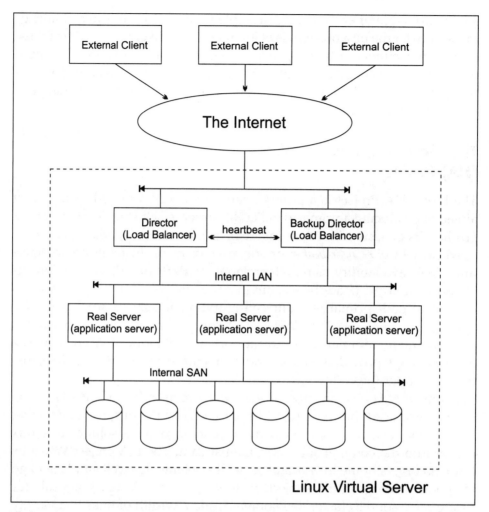

Figure 10.2   The architecture of a Linux Virtual Server Cluster is shown here.

primary load balancer, and are directed to cluster nodes via an internal LAN. The cluster nodes run the actual application code to service the client request, which must return to the client back through the load balancer node.

The LVS applies specific terms to these components. The load balancer being is the *director* and the server nodes in the cluster are the *real servers*. I'll use these terms from now on.

The director is termed a level-four switch. It is a switch in that it alters or switches the route the client request takes to get to a server. *Level four* refers to the Open Systems Foundation (OSF) generic network model, where level four is the level associated with packet routing. At this level the director is only concerned with the destination of the packet, not the content; hence the director is application neutral. It neither knows nor cares what application the packet is destined for, and so requires no application-specific configuration. The director can be configured to do the address switching using either Network Address Translation (NAT), direct IP routing, or an IP tunnel.

Load balancing is achieved using a configurable choice of several different algorithms, depending on which gives the best performance for the usage patterns of a particular cluster. If one of the real servers fails, monitors internal to the LVS will inform the director, and the failed node will be removed from the director's list of available real servers. In this fashion the director performs both a performance management and availability function. The director itself is still a single point of failure, however, so a highly available LVS requires a backup director. In this case some form of heartbeat must be used to monitor for, detect, and recover from failure of the primary director.

The LVS project has over time used several different director monitoring and fail-over mechanisms. The current LVS HOWTO documents the use of several utilities acting in concert. Detection of a failure at the real-server level is done using *mon*, the same network service monitoring utility we saw in Chapter 6, "Monitoring Linux in Production." For heartbeat and failure detection between the directors the LVS uses the *heartbeat* utility from the Linux HA project we just reviewed. IP address takeover by the backup director from the primary is done using a utility called *fake*, which was at one time a separate utility, but now ships as a part of *heartbeat*. To complete a HA LVS implementation, a fault tolerant file system also is necessary for the shared data storage on the internal SAN. The HOWTO suggests the Coda file system, although GFS or InterMezzo as detailed in Chapter 9 should also be viable options.

There is no significant software limitation on the number of real servers in an LVS, and it is useful to note that the real servers need not be Linux machines, as long as they support the necessary application. If non-Linux real servers were used, however, suitable monitors would have to run on them such that a failure would be reported to the director; otherwise the reliability benefit is lost. Although large numbers of real servers are possible, there can be only one director, which may pose scaling problems. As the balancing code is implemented in the kernel, however, it is reasonably efficient and a large director should be able to keep a sizable real-server farm busy with work.

To date, the LVS has seen several successful production applications, including Network Appliances, Inc. (www.internetappliance.com), which markets a Web server appliance that relies on the Linux kernel LVS code at its heart. The LVS project Web site has links to several detailed performance analyses of LVS clusters; it also is the site from which to download the code and follow its progress. The URL is www.linuxvirtualserver.org.

The Red Hat High Availability Server

Red Hat's entry in the HA cluster field has the same architecture as the LVS cluster, and uses some of the same components. Currently built on their v6.2 distribution, the Red Hat HA Server relies on the LVS kernel code to provide scalable and reliable services in the same way an LVS cluster does. Red Hat's cluster uses different availability utilities, however. Heartbeat and failure detection for the directors is provided by the *pulse* utility, while monitoring of the real servers is handled by the *nanny* utility. IP address fail-over for the directors is handled by the *fos* daemon. Red Hat calls this collection of HA utilities when used in conjunction with the LVS kernel code *piranha*. The packaging of *piranha* together with the v6.2 distribution, a kernel compiled to support *piranha* and LVS, a Web-based configuration GUI, and an online support package, together make up the commercial Red Hat HA Server offering. The Red Hat HA Server code is itself all open source, and is available for download directly under the terms of the GPL. Find out more from ha.redhat.com.

VAnessa

VA Network Enhanced Scalable Server Architecture (VAnessa) is a clustering solution sponsored by VA Linux. Two components make up VAnessa, a cluster implementation named *UltraMonkey*, and what VA Linux terms a "Global Load Balancer," named *SuperSparrow*. Like the Red Hat HA Server, UltraMonkey is a variant of the LVS model. The architecture is pure LVS, the load balancing being done by the LVS kernel code. Heartbeating and fail-over for the directors uses *heartbeat*, while monitoring of the real servers is done using *ldirectord*, another open source service monitor with functionality similar to *nanny* and *mon*. The current version of UltraMonkey (v1.0.2) is packaged to work with VALinux' VA-Enhanced v6.2.4 distribution. This is based on the Red Hat v6.2 distribution, so UltraMonkey should also work with a Red Hat v6.2 installation.

The other element of VAnessa is SuperSparrow. This is an interesting piece of code, offering the ability to re direct network client queries to multiple servers that may be widely distributed geographically. The object is to direct the query to the server geographically closest to the client that originated the request, thereby minimizing network distances and, hopefully, improving performance. SuperSparrow uses Border Gateway Protocol (BGP) routing information as the basis for its routing decisions. BGP is the communications protocol used by large volume Internet routers to build routing tables. SuperSparrow needs access to a BGP router, which can be provided either by a Linux server running routing software such as *zebra* (www.zebra.org) or *gated* (open source *gated* implementations are normally included in a Linux distribution). Both support BGP or run from hardware routers with an operating system such as Cisco's Internet Operating System (IOS). Although SuperSparrow is primarily targeted at improving performance, there is no reason why it could not also be used to support a reliable server concept built on geographically separate servers. This would in effect form a dynamic site loss backup solution.

Further information about VAnessa can be found at vanessa.source-forge.net. UltraMonkey information is available from ultramonkey.source-forge.net, and the SuperSparrow nests at supersparrow.sourceforge.net.

FailSafe

FailSafe is an HA cluster solution developed by Silicon Graphics (SGI) for their enterprise servers running SGI's commercial UNIX variant, IRIX. A Linux port of FailSafe was released by SGI in September, 2000. The current version of this port is 1.0.2, which SGI has made freely available under the terms of the GPL. FailSafe is a much more widely ranging clustering solution than either the Linux HA project or any of the LVS variants. Here are the major features of Linux FailSafe:

Cluster scalability. A Linux FailSafe cluster can scale to 16 functional nodes.

Multiple fail-over options. There are several options for failing nodes over to a backup, including designating one spare node as a backup for several production nodes, providing an ordered list of several possible backup servers for each cluster application, prioritizing the importance of specific applications in terms of fail-over processing, or using cascading fail-over lists to provide for the possibility of multiple cluster node failures.

Local fail-over. FailSafe supports attempting to clean up and restart an application locally before resorting to a fail-over to a backup node.

Fine-grain fail-over. In a case of an application failure on a server providing more than one application such that the other applications on the server are still able to run, fine-grain fail-over will move only the failed application to a backup without needing to fail over the entire node.

Dynamic management. Management and configuration of FailSafe and the applications monitors can be done dynamically from a single point of control using a GUI interface.

Hardware Control. Linux FailSafe includes a hardware control facility to support physically resetting failed nodes, ensuring that potential contention for shared resources between a failed node and its backup are avoided. (See the discussion on STONITH in the *Hardware Monitoring and Control* section earlier in this chapter.)

The FailSafe architecture includes all of the elements illustrated in the generic cluster architecture shown in Figure 10.1. FailSafe is primarily a reliability-oriented cluster, thus in contrast to the LVS, it has no load balancing or other performance-oriented features, Instead, it has a greater degree of scalability and a much greater degree of configuration flexibility.

FailSafe maintains a shared database of availability data that is replicated across all nodes in a cluster. It maintains information that is not only node specific, but also application specific, and has the ability to facilitate messaging between application instances necessary to support complex applications such as databases that concurrently access a central data repository. FailSafe also supports a plug-in capability that allows it to tailor monitoring and fail-over behavior to suit specific applications. Support modules are available for generic services such as IP addressing, NFS, Samba, and the Apache Web server, as well as specific enterprise applications including SAP (both the SAP R/3 central instance and the SAP database server are supported) and IBM's db2.

Like the XFS port, the Linux FailSafe port seems to have the active support of SGI, which is good; but with any port the reliability and performance of the parent product may not always be duplicated in the earliest releases of the ported version. The wide-ranging functionality and support of SGI, however, should make FailSafe a major player in the Linux HA arena. The Linux FailSafe project distributes its code under the terms of the GPL from its Web home at oss.sgi.com/projects/failsafe.

Blue Hammer

Blue Hammer is similar to FailSafe in that it is a port of a preexisting commercial product to the open source world. In the case of Blue Hammer, the product is IBM's Parallel Systems Support Programs (PSSP).

PSSP is the management and monitoring infrastructure originally developed for IBM's UNIX-based parallel processing machine, the RS/6000 SP (Scalable Powerparallel) server, the largest computing machine IBM has ever made.

To give you an idea how large an SP can be, the biggest SP now in existence is one of several supercomputers funded under the U.S. government's American Supercomputing Initiative (ASCI) program. Code-named ASCI White, it is located at the Lawrence Livermore Laboratory in California. With 8,192 processors, 6 TB of real memory and 160 TB of disk storage, ASCI White is counted by many to be the largest computer in the world. Other well-known SPs include Deep Blue, the chess champion, and the record-setting Web servers IBM supplied for the last several Olympic games. Until recently PSSP was restricted to use within the specialized hardware environment of an SP. Recently, however, IBM has begun to wean PSSP away from the SP hardware product. Renamed Blue Hammer, PSSP can already be used to support a cluster of large RS/6000 servers without requiring any SP hardware. One of the spin-off benefits of this has been the announced intent to port PSSP outside of AIX (IBM's UNIX variant) into the Linux world under the name Baby Blue Hammer. The first release of Baby Blue Hammer is planned for late 2001.

If, when it arrives, Baby Blue Hammer includes all of the functionality of PSSP, then it will look much like FailSafe, as the software architecture and features list are similar. Baby Blue Hammer would differ from FailSafe, however, in two respects. One is IBM's use of a single server to act as a cluster controller. This machine, termed the Control Workstation (CWS), holds a database of cluster management information and provides a central point of control for cluster operations. The CWS performs a variety of tasks, some of which are optional, as the cluster administrator chooses. Included in the task list are

- Software installation, maintenance, backup, and restoration management
- Node and application health and performance monitoring
- User database administration
- Secure platform for remote administration commands
- Central point of contact and control for configurable, event-driven system monitoring and control infrastructure

This last point deserves further examination. It refers to a functional subset of PSSP called Reliable Scalable Cluster Technology (RSCT). This introduces a distributed database that works in conjunction with monitor daemons running on each cluster node to collect a broad range of operational data and make the data available to clients through an open programming interface. This database is then mated with an event engine, allowing the cluster administrator to choose discrete variables, and set threshold levels above which alarms can be set and automatic recovery actions initiated. This is a sophisticated and well-tried infrastructure that has proved to be successful in building many of the largest UNIX clusters in operation today. While this is very positive, it remains to be seen how much PSSP functionality carries over to the Linux port. As it happens, a large part of PSSP is written in Perl, which will speed the porting task.

The second point of difference between Baby Blue Hammer and FailSafe is that, unlike FailSafe, Baby Blue Hammer should not be expected to include fail-over management capabilities. While it has a sophisticated monitoring ability, in the SP world the task of managing fail-over falls to a separate IBM product, High Availability Cluster Multi Processing (HACMP), and at the current time I am not aware of any plan to port HACMP to Linux. What IBM can offer that FailSafe does not, however, is the promise to port General Parallel File System (GPFS) to Linux in conjunction with the PSSP port. This will make yet another well-proven network file system available to the Linux cluster.

GPFS has been production proven capable of allowing multi terabyte file systems at data transfer rates of as much as 1.2 GB/s. While these rates were obtained in an SP using the very high-speed proprietary SP Switch network technology, these numbers reflect GPFS' ability to effectively spread data transfer overhead across multiple cluster nodes. If one were to build a GPFS cluster using a SAN fabric such as gigabit Ethernet or an FC switch, the network is more likely to be the bottleneck than the file system structure. In the SP, GPFS management is centralized and integrated into the PSSP product, and I would expect that structure to carry over to Baby Blue Hammer.

At the time of this writing, there is no Web site dedicated to this project. Expect news to appear late in 2001 at IBM's open source Web site, oss.software.ibm.com.

Convolo/Kimberlite

Convolo is a commercial cluster offering from Mission Critical Linux Inc., based on the Kimberlite open source cluster developed by the same company. Similar to the Linux HA cluster, Kimberlite is a server pair configuration. The two server nodes are connected to a shared-disk subsystem, typically either a twin-tailed SCSI channel or an FC loop, and operate in either an active-active or active-standby mode.

An active-active cluster implies that both servers support live applications concurrently. If either should fail, the remaining server simply continues to serve the application. In this case the cluster performs both a simple load balancing function as well as supporting failure coverage. If the servers serve different applications, then the surviving server can take over the service provided by the failed server, and vice versa, assuming there is sufficient capacity on each server to do it.

The active-standby configuration, as the name implies would see one active production server backed up by a warm standby unit. Kimberlite uses both an IP network and a hard-wired serial connection for monitoring and control within the cluster pair. Hardware permitting, the serial connection supports STONITH hardware control to prevent contention between servers if a hung server recovers after the application has been failed over.

The commercial Convolo product adds several features to the open source Kimberlite cluster. At the current release of Convolo, v2.0, these features include

- Full NFS fail-over support, including lock fail-over and complete access granting capabilities
- Samba fail-over support
- 90 days of support technical support
- Binary distribution, including easy to use installation and configuration verification utilities
- Configuration GUI
- Noninteractive management interfaces to facilitate integrating Convolo into appliance deployments
- Integration with Mission Critical Linux' other tools for support and remote monitoring and maintenance
- Extensive quality assurance testing
- Hard copy and online documentation

A fully redundant Convolo cluster pair designed to provide no single point of failure hardware redundancy is shown in Figure 10.3.

This arrangement is similar to the generic cluster architecture of Figure 10.1, although additional serial connections in this case include a

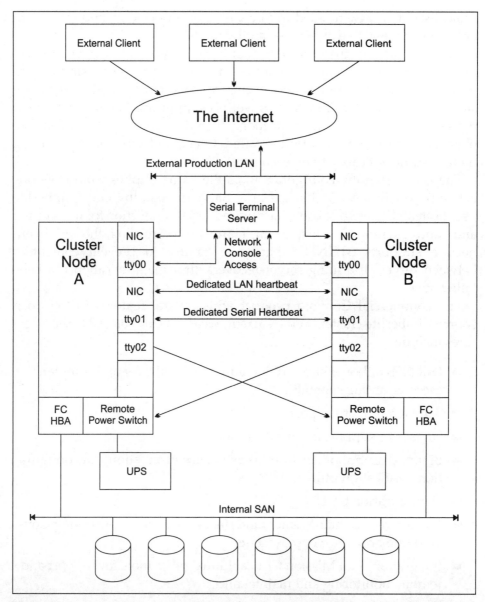

Figure 10.3 This is what a Convolo cluster pair configured with no single point of failure would look like.

terminal server for console access to the nodes, and a separate hardware switch to allow a standard *tty* port to perform STONITH control. This two-node architecture is typical of most cluster pair architectures. More information on Convolo and Kimberlite as well as downloads of the Kimberlite code can be found at www.missioncriticallinux.com.

LifeKeeper (SteelEye)

LifeKeeper is the flagship product of SteelEye Technologies. SteelEye bought LifeKeeper from its original developers, NCR, early in 2000. When supported by NCR, LifeKeeper was successfully marketed to the Fortune 500 market, supporting platforms including Solaris, Windows NT, and NCRSVR4MP, NCR's UNIX offering. In June 2000 the first Linux Life-Keeper port, v3.0, was released, followed by v3.1 in January 2001. Life-Keeper, like FailSafe and Blue Hammer, is a fully scalable cluster, supporting up to 16 nodes in several fail-over configurations (with some configurations supporting more than 16 nodes). A LifeKeeper cluster would have an architecture similar to the generic structure shown in Figure 10.1.

Here is a list of key LifeKeeper features:

- Application Recovery Kits (ARKs) to support off-the-shelf applications and eliminate single points of failure; supported applications include Oracle Net8 Listener, SSL support for Apache Web server, Informix, Sybase, MySQL, MS SQL Server, IBM DB2, MS IIS, MS Exchange, SAP R/3, Sendmail, and Lotus Domino

- Support for Network File System (NFS) as well as NTFS and JFS (journaling file systems), such as *ext3* and *ReiserFS*

- Plug-and-play integration and certified support for servers from multiple vendors, including Compaq, Dell, Hewlett-Packard, and IBM

- Integrated support for Fibre Channel-based SAN storage

- Support for several Linux distributions, including Red Hat 7.0, Caldera eServer 2.3, SuSE 7.1, and TurboLinux (planned for Q2 2001)

- SNMP support allows integration of LifeKeeper with any SNMP-aware network management system, such as HP OpenView and IBM Tivoli

- Tunable heartbeats support fine-tuning failure detection speed and recovery

- Software Developer's Kit (SDK) to enable LifeKeeper customization for customer-specific needs

LifeKeeper also offers an optional add-on, LifeKeeper Data Replication. This is an interesting extension to a cluster product, offering the same network data replication functionality as *drbd*, or *enbd* used to implement a network RAID, as described in Chapter 9. The v3.1 LifeKeeper release has been chosen by Compaq as an availability solution of choice to be promoted for use with ProLiant-based turnkey cluster solutions marketed by Compaq. Further information about LifeKeeper can be found at www.steeleye.com.

Cluster WorX

Cluster WorX is a product of Linux NetworX, a vendor of turnkey Linux cluster solutions. Scaling to large numbers of nodes, Cluster WorX offers a Java-based GUI interface that enables remote monitoring of a variety of hardware and operating system parameters within a cluster. Cluster WorX is marketed in conjunction with Linux NetworX hardware cluster installations, but, as of v2.0, is not available as a stand alone product. Linux NetworX makes these claims for Cluster WorX:

- Complete GUI cluster monitoring
- Complete module power, temperature, network, and process monitoring
- Automatic administrator event notification
- Disk cloning to load OS and applications
- Compatible with SSL and Apache
- Secure remote access with any Java-enhanced browser

Like a Blue Hammer, FailSafe, or LifeKeeper cluster, a Cluster WorX cluster has an architecture similar to the generic structure shown in Figure 10.1. The key difference would is that at the current release, v2.0, Cluster WorX is tied to a turnkey Linux NetworX cluster solution. Further information on Cluster WorX and Linux NetworX clusters can be found at www.linuxnetworx.com.

What You Can Do Now

1. Evaluate your production environment and assess the merits of using a cluster or clusters to improve either the reliability or performance of your production applications.

2. If you decide a cluster would be helpful, evaluate the abilities of each of the cluster implementations reviewed in this chapter to determine which makes the most sense for you.

3. Make a transition plan to move from a non clustered to a clustered environment. Make sure you have a transition path that always has a fallback in case something goes wrong.

4. Install the cluster and become familiar with its mechanisms before going in to production. Be especially careful to thoroughly test the fail-over mechanisms first. Usually the most difficult part of a high availability cluster implementation is not the cluster software or its operation, but the scripts necessary to fail the application over. Make sure to allow time to develop and test these fail-over procedures.

5. Get the most from your new cluster by ensuring that any new applications are implemented within the cluster structure to gain the full benefit of your investment in clustering.

Sample Business Recovery Plan

This appendix outlines a sample Business Recovery (BR) plan to give you a framework for developing your own. I have simplified the process so that you can get a sight of the forest without being impeded by the trees.

Your actual BR plan will no doubt be more complex and take some time to develop, as it should. After all, it is designed to safeguard your most critical business technology and thus should not be something quickly thrown together.

The hypothetical company used for our sample BR plan operates a wholesale-to-retail distribution business from three separate sites. Technology has been leveraged to provide the maximum convenience for customers, who may order goods online, and have the goods delivered from one of the two company warehouses, one of which is close to the head office, the other 500 miles distant. Yours is a competitive business, processing several thousand orders each business day. Your customers value rapid order processing and shipping, and your hope is that the new highly automated system will allow you to process and ship orders faster than your competition. Your customers like the idea, but they have to be sure that the system is reliable; otherwise you will lose their business. The company as a whole employs 50 people, and has annual revenue of $125,000 per employee, for a total gross revenue of $6.25 million.

The head office location has three Linux servers. One is a samba file and print server supporting day-to-day business function applications such as personnel management, word processing, communications, and financial functions such as payroll, receivables, and payables. Most of these applications run on Windows desktop machines, but all of the data resides on the samba file server, and they all print through the Linux print server. The second Linux server at the head office is an online transaction processing business-to-business Web server. This server provides the public Web interface that allows customers to place and track their orders. It must handle all of the financial side of the billing process for the customer, as well as interfacing to the fulfillment system at the warehouses that takes care of maintaining stock and assures delivery to customers. The third Linux server is the network gateway from the head office to the Internet and it implements a firewall. All network traffic in and out of the head office passes through this third machine.

Each of the warehouses has a Linux server hosting the fulfillment software that gets its orders from the Web-based business-to-business application hosted at the head office. This warehouse server takes as input orders to be shipped, and generates inventory debit and credit data as a result of the goods being shipped and received from and to the warehouse. As output, it generates pick lists and assigns shipments to each of the delivery routes running from that warehouse. This system also provides order-tracking information for any currently active order. To protect the Internet communications path from the warehouses to the head office, a second Linux server is installed at each warehouse to function as a firewall. Finally, similar to the head office location, a file and print server supports local PC clients used to record day-to-day operational data such as time cards and absentee reports back to the head office. An encrypted email client is used to do this.

Where to Start

The first thing to do is to produce a network topology diagram. This will help you keep track of each piece of computing hardware and the physical relationship between them. From this you can gain an overall view of the operation. A large-scale diagram showing the overall operation would look similar to Figure A.1.

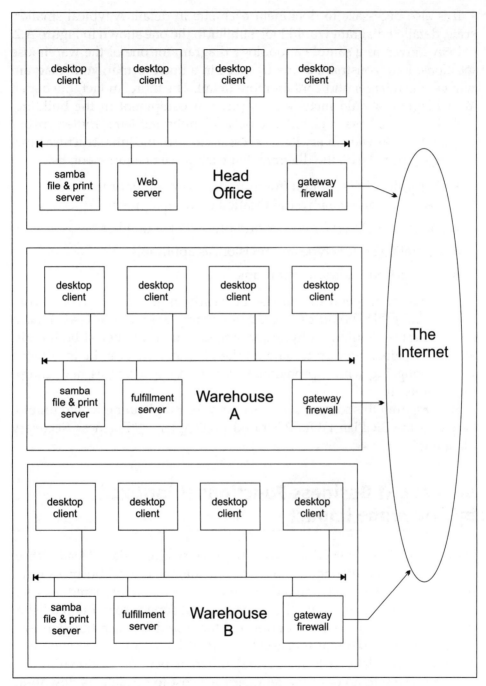

Figure A.1   A large-scale network topology diagram shows an overall corporate operation.

It is also necessary to document each site in detail. A typical smaller-scale, detailed diagram would look similar to the one shown in Figure A.2.

I have given as a sample a topology diagram for one of the warehouse locations. I am constrained due to space in a book format; your diagram will be much larger and contain more detail. The more, in fact, the better. Your diagram should include each piece of equipment in the building, including not only servers, but also network hubs, modems, routers, printers, and UPSs as well. Every item necessary to keep the infrastructure functioning needs to be on the diagram. For each piece of equipment, list:

- A functional description (for example, print server or mailroom LAN hub) and the physical location of the equipment
- Make, model, serial number, and property tag number
- Operating system type and revision, as applicable
- Network addresses, as applicable

Each data connection should also be clearly indicated. The type of connection and cable should be labeled (for example, RS 232 or CAT5). Each network cable should be physically tagged with a number at both ends, and that number kept up-to-date on the diagram. This can be invaluable when debugging wiring problems or when restructuring as new equipment comes in.

Starting from this scenario, here is how your BR planning would unfold, based on the BR Plan HOWTO found in Chapter 1, "Business Recovery Planning."

Step 1: List Business Functions Prioritized by Downtime Impact

Start by dividing your efforts over the three working sites: Head Office, Warehouse A, and Warehouse B. For each site, the critical business functions must be identified, and a downtime cost estimate prepared. At each location, hold meetings with the managers and supervisors. Build a list of the major business functions performed there, and for each function estimate the cost should that function be unavailable as a result of computer downtime. Tabulate costs for several different periods of downtime in order to take into account the tendency for cost to escalate as downtime periods increase, as noted in the text. You can use the sample given in the sidebar "How Much Is This Going to Cost Me?" in Chapter 1 to get you

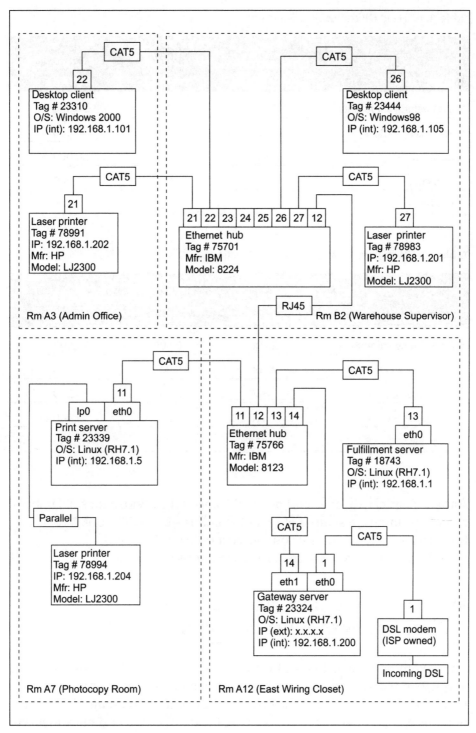

Figure A.2   A smaller-scale network topology diagram details each of our company's sites.

Table A.1   Head Office Business Functions

| | COST OF LOSS ($) | | |
FUNCTION	1-HOUR OUTAGE	4-HOUR OUTAGE	1-DAY OUTAGE
Dispatching shipments	2,500	9,500	36,000
Processing orders	2,000	9,000	36,000
Customer service	800	3,200	30,000
Invoicing	710	2,600	5,200
Payroll	110	500	500

Table A.2   Warehouse A and B Business Functions

| | COST OF LOSS ($) | | |
FUNCTION	1-HOUR OUTAGE	4-HOUR OUTAGE	1-DAY OUTAGE
Dispatching shipments	2,400	8,500	29,000
Receiving shipments	2,000	8,000	24,000
Tracking shipments	800	3,200	19,200
Employee records	520	2,200	2,200
Invoicing	410	1,200	1,200

started. A spreadsheet would be ideal. Table A.1 provides for this; in book format, I can give a sample of what the end result should look like, listing for each location the top five outage cost processes.

Table A.2 shows the results for the warehouses.

Step 2: Identify Data Needed to Keep Critical Business Functions Going

The next thing to do is to take the business functions as listed in Tables A.1 and A.2 and identify the data that is critical to the proper operation of these functions. Table A.3 lists all the business functions in the same Cost of Loss order as before, but this time specifying the data objects and machines crucial to those functions.

Table A.3   Head Office Critical Data and Machines

FUNCTION	MACHINE	DATA OBJECTS
Dispatching shipments	Web server	/usr/local/apache /var/www /opt/b2bapplication/bin /var/opt/b2bapplication/data /etc
	gateway	/etc
Processing orders	Web server	/usr/local/apache /var/www /opt/b2bapplication/bin /var/opt/b2bapplication/data /etc
	gateway	/etc
Customer service	file server	/home /etc
	gateway	/etc
Invoicing	file server	/home /etc
	gateway	/etc
Payroll	file server	/home /etc

Note that the data objects listed are those directories that could be restored from a backup onto a default Linux installation to reproduce the configuration of the original machine. The advantage of the FHS (File system Hierarchy Standard, as described in Chapter 4, "Installing and Configuring for Reliability") is clear here, in that a few critical directories can be seen to hold the majority of the data on each machine that makes it unique. Separating each data object also helps to structure disk storage. More important data can be placed on a RAID, or moved into a server cluster, while less critical data can be held in less expensive ways.

A similar table to that shown for the head office in Table A.3, but for the warehouses looks like that in Table A.4.

Step 3: List What Could Go Wrong

Next you need to work through the list of risks detailed in Chapter 2, "Risk Analysis," and list those that apply to each of your current servers. An

Table A.4 Warehouses Critical Data and Machines

FUNCTION	MACHINE	DATA OBJECTS
Dispatching shipments	fulfillment server	/opt/b2bapplication/bin /var/opt/b2bapplication/data /etc
	gateway	/etc
Receiving shipments	fulfillment server	/opt/b2bapplication/bin /var/opt/b2bapplication/data /etc
	gateway	/etc
Tracking shipments	fulfillment server	/opt/b2bapplication/bin /var/opt/b2bapplication/data /etc
	gateway	/etc
Employee records	file server	/home /etc
	gateway	/etc
Invoicing	file server	/home /etc
	gateway	/etc

examination of the current head office Web server would look like Table A.5.

A similar tally should be made of the current state for all servers.

Step 4: Identify and Prioritize Your High Risk Data

So far in the process we have been gathering data. This step is where things begin to come together. Here we will compare Tables A.1 and A.2 with Tables A.3 and A.4 to attach a cost to the loss of a data entity or a server.

For example, Table A.3 shows that the loss of /var/www on the head office Web server would cause the failure of the customer order processing function and the dispatching of shipments. Table A.1 records the combined cost of the loss of those functions to be $4,500 per hour in the short term, escalating to $72,000 for a 24-hour outage. Contrast this with the loss of /home on the head office file server. Table A.3 indicates that this loss will affect three business functions: customer service, invoicing, and payroll. Table A.1 notes that in the short term, the combined cost of the loss of all three

Table A.5 Head Office Web Server Risk Analysis

HARDWARE RISK	STATUS
Hard disk	Internal SCSI disks, not mirrored
Cooling fans	Single cooling fan in power supply
External power supply	500 VA UPS
Network failure	Single 100BT NIC
Tape drive	Internal 2 GB, 4 mm DAT
Internal power supply	Single, not hot plugable
Internal peripheral card	Standard PCI
RAM or motherboard	Single memory module, motherboard of unknown make
SOFTWARE RISK	**STATUS**
Dynamic data overruns	No current operational monitoring
Daemon crash or race	No current operational monitoring
Bugs and upgrades	As need dictates, no policy
Security breach	No security policy
Viruses and worms	As need dictates, no policy
Boot failure	No boot failure recovery procedure in place
HUMAN ERROR	**STATUS**
Software maintenance	No procedures in place
Software upgrades	Relies on software vendor
NATURAL DISASTER	**STATUS**
Loss of Internet connection	No current backup connection
Power loss	500 VA UPS
Backup site	Offsite backup tapes, no procedure for recovering at a backup site

functions is only $1,620 per hour, compared to a $4,500 per hour loss associated with /var/www. This indicates the /home resource to be less critical in a short-term failure than the /var/www resource. When considering the loss of a machine, more than one business function is sure to be affected. Be sure to add up the costs associated with all the functions lost.

You need to go through a similar process of attaching a cost to the loss of each data resource and server listed in Tables A.3 and A.4, resulting in an ordered list of the most cost critical data and machines. The amount of loss implied in each case is useful to set budgets for the amount of money it would be reasonable to spend to safeguard the resource. For each location, the result would look like Tables A.6 through A.9 with items listed in descending order of liability.

Table A.6   Cost of Data Object Loss: Head Office

| | COST OF LOSS ($) | | |
DATA OBJECT	1-HOUR OUTAGE	4-HOUR OUTAGE	1-DAY OUTAGE
/etc (gateway)	6,010	24,300	107,200
/var/www (Web server)	4,500	18,500	72,000
/opt/b2bapplication/bin (Web server)	4,500	18,500	72,000
/var/opt/b2bapplication/data (Web server)	4,500	18,500	72,000
/usr/local/apache (Web server)	4,500	18,500	72,000
/etc (Web server)	4,500	18,500	72,000
/home (file server)	1,620	6,300	35,700
/etc (file server)	1,620	6,300	35,700

Table A.7   Cost of Server Loss: Head Office

| | COST OF LOSS ($) | | |
SERVER	1-HOUR OUTAGE	4-HOUR OUTAGE	1-DAY OUTAGE
Gateway	6,010	24,300	107,200
Web server	4,500	18,500	72,000
File server	1,620	6,300	35,700

Table A.8　Cost of Data Object Loss: Warehouses

DATA OBJECT	COST OF LOSS ($)		
	1-HOUR OUTAGE	4-HOUR OUTAGE	1-DAY OUTAGE
/etc (gateway)	6,130	23,100	75,600
/opt/b2bapplication/bin (fulfillment server)	5,200	19,700	72,200
/var/opt/b2bapplication/data (fulfillment server)	5,200	19,700	72,200
/etc (fulfillment server)	5,200	19,700	72,200
/etc/ (file server)	930	3,400	3,400
/home (file server)	930	3,400	3,400

Table A.9　Cost of Server Loss: Warehouses

SERVER	COST OF LOSS ($)		
	1-HOUR OUTAGE	4-HOUR OUTAGE	1-DAY OUTAGE
Gateway	6,130	23,100	75,600
Fulfillment server	5,200	19,700	72,200
File server	930	3,400	3,400

Clearly the gateway servers at all locations are the most critical, followed closely by the Web and fulfillment servers. The file servers can take a loss of an hour or two without substantial liability. The next thing to do is to plan defenses to protect these servers.

Step 5: Defend Yourself

Now we know what machines and what data we need to defend, but we need to know what to defend against. To determine that, look back at the risks listed in Table A.5 and apply them against the critical servers and data objects listed in Tables A.6 through A.9.

For the Web and fulfillment servers, it would appear that downtime of even an hour will cause significant loss, so we should take care to guard against all of the perils we can think of that threaten either the machine or the data. In Table A.5, the head office Web server was used as an example. We now know from Table A.7 that this is the second most critical server. Losses for a four-hour outage amount to $18,500, which gives us a pretty good budget to buy insurance. Subject to costing out these defenses, here is what you should consider for this server, based on the material presented in the text. Table A.10 uses the same risk listing from Table A.5 with additional notes detailing what is to be done to defend against loss.

When you are finished, you should have a summary table like this one for each of your servers. Now what remains is to do it.

Table A.10 Head Office Web Server Defense Strategy

HARDWARE RISK	STATUS	DEFENSE
Hard disk	Internal SCSI disks, not mirrored	■ Move storage to external portable enclosure ■ Increase number of drives and configure as RAID array
Cooling fans	Single cooling fan in power supply	■ Source a case allowing multiple cooling fans ■ Monitor in-case temperature
External power supply	500 VA UPS	■ Small UPS may be inadequate to carry server over a long outage; investigate average length of power outage in the area and ensure UPS is large enough to cover ■ Implement a procedure to test the UPS anually
Network failure	Single 100BT NIC	■ Keep a spare NIC on hand; standardize NICs throughout the operation to maximize interchangeability ■ Use only NICs certified by your Linux distributor
Tape drive	Internal 2 GB, 4 mm DAT	■ Ensure that this drive has adequate capacity to handle the data volumes to be backed up

		■ Move the drive to an external enclosure on the file server machine; backups should not be getting in the way of production on this critical Web server ■ Establish and implement a comprehensive backup procedure for all servers and implement it
Internal power supply	Single, not hot plugable	■ Replace with dual-redundant, hot-plugable unit ■ Stock a spare power supply module ■ Consider standardizing power supplies across all servers to maximize interchangeability
Internal cards	Standard PCI	■ As loss potential is high, consider building either a Linux Virtual Server cluster or a high-availability cluster to implement this mission-critical Web server
RAM or motherboard	Single memory module; motherboard of unknown make	■ Otherwise, stock replacement server motherboard and cards, and have procedure in place for repairing a failed server

SOFTWARE RISK	STATUS	DEFENSE
Dynamic data overruns	No current operational monitoring	■ Implement monitors to watch disk usage ■ Make use of disk quotas
Daemon crash or race	No current operational monitoring	■ Implement process table monitor
Bugs and upgrades	As need dictates; no policy	■ Establish policy to ensure timely bug fixes ■ Implement a planning process for the introduction of upgrades ■ Ensure that upgrades are done on a regular basis, so as not to fall too far behind
Security breach	No security policy	■ Establish a security policy and enforce it ASAP!

(continues)

Table A.10   Head Office Web Server Defense Strategy (continued)

SOFTWARE RISK	STATUS	DEFENSE
Viruses and worms	As need dictates; no policy	■ Establish policy on monitoring for and quickly repairing known security weaknesses ■ Consider either subscribing to a service such as Red Hat network, or establish procedure to regularly ensure the latest security patches are in place ■ Regularly perform security intrusion testing
Boot failure	No boot failure recovery procedure in place	■ Put in place a procedure to recover from a failed operating system ■ Test the procedure and ensure that someone is always available who is capable of performing the recovery

HUMAN ERROR	STATUS	DEFENSE
Software maintenance	No procedures in place	■ Establish procedures to govern who does software maintenance, and when ■ Ensure that all maintenance is planned in advance to have minimum effect on production ■ Ensure that plenty of warning is given in advance of software maintenance activity, and always have a path to return to the previous install
Software upgrades	Currently relies on software vendor	■ Ensure that contract with vendor includes performance warranty or penalty clauses to emphasize to the vendor the importance of this application to your company ■ If the vendor is primarily a seller of software, but not of consulting services, ensure that their people are properly qualified ■ Insist that work done by the vendor is fully documented, and that you fully understand what the vendor is doing and why

NATURAL DISASTER	STATUS	DEFENSE
Loss of Internet connection	No current backup connection	■ Investigate the possibility of a second redundant external Internet connection; look into the possibility of a satellite-based link, which is less susceptible to ground-based disaster
Power loss	500 VA UPS	■ Ensure adequate backup power ■ Investigate the viability of small onsite generator in lieu of multiple UPSs
Backup site	Offsite backup tapes; no procedure for recovering at a backup site	■ Establish a disaster recovery site ■ Consider using the warehouse distant from the head office, making sure it would not be liable to be affected by the same disaster as affected the head office ■ Establish a site recovery procedure and test it at least once every two years and after any large configuration change

Step 6: Do It

Cost out what you can afford and implement it. Notice that many of the defenses involve creating procedures and developing policies. These procedures and policies cannot be created once, then left on the shelf to gather dust. They need to be practiced; hence, any procedure needs to have an accountability factor built into it to ensure that it is really being done. Policies and procedures also change with time and need to have built into them a review process to ensure that they keep up with changing times and technologies.

Everything you do needs to be fully and clearly documented. The people you have now will move on in their time, and it is critical that they do not take essential knowledge with them. Good documentation is also critical if problems arise while an employee is ill or on vacation. You cannot afford to have the operations of the company hanging on a single person who alone knows the obscure series of commands to resolve a known problem. It is a great blessing to have good and competent employees, but their knowledge needs to be recorded for the benefit of the company, not held alone in their heads.

Finally, I have concentrated on the technical side of the BR plan in this appendix. Don't forget, however, that despite your best efforts to avoid it, downtime will happen. You need alternate processes in place to maintain the business functions of the company that will be lost when the computer fails. These, too, form a part of a BR plan and cannot be ignored by a prudent manager.

Glossary

AT Attachment   A communications bus (*see* bus) standard for connecting peripheral devices (primarily disks) first introduced by the IBM PC-AT, which became the most common bus used for disk attachment in desktops or small servers until the advent of the PCI bus. *See* PCI.

ATA   *See* AT Attachment.

bash   *See* Bourne Again Shell.

Basic Input Output System   A machine language code stored in read-only memory (ROM) in the hardware of a computer that has all the code necessary for the machine to do basic input/output to devices (BIOS), such as the keyboard and disk drives, without needing access to disk storage.

Berkeley Standard Distribution   The version of UNIX developed over a number of years by the University of California at Berkeley. Most versions of UNIX today, commercial or otherwise, owe a debt to a greater or lesser extent to BSD UNIX.

binary   A numbering system using only the numerals 0 and 1. Digital computer hardware can only distinguish the presence or absence of a voltage, and internally this can be mapped to a mathematical 0 or 1, which is the basis for the way these computers function. Computer programs containing the instructions understood by the computer are commonly known as binaries, as they contain machine instructions that function in this binary mathematical fashion.

BIOS *See* Basic Input Output System.

boot loader *See* Linux Loader.

Bourne Again Shell The default shell supplied by most Linux distributions. It is a modern derivative of the *bsh*, or Bourne shell, named for Steven Bourne, one of the earliest UNIX developers from AT&T Bell Laboratories.

BSD *See* Berkeley Standard Distribution.

bus A communications bus is a standardized hardware component allowing several devices to share a physical grouping of electrical conductors. The most obvious bus in a PC is the series of expansion slots on the motherboard, which are attachment points for the computer's internal peripheral communications bus. *See also* ATA, PCI, and SCSI.

cron A daemon started at boot time on any UNIX systems, *cron*'s task is to wake up every minute and scan a series of data files called crontabs. Each crontab lists tasks and a time or times that these tasks should run. When the scheduled time coincides with the actual time, *cron* executes the task on behalf of the user who created the crontab.

crontab *See* cron.

daemon A term common in UNIX usage that describes an operating system process that is usually started at boot time and runs at all times, supplying a basic function such as name resolution or printer support.

DHCP *See* Distributed Host Control Protocol.

Distributed Host Control Protocol A communications protocol that allows a server to assign IP (*see* Internet Protocol) addresses to client machines upon request. These addresses are not permanent, and DHCP is often used to allow machines to share a limited number of addresses.

DNS *See* Domain Name System.

Domain Name System The distributed database used throughout the Internet to allow a user to refer to another machine on the Internet by a name, such as www.wiley.com, instead of the actual IP address of the machine.

Ethernet Originally developed by Xerox in the 1970s, Ethernet has become the dominant LAN technology.

Fast Ethernet An Ethernet version having a speed of 100 Mb/s.

file system A database that tracks the data associated with all of the data files and directory structure held in a contiguous disk partition. To access any of the files in a file system during normal production use, the file system must be mounted into the logical file system directory tree using the mount command.

General Public License The software license developed by Richard Stallman, creator of the GNU project (*see* GNU). The GPL, also known as a copyleft agreement, defines the concept of open source by requiring software to be distributed with source code (*see* source), and preventing future restrictions on access to the source. More information on the GPL can be found at www.gnu.org.

Gigabit Ethernet   An Ethernet version having a speed of 1 Gb/s.

GNU   An acronym for GNU's Not UNIX, the GNU project (www.gnu.org) was conceived in 1984 by Richard Stallman with the objective of producing a completely free operating system that would be compatible with UNIX. The GNU project today is one of the largest groups of active open source developers.

IDE   *See* Intelligent Drive Electronics.

i-node   A small data entity central to a traditional UNIX physical file system database. Each data file in a file system is assigned an i-node, which holds file metadata (*see* metadata), such as the size, ownership, date stamps, link count, and data block addresses of the file.

Integrated Drive Electronics   *See* Intelligent Drive Electronics.

Intelligent Drive Electronics   Refers to the generic technology of integrating the drive controller, which in older technologies was a separate peripheral card, into the disk drive itself. The term is commonly used incorrectly to refer to a drive made to conform to the ATA bus, as ATA drives commonly have an integrated drive controller.

Internet Protocol   The addressing standard used in the Internet to uniquely identify a process running on any server on the Internet. The most familiar element of the IP is the 48-bit IP address required to identify an Internet server machine. The Internet Protocol is described in RFC791, RFC2460, and other RFCs.

IP   *See* Internet Protocol.

kernel   The core program code for an operating system, loaded into memory from a disk or network at the beginning of the boot process. The kernel handles core functions such as sharing the CPU capacity between multiple processes, managing real memory, performing I/O to physical devices, and in the case of most UNIX variants, managing network traffic.

Korn Shell   Named for its author, David Korn, the Korn shell adds to the syntax of the Bourne shell extra functionality from the C shell (the default shell in BSD UNIX) as well as functionality native to only itself. A version of the Korn shell called *pdksh* is available in the public domain, and is included in many Linux distributions.

ksh   *See* Korn Shell.

LAN   *See* Local Area Network.

LILO   *See* Linux Loader.

Linux Loader   The most popular of several boot loaders commonly used by Linux distributions. It is the job of a boot loader to map the physical location of the binary code for the kernel, and make sure that information is available to the BIOS in order to allow the BIOS to find and load the kernel into memory at boot time.

Local Area Network   Any communications network considered to be local in scope, usually connecting computers within an office where distances rarely exceed a few hundred feet. See also Ethernet.

MD5   *See* Message Digest 5.

Media Access Control   A term referring to the requirement inherent in any communications network to control which network device can use the network at any one time. The term MAC is commonly used inaccurately to refer to the hardware address of a NIC (*see* Network Interface Card), which is a unique number assigned to each NIC at the hardware level to identify the card to the access control software.

Message Digest 5   An algorithm that takes a block of text, commonly an email message or a data file, and produces a 128-bit fingerprint of the data, such that if the data itself is changed, the fingerprint will also change. It is used primarily in the creation of digital signatures, and is described fully in RFC1321.

metadata   The data held in a file system that is not file data, but is rather administrative data needed by the file system to properly store and manage the file system. The most obvious example of metadata is the i-node (*see* i-node).

mount   The command used to make a file system visible to regular user processes. It must be issued with super user privilege, and associates the root directory of the file system directory tree held in the partition being mounted with a pre-existing directory entry in the current logical file system.

Network Interface Card   The peripheral card used to connect a PC to a communications network.

NIC   *See* Network Interface Card.

NVRAM   *See* Random Access Memory.

partition   Disks are divided into contiguous sections of storage space termed partitions. The starting and ending point of each disk partition is defined in a partition table stored on the disk.

PCI   *See* Peripheral Connection Interface.

pdksh   *See* Korn Shell.

Peripheral Connection Interface   The type of bus (*see* bus) most commonly used on current PCs, the successor to the AT bus.

PGP   *See* Pretty Good Privacy.

PostScript   A proprietary page description language developed by Adobe Systems. PostScript allows an application program to describe the exact appearance of a printed page of output in a language not specific to any physical printer. A PostScript printer must read and translate the instructions in the PostScript data file to instructions that the printer requires to create the desired output. PostScript has become a de facto standard in the desktop publishing and graphic arts industries.

Pretty Good Privacy   An open source implementation of an asymmetric key encryption system specifically oriented towards securing email. PGP has a colorful history of legal actions, concerning the legality of exporting encryption software from the United States or Canada, and also questions concerning patents held on several relevant encryption algorithms. PGP has weathered all these storms and is currently one of the more popular email privacy packages.

Random Access Memory   The physical memory storage that is used by the CPU to store all binary and application data that it needs to operate on. RAM is volatile; that is, anything stored in RAM will be lost if the computer loses power. However, a special type of RAM known as NVRAM can retain data over a power loss.

Red Hat Package Manager   A package management system allowing source code for a program to be packaged along with compiled binaries and the instructions for compiling them. It incorporates a database to track versions, as well as verify the names of the files in a package and the data integrity of those files.

Request for Comments   The documents managed by the Internet Engineering Task Force. In 1969 the originators of today's Internet started a series of collaborative notes that have become what is in effect a set of de facto standards for a wide range of Internet-related technical issues. The definitive collection of RFCs is maintained at www.rfc-editor.org.

RFC   *See* Request for Comments.

root file system   The file system that is the first mounted during the boot process. It contains the top-level directory hierarchy of the logical file system structure, and also the majority of the operating system configuration data.

root user   UNIX has always relied on a special user account that is not subject to any security restriction as it's a top-level administrative account. The person holding the password for this account is termed the super user; the actual login name for this account has traditionally been *root*, although strictly speaking super user privilege is given to any user account assigned the numerical user ID 0.

rpm   *See* Red Hat Package Manager.

Samba A public domain Server Message Block file server program, SMB is the file system structure used by Microsoft's Windows family of operating systems. Hence, a Linux server running Samba will appear to a Windows client as if it were a Windows file or print server.

script A shell script is an ASCII text file containing a series of commands, all of which are valid commands that could have been typed at a shell command line. The shell can be directed to run this script, in which case the commands in the script run automatically in sequence, as if they had been typed at a command line. The batch file in DOS is based on this UNIX concept.

SCSI *See* Small Computer Systems Interface.

shell A program that gives the user a command line interface to the operating system. Different shells have the ability to remember previous commands, automatically search directories for commands, or complete partial filenames and perform other actions to make it easier to work from a command line. The shell is not a part of the kernel, but is an additional process that runs under kernel control. *See* bash and ksh.

Small Computer Systems Interface An ANSI standard for a parallel data transfer bus for attaching peripheral devices, such as disks and tape drives, to a computer. A single SCSI bus will accommodate several devices, at relatively high transfer rates. The SCSI standard has seen widespread use for a number of years, and several variations on the original standard now exist. A SCSI bus disk storage system will generally yield better overall performance than an ATA bus.

source Source code is instructions written in a programming language such as C, Java, or FORTRAN, which define a computer program. In languages such as C and FORTRAN, the source code must be compiled into a binary (*see* binary).

super block A data object that is part of the metadata of a file system, the super block holds summary information concerning the allocation state of each data block as well as other global file system information.

super user *See* root user.

Uninterruptible Power Supply A hardware device incorporating a battery that is capable of supplying power to a computer during a failure of the external power supply to the building.

UNIX Not an acronym, rather it is a corruption of MULTICS, an early multiprocessing operating system known to the inventors of UNIX at Bell Labs in the late 1960s. While UNIX was developed by employees at Bell Labs, antitrust judgments prevented Bell from selling software. Consequently, UNIX was made available to the academic community at no cost. In the 1970s and 1980s it grew to become the de facto standard academic operating system. Since then, various commercial and non-commercial variants have become among the most widely used operating systems in the world. Linux could be considered one of the most significant non-commercial UNIX variants.

UPS   *See* Uninterruptible Power Supply.

X Windows   The X Windows system (commonly abbreviated to simply X) is a client/server graphics user environment developed in the 1980s at the Massachusetts Institute of Technology. X is a communications protocol allowing a process running on one machine to transfer a complete description of the graphical output it wants displayed to another machine on a network. The second machine displays the output, and can accept input from a user via a pointing device, such as a mouse, and send that input back to the client process running on the server machine. Most UNIX server networks use X as the means to provide a graphical user interface (GUI) to the end user.

Index